Hidden Secrets
of the
Eastern Star

The Masonic Connection

by Dr. Cathy Burns

SHARING
212-S East 7th Street
Mt. Carmel, Pennsylvania 17851-2211

TABLE OF CONTENTS

1. A Brief History of the Eastern Star 5

2. The Masonic Connection 11

3. The Eastern Star and Christianity 23

4. His Star in the East 45

5. The Pentagram 77

6. A Look at Baphomet.. 97

7. Symbolism of the Eastern Star....................... 145

8. More Eastern Star Symbolism 181

9. Gavel, Clasped Hands and Veil 211

10. Eastern Star Goddesses.................................... 229

11. What is the Cabalistic Motto? 253

12. Is Death a Victor? 279

13. Secrecy and the Eastern Star........................... 291

14. The Four Elements 307

15. A Look at the Rainbow Girls 341

Endnotes 373

Bibliography 465

1. A BRIEF HISTORY OF THE EASTERN STAR

The Eastern Star: These words prompt numerous questions. Who founded it? What is it? Is it a secret society? Is it a religious organization? Is it compatible with Christianity? What does their motto "We have seen His star in the East and have come to worship Him" mean? Who is represented by this star? Is the Eastern Star based on the Bible? Can anyone join or are there special requirements that must be met? Is there a Masonic connection? What is the "Cabalistic Motto"? Are there secret passwords and signs of recognition?

All these questions and more will be answered in this book. We'll take a peek inside the Lodge Room, a brief journey through the five degrees, a look at some of the symbolism used, and then see how it all compares to the teachings of the Bible. The Eastern Star claims to be "the largest organization upon the face of the globe to which both men and women are eligible,"[1] so a closer examination of this group should prove beneficial.

The Eastern Star claims Dr. Rob Morris as its founder. He was born August 31, 1818, to Robert Peckham and Charlotte Lavinnia Shaw. His birth name was Robert William Peckham. His parents separated in 1821, and he remained with his father until his father's death in 1825. Robert then went to live with John Morris and later took his foster father's last name as his own.[2] Afterward, he changed his name "Robert" to "Rob" so as not to be confused with the signer of the Declaration of Independence whose name was also Robert Morris.[3]

On March 5, 1846 Rob Morris was made a Mason and he eventually "received the 'Ladies Degrees,' which later became the basis of his work in formulating the Eastern Star degrees."[4] Morris was involved in many Masonic undertakings. In 1853 he started publishing the *Kentucky Freemason*, the name of which was later changed to *The American Freemason*. His first book on Masonry was *The Lights and Shadows of Freemasonry* which was printed in 1852.[5] Morris "was a very large contributor to many Masonic periodicals, and a number of newspapers and magazines."[6]

> He had given to the world over three hundred Masonic lyrics and seventy-four volumes of Masonic literature, more than fifty Eastern Star poems and a number of volumes designed to perfect the Order which he had originated.[7]

We are also informed:

> Rob Morris was, during his lifetime, probably the widest known Mason in the country, if not in the world....a greater part of his life was devoted to Masonic research and to the dissemination of Masonic knowledge.[8]

Morris, "a Mason in high standing,"[9] "advanced in every branch of Freemasonry, becoming Grand Master of the Grand Lodge of Kentucky on October 12, 1858."[10] He also "received the Rite of Memphis, so far as the ninetieth degree...."[11] By the time of his death on July 31, 1888, he had accrued a large number of honorary degrees and memberships both in America and abroad. He "at one time recalled a list of one hundred and forty-three regular degrees and orders in Masonry, whose covenants he had assumed."[12]

SHROUDED IN MYSTERY

Although it is widely claimed that Morris was the founder of the Eastern Star, in *History of the Order of the Eastern Star*, we are notified: "The real origin of the Eastern Star, like Masonry, will always be shrouded in mystery....it will be seen that perhaps it had a French origin, as early as 1730."[13] Lucien V. Rule, a Masonic author, explains:

> At what period and by whom the Eastern Star was invented history fails to record....But enough is known to warrant the statement that it was in existence long before Rob Morris knew anything about Masonry. However, when he received it, it was undoubtedly the merest skeleton of what it is now.[14]

For at least 250 years there have been androgynous groups (especially in France) where both men and women could participate. A number of these societies were created by Masons,[15] but "[w]hile adoptive lodges were formed wherever French Freemasonry exerted an influence, they were never established in England or in America."[16] Morris, taking his cue from the French, developed his own version of the Adoptive Rite or Androgynous Masonry, known today as the Eastern Star.[17] The influence from the French "is noticeable in the development of the Eastern Star degrees, but the *manner* in which the system was attached to the Freemasonry of the period is *distinctly original*." [Emphasis in the original][18] In 1852, Morris acknowledged that he had borrowed from the French system.

In the September 15, 1852 issue of *The American Freemason,* a magazine published by him, he maintained: "The degree is of French extraction, and has all the embellishments of that fanciful race."[19] Two years prior to this, he admitted:

> The five Androgynous degrees, combined under the above title, are supposed to have been introduced into this country by the French officers who assisted our Government during the struggle for liberty.[20]

Willis D. Engle, one of the active workers in the early formation of the Eastern Star, reveals: "The fact is that brother Morris received the Eastern Star degree at the hands of Giles M. Hillyer, of Vicksburg, Mississippi, about 1849."[21] Mary Ann Slipper, an Eastern Star writer, claims:

> The Order of the Eastern Star is not a new idea, we can trace back for two centuries Orders with a similar idea. It has been asserted that in Boston, Mass., the O.E.S. held a session there in May, 1793. A very definite statement has been made that this Order performed a great charitable service during the war of 1812.[22]

In *The Adoptive Rite Ritual,* arranged by Robert Macoy, we find:

> Many systems of the Adoptive Rite have, from time to time been introduced into the United States with varied success, but none of which seemed to possess the elements of permanency until the introduction of the Order of the EASTERN STAR, which was established in this country during the year 1778. [Emphasis in the original][23]

In spite of a number of references to the contrary, by 1877, Morris insisted:

> I wrote every word of the original lectures and composed the songs. For twenty-eight years I have been communicating it as my own origination. I am the founder of the system and no one can show any proof of its existence prior to 1849.[24]

Regardless of whether Morris just revised the Eastern Star ritual or actually wrote the entire degrees, he is usually credited with being the founder of the Eastern Star in the year 1850.[25]

"In 1855, Rob Morris inaugurated a Supreme Constellation, claiming that 'no such attempt upon national basis has heretofore been made in America.'"[26] This Supreme Constellation was headed by Morris who called himself the "Most Enlightened Grand Luminary."[27] By 1855, 75 charters had already been granted.[28] In 1868 Rob Morris visited the Holy Land to do some research work,[29] so he relinquished control of the Eastern Star to Robert Macoy who was also a Mason.[30]

REVISED AND ALTERED

It was under Macoy's direction, that the Eastern Star was finally composed of chapters[31] and became arranged more orderly.[32] However, under Macoy some opposition also resulted because he was charging an exorbitant rate, allowing him to make an income of several thousand dollars a year just from selling charters, rituals, and jewels. We are told that he "soon amassed quite a fortune for himself. He granted Charters freely and sold books and supplies at his own prices."[33] In addition, he frequently changed the ritual.

That [ritual] in use in 1874 was revised and materially altered in 1875, so that previous editions were useless when the later was used, and, in 1876, he issued another differing still more from previous ones; even the different editions of the syllabus gave radically different directions as to the manner of giving the signs....[34]

Because Macoy gave out charters freely, the Eastern Star soon had hundreds of Chapters, with thousands of members.[35] This phenomenal growth made it necessary for the complete organization of a General Grand Chapter in order "to obtain permanency and uniformity of the ritual,"[36] with a preliminary session being held on November 15, 1876.

The General Grand Chapter has territorial jurisdiction over both the Americas, and all islands adjacent thereto, except the states of New York and New Jersey, and has concurrent jurisdiction over Europe and Africa with Scotland, except the British Dominions therein....

Each Grand Chapter controls its own finances and is subservient to the General Grand Chapter, only in so far as Ritual, Code, and general supervision is concerned.[37]

INTERNATIONAL EASTERN STAR TEMPLE

WASHINGTON, D. C.

The plan for the International Eastern Star Headquarters to be in Washington, D. C. was introduced at the Triennial Assembly held in Seattle, Washington in 1919. It was decided that each Grand Chapter would be responsible for one dollar per member to make this International Headquarters a reality.

The former Perry Belmont Mansion was bought and on February 24, 1937 this building was dedicated as the International Eastern Star Temple. Delegates and distinguished Masters were present from all parts of the world.

2. THE MASONIC CONNECTION

It is claimed that the Order of the Eastern Star is not a Masonic organization. *The Greenwood Encyclopedia of American Institutions: Fraternal Organizations* maintains: "Although Masonically linked, this female group is not Freemasonry."[1] One Masonic booklet emphasizes: "Definitely is not a Masonic organization, although ritual and practice are definitely Masonic in spirit, altruistic and charitable."[2] In an address given by the Worthy Matron to the Eastern Star initiate, it is explained: "We are not a part of the Masonic institution...."[3] This statement, however, continues: "**...YET WE ARE CONNECTED WITH MASONRY BY INTIMATE AND TENDER TIES.**" [Emphasis mine throughout][4] One ritual I've read goes even further than this by claiming: "Ladies, you are connected with Masonry by ties far more intimate and tender than you are aware of, **OR THAN I CAN EVEN INFORM YOU OF.**"[5] The initiate is also told by the Worthy Matron: "I desire to inform you as to your true relationship to the Masonic fraternity. A little knowledge of the real nature and purposes of Masonry will help you to understand this."[6] Obviously, then, there is a definite link between the Eastern Star and Masonry. In fact, it is through the granting of the Eastern Star degrees, that the "ladies are adopted into the Masonic communion...."[7] Even the five colors used in the Eastern Star ritual represent "a five toned cord of the tie that binds us to the Masonic teachings."[8]

Besides the definite association just mentioned, we find that there is a prerequisite that must be met before any person can join the Eastern Star. A man must be at least a Master Mason, meaning that he must have taken the first three Masonic degrees and must be in good standing. A woman can only join if she has a Master Mason as a close relative and is at least 18 years old.

Only the wives, daughters, sisters, mothers, and widows of third degree Masons in good standing can join.[9] Some widows are even forbidden to unite with the Eastern Star if they have remarried men who are not presently Master Masons.[10]

BETRAYING MASONIC SECRETS

Not only must there be a Masonic relationship before a woman can belong to the Eastern Star, but a Master Mason (or higher) must preside at all meetings where degrees are conferred.[11] In fact, there must be at least two (one book says three) Master Masons as officers.[12] One encyclopedia informs us:

> From its beginning, the OES [Order of the Eastern Star] has been an organization directed by Freemasonry. Not only were its rituals written and revised by Masons, but Masonry has always kept a watchful eye on the order by having one of its members serve as a patron in each OES subordinate chapter.[13]

Furthermore, when the Associate Matron is explaining to the initiate about the Worthy Patron's badge, she declares: "His badge of office is the Square and Compass within the Star, **EMPHASIZING THE CONNECTION** between the Masonic Fraternity and the Order of the Eastern Star."[14] Later in this ceremony, it is once again reiterated:

> Your **CONNECTION WITH THE MASONIC ORDER,** and the recommendations which you bring, assure us that you are worthy to be entrusted with the light and knowledge of our Order.[15]

Interestingly, Morris was accused by other Masons of "betraying Masonic secrets"[16] when he first tried writing a degree for women.

The Spirit of Freemasonry

This correlation between the Eastern Star and Masonry is extremely important. One Eastern Star ritual book by F. A. Bell informs us: "The Order of the **EASTERN STAR IS MODELED AFTER FREE-MASONRY** to a certain extent, and has been called Adoptive Masonry, or the Adoptive Rite."[17] In the *Adoptive Rite Ritual* by Robert Macoy, we are told: "These ladies are said to have been *adopted* into the Masonic communion...." [Emphasis in the original][18]

Therefore, to properly understand the Eastern Star, we must also take a look at the Masonic organization.

DEATH AND RESURRECTION

The third degree of Masonry culminates with a death and resurrection ceremony. Since this is the main highlight of the three degrees, we will deal with this in more detail.

This ritual relates the myth of a person called Hiram Abiff. He is supposed to have been the man who built Solomon's Temple. According to the Masonic legend, he promised his workmen that when the Temple was finished, he would give them the secrets of a Master Mason which would allow them to earn higher wages. As the Temple neared completion, the men became impatient and demanded that Hiram give the secrets to them. Since the work was still incomplete, Hiram refuses to do so. Three of these men then decide to take matters into their own hands and when they find Hiram alone, they threaten to kill him if he does not reveal the secrets to them. The third man states:

> You have...escaped "Jubela" and "Jubelo"; me you cannot escape; my name is "Jubelum!" What I purpose, that I perform. I hold in my hand an instrument of death; therefore, give me the Master's word, or I will take your life in a moment![19]

When Hiram once again refuses, Jubelum kills him. The three men, realizing what they had done, then flee into hiding. Back at the Temple site, it is soon discovered that Hiram is missing. King Solomon then dispatches 12 Fellow Crafts (this is the name of the second degree in Masonry) to search for Hiram. Eventually the body is discovered and word is sent to King Solomon who commands them to raise the corpse. An Entered Apprentice (the name of the first degree in Masonry) goes to the body and tries to raise it using the grip of the first degree. This doesn't work so he returns to Solomon. This time Solomon sends a Fellow Craft to raise Hiram. He also fails to raise him although he has used the grip of the second degree. Finally, King Solomon goes to Hiram himself, and with the "strong grip of the lion's paw" (the grip of the third or Master Mason degree), he is able to raise Hiram.[20]

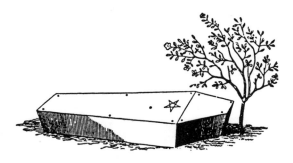

This Masonic ceremony, which cannot be found in the Scriptures, is enacted by every Mason who takes the third degree. Masonic author, A. T. C. Pierson, admits:

> The Masonic legend stands by itself, *unsupported by history* or other than its own traditions; yet we readily recognize in Hiram Abiff the Osiris of the Egyptians, the Mithras of the Persians, the Bacchus of the Greeks, the Dionysius of the fraternity of the Artificers, and the Atys of the Phrygians, whose passion, death and resurrection were celebrated by these people repectively (sic). [Emphasis in the original][21]

The Masonic candidate himself represents Hiram, who is slain, buried, and then resurrected. Most Masons who have performed this ritual have no idea whatsoever what is actually being represented, but in the Ancient Mysteries of paganism, there were always death and resurrection ceremonies symbolizing the decease and reappearance of a pagan god. Since Masonic author, F.

A. Bell, referred to the Eastern Star as the "Ancient Mysteries,"[22] we have every right to point out the correlations within Masonry, the Eastern Star, and the Ancient Mysteries.

When a candidate reenacts this death and resurrection custom, he is actually participating in a pagan activity which symbolizes the relationship between the initiate and the god, thus making the candidate equivalent to a divine or godlike being. This action brings to mind Satan's "promise" (actually it was a lie) to Eve in the Garden of Eden. He told her that if she would disobey God and partake of the fruit of the tree of the knowledge of good and evil, she would become as a god (see Genesis 3:1-7).

BLOOD OATHS TAKEN

There are also blood oaths that are taken by Masons for each degree that they advance. The first degree oath, in part, proclaims:

> ...binding myself under no less penalty than that of having my throat cut across, my tongue torn out by its roots, and my body buried in the rough sands of the sea, at low-water mark, where the tide ebbs and flows twice in twenty-four hours, should I ever knowingly violate this my Entered Apprentice obligation.[23]

Second degree Masons repeat the following:

> ...binding myself under no less penalty than that of having my breast torn open, my heart plucked out, and placed on the highest pinnacle of the temple there to be devoured by the vultures of the air, should I ever knowingly violate the Fellow Craft obligation.[24]

Finally, the third degree oath declares:

...binding myself, under no less penalty than that of having my body severed in two, my bowels taken from thence and burned to ashes, the ashes scattered before the four winds of heaven, that no more remembrance might be had of so vile and wicked a wretch as I would be, should I ever, knowingly, violate this my Master Mason's obligation.[25]

ALL of these oaths and the death and resurrection ceremony are **REQUIRED** by a man **BEFORE** a woman relative of his may have the "privilege" of joining the Eastern Star! In fact, the Eastern Star is only a Masonic "cover-up" to keep the women from complaining about the Masonic lodge.

I will explain this in a minute, but I do want to stress that the majority of men and women who join these organizations most likely **HAVE NO IDEA WHATSOEVER** about what is being represented or promoted in the Lodge rooms. Lynn F. Perkins, in his Masonic book, points this out about Masonry:

It should be carefully noted that the **PURPOSE** of the Ritual is just as much **TO CONCEAL** as to reveal the secret science that **LIES BEHIND** and within the outward and literal forms and symbols. The true wisdom is **CONCEALED, HIDDEN,** not only from those who do not join the Masonic Order but also from those who "take" the degrees; and it will remain "hidden" until each Mason seeks revelation and finds the Truth for himself. There are no interpretations in the Ritual; they have to be sought elsewhere.[26]

Countless men are totally unaware that a blood oath will be required of them at their initiation. Furthermore, numerous men have no indication as to what the death and resurrection ritual really involves or what it represents. I know fine men and women who belong (or have belonged) to the Masonic Lodge and the Eastern Star (including several of my own relatives over a number of generations) and I doubt if any of them realize what is being symbolized there. Many of these people are good-living, moral individuals who attend church and are kind neighbors. Most of them would never knowingly belong to any organization that would undermine their morals or religious beliefs. Multitudes of these men and women are innocent "victims."

The purpose of this book is not to criticize or condemn these innocent human beings but to show them what their organizations actually teach from their own rituals, manuals, and assorted works. I have nothing against individual persons, but rather against the fraternity which practices deception. This book, therefore, is an honest review of tens of thousands of pages of research material dealing with the Eastern Star and Masonry.

LET'S APPEASE THE WOMEN!

As I just mentioned, the Eastern Star was only started to appease the wives of Masons. Many women were complaining that the Masonic Lodge was causing a division in their homes because the men were forbidden to tell their wives what they were doing in the Lodge. Also, the wives didn't like the idea that lots of money was being taken for initiation and regalia fees, especially since there was so much secrecy involved. Husbands and wives who shared everything with each other were prohibited from discussing this particular aspect of their lives, yet the wives were expected to be supportive of their husbands' organization. If the men wished to continue the secrecy of their Lodge, they knew that they had to offer something to their wives that would placate them, and so the idea of the Eastern Star was born.

Bell's Eastern Star Ritual states:

The Masonic Order is strictly a secret society and a Mason may not disclose the mysteries of the order even to members of his family. The Order of the Eastern Star is the result of a desire on the part of the Masons to afford the women of their families **AS FAR AS POSSIBLE** the benefits and privileges of Freemasonry, and **ALSO TO SECURE THE HELP AND CO-OPERATION OF THE WOMEN IN THEIR BENEVOLENT PROJECTS.**[27]

In fact, in the preliminary address given by the instructor during the Eastern Star initiation, the women are (or, at least, were at one time) told:

LADIES: We meet and welcome you here for a **DOUBLE** purpose. *First, that we may* inform you as to your true **RELATIONSHIP TO THE MASONIC FRATERNITY,** and thus **REMOVE ANY PREJUDICES** that you may have entertained against us....

It must be plain enough to every wife and daughter and sister of a Mason that there is something in Masonry, known only to the brethren, which is very delightful and precious to them. This oftentimes provokes the question, Of what use is Masonry to the ladies? As it separates man and wife to some extent by giving the man certain secrets and duties which the wife cannot share, the ladies sometimes take umbrage against Masonry, and even become its enemies, and oppose it violently as something contrary to the laws of God and man. A little knowledge, however, of the real nature and purposes of Masonry will remove all this, if there is any of it existing in the mind of any lady present....

But now it is necessary that we should show you why **LADIES, TOO, SHOULD LOVE MASONRY,** and should be, as many of them are, its warmest friends and defenders. [Italics in the original; Caps and bold added][28]

Another source states:

In addition, the development and spread of the Order of the Eastern Star, an organization composed of female relatives of Masons, mitigated women's resentment of the order, as it allowed them to duplicate their husbands' experience of secrecy, ritual, and sociability.[29]

The degrees of the various Orders, dependent upon the Masonic Fraternity for the elegibility (sic) of those seeking its benefits, has (sic) been framed and established...for inciting the influence of women toward the purposes of the Masonic institution....[30]

The individual accredited with the founding of the Eastern Star, Rob Morris, himself remarked:

From the period of my initiation into Masonry I had entertained the desire of introducing the female relatives of Masons into closer relationship with the Order. Through the immense influence of women, so much might be done to bring the performances of Freemasons nearer their professions.[31]

In fact, Dr. Morris wrote the following poem to show why he founded the Eastern Star:
"To **WIN** the love of **WOMEN TO OUR CAUSE,**—
The love of mother, sister, daughter, wife,—
To **GAIN HER ADMIRATION OF OUR LAWS;**
This were the greatest triumph of our life.
For this we well may work and well agree;
No emblem on our Trestle Board so rife
But would the brighter shine could we but see
On woman's breast its rays—that fount of purity.
Ladies, the hearts of Masons are sincere;...
Then lend your brightest smiles **FREEMASONRY TO BLESS!**"[32]

DEFENDING MASONRY

One final quotation should suffice to prove that the Eastern Star was organized for the benefit of propagating Masonry (and not really so much for the female relatives).

> As Freemasons, we earnestly solicit your good will and encouragement in the work which we are engaged. I have proved to you that it is for your good **AS MUCH AS OURS** that we are doing the Masonic work. Then, ladies, help us. **HELP US BY DEFENDING OUR PRINCIPLES** when you hear them attacked, and speaking ever a kind word in our behalf.[33]

Thus we can see from a number of pro-Eastern Star and pro-Masonic sources that the Eastern Star is really for the **ADVANTAGE AND FURTHERANCE OF MASONRY.** If the women have their own organization which satisfies some of their curiosity, then they will not be so quick to interfere with their husbands' involvement with Masonry nor will they feel so left out. This attitude helps to promote Masonic goals and serves to advance the Masonic cause. Another Eastern Star book reiterates: "In establishing the Eastern Star he [Rob Morris] emphasized the high moral status of Masonry." [34] *Bell's Eastern Star Ritual,* which is billed as the "most authentic" ritual,[35] mentions that the Eastern Star:

> ...has come to be looked upon as "a strong right arm of Masonry," assisting nobly in its charitable enterprises, helping to secure Masonic Temples, and adding much to the social life of the fraternity.[36]

Because of this Masonic connection, we will look at the Masonic organization from time to time throughout the remainder of this book.

3. THE EASTERN STAR AND CHRISTIANITY

Is the Eastern Star compatible with Biblical Christianity and are the degrees really based on the Bible? These are important questions that must be faced honestly. We are told that the Eastern Star is a Christian association[1] and that it "is impregnable to the profane, the vicious, and the sceptics of christian (sic) faith."[2] We are further advised that "none can consistently become its members, whether male or female, save those who at least believe in Jesus Christ."[3]

> The Eastern Star degree is not adapted to the Jewish brethren or their female relatives, though they may receive it if they choose. If any offer to attend they ought to be informed that it is purely christian (sic).[4]

Even one of the Landmarks of the Eastern Star is: "Its lessons are Scriptural; its teachings are moral; and its purposes are beneficent."[5]

While at one time the Eastern Star claimed to be a Christian or a religious organization, in the 1989 "Follow the Star" pamphlet, we are now informed that the "Eastern Star is a social Order comprised of persons with deep religious convictions and spiritual values, but is not a religion."[6]

Before we look at the Eastern Star degrees, let's see how Rob Morris felt about Christianity as well as other religions. He wrote in *The Lights and Shadows of Freemasonry*:

> As so large a proportion of American Masons are professing Christians...I have not hesitated frequently to "name the name of Jesus" in this volume, although no one has so often and publicly demonstrated that Freemasonry was ten centuries old when the Star of Bethlehem arose.[7]

MORRIS ADMIRES MOHAMMED

Doesn't that sound wonderful? Rob Morris mentions the name of Jesus, but then he goes on to add:

> At the same time I have fully expressed my admiration for much of the character and many of the precepts of Mohammed, as embodied in the Koran. Avoiding the doctrinal points and, read in the spirit of fraternal love, as illustrated in the lectures of Freemasonry, that remarkable book, the Koran, might justly be taken as a comment upon the much older, far wiser, and most remarkable book ever written, THE OLD TESTAMENT of the Hebrew dispensation. [Emphasis in the original][8]

Oh, so now we see that even though Morris mentions Jesus, he also admires Mohammed and the Koran. Additionally, he dedicated his book to "His Excellency, Mohammed Raschid."[9] He ends the dedication with these words:

> Our earthly lot differs most widely. Your name is spread afar as one to whom God has intrusted the government of a people. Our forms of faith are diverse. In language, customs, and modes of thought, we are cast in different moulds; but in Masonic UNITY we are one, and one in Masonic FAITH. As our hopes and aims and labors are one, we, trusting in one God, and doing, each of us, what we believe to be His expressed will, do humbly expect a common reward when we have passed that common lot which none can escape. To the Divine power, therefore, I tenderly commend your Excellency, both for this world and for that which is to come. [Emphasis in the original][10]

It is important to know Morris' view about Scriptures. It is also of interest to note that he believes that even though Raschid has a diverse faith, he will receive the same reward as Morris will when this life is over. This viewpoint, of course, carries over into the Eastern Star ritual.

The Eastern Star is composed of five degrees, each one taken from a passage of Scripture.[11] The names of these degrees are Adah (referring to Jephthah's daughter), Ruth, Esther, Martha, and Electa (pertaining to the "Elect Lady" mentioned in II John 1:1). During the initiation, many Scriptural references are read. Hymns are also sung, some of them being: Brighten the Corner Where You Are; Bringing in the Sheaves; Jesus Wants Me for a Sunbeam; Bring Them In; Washed in the Blood of the Lamb; Jesus Loves Me; It's the Old Time Religion; The Light of the World Is Jesus; and Calvary's Stream Is Flowing.[12] Their motto is: "We have seen His star in the East, and are come to worship Him."[13]

RELIGIOUS FACADE

These statements, Scripture references, hymns, and motto make it sound like the Eastern Star is an organization based on the tenets and doctrines of Christianity. Of course, this is exactly what it is intended to convey, but under this facade an altogether different organization is seen to exist! Just because one quotes a lot of Scripture does not make that person a Christian. The devil, like Albert Pike, the Eastern Star members, Masons, etc., quoted (or misquoted) much Scripture, but the devil certainly was not a Christian! Paul warned the Corinthian church that many would corrupt the Word of God (II Corinthians 2:17).

As we compare the Scripture references used to the explanations given throughout the Eastern Star ritual, we can easily recognize that the precious Word of God has been added to and that untrue and incorrect details have been inserted. For example, let's start with the first degree—that of Adah.

During the initiation ceremony (which, by the way, cannot be conferred until after the initiation fee has been paid),[14] the story of Jephthah, the ninth judge of Israel, is expounded. Using the narrative found in Judges 11, the candidate is told the story of how Jephthah vowed a vow unto the Lord that if the Lord would help him be victorious over the enemy "that whatsoever cometh forth of the doors of [his] house to meet [him]...shall surely be the Lord's..." (Judges 11:31). The Lord gave Jephthah the victory and as he returned from the battle, the first greeting came from his daughter (to whom the Eastern Star has given the name Adah). Jephthah's triumph was overshadowed when he realized that his daughter was the one whom he had vowed to give to the Lord. When Jephthah told his daughter of his vow, she compliantly said that he should fulfill his promise. So far the Eastern Star ritual agrees with the Biblical account.

ADAH —Jewels and Regalia

We are told that "none of the traditions of the Eastern Star contradict the text of Scripture" but that they:

> ...extend the Scriptural history, and they throw important light upon the passages referred to...there is no shade of discrepancy between these Lectures and the generally-received understanding of the Bible. Of this, the pious Christian may be well assured, even in advance of a perusal.[15]

Is this true? We shall see as we proceed with the story of Jephthah's daughter.

ONLY ACCEPTABLE SACRIFICES

The Eastern Star ritual continues with the explanation how Jephthah offered his daughter for a burnt sacrifice to fulfill his vow.[16] Many Bible scholars do not believe that Jephthah actually killed his daughter but that he dedicated her to the service of the Lord. The phrase in question is: "whatsoever cometh forth...shall surely be the Lord's, and I will offer it up for a burnt offering" (Judges 11:31). However, not just anything that would meet Jephthah would be allowed. Only certain animals were acceptable sacrifices to the Lord, so if an unclean animal would have been the first to meet him, it would not have been an acceptable offering. In fact, offering such an animal would have been displeasing to the Lord. In Leviticus 1 we see that the offering that was to be sacrificed had to be "without blemish" (verses 3 and 10) and Leviticus 27:11 mentions an unclean beast "of which they do not offer a sacrifice unto the Lord." With this in mind, Jephthah must have known that not just any animal would be suitable. He also was most likely aware of the possibility that a human being would be the first to greet him, so his vow included that it "shall surely be the Lord's."

Adam Clarke, a Bible scholar, tells us that, according to the most accurate Hebrew scholars, the translation of the Hebrew (the language in which the Old Testament was originally written) for Judges 11:31 is: "I will consecrate it to the Lord, or I will offer it for a burnt-offering...."[17] When the rest of the passage is read, it seems very likely that Jephthah did not offer his daughter as a burnt offering but consecrated her to the Lord. Verse 37 mentions his daughter's request to have two months to "bewail her virginity." Furthermore, in verse 39 we see that she "returned unto her father, who did with her according to his vow which he had vowed: and she knew no man" meaning that she remained a virgin.

Why is this important? First of all, human sacrifices were condemned by God (see Jeremiah 7:31, Ezekiel 16:20-21, Deuteronomy 12:31, 18:10, etc.). Second, in Bible times, it was the hope of a young woman to be the individual selected as the mother of the Messiah. Since this was Jephthah's only child, and she was consecrated to perpetual virginity, his posterity would be cut off, thus ending forever his chance of having the Messiah come through his bloodline. This indeed was a great sacrifice.[18]

WAS JEPHTHAH A MASON?

Completely disregarding this issue, the Eastern Star ritual goes into great detail over the so-called sacrifice of Adah. What's worse is that it is claimed that Adah willingly allowed Jephthah to sacrifice her in order that her father would not break his **MASONIC** vow! You see, it is claimed that Jephthah was a Mason.[19] Not only is this Scripturally incorrect and unfounded, it is also historically inaccurate since modern Masonry did not begin until 1717.

ASTROLOGY FORBIDDEN

Of course, the first degree of Adah is not the only ritual that is added to. The third degree is that of Esther. One Eastern Star book, explaining about Esther, comments:

> Astrologers, at her birth, foretold to the anxious parents that their babe was born for high honors; that she should wear a diadem, and share the royal sceptre; that she would shine among the constellations of rank, a "star" of the first magnitude, prominent through histories of civilized and barbaric ages.[20]

Since astrology (or the observing of times) is forbidden in numerous passages of Scripture (see Deuteronomy 18:10-12; Isaiah 47:13-14; Jeremiah 10:1-2; II Kings 17:17; 21:6; Leviticus 19:26; II Chronicles 33:6; Jeremiah 27:9; 29:8; Acts 16:16-18, etc.), it is highly doubtful that Esther's parents would have even considered consulting an astrologer. Other books claim Esther's husband, King Ahasuerus, was a Mason.[21] The ceremony itself states:

> The more intimately the King became acquainted with her mental powers, the more he respected them. There was no problem of state so intricate that she was not able to solve. In time she became his confidant, and shared with him in the greatness of his kingdom.[22]

The ritual continues, mentioning that as soon as Esther found out about the edict against the Jewish people, she resolved to save her race.[23]

The King had often admitted his indebtedness to her counsels, and pledged his royal word to grant her any request she might make of him, even "to the half of the kingdom," and Esther now resolved to test his sincerity, and appeal to him, even at the risk of her own life, to reverse the horrible edict.[24]

We are told that the day Esther had chosen to see the King was a day of Grand Council where the Persian governors, princes, and officers were gathered together. No one was to see the King unless they were bidden and Esther had not been bidden, but she entered the King's presence nonetheless. The King was angry with her, and "he commanded the guards to lead her forth and execute the law upon her without delay."[25] "Were it my mother, she should die. Take her at once to the courtyard and put her to death,"[26] King Ahasuerus commands, but Esther giving a prearranged signal understood between them, made the King change his mind and he granted Esther her request.[27]

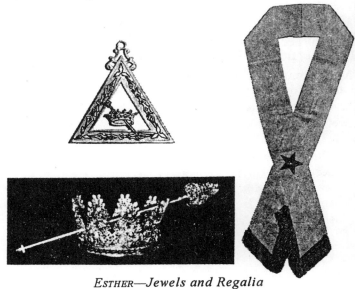

ESTHER—*Jewels and Regalia*

EASTERN STAR'S DISCREPANCIES

Let's pause long enough to look at some of the discrepancies between what the ritual teaches and what the Bible states. First of all, most of the ritual books I've read claim that Mordecai was Esther's uncle.[28] According to the Bible, Esther was Mordecai's "uncle's daughter" (Esther 2:7), making Mordecai Esther's cousin, not her uncle. We also notice that when the edict was pronounced against the Jewish people that Esther did not immediately resolve to save her people as the Eastern Star ritual asserts. When Mordecai sent a message to Esther to inform her what was decreed against the Jewish people and requested that she approach the King, Esther replied to Mordecai that no one could see the King and live except those to whom he held out his sceptre and she reminded Mordecai that the King had not even called for her in the past 30 days. When Mordecai heard this news he sent the messenger back to her warning her that she would not be able to escape if all the other Jews were killed. Finally, Esther sent word to Mordecai that he was to gather all the Jews together and fast and pray for her for three days and that she and her maidens would do likewise. After that, and only after that, would she approach the King to speak on behalf of the Jews.

When the three days were expired Esther went in to the King and:

> ...it was so, when the king saw Esther the queen standing in the court, that she obtained favour in his sight: and the king held out to Esther the golden sceptre that was in his hand. So Esther drew near, and touched the top of the sceptre (Esther 5:2).

Nowhere is there a hint that the governors, princes, and officers were gathered at the palace that day. Nowhere is there any hint that the King was angry at Esther. In fact, it says that she obtained the King's favor. Nowhere is it mentioned that there was any prearranged signal given, nor does the Bible tell us that the King had **OFTEN** promised Esther up "to the half of the kingdom" and that Esther now came to prove his statement. Nowhere is there any clue that Ahasuerus was a Mason. Nowhere can it be ascertained that Esther was the King's confidant, especially since Esther told Mordecai that the King had not called for her in the past 30 days. Had she been the confidant that the ritual avows she was, the King would certainly have had to consult with her frequently and would not have left her alone for 30 days at a time.

The Eastern Star lecture contends that Ahasuerus:

> ...made frequent declarations of his attachment to her [Esther], and the readiness and liberality with which he would acknowledge it whenever demanded. He vowed to her, that no sacrifice would be deemed by him too great for this end, even though it involved the half of his kingdom; and he instructed her, in the event of her wishing to claim this promise, to clothe herself in the apparel of her station,—the white silken robes and the crown royal of the Queen, and thus attired, to come boldly before him. And he swore, with arm uplifted to JEHOVAH—that God whom his

Masonic instructor had taught him to adore as supreme,—that wherever he might be, or in whatever business engaged, if she would appeal to him in this manner, he would grant her request, be it what it might, even to the half of his kingdom. [Emphasis in the original][29]

Had this been the case, Esther would not have feared making her request known nor would she have had all the Jews fasting for her for three days prior to her entreaty because she would have been confident that the King would fulfill his promise. Esther would not have told Mordecai of the seriousness of approaching the King without being called (which could have resulted in her death). Again we see that the Eastern Star ceremony contradicts the Biblical account which it claims to enhance. So, as should be obvious, there is a great deal of difference between what the ritual teaches and what the Bible declares, even though the Eastern Star remarks that "there is no shade of discrepancy."[30]

ELECTA NOT IN SCRIPTURES

In an Eastern Star book entitled *The Ladies' Friend*, G. W. Brown claims: "The **COMPLETE HISTORIES** of these five female characters you will read for yourselves in the Scriptures."[31] Yet, several pages later, the author admits:

The last of these five female characters, whose virtues and misfortunes make up the glory of the Eastern Star, is Electa. **NO ACCOUNT OF THIS CELEBRATED WOMAN IS GIVEN IN THE SCRIPTURES;** we are entirely indebted for what we know of her to Masonic tradition.[32]

Another Eastern Star book also alleged that the "Five Degrees of the Order of the Eastern Star are founded on the Holy Scriptures,"[33] but the degree of Electa has no Scriptural basis whatsoever. One book, however, does admit that the "character portrayed is a purely fictitious one, to which the name of Electa is given...."[34] The name Electa is not to be found in the Bible, nor is any of the ritual that is passed on to the initiates. The name is derived from II John 1:1 where John writes: "The elder unto the elect lady and her children, whom I love in the truth; and not I only, but also all they that have known the truth."

An old Eastern Star ritual book mentions that Electa was the "friend of St. John and wife of Gaius, Past Grand Master of Masons."[35] Electa, according to the Eastern Star books, was reared as a pagan and worshiped idols but she, as well as her husband and her household, converted to Christianity, even though she knew that to do so could mean death and persecution. She opened

ELECTA—Jewels and Regalia

her home to the persecuted and willingly shared her wealth with others.[36]

One day, according to the story told by the Eastern Star, a law went into effect requiring that "all who professed the religion of Christ should be made to renounce it under penalty of death."[37]

> It was at a period when all manner of persecution awaited those who professed the Christian faith. Imprisonment, scourgings, loss of property and often the loss of life was the price paid by those who gave in their adhesion to Christ. Electa and her family, however, were spared for many years. The Masonic influence which her husband so largely shared, made friends amongst those who would otherwise have persecuted them; and although they were often scorned and pointed at as the followers of a crucified Saviour, yet no other evil befell them.[38]

Eventually, however, the time came when the Roman soldiers went to Electa's home and demanded that she throw a cross on the ground and step on it. Instead, Electa hugged the cross to her bosom, showing that she would never deny her Christian faith even in spite of persecution.[39] The Eastern Star lecture explains: "Their [the Roman soldiers'] commander, a Mason, endeavored to save Electa, by inducing her to submit to the test, but in vain."[40]

> He besought her therefore, ardently, to recant from Christianity. He told her the **RECANTATION WAS A MERE FORM,** which need not indeed affect her private opinions and handed her a Cross which he bade her throw upon the floor and put her foot upon it, assuring her that he would then leave her without danger, and **MAKE REPORT THAT SHE HAD RECANTED.**[41]

Refusing to do so:

She was, therefore, thrown into a loathsome dungeon, with her family; and her splendid mansion and possessions totally destroyed. For a twelvemonth [1 year], they were fed in that prison by the Masonic charity; then they were visited by the Judge, a humane man and a Mason, who, like the commander, proposed the test as a means of escape, still available. But it was steadfastly spurned, and though worn by sufferings, Electa begged for that one favor, that their martyrdom might not be delayed from any expectation that any of them would renounce their religion—for they never would.

They were then dragged forth and scourged nigh unto death. After this, they were taken to the top of the nearest hill and crucified.[42]

While religious persecution of this nature has happened many times in the past, and is still taking place today in many areas of the world, the narration as given in the lecture, is not an actual fact. Moreover, there are several items that are definitely not Scriptural, even though we are informed "that none of the traditions of the Eastern Star contradict the text of Scripture."[43] The lecture alleges that St. John, Gaius, and several of the Romans were Masons. As I've already pointed out, modern Masonry was not started until 1717, which makes these claims untrue.

MASONIC HONESTY?

We also get a glimpse into the character traits of some Masons, which I find quite fascinating. Although Masonry claims to be tolerant of all religions, the Roman commander, a Mason, demanded that Electa deny her Christian faith.[44] Consider the statement: "The Masonic influence which her husband so largely shared, made friends amongst those who would otherwise have persecuted them...."[45] Here we see that their Masonic friends were persecutors and would have persecuted Electa and her family for their religious faith had Electa's husband, Gaius, not been a Mason. Some religious toleration!

Notice also that the Masonic commander told Electa that "the recantation was a mere form," which was, of course, a lie. He further said that he would report that she had recanted, even though he declared that the recantation "need not indeed affect her private opinions." If this were true that the recantation did not affect her private opinions, then by reporting that she had recanted (thus implying that she had given up Christianity), he would have been lying to his official. Either way, this Mason was far from being truthful. So much for Masonic honesty! Furthermore, the judge is proclaimed as "a humane man and a Mason,"[46] yet, he, too, insisted that Electa deny her faith, again showing the intolerance for the Christian religion. Since the fate inflicted upon Electa and her family was probably left in the hands of this judge, I can only wonder what Masonry means by "humane" when we see the cruel tortures that these Christians were put through, including destruction of property, scourging, and crucifixion. All this was implemented by "brother" Masons!

MORE CONTRADICTIONS

Of all things, this lecture starts like this:

The Evangelist John, one of the Patron Saints of Masonry, and one of the acknowledged pillars of the early Christian Church, was the successor in the Grand Mastership, of Gaius, the husband of Electa. **THE EARLY CHRISTIANS WERE MUCH INDEBTED TO MASONRY,** whose principles united them together, and whose votaries **PROTECTED THEM FROM THE SWORDS** of their enemies.[47]

How could the early Christians be indebted to Masonry when this was the very organization that was fueling their persecution and was partially the cause of their martyrdom? Another contradiction is found in the idea that John was a Christian but nowhere are we told that he was singled out for persecution. He seemed to be able to meet freely with the very people who were killing the Christians. Surely John would have been as well known (or better known) than Electa and would have also come under Masonic persecution. Yet when Gaius was imprisoned and killed, the Masons chose another Christian, John, to become the Grand Master of the Lodge to replace Gaius.

Moreover, before Electa's imprisonment and subsequent death, the lecture claims St. John had promised her that he would "institute a Degree to be entitled after [her] name, which shall perpetuate [her] history...."[48] Can you imagine John going back to the same group of people who were instrumental in putting to death Electa and Gaius, and instituting a degree in Electa's behalf? If Christians were so hated, persecuted, and killed, how could John institute a sign for Electa's sake? This would be pure insanity on John's part to ask these Masons to honor a person who would be considered a heretic to them. Nevertheless, the ritual contends:

> True to his word, the Grand Master St. John, upon receiving intelligence of her triumphant death, made known his promise to the Fraternity in Grand Lodge assembled, and established the Degree of Electa, announcing for its sign, the CHRISTIAN'S HAILING SIGN, a remembrance of the manner of her death. [Emphasis in the original][49]

Consider, too, the foolishness of these pagan Masons accepting the "CHRISTIAN'S hailing sign" when they were persecuting and killing the Christians. Accepting such a sign would have been equivalent to Hitler agreeing to honor the Jews after he had ordered them killed. Also note, if St. John introduced this degree in approximately 90 A.D. (as the ritual maintains), then Rob Morris did not invent it, as he claimed he did. If Morris is indeed the inventor of this Degree, then St. John did not introduce it to the Grand Lodge, as Morris claimed he did. Either way, Morris is lying! Again, we can see Masonic "honesty" in action (or should I say dishonesty as usual)?

MASONIC DATES CONFLICT

Another example of so-called Masonic honesty can be found in a book entitled *History of the Order of the Eastern Star.* It asserts: "The Masonic Order dates its origin back to the reign of King Solomon, who ascended the throne 1015 years before the Christian era...."[50] Of course, as I stated earlier, the modern founding of the Masonic organization only dates back to 1717. In this same book, we find the following statements:

> She [Adah, daughter of Jephthah] was a Mason's daughter....[51]

> Her [Ruth's] husband, Mahlon was a citizen of Bethlehem, who had taken up his residence in the land of Moab where he died. He was a Freemason.[52]

> The owner of the field—Boaz by name—was as famed for his liberality as for his wealth. He, too, was a Mason, and had long tutored himself by the sublime principles of that Order, of which he was an honored member, to divide his bread with the suffering poor.[53]

> The Masonic history of Ruth ends here; but the Scriptural account goes on to say that she became the wife of this generous man [Boaz] and Mason, and that through a long line of posterity, Christ, according to the flesh, was her son.[54]

Did you notice a problem? First the book claims the Masonic Order dates back to **KING SOLOMON'S REIGN,** but then it goes on to maintain that Jephthah (born approximately 1161 B.C.),[55] Mahlon (died approximately 1261 B.C.),[56] and Boaz (married to Ruth in approximately 1251 B.C.)[57] were all Masons! The dilemma is that all these men lived several generations **BEFORE** Solomon was even born in approximately 1015 B.C.[58] In fact, Boaz was the great great grandfather of Solomon! How then, could Boaz have "long tutored himself by the sublime principles of that [Masonic] Order" when that Order was not even in existence? Also, the declaration that the "Scriptural account goes on to say that" Boaz was a Mason is an obvious untruth.

Although much more could be said about these five degrees (such as the Eastern Star's pronouncement that Lazarus was a Freemason[59]) it should be evident by now that the degrees are not only not Scriptural, but they also contain outright lies, exaggerations, and misstatements. Additionally, there arises a theological problem in the degree of Adah, where Jephthah says to Adah: "My daughter! there is another world, where the errors of this life shall be forgiven, and sorrow lost in universal joy. I will meet you there."[60] The Bible clearly teaches us that there is no second chance for salvation or rectifying transgressions. "It is appointed unto men once to die," says the writer of Hebrews, "but after this the judgment" (Hebrews 9:27). However, the statement supposedly made by Jephthah insinuates that there will be another chance in the next world "where the errors of this life shall be forgiven." Remarks of this nature can give the initiate the feeling that there is no need in this life to worry about repenting of sins now since there will be another chance later on. A belief like this can have dangerous spiritual consequences.

QUEEN OF THE SOUTH

In addition to the five degrees mentioned above, there is an honorary degree called the Queen of the South, also written by Rob Morris.[61] The setting is in a place called a Palace with the Queen of Sheba entreating King Solomon to give recognition to women.[62] She pleads:

> The basic secrets of Freemasonry we do not seek to learn. We do not wish to make unreasonable demands upon our fathers, brothers, or husbands as Master Masons. Yet when we are told that we are intimately bound to the Masonic fraternity by ties most tender and lasting, we seek some tokens of recognition whereby we may know Masons and be known of them as sharing in the Masonic privileges. Whatever knowledge is of advantage to us for the advancement of womankind, that we desire to know, and Masons will find us worthy of the trust reposed in us.[63]

As the Queen finishes her speech, she declares:

Inviolably in my heart of hearts I will treasure what you have given me this hour, and this tongue shall be torn from its place before the least of your secrets shall be unlawfully made known.[64]

We might ask, "What are the secrets that cannot be made known?" The Master Mason's obligation reveals:

Furthermore, that I will keep the secrets of a worthy brother Master Mason as inviolable as my own when communicated to and received by me as such, murder and treason excepted.[65]

William Meyer explains:

Murder and treason are crimes and so the candidate agrees to conceal crimes of a lesser nature than murder and treason when committed by a brother Master Mason. The Eastern Star "Queen of the South" agrees that her "tongue shall be torn from its place," before the least of any Master Mason's secrets, (whether this be adultery, prostitution, theft, or knavery) be unlawfully revealed by her, to the proper authorities or to a non-Mason, even though such non-Mason be her own husband....

Nor dare the "sister" complain when "brother" husband goes on the primrose path, for should he be expelled from the lodge, she goes out too, unless she could induce some other brother to become her sponsor. A most ingenious way to make these women keep their mouths shut![66]

In addition to swearing this oath, we discover that the degree, although sounding like it might be based on

Scripture, is not. The Queen of Sheba who comes to Solomon in this degree is called Bathsheba.[67] This Queen, when addressing Solomon, refers to herself as "the Queen Mother"[68] and begs Solomon to "Harken unto me, oh my son."[69] It is true that Solomon's mother's name was Bathsheba, but Bathsheba **WAS NOT** the same person as the Queen of Sheba! The Bible clearly reveals that the Queen of Sheba was from another country:

> When the queen of Sheba heard of the fame of Solomon, she came to prove Solomon with hard questions at Jerusalem...and when she was come to Solomon, she communed with him of all that was in her heart....So she turned, and went away to **HER OWN LAND,** she and her servants (II Chronicles 9:1, 12; I Kings 10:1, 13; See also: Matthew 12:42 and Luke 11:31).

Once again, it should be clear that the Eastern Star uses (or rather abuses) the Bible to make the ritual **SOUND** like it is Scriptural when, in actuality, it is not.

The Lord, speaking through Isaiah, proclaimed:

> This people draw near Me with their mouth, and with their lips do honour Me, but have removed their heart far from Me, and their fear toward Me is taught by the precept of men....Woe unto them that seek deep to hide their counsel from the Lord, and their works are in the dark, and they say, Who seeth us? and who knoweth us? (Isaiah 29:13, 15; Matthew 15:8; Mark 7:6).

4. HIS STAR IN THE EAST

"We have seen His star in the East, and are come to worship Him."[1] The Eastern Star initiates are told that this phrase refers to the star of Bethlehem[2] that the wise men followed to find Christ (Matthew 2:2). "The five-pointed star is often called the Star of Bethlehem... that, at the time of the birth of Jesus, a star guided the Magi to Palestine...."[3] Is this really what is meant by this statement or is there another, more esoteric meaning? This same reference explains:

...ASIDE FROM THIS TIME-HONORED TRADITION that, at the time of the birth of Jesus, a star guided the Magi to Palestine, there is a deep ethical and spiritual suggestiveness in this beautiful emblem which may be profitably **CONSIDERED FROM MORE THAN A SINGLE STANDPOINT.**[4]

So, we can see that there is a "spiritual suggestiveness" **ASIDE** from (or in **ADDITION** to) the tradition of the Star of Bethlehem. What, then, does this Star **REALLY** symbolize?

In the *Worthy Matrons' Hand Book,* is a poem that is revealing. It reads:

"You all know of that star of the East,
And the story the 'Wise Men' told;
How it proclaimed to the world a new light,
That bright, wondrous star of old.
We, **TOO,** have a star to worship,
Giving hope, and light by the way,
If we only obey its teachings,
And practice its precepts each day."[5]

Notice that this poem insinuates that the Eastern Star star is a **DIFFERENT STAR** than that star of the

East. It mentions the "star of the East," then adds: "We, **TOO,** have a star to worship," which makes a differentiation between the **TWO** stars!

First of all, the star of Bethlehem could not have been an "eastern star," since most biblical expositors agree that the magi came **FROM** the east, and that therefore a star over Judea would be in the western sky to their viewpoint. Some scholars feel that the passage means that the magi were "in the east" when the (sic) saw the star—others say that the term "in the east" can also be translated alternately as "seen when it rose," meaning that they saw the star as it rose.[6]

The Greek word for "east" is "anatole" and means "a rising of light," but it can also imply "the east." So, from a Scriptural analysis, we can see the "Eastern Star" is not the same star as mentioned in Matthew 2:2. However, we find even more revealing information in Masonic literature.

It is justifiable to research Masonic literature for the meaning of symbols since one Eastern Star book by Mary Ann Slipper explains:

Masonry, the oldest of all secret orders which have survived the passing of the years, employs a most elaborate system of symbols in the ritualistic work.

SEVERAL OF THE SAME SYMBOLS HAVE BEEN BORROWED FOR USE IN THE ORDER OF THE EASTERN STAR...THE FIGURE OF

THE SYMBOL SLIGHTLY CHANGED, BUT THE IDEA ASSOCIATED WITH THE SYMBOL KEPT INTACT.[7]

THE BLAZING STAR

With this in mind, let's proceed. The Masonic Service Association, an organization that supplies lodges with brief lectures for lodge meetings, publishes *The Short Talk Bulletin,* which is called "one of Masonry's most outstanding regular publications."[8] Turning to the outline section of *The Short Talk Bulletin* entitled "Blazing Star" we find: **"NOT** the Star of Bethlehem."[9] This outline also lists the Blazing Star as "A **HEX** sign" and "A Symbol of Deity."[10] Now, the Bethlehem Star announced the birth of Jesus Christ, but if the Blazing Star (the star used in both Masonry and the Eastern Star) is a **HEX** sign and a symbol of Deity but is not the Star of Bethlehem, who or what does this Star represent? In other words, this Star is a symbol of Deity[11]

OUTLINE FOR A SHORT TALK

I. Introduction: Definitions

    A. A lodge "ornament"

    B. A 5-pointed star

    C. Not the Star of Bethlehem   *NOTE*

II. Antiquity of This Symbol

    A. Used by ancients

    B. Greek *pentalpha*

    C. A hex sign

III. Use in Freemasonry

    A. Symbol of prudence

    B. The "true Freemason"

    C. The "glory in the center"

    D. Divine radiance

    E. A symbol of Deity

IV. The Pentalpha

    A. Origin of the term

    B. Five, a mystic number

    C. Its power of regeneration

    D. The "triple triangle"

V. Importance to Speculative Masons

    A. Geometry

    B. Construction of pentalpha

    C. Ratios and relationships

VI. Conclusion

    A. Regenerative nature of the star

    B. Moral idea illustrated

but since the Deity represented by this Star is not the same star that announced the birth of Christ, this Star is a representation of some other Deity! Let's look at another Masonic source as we continue to investigate this Star.

Albert Mackey admits:

The *Blazing Star* is said by WREN to be "commemorative of the star which appeared to guide the wise men of the East to the place of our Savior's nativity." This, which is one of the ancient interpretations of the symbol, being considered as too sectarian in its character and unsuitable to the universal religion of Masonry, has been omitted since the meeting of grand Lecturers at Baltimore in 1842. [Emphasis in the original][12]

Since Rob Morris, the founder of the Eastern Star, was a very knowledgeable Mason, and since he was made a Mason four years **AFTER** the Baltimore meeting, he should have been (and most likely was) aware that the Blazing Star or the Star in the East **DID NOT** represent the star that guided the wise men to the place where Christ was. As can be seen from the above quotation, the idea of the star representing Christ's birth was "considered as too sectarian" and so this explanation was **OMITTED** in 1842. The Eastern Star was not founded until 1850!

PRUDENCE IS A SERPENT

Masonic author, George Oliver, claims that the Blazing Star:

...is an emblem of that Prudence which ought to appear conspicuous in the conduct of every mason; but it is more especially commemorative of that Star which appeared in the East, to guide the wise men to

Bethlehem, to proclaim the birth and the presence of the Son of God.[13]

He adds that the "Great Architect of the universe is therefore symbolized in Freemasonry by the Blazing Star, as the herald of our salvation."[14] That **SOUNDS** okay, doesn't it? The Blazing Star is an emblem of Prudence and the "herald of our salvation," says Oliver and other Masons.[15] Later, however, Oliver explains to us what Prudence was:

> Prudence was the third emanation of the Basilidean deity, Abrax and it was denominated, on account of its value and importance to man in a state of probation, the Logos, or Word.[16]

Francois Ribadeau Dumas mentions that the god of prudence in Egypt is the serpent.[17] In *The Short Talk Bulletin* we find:

> In some Masonic rituals of the eighteenth century the blazing star was regarded as a symbol of prudence....Some writers have seen in this interpretation a "persistence" of ideas from the dawn of recorded history to the present. The ancient Egyptians worshipped as one of their gods the Dog Star....The star was given credit for such salvation and thus became a symbol of prudence.[18]

Eliphas Levi alleges that the astral light was represented by the Gnostics:

> ...as the burning body of the Holy Ghost, and this was which was adored in the secret rites of the Sabbath or the Temple under the symbolic figure of Baphomet, or of the Androgyne Goat of Mendes.
>
> This ambient and all-penetrating fluid, this ray detached from the sun's splendour, and fixed by the

28TH DEGREE — KNIGHT OF THE SUN

We find another explanation in the lecture for the Rose Croix Degree:

The serpent... the Phoenicians... deemed to be immortal... becoming young... by entering into and consuming himself. Hence the Serpent in a circle, holding his tail in his mouth, was an emblem of eternity (p. 278);

and further in the lecture of this degree:

There is a Life-Principle of the world, a universal agent, wherein are two natures and a double current, of love and wrath. ...It is a ray detached from the glory of the Sun,... It is the body of the Holy Spirit, the universal Agent, the Serpent devouring his own tail (p 734).

weight of the atmosphere and by the power of central attraction, this body of the Holy Ghost, which we call the Astral Light and the Universal Agent, this electro-magnetic ether, this vital and luminous caloric, is represented on ancient monuments by the girdle of Isis, which twines in a love-knot round two poles, by the bull-headed serpent, by the serpent with the head of a goat or dog, in the ancient theogonies, and by the **SERPENT DEVOURING ITS TAIL, EMBLEM OF PRUDENCE AND OF SATURN.** It is the winged dragon of Medea, the double serpent of the caduceus, and the tempter of Genesis; but it is also the brazen snake of Moses, encircling the Tau, that is, the generative lingam; it is the Hyle of the Gnostics, and the double tail which forms the legs of the solar cock of Abraxos. Lastly, it is the devil of exoteric dogmatism....[19]

DOG STAR REPRESENTED

Aha! All of a sudden the meaning is not what we thought it was, is it? The symbol of the Blazing Star actually represents the Dog Star. In just a moment we will cover the Dog Star in greater detail. For now, to find out more of what Oliver means, we need to know who Abrax was. Abrax (also Abrac, Abracax, Abraxas, Abrasax, Abraxis, and Abraxos) was the name of the Gnostic god,[20] the "Protective Serpent,"[21] and a symbol of the Sun.[22] "The word engraved on a gem or stone is considered by occultists to constitute a very potent charm."[23] From Abraxas comes the word "Abracadabra."[24] In *A Dictionary of Symbols,* we find this about the word Abracadabra: "This magic word has also been related to the Abracax (Abraxas, Abrasax) of the Gnostics. It is in reality one of the names of the sun-god, Mithras."[25] According to the *Masonic Quiz Book,* it "formerly was worn as an amulet against certain diseases....At some times a form of incantation."[26]

Albert Pike, probably the most well-known and respected Masonic authority of all time,[27] declares the following about the Blazing Star:

> ...to make it commemorative of the Star that is said to have guided the Magi, is to give it a meaning comparatively modern. Originally it represented SIRIUS, or the Dog-Star, the forerunner of the inundation of the Nile; the God ANUBIS, companion of ISIS in her search for the body of OSIRIS, her brother and husband. Then it became the image of HORUS, the son of OSIRIS, himself symbolized also by the Sun, the author of the Seasons, and the God of Time; Son of ISIS, who was the universal nature, himself the primitive matter, inexhaustible source of Life, spark of uncreated fire, universal seed of all beings. It was HERMES, also, the Master of Learning, whose name in Greek is that of the God Mercury. It became the sacred and potent sign of character of the Magi, the PENTALPHA, and is the significant emblem of Liberty and Freedom, blazing with a steady radiance amid the weltering elements of good and evil of Revolutions, and promising serene skies and fertile seasons to the nations, after the storms of change and tumult. [Emphasis in the original][28]

Here Pike is saying that the idea of the Blazing Star guiding the Magi is only a comparatively modern meaning, but that **ORIGINALLY** this Star represented Sirius. This is some admission—especially once you realize just **WHAT** Sirius implies! Pike explains that the "Blazing Star in our Lodges...represents Sirius, Anubis, or Mercury, Guardian and Guide of Souls. Our Ancient English brethren also considered it an emblem of the Sun."[29] Some other names for this so-called "Star of Bethlehem," then, are the Blazing Star, Dog Star, Sirius, Anubis, and Mercury. Pike also calls this Dog Star Horus[30] and Sothis[31] Other sources list this Star as: Star of Isis,[32] Star in the East,[33] Star of the

Annunciation,[34] Canis Major,[35] Sept,[36] Sihor,[37] Star of the White Spirits,[38] Star of Isis-Sothis,[39] Star of Hathor,[40] Star of Horus,[41] Nile star,[42] Morning Star,[43] Canicula,[44] Sothos,[45] Sothis,[46] Septet,[47] Thotes,[48] Star of Set,[49] Star of Nuit,[50] Thot (or Thoth),[51] Thor,[52] Taaut (or Thaaut),[53] Thayuat,[54] AEsculapius,[55] Hept,[56] Tahaut,[57] Seirios,[58] Seitois,[59] Rubeola,[60] Hannobech,[61] Lucifer,[62] and Set.[63]

Checking these other designations for the Dog Star provides some astonishing information. For instance, one of the names of the Dog Star is Sirius.[64] William Schnoebelen, a former witch, Satanist, and Mason, points out that Sirius "is the most significant star in Satanism. It is sacred to the god, Set."[65] This, of course, is not just one man's opinion, either. A witchcraft magazine, *Circle Network News,* relates:

> Those who practise Witchcraft with an Egyptian flavour, or are of ceremonial bent, will no doubt join in the celebration of the rising of Sothis (Sirius) the star of Isis on the 23rd of July [1984].

> This night, from Amenti [the underworld or hell[66]], shall Seth [Set], God of the underworld, release her, and she shall rise, the Star of Isis, Sothis in all her beauty.[67]

Another occult magazine, *Sphaera Imaginatio,* announces:

> The summer solstice coincided with the Dog-Star (Sothis) rising with the sun...Sirius-Sothis being the star of the Goddess Isis.[68]

Texe Marrs, an expert on the New Age movement, reports:

> Throughout the centuries Sirius has been recognized by most occultists and esoteric teachers as the location

where Lucifer and his hierarchy dwell. In Christian terminology, Sirius is simply a secretive codeword for "hell."[69]

It is interesting to note that Venus also "became the goddess of the Dog Star, Sirius...."[70] Venus, by the way, is another name for Lucifer![71] Sirius is so important to the occultists that a New Age organization even named their society the Sirius Community and their newsletter is called the *Sirius Journal.*[72] This group was started by former members of the Findhorn Community located in Scotland.

LUCIFERIC INITIATION

Another former member and co-director of the Findhorn Community was David Spangler.[73] Spangler seems to be quite enthralled with Lucifer. He writes:

Lucifer prepares man in all ways for the experience of Christhood and the Christ prepares man for the experience of God....But the light that reveals to us the presence of the Christ, the light that reveals to us that path to the Christ comes from Lucifer. He is the light giver....it is his light that heralds for man the dawn of a greater consciousness....

Lucifer works within each of us to bring us to wholeness, and as we move into a new age, which is the age of man's wholeness, each of us in some way is brought to that point which I term the Luciferic initiation, the particular doorway through which the individual must pass if he is to come "fully" into the presence of his light and his wholeness.[74]

Later in the book he says:

Lucifer came to give us the final gift of wholeness. If we accept it then he is free and we are free. That is the Luciferic initiation. It is the one that many people now, and in the days ahead will be facing, for it is an initiation into the New Age.[75]

It should be easy to see that the admiration of Lucifer and Sirius in the New Age movement and Masonry is well established. Masonry, by the way, is part of the New Age movement. In the August 1992 *Scottish Rite Journal* (which is "the oldest American Masonic publication"[76]), is an interesting notation. There is an article bragging that a Masonic section on Compuserve can now be reached. How do you get this information? "To access the Masonic section, log onto CompuServe, GO Newage, Section 8 (Masonry.)"[77] In other words, to obtain this information you must type "GO Newage." Many other examples can be cited. For instance, for 87 years the title of the official monthly publication for the Southern Jurisdiction of Masonry's Masonic magazine was *The New Age*. Recently, however, they changed their name to *The Scottish Rite Journal*.[78]

JANUARY • 1989 • VOLUME XCVII, NUMBER 1

The former head of the Southern Jurisdiction of Masonry was Henry C. Clausen. In his book, *Emergence of the Mystical,* he penned: "We look toward a transformation into a **NEW AGE** using, however, the insights and wisdom of the ancient mystics."[79] Even one Masonic author, Lynn F. Perkins, wrote a book entitled *Masonry in the New Age.* He eagerly relates:

> What a great day it will be when the youth of the **NEW AGE,** educated outside of the lodges in the teachings of the "Cosmic Viewpoint," will flock into the lodges of Masonry to receive further instruction (Light) from competent teachers of philosophic Masonry!! The future of Masonry is, indeed, bright with the promise of a revival of its true purpose and mission in a **NEW AGE** setting!...Let **NEW AGE** Peace and Brotherhood appear on earth as it is in the heavens!!! "So Mote It Be."[80]

THE GOD OF THE EASTERN STAR

Returning to the Dog Star, we find that another name for this Star is Mercury.[81] In Roman mythology Mercury:

> ...was the god of commerce and travel, and the patron of thieves, gamblers, and ambassadors. The Greeks called him Hermes or Cyllenius, because he was born on Mount Cyllene, in Arcadia. He was the son of Jupiter (Zeus) and Maia, a daughter of Atlas. Pan, the god of shepherds, was the son of Mercury.[82]

Apollo gave him:

> ...a magic wand called the *caduceus.* Mercury used this to guide the souls of the dead to the Lower World. He also could control the living and the dead with it, or turn anything to gold. [Emphasis in the original][83]

In one book on mythology, you will find Mercury "seated naked on a rock...."[84] A book on witchcraft informs us that Mercury was the "inventor of incantations [and] was wont to be invoked in the rites of magicians...."[85] Mercury was also one of the names of gods invoked in Roman Necromancy.[86] Necromancy is sorcery or communication with the dead. Another book mentions that Mercury was "the conductor of the dead to Hades [hell]."[87] Pike, of course, claims that Mercury is the "Guardian and Guide of Souls."[88] Do you want a god that is conjured up by magicians and is the conductor of the dead to hell to be the "Guardian and Guide" of **YOUR** soul?

Are you beginning to get a picture of the god that is being portrayed in the Eastern Star? Their god has magical powers. He is the god of the underworld (hell) and the patron of thieves and gamblers. Note also that Mercury's son is Pan.[89]

> The god Pan is a symbol of nature, and is usually
> represented with horns (expressive of the sun's rays
> and of the aggressive force of Aries) and with legs
> covered with hair (denoting the vitality of base forces,
> earth, shrubs and the instincts). In astrology, Pan is
> one aspect of Saturn, and is also equated with Satan
> and with life in its involutive, and, in particular, its
> base, aspects.[90]

The   P-3
God
PAN

PAN, Greek god of nature, forests, pastures, flocks, and shepherds. His horns are expressive of the sun's rays, and legs covered with hair denote base forces. Pan is sometimes equated with Satan and life's lower instincts, or the left hand path.

Since Pan is represented with horns it is no wonder that he is called the "Horned God" by the witches.[91]
PAN WAS THE PATRON SAINT OF SEXUAL PASTIMES....He often tried to capture women, and because of his lustfulness, they lived in such fear of him that his name is still associated with fear, in the adjective "panicky" and the noun "panic."[92]

GOD OF LUST

In *The Satanic Bible* Pan is called the "Greek god of lust" who was "later relegated to devildom."[93] "...Pan appears conventionally with horns and a hand on a naked nymph."[94] "He was Pan the unhappy lover, Pan the mischief-maker, Pan the author of sudden **SEXUAL FORAYS AGAINST GIRLS AND BOYS ALIKE.**"[95] The last statement reveals to us that Pan is an adulterer, homosexual, and bisexual. "In fact," says Charles G. Berger, "we are told that practically all of the gods had homosexual love affairs."[96] He continues:

Not only were women offered for the use of men, but male prostitutes, sodomites, or *kadhish* (consecrated males), were provided for those who wished to satisfy their perverted inclinations in that manner. That the sodomites might be made more effeminate and pleasing, they were sometimes depilitated. In Yucatan the god Chin instituted and sanctified homosexuality. Tahiti had special divinities for homosexual worship.[97]

Although sex worship often degenerated into licentiousness, it gradually developed in such a manner that the sex element became less and less conspicuous....After a time the very knowledge of the connection of sex with religion became a part of the religious mysteries which was carefully **KEPT FROM THE COMMON PEOPLE, AND WAS**

REVEALED ONLY UNDER THE MOST SOLEMN VOWS OF SECRECY to persons who had previously proved themselves to be worthy of being entrusted with such an important secret. Later the knowledge was recognized, forgotten, and lost to all except a few scholars who carefully kept it, and from whom we may learn.[98]

SYMBOLS ARE DISGUISED

What a perfect description of how Masonry and the Eastern Star, among other mystery religions, have concealed and shrouded the sexual connotations under the guise of symbolism! Berger explains:

At first, in art, the sex organs were represented by pictures of them, but as man developed and ideas of morals changed, such representations seemed offensive or crude, and they were therefore **GRADUALLY MODIFIED UNTIL THE SYMBOLS COULD SCARCELY BE RECOGNIZED AS SEXUAL** in origin. **OTHER EXPLANATIONS AND MEANINGS WERE INVENTED FOR THE MASSES,** who were not supposed to understand the **TRUE MEANINGS.** Thus, **SYMBOLS CAME TO HAVE TWO MEANINGS,** the esoteric and the exoteric. The **ESOTERIC** meaning was the true or original meaning, **UNDERSTOOD BY ONLY A FEW** and closely guarded by them. The exoteric meaning was the invented, or modified, explanation intended for the many. The sacred mysteries, which are often mentioned in connection with many ancient religions and which were closely guarded by the initiate, concerned esoteric meanings in the religions of previous times. These sacred mysteries very often were merely continuations of the simpler forms of early sex worship carried on by a select few.[99]

The Blazing Star (or the Pentagram) just happens to be one of these disguised sexual symbols. Former

Sovereign Grand Commander of the Southern Jurisdiction of Freemasonry, Henry C. Clausen, points out:

> The **BLAZING STAR** found in the center of the temple floors indicated the search of the adepts into the heavens for the sign of a brilliant, luminous star. When this appeared, they would warn the people of the lowlands that danger was approaching so they could go to high ground and escape the overflowing waters of the Nile which, in turn, would **FERTILIZE** the flooded earth. This of itself was considered a demonstration of the **OSIRIAN TRIAD** whereby **OSIRIS,** the Sovereign of the Sun and of the Lower Regions and Judger of Souls would **UNITE** with **ISIS,** personifying **FERTILITY** and the rich, black land of the Nile Valley, and from this **UNION** there would come **HORUS,** the Son, representing the new harvest of luxuriant abundance.[100]

In fact, the Pentagram is called "The Great Rite" in witchcraft. Witches Janet and Stewart Farrar report:

> The couple enacting the Great Rite are offering themselves, with reverence and joy, as expressions of the God and Goddess aspects of the Ultimate Source....They are making themselves to the best of their ability, channels for that divine polarity on all levels, from physical to spiritual. That is why it is called the Great Rite.... "Ritual sexual intercourse," says Doreen Valiente, "is a very old idea indeed— probably as old as humanity itself."...The Great Rite invocation specially declares that the body of the woman taking part is an altar, with her womb and generative organs as its sacred focus, and reveres it as such....The High Priestess then lays herself down towards the altar, and her arms and legs outstretched to form the **PENTAGRAM.**[101]

THE CADUCEUS

Earlier we mentioned that Mercury (or Hermes) had a magic wand called a caduceus, which was a staff entwined by two serpents.[102] Pike explains the caduceus like this:

> It was originally a simple Cross, symbolizing the equator and equincoctial Colure, and the **FOUR**

> **ELEMENTS** proceeding from a common centre. This Cross, surmounted by a circle, and that by a crescent, became an emblem of the Supreme Deity—or of the active power of **GENERATION** and the passive power of **PRODUCTION** conjoined,—and was appropriated to Thoth or Mercury. It then assumed an improved form, the arms of the Cross being changed into wings, and the circle and crescent being formed by two snakes, springing from the wand, forming a circle by crossing each other, and their heads making the horns of the crescent; in which form it is seen in the hands of Anubis.[103]

The caduceus, says Pike, additionally symbolizes the four elements. J.E. Cirlot gives us a fuller explanation:

> The caduceus also signifies the integration of the four elements, the wand corresponding to earth, the wings to air, the serpents to fire and water (by analogy with the undulating movement of waves and flames)....According to esoteric Buddhism, the wand of the caduceus corresponds to the axis of the world and the serpents refer to the force called Kundalini, which, in Tantrist teaching, sleeps coiled up at the base of the backbone—a symbol of the evolutive power of pure energy.[104]

The four elements figure prominently in witchcraft and will be discussed elsewhere in this book.

Did you notice that the caduceus "became an emblem of the Supreme Deity"[105] and that it represented "the active power of generation and the passive power of production conjoined"?[106] In other words, this emblem is a veiled symbol for the sex act and it is this symbol that represents the Supreme Deity of the Masons (and, by extension, the Eastern Stars as well)! Eliphas Levi, the **OCCULTIST** whom Albert Pike plagiarized in *Morals and Dogma*[107] (which we are told by Masonic author Lucien V. Rule "is the greatest single work on author Lucien V. Rule "is the greatest single work on Masonic philosophy ever given to the world"[108]), also mentions that the god Mercury was assigned "to the parts of **GENERATION.**"[109] Of course, one Masonic symbol after another has this sexual connotation, but in spite of the sexual innuendoes, Past Master Albert L. Woody, Grand Lecturer in Illinois, tells us:

> As late as 1812, in Pennsylvania, the Deacons in procession carried columns—the **SAME** columns which now rest on the Wardens' pedestals. Deacons first carried blue rods tipped with gold, symbolizing friendship and benevolence; later these were tipped with a **PINE CONE** in **IMITATION OF THE CADUCEUS** of Mercury, the messenger of the gods.[110]

Another Masonic book, after explaining about the caduceus, brags: "The rod of the Master of Ceremonies is an analogue [equivalent or parallel]."[111] Masonic author and **OCCULTIST,** Manly Palmer Hall (who gave instructions on how to **CONJURE UP DEMONS**[112]), states: "The **PINE CONE IS A PHALLIC SYMBOL** of remote antiquity."[113] I find this quite interesting since in witchcraft a phallic wand is supposed to be carried for fertility festivals. Stewart Farrar, a witch, says that how visually explicit this symbol is, is up to the individual witchcraft groups, but "One traditional symbol is a plain wand tipped with a pine-cone...."[114] Doesn't the connection between Masonry and witchcraft become quite evident? Gerald Gardner, **BOTH A MASON AND A WELL-KNOWN WITCH,** "goes so far as to say that **WITCHCRAFT IS THE ORIGINAL LODGE.**"[115] Gardner, like many other Masons and witches, had a "heavy sexual emphasis"[116] in his brand of witchcraft.

> Gerald Gardner's rites also included ritual scourging and sexual intercourse between the High Priest and Priestess. He insisted that witchcraft (or "wicca")

Not only is there a link between Lucifer and Sirius but the relationship of Sirius with fertility can be observed. The book, *Egyptian Mythology,* denotes that Hathor's:

> ...connections with **FERTILITY** naturally led to her association with the rise of the Nile and the **DOG-STAR SOTHIS [SIRIUS],** when she was represented lying in a ship as a cow with a star between her horns.[118]

For more information and documentation about the sexual connotation of Masonic symbolism, see my book *Hidden Secrets of Masonry.*[119]

HERMES IS MASONIC REDEEMER

Mercury was a Roman god but in Greece he was called Hermes.[120] Hermes, too, was regarded as the "conductor of the dead to Hades [hell]."[121] It was believed that "Hermes could also lead back the souls of the dead into the world of light."[122] Of course, this is an unscriptural view since the Bible clearly specifies that "it is appointed unto men once to die, but after this the judgment" (Hebrews 9:27). Once one's eternal destiny has been settled, there is no way that anyone can leave hell and enter into heaven or the "world of light." Luke 16:26 mentions that "there is a great gulf fixed: so that they which would pass from hence to you cannot; neither can they pass to us, that would come from thence."

It was Hermes who was an astrologer[123] and who was also attributed with initiating men into magic[124] and "the founder of occult science, especially Alchemy."[125] Pike states:

> Among the sciences taught by Hermes, there were secrets which he communicated to the Initiates only upon condition that they should bind themselves, by

a terrible oath, never to divulge them, except to those who, after long trial, should be found worthy to succeed them. The Kings even prohibited the revelation of them on pain of death. This secret was styled the Sacerdotal Art, and included alchemy, astrology, magism [magic], the science of spirits, etc.[126]

Another Masonic book notifies us that Hermes was "the Bringer of Light."[127] Pike remarks that **HERMES IS** "the personification of Light and the Son, the Mediator, **REDEEMER AND SAVIOUR.**"[128] Alice Bailey, an occultist, reiterates that Hermes "was the first to proclaim Himself as 'the Light of the World.'"[129] Are you beginning to see that when Masons are told they are "sons of light" or when they are "brought to light" that their "light" comes from a false god and not from the God of the Bible? In fact, in the Atrium (or the center court of the Temple) at the House of the Temple, the headquarters of the Supreme Council of the Southern Jurisdiction of Freemasonry, can be found:

...four huge Doric columns of polished green Windsor granite on both sides of the Atrium. Each column is in four sections and weighs 24 tons. In front of each column is a bronze candelabrum standard in the form of Hermes—the **BRINGER OF LIGHT** in the ancient Greek religion.[130]

It seems perfectly fine for Masons to have the symbolism of false gods in their Temple, but they don't want to mention the name of Jesus since that might be offensive to some Masons! Shouldn't the mention of false gods be offensive to Christians? Does this sound like the Eastern Star and Masonry are really compatible with Christianity?

LUCIFERIAN, MAGICIAN,[131] **AND OCCULTIST,**[132] Helena Petrovna Blavatsky, reveals this about Hermes:

SATAN OR HERMES ARE ALL ONE.... He is called the Dragon of Wisdom...the serpent...identical with the god Hermes...inventor of the first initiation of men into magic...the author of serpent worship.[133]

Hermes, like his Roman counterpart, Mercury, carries a staff entwined with serpents. Joseph L. Henderson relates:

These are the famous Naga serpents of ancient India; and we also find them in Greece as the entwined serpents at the end of the staff belonging to the god Hermes. An early Grecian herm is a stone pillar with a bust of the god above. On one side are the entwined serpents and on the other an erect phallus. As the serpents are represented in the act of **SEXUAL UNION** and the erect phallus is unequivocally sexual, we can draw certain conclusions about the function of the herm as a symbol of fertility.

But we are mistaken if we think this only refers to biological fertility. **HERMES** is Trickster in a different role as messenger, a god of the cross-roads, and finally the **LEADER OF SOULS TO AND FROM THE UNDERWORLD.** His phallus therefore penetrates from the known into the unknown world, seeking a spiritual message of deliverance and healing.[134]

[Hermes] had many amorous adventures. Among the goddesses he was, it appears, the lover of Persephone, Hecate and Aphrodite. Among the nymphs, whom he pursued in the shady depths of forests, his conquests were wider. By them he had a numerous progeny....[135]

Hermes was called the "lord of the phallus and male and female at once."[136] This sexual union, as I mentioned earlier, is very prevalent in Masonic symbolism. The symbol used in Masonry is disguised under the form of the cube or cubical stone. Albert G. Mackey, a well-known and highly revered Mason, claims: "Among the pagan mythologies, Mercury or Hermes, was always represented by a cubical stone...."[137] This statement insinuates that Masonry must also be a pagan mythology since Masons use this symbol under the emblem of a rough and smooth (or perfect) ashlar.[138] It's no wonder, then, that these gods are purported to have many sexual encounters, nor is it a great astonishment to learn that these encounters are not only with girls but also with boys. Sexual perversions of all kinds have always been associated with mythology, witchcraft, and Satanism.

PRAYER TO HERMES

Knowing what has been revealed about Hermes (or Mercury), would you be surprised to learn that in 1829 Albert Pike wrote a **HYMN** to the god Hermes? In part, it reads:

"TO HERMES

Hear, white-winged Messenger!...
Thou, who dost teach
Quick-witted thieves the miser's gold to reach,...
Young Rogue-God Hermes! always glad to cheat
All Gods and men,—with mute and noiseless feet
Going in search of mischief; now to steal
The spear of Ares, now to clog the wheel
Of young Apollon's car, that it may crawl
Most slowly upwards!...
LET US EVER BE
UNDER THY CARE,
**AND HEAR, OH HEAR, OUR SOLEMN,
        EARNEST PRAYER."**[139]

Here Pike acknowledges that he is well-versed in mythology and knows that Hermes is considered as a cheat and a rogue, but turns right around and requests that Hermes ever keep him in his care and hear his prayer! Notice to whom he is praying. Remember, too, that Albert Pike is the man who wrote the Masonic rituals from the 4th to the 33rd degrees.[140] Of great interest may be the fact that the acclaimed founder of the Eastern Star, Rob Morris, was also a friend of Albert Pike![141]

MASON CONJURES UP DEMONS!

The Egyptian god, who is equivalent to the Roman Mercury and the Greek Hermes, is Thoth (or Thot).[142] According to *The Satanic Bible,* Thoth is the "Egyptian god of magic."[143] It was Thoth, with his powers of magic, who:

> ...taught Isis the many spells which were to earn her the title of **GREAT ENCHANTRESS.** Thoth's spells enabled Isis to **RESTORE OSIRIS TO LIFE** and to conceive by him after his murder.[144]

Not only was Thoth the god of magic but he was also the god of the dead.[145] Once again, we can see the connection with Masonry since the Masonic rituals, especially the death and resurrection ceremony of the third degree, is a portrayal of the death and resurrection of the Egyptian god Osiris.[146] For instance, Masonic author, George H. Steinmetz, writes: **"UNQUES-TIONABLY OUR THIRD DEGREE DERIVES FROM THE MYSTERIES OF OSIRIS** or from the still more ancient legend from which the Osirian myth itself originated."[147]

"Thoth himself was supposed to have written with his own hand a book of magic and the forty-two volumes which contained all the wisdom of the world."[148] Other references state that he "was credited with considerable magic powers,"[149] taught people the occult arts,[150] and was the originator of alchemy.[151] (Alchemy is magic.[152]) Thoth is attributed with creating "the Tarot cards which may also be used as amulets."[153]

Thoth is one of many gods mentioned as a witchcraft deity:

> When envisioning the Goddess and God, many of the Wicca [practitioners of witchcraft] see Them as well-known Tammuz, Hecate, Ishtar, Cerridwen, **THOTH,** Tara, Aradia, Artemis, Pele, Apollo, Kanaloa, Bridget, Helios, Bran, Lugh, Hera, Cybele, Inanna, Maui, Ea, Athena, Lono, Marduk—the list is virtually endless. Many of their deities with their corresponding histories, rites and mythic information, furnish the concept of deity for Wiccans.[154]

John Yarker, a Mason and author of *The Arcane Schools,* informs us that Thoth and Hermes were also known by the name of Marduk.[155] Marduk was the "god of magicians and magic arts."[156] Yarker adds that "the Biblical Nimrod is one with Marduk, the beginning of whose kingdom was Babel...."[157] In other words, Yarker is identifying Thoth with Nimrod, the builder of the Tower of Babel! (See Genesis 10:8-11 and 11:1-9.) Of course, the building of the Tower of Babel was displeasing to God, but Masons take great pride in this endeavor. Arthur Edward Waite, a **MASON, GOLDEN DAWN MEMBER,**[158] **OCCULTIST,**[159] **AND A SORCERER** who "taught people through his books **HOW TO CONJURE UP DEMONS AND SELL THEIR SOULS TO THE DEVIL,"**[160] writes: "As regards Masonry, **BABEL** of course **REPRESENTED A MASONIC ENTERPRISE...."**[161]

Another Masonic writer, George Oliver, claims that Thoth "was the great grandson of Noah."[162] From the

Bible we learn that Nimrod, the rebel against the true God, was Noah's great grandson (Genesis 10:1, 6-10 and I Chronicles 4:1, 8-10), so this is just another indication that some Masons believe that Thoth was Nimrod.

The Phoenician name of Thoth is rendered as Taaut (also Taut or Thaaut).[163] **PIKE BRAGS THAT THIS GOD IS STILL PREVALENT IN MASONRY AND IS REPRESENTED BY THE MASTER OF THE LODGE** (the Orator)![164] He also states: "According to Sanchoniathon, TAAUT, the interpreter of Heaven to men, attributed something divine to the nature of the dragon and serpents...." [Emphasis in the original][165] He "was the author of the worship of serpents among the Phoenicians."[166]

GOD OF THE UNDERWORLD

Another god that is mentioned in relation to the **BLAZING STAR** is **ANUBIS,** the "God of dark wisdom."[167] Pike tells us: "Isis was also aided in her search [for Osiris] by Anubis, in the shape of a dog. **HE WAS SIRIUS OR THE DOG-STAR...."**[168] It was Anubis who supposedly guarded "the gates of death"[169] and he "was associated with magic and divination."[170] One catalog describes Anubis like this:

God of the dead, Anubis opened the roads to the other world and presided over embalmments. After the funeral, Anubis would take the dead by the hand and introduce him into the presence of the sovereign judges where the soul of the deceased would be weighed.[171]

It was Anubis' duty to attend to the ritual preparation of bodies, to weigh the heart of every man on the scale of justice, and to judge a man's good and bad deeds on earth.[172]

Not surprisingly, Anubis is one of the gods adored in witchcraft. One witchcraft magazine tells how to make an Anubis protection amulet. After the instructions are given, the writer of the article then adds: "Anubis can be anyone's best friend, (He's definitely mine!) even if He is considered by many to be the most ominous God of the Underworld [hell]."[173] Personally, I don't need (or want) the protection of the "God of the Underworld"! Do you?

The description of Anubis given above clearly signifies to us that this god cannot possibly be the God of the Christians. For one thing, the Bible definitely states that "God is not the God of the dead, but of the

The Egyptian initiation mystery raised the god Anubis, which was represented as a jackal, to the rank of 'Superior of Mysteries'

living" (Matthew 22:31-32, Mark 12:26-27, and Luke 20:37-38). Notice also that Anubis is depicted in the shape of a dog (or a jackal).[174] Other gods previously mentioned were Thoth, Set, Horus, and Pan. Thoth was illustrated as an ibis-headed man, a baboon, or sometimes as a "dog-headed ape" or a "dog-headed baboon."[175] Set was "represented by the head of a strange-looking animal that may have been a cross between a donkey and a pig"[176] and was also worshiped under the crocodile and hippopotamus forms.[177] Horus was symbolized as a hawk or falcon[178] and Pan was portrayed as "half-goat, half-man."[179]

You see, the "gods were originally believed to be animals or birds—and in later years were anthropomorphized and pictured with human bodies with the head of the animal or bird."[180] Of course, the Bible speaks about such a situation. Romans 1:21-23 and 25 state that:

...when they knew God, they glorified Him not as God, neither were thankful; but became vain in their imaginations, and their foolish heart was darkened. Professing themselves to be wise, they became fools, And changed the glory of the uncorruptible God into an image made like to corruptible man, and to birds, and fourfooted beasts, and creeping things....Who changed the truth of God into a lie, and worshipped and served the creature more than the Creator, who is blessed for ever.

This passage continues:

For this cause God gave them up unto vile affections: for even their women did change the natural use into that which is against nature:...And even as they did not like to retain God in their knowledge, God gave them over to a reprobate mind, to do those things which are not convenient; Being filled with all unrighteousness, fornication, wickedness, covetousness, maliciousness; full of envy, murder, debate, deceit, malignity; whisperers, Backbiters, haters of God, despiteful, proud, boasters, inventors of evil things, disobedient to parents, Without understanding, covenantbreakers, without natural affection, implacable, unmerciful... (Romans 1:26-28-31).

It's no wonder, then, that all kinds of unrighteousness follow such a worship of pagan gods for the gods that are being revered are themselves portrayed as doing evil acts. Just a quick glance at mythology will show the gods lying, cheating, committing fornication, adultery, murder, and such like. This is certainly a completely different lifestyle from the righteous life Christ lived (see Hebrews 7:26). Peter also admonishes us: "But as He which hath called you is holy, so be ye holy in all manner of conversation; Because it is written, Be ye holy; for I am holy" (I Peter 1:15-16).

EGYPTIAN WITCHCRAFT SCENE

Also presented in the description of Anubis is the idea that if good deeds outweigh bad ones, the person is rewarded and vice versa. A book printed by the Masonic Publishing and Manufacturing Company reveals:

A painting of the Funeral Ritual represents the judgment of a soul; it advances toward the goddess *Thme,* who wears an ostrich feather on her head; beside this divinity of justice and truth, appears the scale in which *Anubis* and *Horus* weigh the actions of the deceased—they place in one side the ostrich feather, and in the other the vase containing the heart; if the weight of the heart is greater than that of the ostrich feather, the scale descends, and the soul is received in the celestial courts; above this scene appear the forty-two judges of the souls seated, and having the head ornamented with the ostrich feather. [Emphasis in the original][181]

What is interesting about this explanation is that **THIS "EGYPTIAN WITCHCRAFT" SCENE**[182] **IS ACTUALLY PORTRAYED IN THE MASONIC LODGE** in the 31st degree[183] and the balance scale is one of its symbols. In this Masonic degree the "candidate

Inspector Inquisitor, Thirty-first Degree

is brought into the Court of the Dead to be judged for actions while living and to determine if he deserves to dwell among the gods."[184] This is a teaching that is contrary to God's Word, for we can never be saved by works. II Timothy 1:9 mentions that God "hath saved us, and called us with an holy calling, **NOT ACCORDING TO OUR WORKS,** but according to His own purpose and grace, which was given us in Christ Jesus before the world began." In Titus we are told: **"NOT BY WORKS OF RIGHTEOUSNESS** which we have done, but according to His mercy He saved us, by the washing of regeneration, and renewing of the Holy Ghost" (Titus 3:5). Of course, just a few verses later we find "that they which have believed in God might be careful to maintain good works" (Titus 3:8). We also know that many profess "that they know God; but in works they deny Him, being abominable, and disobedient, and unto every good work reprobate" (Titus 1:16), but good works alone will not get us to heaven. As Paul wrote: "For **BY GRACE ARE YE SAVED THROUGH FAITH;** and that not of yourselves:

it is the gift of God: Not of works, lest any man should boast" (Ephesians 2:8-9). However, once we are saved, we will want to obey God's commands and work for Him out of love for God, but our works cannot save us. "Even so faith, if it hath not works, is dead, being alone" (James 2:17).

So far we have looked at several representations for the "Eastern star." Masonic author, Albert Churchward, even reveals that the Star of Annunciation (or the Dog Star) was actually heralding "the birth of Horus"![185] This, then, is the star to which the Eastern Stars refer when they say: "We have seen His star in the east and are come to worship Him"! As Masonic author, John T. Lawrence, explains:

> **STAR-WORSHIP,** or Sabaism, is a very ancient form of religion. **EACH STAR WAS THE ABODE OF SOME HERO OR SOME GOD,** once incarnate on the earth. The connection of the stars as they ascended and descended in the heavens, with terrestrial phenomena, was probably noticed in very early periods, such, for instance, as the coincidence of the periodical rising of the Nile with the emergence from the sun's rays or the helical rising of the **DOG-STAR.**[186]

You should now be able to see that the Eastern Star **IS NOT** the star of the Bible but of another god. Of course, there is more—much more—to learn about this Star. In the next chapter we will discuss the Star's correlation with yet another god—the god Set. We will also discover the meaning behind the five-pointed star (pentagram) used in the Eastern Star, Masonry, Wicca (witchcraft), and Satanism.

5. THE PENTAGRAM

In the last chapter we discovered that the so-called "Star of Bethlehem" has numerous names and associations. We found out that Albert Pike said the idea that this star was "commemorative of the Star that is said to have guided the Magi, is to give it a meaning comparatively modern."[1] Albert Churchward, a Mason of high rank, adds that "the allusion as the star which guided the 'wise men,' etc., is a **RECENT** version...."[2] The Masonic Service Association, the publisher of *The Short Talk Bulletin* for Lodge discussion, also specifies that this Star is "Not the Star of Bethlehem."[3] So we know that if this Star is not the Star that guided the wise men, then it must have another meaning. This *Short Talk Bulletin* gives us a hint of another meaning when it lists this Star as "A **HEX** sign" and "A Symbol of Deity"![4]

Of course, one of the most sinister aspects of this star is its correlation with the god Set.[5] "Set was the ancient Egyptian god of evil. He was also known by the names Seth and Sutekh. He was a wicked and powerful god who often used witchcraft to achieve his aims."[6] Additionally, the name **SET** (or Sut) is another name for **SATAN!** Proof of this can be found by turning to Masonic writer, Albert Churchward, in which he states: "Set or Sut, according to Plutarch, is the Egyptian name of Typhon—*i.e.* Satan of the Christian Cult."[7] John Yarker, another Masonic author agrees when he stated that **SET WAS "A DEVIL** identical with Typhon."[8] Yet another book, *Freemasonry and the Ancient Gods,* authored by Mason J. S. M. Ward, reveals that Set was "regarded as evil, because he represented darkness."[9] In *The Adelphi Quarterly,* a New Age magazine, we are notified: "The word 'Satan' comes from the Egyptian god of the underworld, Set or Seth."[10]

Further proof of the relationship between Set and Satan can be found in *The Satanic Bible,* written by

Anton LaVey, the founder of the first Church of Satan. Under the enumeration of "The Infernal Names" for Satan is listed "Set."[11] By the way, among this itemization is also the name of "Thoth."[12] Remember, Thoth is one of the other names given for the **EASTERN STAR** known as **SIRIUS**.[13] On another page in this Satanic "bible," "Set" is described as the "Egyptian devil."[14] In *Treasury of Witchcraft* is included a listing of other names for Satan, one of which is Set.[15] Another New Age book (which praises Lucifer) describes Set as "the early Egyptian god of death, evil, and hell."[16] Additionally, occultist, New Ager, and Theosophist, Helen Petrovna Blavatsky, links Set and Satan together when she writes:

> ...Hermes, the god of wisdom, called also Thoth, Tat, Seth, Set and *Sat-an;* and that he was, furthermore, when viewed under his bad aspect, Typhon, the Egyptian Satan, who was also *Set.* [Emphasis in the original][17]

Michael Aquino "has written that Set is the oldest formulation of the being now called Satan, the embodiment of the sense of alienation and loneliness which man feels from the universe."[18]

TEMPLE OF SET

Before continuing with more characteristics of Set, let's take a brief look at who Michael Aquino is. Aquino had been a member of Anton LaVey's Church of Satan.[19] After leaving LaVey's church, he started his own organization called the Temple of Set[20] and his newsletter is entitled *The Scroll of Set.* The split between LaVey and Aquino was partially due to their individual conception of Satan. LaVey believed that Satan was just a symbol but Aquino contended that Satan, in the form of Set, was an absolute reality.[21] Aquino even has the number 666 tattooed on his forehead.[22]

Michael Aquino—Notice the Pentagram (Baphomet).

In spite of Aquino's beliefs and his status as a Satan worshiper, he was also a United States Army Lieutenant Colonel who served in Psy-Op operations.[23] When Aquino appeared on the Oprah Winfrey Show, he described Satanists as "very decent, very law-abiding people [with]...a very high set of personal ethics...[who have] nothing to do with evil."[24] Yet Aquino seems to contradict himself when he points out "that the essence of Satanism is an arrogant and hostile rebellion against universal law."[25] Just how "decent" and "law-abiding" Aquino is, came out a few years ago when he was accused of sexual molestation of a child.[26] Actually, it is not surprising to see charges of sexual abuse in such a cult since the god he worships promotes and endorses sexual permissiveness. In fact, knowing the abominable background of Set, it is no shock to discover that in "ancient Egypt, Set was worshiped with obscene, homosexual rituals."[27] We are told that the rituals performed for Set and Sirius were so horrible and debased "that later rulers of Egypt defaced their temples and obelisks and tried to drive them from the land."[28] In mythology we find that Set himself was involved in incest for he married his sister, Nephthys.[29] Set was also involved in adulterous affairs for he had at least two other consorts: Septet and Khekhsit.[30] Septet, by the way, is another name for the Dog Star,[31] again showing a **CONNECTION BETWEEN SET AND THE STAR USED IN THE EASTERN STAR.**

EASTERN STAR EMBLEM

Set is likewise portrayed as the "Devil of Darkness,"[32] "Prince of Darkness,"[33] and "the Lord of the Underworld."[34] It is stressed that the "Underworld" of which Set is in charge, is not Hades, but Tartarus, for "Tartarus is the hell of the damned and it was of this world that Set was the Lord."[35] Set's symbol is the **INVERTED PENTAGRAM!**[36] What symbol did Aquino choose for his Temple of Set? The inverted pentagram,[37] of course. What is incredible is that **THIS IS THE STAR THAT HAS BEEN CHOSEN FOR THE EMBLEM OF THE EASTERN STAR** (except in New York state[38])!

The pentagram is known by several other names:

Celtic priests called it the **WITCH'S FOOT.** In the Middle Ages it became known in Britain and elsewhere in Europe as the goblin's cross, **DEVIL'S SIGN,** and the **WIZARD'S STAR.** Among the druids of Great Britain, it was the blasphemous sign of the Godhead.[39]

"It is also Solomon's seal....In ancient times it was a magic charm amongst the people of Babylon."[40]

It was one of the most important symbols of the Pythagoreans, for whom its mathematical properties were most significant as the pentalpha, but who also fashioned it into trinkets to be used as talismen to ward off evil spirits, ill health, or misfortune. This symbolism persisted throughout the centuries of European history; in Germany, for example, it became the *Druttenfuss,* a **HEX SIGN** to prevent witches and goblins from entering barns and cottages.[41]

The pentagram, as mentioned, was a symbol of the Pythagoreans who were followers of Pythagoras.[42] Pythagoras is a widely recognized figure in Masonry.[43] For instance, Masonic author, J. D. Buck, brags:

Modern Freemasonry honors as its ancient great teachers Zoroaster, **PYTHAGORAS,** Plato, and many others, and in some of its degrees gives a brief summary of their doctrines. **MASONRY,** in a certain sense, includes them all, and has **ADOPTED THEIR PRECEPTS.** They were all initiates in the mysteries, and fundamentally their doctrines were the same. All taught the existence of the G.A.O.U. (sic), the immortality of the soul, and the unqualified Brotherhood of Man; and with these primitive and fundamental truths Masonry is in full accord.[44]

Who was Pythagoras?

[He] was as much a **MAGICIAN** as he was a mathematician, and in his pursuit of an answer to the mystery of life, he developed an avid following.

He founded a **SECRET SOCIETY,** whose members had to go through a difficult initiation and then adhere to strict rules that demanded of them silence, abstinence, vegetarianism, and deep self-analysis.[45]

Pythagoras "was also an **OCCULTIST,** a product of **PAGAN** Greek culture. He was the founder of a brotherhood that believed in **REINCARNATION.**"[46] In the *Masonic Quiz Book* we are informed that the druids were a "Celtic religious sect whose doctrines were the same as those of Pythagoras."[47] In spite of this (or perhaps **BECAUSE** of this), Pythagoras "is referred to in the Masonic ritual as the Masons' 'ancient friend and brother.'"[48] In fact, it was Apollonius of Tyana who "early became a disciple of the Pythagorean creed."[49] (More about Apollonius will appear in the next chapter.)

POWER OF THE PENTAGRAM

The pentagram is also sometimes called a pentacle or pantacle. Webster's Dictionary says that the pentacle (or pentagram) is a "5-pointed or sometimes 6-pointed star used as a **MAGICAL** symbol." Witches Janet and Stewart Farrar describe the pentagram like this: "a five-pointed star, one of the **MAIN SYMBOLS OF WITCHCRAFT AND OCCULTISM** in general."[50] A book on numerology agrees that the pentagram "is used in many ritualistic ceremonies including witchcraft."[51]

One witchcraft magazine explains:

The five-pointed star is one of the world's oldest symbols and it has been used in many cultures since ancient times as an amulet to bring good fortune and ward off harm. Most **WICCAN** [witchcraft] **PRACTITIONERS ALSO WEAR IT** today as a symbol of their religion....In the Wiccan religion, the five points of the **PENTAGRAM REPRESENT THE FIVE ELEMENTS** of Nature—Earth, Air, Fire,

Water, and Spirit—with the top point corresponding
to Spirit, the unifying element....A Pentagram inscribed
on a platter is called a Pentacle. Pentacles are used
as ceremonial tools for the Element Earth and placed
above windows and doorways to bless and protect a
dwelling.[52]

Sybil Leek, a well-known **WITCH,** declares that
the "pentagram has always been used in ritual **MAGIC**
and in the **WITCHCRAFT** rites of healing."[53] New
Ager Dick Sutphen agrees that the "pentacle holds an
important place in ritual **MAGIC."**[54] Another book on
witchcraft mentions:

The pentacle, the five-pointed figure, contained mystic
symbols, used especially in **DIVINATION** and the
CONJURATION OF SPIRITS. The pentalpha, a
design formed by interlacing five A's, was also in
similar use. To **SUMMON DEMONIAC HELP,** the
pentagram was fashioned: a five-pointed geometric
figure.[55]

International Imports produces an occult catalog. This
company sells altar covers with pentagrams on them—
a "circled pentagram for white magic occult work;
**INVERTED PENTAGRAM FOR BLACK MAGIC
RITUALS."**[56] Elsewhere this catalog advertises occult
jewelry with a pentagram. It adds that the pentagram is
the "most powerful of all occult talismans....It is alleged
that it is more powerful than the cross...."[57] We are also
told that the **INVERTED PENTAGRAM IS "A SIGN**

FOR EVIL."[58] Gary Jennings, in his book, *Black Magic, White Magic*, reveals that:

> ...the most powerful and respected of all magical symbols was the pentagram—the figure of five sides and five angles....The belief was that if this figure were drawn with a single angle...**POINTING DOWN, THE SIGN REPRESENTED SATAN** and thus was **USED FOR INVOKING EVIL SPIRITS.**[59]

In the *Dictionary of Mysticism*, we learn that the pentagram:

> ...is considered by occultists to be the most potent means of conjuring spirits. When a single point of the star points upward, it is regarded as the sign of the good and a means to conjure benevolent spirits; when the **SINGLE POINT POINTS DOWN** and a pair of points are on top, it is a **SIGN OF THE EVIL (SATAN)** and is **USED TO CONJURE POWERS OF EVIL.**[60]

Laurie Cabot, another **WITCH,** explains: "It really isn't that difficult to distinguish the Craft from Satanism. Witches wear the pentacle with the point up. **SATANISTS REVERSE IT WITH THE POINT DOWN....**"[61]

> The **PENTAGRAM** is a very important symbol **USED IN CALLING DEMONS** and as an aid in the casting of spells. When pointed skyward, the star symbolizes the power of witchcraft. Most Wiccans—(witches/ warlocks) believe that their power comes from such elements as the earth, sky and wind.[62]

THE PENTAGRAM AND EASTERN STAR

It should be obvious by now that the occultists, New Agers, magicians, Satanists, and witches all claim the pentagram as one of **THEIR** symbols and hold it in high regard. "Symbols," we are told, "are representative of ownership."[63] In fact, Fred and Jill Buck from the Magi Craftsmen, announce: "The Pentagram is one of the most powerful symbols for the **NEW AGE**."[64] Additionally, a witchcraft magazine was even entitled *Pentagram*.[65] The pentagram (or five-pointed star) can be drawn in two ways—with one point facing up or with two points facing up (known as the inverted or Satanic pentagram).[66] "When pointing down, as on the front of the Satanic Bible, the star signifies the Church of Satan, symbolic of power from Hell."[67] As can be seen, this star is a crucial ingredient in the occult, Wicca (witchcraft), and Satanism and the fashion in which this star is placed is highly illuminating. Bill Schnoebelen "emphasized that **TO THE MAGICIAN, THE INVERTED PENTAGRAM HAS ONE USE ONLY,** and that is to **CALL UP THE POWER OF SATAN** and bring the Kingdom of the Devil into manifestation on earth."[68]

The pentagram also plays an important role in **MASONRY AND THE EASTERN STAR.** Are Masons aware of the connotation of this star or do they ignorantly use this symbol? Let's turn to Masonic writers to see what they tell us about the meaning of the pentagram and the position in which it is drawn.

We'll start with a quotation from Manly Hall, a 33° **MASON AND AN OCCULTIST.** He points out:

The **PENTAGRAM IS USED EXTENSIVELY IN BLACK MAGIC,** but when so used its form always differs in one of three ways: The star may be broken at one point by not permitting the converging lines to touch; it may be inverted by having one point down and two up; or it may be distorted by having the points of varying length.

When used in **BLACK MAGIC, THE PENTA-GRAM IS CALLED** "the sign of the cloven hoof," or the **FOOTPRINT OF THE DEVIL.** The star with two points upward is also called the "Goat of Mendes," because the inverted star is the same shape as a goat's head. When the upright star turns and the upper point falls to the bottom, it signifies the fall of the Morning Star.[69]

S. R. Parchment, in his book *Ancient Operative Masonry,* states that:

...the **PENTAGRAM** represents the liberated spirit. When the star is shown point upward, it is considered the symbol of the white magician who is able at will to leave the body [an out of the body experience] by way of the head; **WHEN DOWNWARD, BLACK MAGIC.**[70]

The Golden Dawn, a book labeled as "THE MOST IMPORTANT OCCULT BOOK EVER PRINTED," [Emphasis in the original][71] was written by Israel Regardie. In it we are notified that the pentagram:

...with the **SINGLE POINT DOWNWARDS...IS A VERY EVIL SYMBOL.** The Head of the Goat, or **DEMON'S HEAD,** representing the abasement of reason beneath the blind forces of matter, the elevation of anarchy above order, and of conflicting forces driven by chance above God.[72]

The Golden Dawn, by the way, was a secret "occult society which gathered around the use of magic and the writings of Eliphas Levi."[73] Its membership "included such notables as W. B. Yeats, Aleister Crowley, Dion Fortune, Algernon Blackwood, Arthur Machen, Lady Frieda Harris, Brodie Innes, S. L. McGregor Mathers, Sax Rhomer, A. E. Waite, Evelyn Underhill...W. Wynn Westcott,"[74] and Paul Foster Case.[75] At least five of the people listed (S. L. McGregor Mathers, Aleister Crowley, Arthur Edward Waite, W. Wynn Westcott, and Paul Foster Case) were **MASONS**. It was at Aleister Crowley's invitation that Regardie went to "work as his secretary and studied with him."[76] Crowley will be discussed in more detail in the next chapter, but you can once again see that the Masons **KNEW** that the inverted pentagram was an evil symbol.

THE TWO PENTAGRAMS

In *The Brotherhood of the Rosy Cross* by Arthur Edward Waite, we find the following instruction given in one Rosicrucian degree:

> After these and other lucubrations the uppermost point of a Pentagram was pressed against his breast; he was told to trust in Adonai and to be centred (sic) in the thought of God; to take heed lest he prove a traitor, whether to God and His light or the Brethren, for the two avenging points of the Pentagram would then be turned against him and the powers of the evil ones let loose.[77]

Henry L. Stillson and William J. Hughan, in *History of Freemasonry and Concordant Orders*, describe the pentagram like this:

> This star represents GOD, all that is *pure, virtuous,* and *good,* when represented with one point upward:

but when turned with one point down it represents EVIL, all that is opposed to the *good, pure,* and *virtuous;* in fine, it represents the GOAT OF MENDES. [Emphasis in the original][78]

This book goes on to explain:

The Holy and Mysterious Pentagram, called in the Gnostic schools the Blazing Star (L'Etoile flamboyante), is the sign of Intellectual Omnipotence and Autocracy.

It is the star of the Magi; it is the sign of THE WORD MADE FLESH, and according to the direction of its rays [meaning with one or two points up], this absolute symbol represents Good or Evil; Order or Disorder, the blessed Lamb of Ormuzd (Ahuro-Mazdao), and Saint John, or the accursed Goat of Mendes....

It is initiation or profanation; it is Lucifer or Vesper, the morning or the evening star.

It is Mary or Lilith, victory or death, light (day) or darkness (night). When the Pentagram elevates two of its points, it represents Satan, or the goat of the Mysteries; and when it elevates one of its points only, it represents the Saviour, goodness, or virtue." [Emphasis in the original][79]

Let's break this statement down into two columns: one column for the associations with the one point up

This star represents GOD, all that is *pure, virtuous,* and *good,* when represented with one point upward: but when turned with one point down it represents EVIL, all that is opposed to the *good, pure,* and *virtuous ;* in fine, it represents the GOAT of MENDES.

pentagram and the other column for the relationships with the two points up pentagram.

ONE POINT UP PENTAGRAM	TWO POINTS UP PENTAGRAM
Good	Evil
Order	Disorder
Lamb of Ormuzd (Ahuro-Mazdao [Ahura Mazda])	Goat of Mendes
Initiation	Profanation
Lucifer	Vesper
Morning Star	Evening Star
Mary	Lilith
Victory	Death
Light (day)	Darkness (night)
Saviour, goodness, virtue	Satan or the goat of the Mysteries

Did you notice that even under the so-called "good" pentagram that Lucifer is listed as well as the god Ahura Mazda? Also take notice that with this listing Lucifer would be considered as the Saviour and the Morning Star. Of course, this isn't really surprising since Masons themselves (and others) tell us that Lucifer (or Venus) is the Light-bearer and the Morning Star.[80] Another interesting note is that Ahura Mazda (a god mentioned in the higher degrees of Masonry) is considered to be a **GOD OF LIGHT**.[81] Additionally, Albert Pike claims:

> Ahura-Mazda himself is the living WORD; he is called "First-born of all things, express image of the Eternal, very light of very light, the Creator, who by power of the Word which he never ceases to pronounce, made in 365 days the Heaven and the Earth." [Emphasis in the original][82]

Ahura-Mazda, then, is the "WORD MADE FLESH" that is being referred to, and not Jesus Christ. You see, when Masons who believe they are Christians hear about the "word made flesh" and the "Saviour" they most likely think these phrases refer to Christ, but Masons who have advanced to the highest degrees and have studied Masonic works and symbolism reveal to us that phrases like these **DO NOT** refer to Christ but to pagan gods.

INTENTIONALLY MISLED

Furthermore, it is **DELIBERATELY PLANNED** that the average Mason does not find out about these occultic and pagan aspects of Masonry. Pike admits:

> The Blue Degrees [the first three degrees of Masonry] are but the outer court or portico of the Temple. Part of the symbols are displayed there to the Initiate, but he is **INTENTIONALLY MISLED BY FALSE INTERPRETATIONS.** It is not intended that he shall understand them; but it is intended that he shall **IMAGINE** he understands them. Their **TRUE EXPLICATION IS RESERVED FOR THE ADEPTS** [those who have advanced to the highest degrees in Masonry]....It is well enough for the mass of those called Masons, to imagine that all is contained in the Blue Degrees; and whoso attempts to undeceive them will labor in vain....[83]

Did you notice Pike's words? He clearly informs us that "it is intended that he shall imagine he understands" the degrees, but the real explanation is concealed from the Mason. Because of the lies, the deception, and the cover-up, most Masons really do not understand what is being taught in the lodge.

Elsewhere, Pike adds:

> **MASONRY,** like all the Religions, all the Mysteries, Hermeticism and Alchemy, **CONCEALS** its secrets from all except the Adepts and Sages, or the Elect,

and **USES FALSE EXPLANATIONS AND MISINTERPRETATIONS OF ITS SYMBOLS TO MISLEAD** those who deserve only to be misled; to conceal the Truth, which it calls Light, from them, and to draw them away from it.[84]

Returning to the "good" pentagram, we have discovered that it is used by witches, occultists, New Agers, and magicians for magic rituals and that it represents Lucifer. As you can see, there's nothing "good" about this pentagram, but the "evil" pentagram has an even more sinister connotation. Sad to say, it was the evil pentagram that Rob Morris, the person credited with the founding of the Eastern Star, had chosen for this organization. Before looking at some of the evil aspects of the pentagram with two points facing upward, you are probably wondering if Mr. Morris knew what he was doing. Did he have any idea of the meaning of the symbol he selected?

MORRIS' MASONIC RECORD

First of all, we must realize some of Morris' involvement in Masonry.

He was exalted to the degree of Royal Arch in Lexington, Mississippi, in 1848; accepted as Royal and Select Master in 1849; made a Knight Templar at Jackson, Mississippi, in 1850; received the Scottish Rite degrees to the thirty-second degree in 1854. He received the Rite of Memphis, so far as the ninetieth degree, in New York, in 1864, and the Encampment Order of English Templary in Canada, in 1857. He also received a very large number of the honorary appendages to Masonry, such as the three official orders of Royal Arch Masonry, Past Eminent Commander, Past Grand Commander, Grand High Priest, Past Grand Commander-in-Chief 32nd degree. The Masonic and Military Orders of the Knights of

Rome, and the Red Cross of Constantine were communicated to him in 1857, and afterwards in 1873.[85]

His honorary degrees and complimentary memberships numbered nearly one hundred and fifty.[86] "He contributed to columns in **ALMOST EVERY** Masonic publication."[87] We are also told that:

> ...having spent most of the strength, thought and wisdom of his early manhood in a **CLOSE STUDY OF THE RITUALS, CODES, PRINCIPLES AND TENETS OF MASONRY,** he was conceded to be **ONE OF THE MOST VERSATILE AND LEARNED MASONS OF HIS DAY.**[88]

Obviously, Morris was well-versed in Masonic ideas and he certainly should have known the connotation of the symbol he designated for the Eastern Star.

Willis D. Engle was one of the early members and researchers of the Eastern Star[89] as well as the first Secretary of the General Grand Chapter of the Eastern Star.[90] In his book entitled *A General History of the Order of the Eastern Star,* he informs us:

> Some discussion has been had as to the origin and propriety of the latter position, as mythological teaching is that the star with one point up is an emblem of good, while with two points up it is an emblem of evil. Brother Morris, was perhaps, not lacking in mythological lore when he penned the directions for forming the star with one point toward the east, but it will be easily seen that by the later development, in doing away with the outer points, the mythological significance of the star was altered without design, and probably by persons that were ignorant of the fact, and that it stood for the goat of Mendes. But in this particular, as in many others, brother Morris was

not consistent, as in the tessera he placed the star with two points up.[91]

The Tessera is a metallic object in the form of a Five-pointed Star, the points being so disposed that one is directed downwards, on the front of which appears the Lion, the symbol of this Order,—on the back the name of the Stella (or Protector) who presents it, and the name and number of Constellation of which she (or he) is or was last a Member.[92]

The letters spell "AREME." (Chapter 10 explains more about Areme.)

Isn't it interesting that the inverted (or Satanic) pentagram used as the tessera has a lion on the front of it? It says that the lion is "the symbol of this Order."[93] Could this lion be the same one that the Bible warns us about when it cautions us: "Be sober, be vigilant; because **YOUR ADVERSARY THE DEVIL, AS A ROARING LION,** walketh about, seeking whom he may devour" (I Peter 5:8)? We must remember that the lion in Masonry **DOES NOT** refer to Christ. In *What? When? Where? Why? Who? in Freemasonry,* published by the Masonic Service Association, we find:

The idea of a resurrection is curiously interwoven with the **LION** in all ages and was **CONNECTED WITH RESURRECTION LONG BEFORE THE MAN OF GALILEE** walked upon the earth. In ancient Egypt, **A LION RAISED OSIRIS** from a dead level to a living perpendicular by a grip of his paw; Egyptian carvings show a figure standing behind the Altar, observing the raising of the dead, with its left arm raised, forming the angle of a square. The **LION OF THE TRIBE OF JUDAH,** considered as signifying a coming redeemer who would spring from the tribe, or meaning the King of Israel who built the Temple, or symbolizing the Christ, **MUST NOT BE CONFUSED WITH A MODE OF RECOGNITION.**[94]

Notice that we are forewarned that we are not to confuse the lion that represents Christ with the lion being signified in Masonry!

Many years after the inverted pentagram was chosen as the Eastern Star symbol, a special meeting on this subject was held and:

> ...the officers decided to keep the emblem, since as they said, "This emblem, which has been our symbol, although a **SIGN OF EVIL,** has been redeemed by THE GOOD WORKS OF OUR MEMBERS"!![95]

In spite of the officers' decision, the star has not been redeemed. It is still considered as an evil sign as can be seen from a *Short Talk Bulletin,* entitled "Symbolism" (which was reprinted in 1982):

> The five-pointed star—point up—is a very ancient symbol of man, and was used by the old sages to

designate the absolute sign of human intelligence. It
refers to the spiritual element predominant in man,
while the same figure with **TWO POINTS UP
REFERS TO THE GOAT OF MENDES**—or that
the beast is in the ascendant.[96]

GOAT OF MENDES

Since we have been informed several times by
Masonic authors that the inverted pentagram refers to
the Goat of Mendes, let's take a look at what this goat
represents. In *A Dictionary of Symbols* we notice that
the he-goat is associated with the devil.[97] Mendes was
an "Egyptian god resembling Pan; he was worshipped
in the form of a goat."[98] One witchcraft organization,
Nuit Unlimited Imports, sells a Goat of Mendes T-shirt.
They mention that this goat is also known as Baphomet.[99]
Describing Baphomet, we find that this:

> ...art work was drawn by Eliphas Levi, the foremost
> **OCCULT** authority of the 19th century. Symbols
> were included relating directly to ceremonial **MAGIC**
> and identified with Baphomet. Much of the same

symbols carry forward as on the **DEVIL CARD** in the Thoth deck of Crowley.

The **GOAT OF MENDES** itself is known as the **"GOD OF THE WITCHES"**....[100]

So, this is the god, the "God of the Witches," that is being worshiped by the Eastern Star women and men when the inverted pentagram is displayed. Do the Eastern Stars know they are worshiping Baphomet in their meetings? Of course not, and this is **PRECISELY** what the higher echelon of Masonry wants to keep secret from these people, but there's so much to learn about Baphomet, so let's spend a little time seeing what we can uncover about him in the next chapter.

6. A LOOK AT BAPHOMET

We have already been informed that the picture of Baphomet was drawn by Levi.[1] Who was Eliphas Levi? Levi, whose real name was Alphonse Louis Constant,[2] acquired an education at the Seminary of Saint Sulpice and:

> ...apparently studied Latin, Greek, and Hebrew. He subsequently took minor orders, and became a deacon of the Roman Catholic Church. Coming under the influence of an eccentric, if not mad, prophet named Ganneau, he soon abandoned the strictures of the Church.[3]

His marriage to 16-year-old Noemie Cadiot resulted in two children, but both of their children died and the marriage soon ended by Noemie leaving Levi.[4]

> According to a friendly account, the deserted magus [magician or sorcerer] betook himself to books, and gave himself up altogether to the **OCCULT** sciences. M. Chauliac, on the other hand, depicts him as **INVOKING THE DEVIL** in order to procure her return.[5]

About this time, the:

> ...Abbe Constant, for a second time repudiating his name, assumed the title of the Magus Eliphas Levi, giving consultations in great number to credulous clients, who paid as much as twenty-five francs a time for a prediction from Lucifer.[6]

Levi "claims that he received from the 'spirits' a magic book, pentacles and other things. He was interested in alchemy and the Cabbala."[7] Rex R.

BLACK MAGIC AND PACTS

Symbols play a vital role in infernal conjuration. Above, the Goetic Circle of Pacts, drawn by Eliphas Levi *in the 19th century, is supposed to be used when the sorcerer is to make a pact with the Descending Hierarchy. The three circles in the center are the standing positions of the sorcerer and his apprentices. The skull must be from a parricide, the horns from a goat, the bat must have been drowned in blood, and the black cat, whose head is placed opposite the skull, must have been fed on human flesh.*

The seal and characters of Lucifer, from the Grimorium Verum, *a 16th century book of demonic magic. The characters are supposed to be written on parchment with the blood of the sorcerer, and worn by him at all times during the conjuration.*

Hutchens, 33° Mason, and Donald W. Monson, 32° Mason, also confirmed that Levi was an **OCCULTIST** in their book *The Bible in Albert Pike's Morals and Dogma*. They state that he "entered upon the **OCCULT** studies which would encompass his labors for the rest of his life."[8]

The Dictionary of Satanism tells us that Levi was a:

> ...French **MAGICIAN** and author of works on the **OCCULT**. Eliphas Levi...claimed to have summoned up the **GHOST OF APOLLONIUS** of Tyana in London in 1854. Born in Paris about 1810, he is said to have been reincarnated as Aleister Crowley.[9]

There are several issues raised in this quotation that need some explanation. You will notice that **LEVI WAS A MAGICIAN AND AN OCCULTIST,** but why would he want to conjure up the ghost of Apollonius? Apollonius, you see, was also a magician and occultist who used talismanic jewels and also taught his disciples how to use them.[10] In *Witches and Sorcerers* we find:

> Apollonius of Tyana...was one of the most baffling of the magicians. His miracles were those of the traditional Oriental wizards and priests, with several more added. Some of his magical activities were so amazing that clerics have said that he was placed on this earth by Satan in order to attempt, by diabolical arts, to eclipse the miracles of Christ.[11]

He was "one of the earliest historical figures that pagans sought to establish as an anti-christ."[12] Ammianus Marcellinus indicates that Apollonius was "an example of a human endowed with a particularly strong guardian spirit...."[13] Manly Hall, also an **OCCULTIST and 33° MASON,** wrote a book called *The Phoenix,* in which appears a chapter about Apollonius. This chapter is entitled "Apollonius, 'The Antichrist.'"[14] Apollonius was a foe of Christianity[15] yet this is the person whom Levi claims to have summoned from the dead.[16]

CROWLEY: OCCULTIST AND MASON

Aleister Crowley's name was also mentioned in a previous quotation. Crowley was the most influential Satanist of all time and. Eliphas Levi had such a profound influence on Crowley, that Crowley actually believed that he was Eliphas Levi reincarnated. Crowley even translated one of Levi's books.[17] "The influence of Levi can be seen not only on Freemasonry, but also upon modern Satanism. It can also be said of **CROWLEY** that he was an **OCCULTIST AND A FREEMASON.**"[18] Yes, Crowley was a Mason, and even the May 1993 issue of *The Scottish Rite Journal* admitted that Crowley was an occultist,[19] so let's delve a little deeper into his background.

Crowley referred to himself as the Beast (taken from Revelation) and used the symbol 666.[20] In a book entitled *Necronomicon,* which gives an acknowledgement to the "Demon PERDURABOO"[21] for his help, we find: "Indeed, **CROWLEY HAD** nothing but **ADMIRATION FOR** the Shaitan **(SATAN)** of the so-called 'devil-worshipping' cult of the Yezidis of Mesopotamia...."[22] Perhaps, then, it is not surprising to find in *Magicians of the Golden Dawn* that the "most powerful magician to be trained in the original Order [of the Golden Dawn] was probably Aleister Crowley ('Perdurabo')."[23] Notice that Crowley took the name "Perdurabo"—the same name accredited to a demon in the *Necronomicon.* Also observe that Crowley admired Shaitan or Satan. It may surprise you to learn that in "India in fairly modern times, a meeting place for [Masonic] Lodges was called a Shaitan Bungalow. The superstition was that the evil spirit was a factor in secret orders."[24]

Concerning Crowley, Ellic Howe writes:

> While still an undergraduate at Cambridge Crowley wanted "to get into personal communion with the devil" and required a manual of technical instruction. A bookseller produced a copy of A. E. Waite's *The Book of Black Magic and Pacts*.... He then discovered Mathers's *The Kabbalah Unveiled,* but found it heavy going.[25]

Remember that both Waite and Mathers were also **MASONS AS WELL AS OCCULTISTS** and Crowley has also been labeled as a Satanist by numerous authors![26]

Crowley was a sex pervert (including both homosexual and heterosexual contacts[27]) who felt that he could harness power through the sex act.[28] Colin Wilson remarks:

> Crowley set about performing **SEXUAL MAGIC** with diligence, **SODOMISING** Victor Neuberg in Paris in 1913 as part of a magical ceremony. He also practised sexual magic with a companion of Isadora Duncan's, Mary D'Este Sturges, and they rented a villa in Italy for that purpose. He also took a troop of chorus girls to Moscow— they were called the Ragged Ragtime Girls— and had a violent affair with another "starving leopardess" of a girl, who needed to be beaten to obtain satisfaction. Crowley claims it was his first relationship of this sort, but it was not the last. Physical sadism was another taste he acquired. He opened a Satanic Temple in a studio in Fulham Road, and an American journalist described the number of aristocratic female disciples who

frequented it. Crowley had now filed his two canine teeth to a sharp point, and when he met women, was inclined to give them the "serpent's kiss," biting the wrist, or occasionally the throat, with the fangs. Symonds also mentions that he had a habit of defecating on carpets, and explaining that his ordure was sacred, like that of the Dalai Lama.[29]

Wilson continues:

Crowley covered the walls with paintings of people having sex in every position, and painted his studio—which he called the Chamber of Nightmares—with **DEMONS**. He was convinced that an adept could only become free of the need for drugs by taking them freely and mastering the need for them; so piles of cocaine were left around for anyone to take like snuff, while heroin was supplied by a trader from the mainland.[30]

Crowley's sexual desires did not stop even here. Arthur Lyons, in his book, *Satan Wants You*, reveals:

During one ritual in 1921, he induced a he-goat to copulate with his constant female companion and "Scarlet Woman," Leah Hirsig, then slit the animal's throat at the moment of orgasm.[31]

CROWLEY OFFERED HUMAN SACRIFICES

To top off his abominations, Crowley was involved in a large amount of **HUMAN SACRIFICES**. "He is said to have taken part in 150 ritual **MURDERS,** most of whom were children."[32]

Yet, in spite of this perversion, Arthur Lyons, in his *The Second Coming: Satanism in America*, tells us that Crowley was the hero for the admirers of the occult and Satanic cults.[33] He writes:

It may be said safely that Crowley is the germinal core of some neo-Satanic groups today. The head of one such group I found, for example, actually claims to be the reincarnation of Crowley, while at the same time claiming to be the incarnation of Satan, two statements which are only reconcilable if Crowley is assumed to have been a manifestation of the Devil.[34]

It's no wonder, then, that Anton LaVey, the founder of the Church of Satan, was highly influenced by Crowley. Lyons contends:

LaVey's conception of magic is strongly colored by elements of Crowleyanity....LaVey's lesser and greater magic are merely pure biological applications of Crowley's magick, which neatly clip off the supernatural realm to which Crowley's definition also applies.[35]

Crowley's hatred of Christianity can be seen for when "he baptized a frog as Jesus Christ and crucified it on a cross,"[36] he chanted the following:

"...Lo Jesus of Nazareth, how thou art taken in my snare. All my life long thou hast plagued me and affronted me, in thy name—with all other free souls in Christiandom (sic). I have been tortured in my boyhood; all delights have been forbidden unto me, all that I had was taken from me, and that which is owed to me they pay not—in thy name. Now at last I have thee; The Slave-God is in the power of the Lord of Freedom [referring to Crowley]. Thine hour is come; as I blot thee out from this earth, so surely shall the eclipse pass; and Light, Life, Love, and Liberty be once more the law of Earth. Give thou place to me, O Jesus; thine aeon is past; the age of

Horus is arisen by the Magic of the Master the
Great Beast."[37]

Crowley, who founded a number of witchcraft
organizations, believed that the "religious experience
was achieved through sexual perversions of all
descriptions, as do most satanists."[38] Crowley even:

> ...took the name Baphomet when he assumed
> leadership of the occult/Masonic organization,
> the O.T.O. (Order of Eastern Templars). Crowley
> wrote of Baphomet as representing a type of
> phallic god.

> Kenneth Grant, the modern world leader of the
> O.T.O., claims that Baphomet conceals a formula
> of homosexual sex magic from the Templars.[39]

Levi, too, "stressed magic as a means to power
and emphasized sex and drug abuse."[40] Colin Wilson
mentions in *The Occult* that "magic and sex remained
in close association...."[41]

SEX AND DRUG ABUSE

It's no surprise, then, to learn that Eliphas Levi
(as well as Aleister Crowley) emphasized sex and
drug abuse.[42] Both of these items figure prominently
in Satanism. In fact, Levi's drawing of Baphomet
shows his emphasis on sex, for he made Baphomet
as an androgynous (meaning both male and female)
figure.[43] Satan, like Baphomet, "is often pictured as
a hermaphroditic deity, having a male phallus and
the breasts of a woman."[44] "The winged staff between
Baphomet represents the phallus."[45] The goat is one
of the symbolical animals of Hermetic magic, says
Levi, and it is the "symbol of generation."[46] In a

Baphomet

Horns: Represent the waxing and waning moon. The center horn - Magical light of the universe, or Universal Intelligence, the God/Goddess power always available when we learns how to use it.

Head of the goat: Symbolizes much the same as the sacrificial goat of the Bible. Here, however, it also acts as a reminder that man must make certain sacrifices before achieving complete illumination or "One-ness."

Beard: Symbolizes the "Grand Old Man" of the Cabalists as well as agelessness or timelessness.

Pentagram on the forehead: Light and the Cabala, the Tree of Life, a sacred symbol of man.

Right hand pointing up: Power used for good, or power being taken from above to be transferred to manifestation.

Left hand pointing down: Man has free will yet the power can be misused. Power drawn from the right hand transferred to the left for material manifestation. The right and left hand also signify the balance between Mercy and Justice

Breasts: One feminine, one masculine symbolizing both attributes found in man, as this androgynous figure represents humanity.

Caduceus: Eternal life.

Scales on the body: The emotional side of man, the water element

Feathers: Symbolizes that which is mercurial and volatile. The fire element.

Cloven hooves: The animal nature of man, the concept that we may not have fully evolved out the beast kingdom. The element of earth.

Circle surrounding belly: Atmosphere and centering in ones current environment.

Wings: Man's struggle to rise above his environment. The air element.

Half Sphere on which the figure sits: Represents his universe, of only half of which is shown because man is still learning to rule his universe.

book on witchcraft, *The Complete Book of Witchcraft and Demonology,* we find a picture of Baphomet. The caption states that he is the "horned god of the witches, symbol of sex incarnate."[47] This picture, by the way, shows Baphomet making the Devil's triad with his right hand.

Starhawk, a witch, boasts:

> The God of the Witches is sexual—but sexuality is seen as sacred, not as obscene or blasphemous. Our God wears horns—but they are the waxing and waning crescents of the Goddess Moon, and the symbol of animal vitality. In some aspects, He is black, not because He is dreadful or fearful, but because darkness and the night are times of power, and part of the cycles of time....

> The God of the Witches is the God of love. This love includes sexuality, which is also wild and untamed as well as gentle and tender. His sexuality is fully *felt,* in a context in which sexual desire is sacred, not only because it is the means by which life is procreated but also because it is the means by which our own lives are most deeply and ecstatically realized. In Witchcraft, sex is a sacrament, an outward sign of an inward grace. [Emphasis in the original][48]

Levi, like Crowley, has made some blasphemous and anti-Christian statements. Below are a few excerpts from the writings of Levi.

▲ The devil is God upside down.[49]

▲ We approach the domain of black magic. We are about to assail, even in his withdrawn sanctuary, the darksome deity of the Sabbath, the formidable goat of Mendes, the phantom full of horrors, the dragon of every theogony, the Ahriman of the Persians, the Typhon of the Egyptians, the Python of the Greeks, the old serpent of the Jews, the bearded idol of mediaeval alchemists, the Baphomet of the Templars. Let us declare, for the education of the uninitiated, for the satisfaction of M. le Comte de Mirville, for the justification of Bodin the demonologist, and for the greater glory of the Church, which has persecuted the Templars, burned the magicians, and excommunicated the Freemasons, let us say boldly and loudly, that all initiates of the occult sciences—I speak of the inferior initiates and the betrayers of the Great Arcanum—have adored, do, and will always adore that which is signified by the frightful figure of the sabbatic goat.

Yes, in our profound conviction, the grand masters of the order of the Templars adored **BAPHOMET,** and caused him to be adored by their initiates; yes, there have existed, and there may still be, assemblies presided over by this figure, seated on a throne and with a flaming torch between its horns; only the worshippers of this sign do not think it the **REPRESENTATION OF THE DEVIL** as we do [!], but rather that of the god Pan....[50]

▲ The terrible Baphomet is, in fact, like all monstrous enigmas of ancient science, nothing more than an innocent and even pious hieroglyph. Let us declare emphatically, to combat the remnants of Manichaeanism, that Satan, as a superior personality and power, has no existence.[51]

▲ What is more absurd and more impious than to attribute the name of Lucifer to the devil, that is, to personified evil? The intellectual **LUCIFER IS THE SPIRIT OF INTELLIGENCE AND LOVE;** it is the paraclete, it is the Holy

Spirit, while the physical Lucifer is the great agent of universal magnetism.[52]

▲ [Levi has Jesus speaking to Satan, saying] "But thou shalt be called Satan no longer, thou shalt reassume the glorious name of Lucifer, and I will set a star upon thy forehead and a torch in thy hand....I will give thee the sceptre of earth and the key of heaven."[53]

▲ Thus **SATAN** is not the ruler of the realm of shadows, he is the agent of light behind a veil. He **IS OF SERVICE TO GOD, HE PERFORMS GOD'S WORK: GOD HAS NOT REJECTED HIM,** for he holds him still in his hand....What is the Devil, then, in the final analysis? **THE DEVIL IS GOD WORKING EVIL.**[54]

Some of Levi's private correspondence appeared in numerous issues of the Theosophical magazine entitled *Lucifer.*[55] We have already learned that he was an occultist and magician. In fact, "Rosicrucians, ritual magicians and witches all would look to Levi for direction, even as they formed highly differentiated groups."[56] With such blasphemous statements as printed above, would it come as a surprise to you that Eliphas **LEVI WAS ALSO A MASON?** He became a Mason on March 14, 1861, and was initiated in the Lodge Rose du Parfait Silence.[57] There was even a:

...tribute to Eliphas Levi in a Masonic Cyclopedia. The author of the Royal Masonic Cyclopedia, Kenneth Mackenzie, was another man in a league with Levi, Pike, Crowley, and many others who can be truly called, both Occultists and Freemasons.[58]

MASONIC BOOK MUST BE RETURNED

Arthur Edward Waite, a Mason, writes: "Albert Pike was a disciple of Eliphas Levi, the French occultist...."[59] What's more, Albert Pike, a highly respected Masonic writer, even plagiarized much of Levi's works for his own book entitled *Morals and Dogma.*[60] This book (until recently) was given to each Mason when he was initiated into the higher degrees of Masonry. One former 33° Mason said that at his 32° initiation the Masons were presented with this book. He states:

We were told that it was *the* source book for Freemasonry and its meaning. We were also told that it must never leave our possession, and that arrangements must be made so that upon our deaths it would be returned to the Scottish Rite. [Emphasis in the original][61]

Although many **MASONS** deny knowing anything about Albert Pike, the higher levels of Masonry **KNOW** about him and **HIGHLY REVERE HIM.** In a *Short Talk Bulletin* entitled "Albert Pike," we are told: "Those who do not know Masonry often think of him as a man whom history passed by and forgot." However, this booklet adds:

He was the **MASTER GENIUS OF MASONRY** in America, both as scholar and artist. No other mind of equal power ever toiled so long in the service of the Craft in the New World. No other has left a nobler fame in our annals.[62]

Speaking of Pike's book, *Morals and Dogma,* this booklet maintains that it is:

...a huge manual for the instruction of the [Scottish] Rite....It ought to be revised...since it is too valuable to be left in so cumbersome a form, containing as it does **MUCH OF THE BEST MASONIC THINKING** and writing in our literature.[63]

The booklet continues:

NO PURER, NOBLER MAN HAS STOOD AT THE ALTAR OF FREEMASONRY or left his story in our traditions. He was the **MOST EMINENT MASON IN THE WORLD**....Nor will our Craft ever permit to grow dim the memory of that stately, wise, and gracious teacher....[64]

Reprinted, December 1988

Vol. I   JULY, 1923   No. 7

THE SHORT TALK BULLETIN

OF THE

MASONIC SERVICE ASSOCIATION

OF THE

UNITED STATES

ALBERT PIKE

THE MASONIC SERVICE ASSOCIATION
OF THE UNITED STATES

VOL. XXXIV   FEBRUARY, 1956   No. ➡ 2

The
SHORT TALK BULLETIN.

THE BROKEN COLUMN

THE MASONIC SERVICE ASSOCIATION
OF THE UNITED STATES
Reprinted, January, 1985

Vol. VI   MAY, 1928   No. 5

THE SHORT TALK BULLETIN

OF THE

MASONIC SERVICE ASSOCIATION

OF THE

UNITED STATES

THE LEGEND OF THE LOST WORD

TO BE READ IN LODGE

PUBLISHED MONTHLY BY
THE MASONIC SERVICE ASSOCIATION
OF THE UNITED STATES
Silver Spring, Maryland 20910-4785
Tel: (301) 588-4010

Reprinted, March, 1986

This *Short Talk Bulletin* was originally published in July 1923, but it was reprinted in December 1988, showing that **MASONRY STILL CLAIMS PIKE AS ONE OF THE BEST MASONS EVER TO LIVE** even though he has been dead for over 100 years now.

HEAD OF MASONRY PRAISES PIKE

Of course, there has been **MORE RECENT PRAISE OF ALBERT PIKE**—this time coming from the very head of the Southern Jurisdiction of Masonry, C. Fred Kleinknecht, who is the Sovereign Grand Commander. In the January 1989 issue of *The New Age,* Kleinknecht mentioned that the "apex of our teachings has been the rituals of our degrees and *Morals and Dogma*...."[65] Pike, by the way, wrote some and rewrote others of all the rituals from the 4th through the 33rd degrees.[66] In the November 1992 issue of *The Scottish Rite Journal* (this magazine was called *The New Age* from 1903 until 1990), Kleinknecht again heaps praise on Pike and his book. He brags:

> Correctly understood, Albert Pike's *Morals and Dogma* provides our Brethren a stimulus to thought, a source of inspiration, and even an aid to Scottish Rite growth. Pike's great work is not the book of an hour, a decade, or a century. **IT IS A BOOK FOR ALL TIME....**
>
> Abandon *Morals and Dogma?* Never![67]

Kleinknecht adds that Pike had a "personal and profound faith as a Christian."[68] Eliphas Levi also claims to be a Christian.[69] Of course, the Bible tells us in Titus 1:16: "They **PROFESS** that they know

God: but **IN WORKS THEY DENY HIM,** being abominable, and disobedient, and unto every good work reprobate." Obviously, Levi's and Pike's Christianity is not the Christianity of the Bible, especially when Pike writes:

> LUCIFER, the *Light-bearer!* Strange and mysterious name to give to the Spirit of Darkness! Lucifer, the Son of the Morning! Is it *he* who bears the *Light,* and with its splendors intolerable blinds feeble, sensual, or selfish Souls? Doubt it not! for traditions are full of Divine Revelations and Inspirations.... [Emphasis in the original][70]

In fact, this quotation is one of those partially plagiarized from Levi, well-known occultist and Mason. Levi remarked:

> Lucifer! The Light-Bearer! How strange a name is given to the spirit of darkness! What, is it he who bears light and also blinds weak souls? Yes, doubt it not, for traditions are full of divine revelations and inspirations.[71]

LUCIFERIAN BROTHERHOOD AND MASONRY

Eliphas Levi and Albert Pike aren't the only ones who claim that Lucifer is the Light-Bearer. Anton LaVey tells us that Lucifer is "bearer of light" and "the spirit of the air."[72] In Ephesians 2:2 we see that Satan is referred to as the "prince of the power of the air," however, he is not some great god to be honored but rather is "the spirit that now worketh in the children of disobedience." The Bible also warns us that many people will come as the "apostles of Christ" but that they are in reality "false apostles" and "deceitful workers." Since Satan himself comes as "an angel of light," we are told that "it is no great thing if his ministers also be transformed as the ministers of righteousness; whose end shall be according to their works" (II Corinthians 11:13-15).

Manly Palmer Hall is another Mason who praises Lucifer. In his book, *The Lost Keys of Freemasonry,* he explains:

> When the Mason learns that the key to the warrior on the block is the proper application of the dynamo of living power, he has learned the mystery of his Craft. The **SEETHING ENERGIES OF LUCIFER** are in his hands and before he may step onward and upward, he must prove his ability to properly apply energy.[73]

How does Scottish Rite Masonry feel about Hall? You can judge for yourself from the following obituary notice that appeared in the November 1990 issue of *The Scottish Rite Journal.*

> Illustrious Manly Palmer Hall, often called **"MASONRY'S GREATEST PHILOSOPHER,"** departed his earthly labors peacefully in his sleep on August 7, 1990, in Los Angeles, California....Brother Hall...devoted his life to lecturing, teaching, editing, and writing on all aspects of Freemasonry.

> ...He is best known for writing *The Lost Keys of Freemasonry* (1923), *The Dionysian Artificers* (1926), *Masonic Orders of Fraternity* (1950) and of course, his monumental *Encyclopedic Outline* of Masonic history, philosophy and related subjects....

> ...Brother Hall...received the Scottish Rite's highest honor, the Grand Cross in 1985 **BECAUSE OF HIS EXCEPTIONAL CONTRIBUTIONS TO**

MACOY / 106

THE LOST KEYS OF FREEMASONRY or, The Secret of Hiram Abiff
by Manly P. Hall, 33°

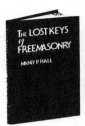

A book for the Mason and non-Mason. As a contribution to Masonic idealism, revealing the profounder aspects of an ancient fraternity which has always wrought for the benefit of mankind, the book is one to read over and over again.

The Egyptian Initiate has been added to this edition and readers will find it intensely interesting and enlightening.

Hard cover with jacket. 136 pages. Illustrations.

ISBN-0-88053-044-8   M300 $9.50

(Less 25% on 5 or more, plus postage)

MANLY P. HALL'S LITERARY MASTERPIECE
Diamond Jubilee Edition
The Secret Teachings of All Ages

AN ENCYCLOPEDIA OF MASONIC, HERMETIC, QABBALISTIC AND ROSICRUCIAN SYMBOLICAL PHILOSOPHY:

Interpretation of the secret teachings concealed within the rituals, allegories and mysteries of all ages.

Now available in its original size and format, (12-1/4" x 18-1/2" x 1-3/4"), including 54 color plates and over 200 black and white cuts.

Forty-six revealing chapters on the ancient and modern mystery teachings and esoteric philosophy.

Contains information on ATLANTIS AND THE GODS OF ANTIQUITY; LIFE AND WRITINGS OF THOTH HERMES TRISMEGISTUS; INITIATION OF THE PYRAMID; THE VIRGIN OF THE WORLD; SUN, A UNIVERSAL DEITY; ZODIAC AND ITS SIGNS; BEMBINE TABLE OF ISIS; WONDERS OF ANTIQUITY; THE LIFE AND PHILOSOPHY OF PYTHAGORAS; PYTHAGOREAN MATHEMATICS; HIRAMIC LEGEND; STONES, METALS, AND GEMS; and much, much more!

    LIMITED EDITION   O702—$150.00

Also, available in 1/3 reduced facsimile with black and white illustrations. Comprehensive index. 229 pages. Cloth.   O701 $37.50
Also, available in paper back.   O700 $27.50

MASONIC ORDERS OF FRATERNITY
by Manly P. Hall, 33°

Particular emphasis upon the 17th and 18th century revivals of the Mystery rituals of Antiquity. Such names as the Comte de St. Germain, Cagliostro, Louis Claude de St. Martin, Dr. John Dee and the French Voltaire, as well as information about the mysterious rituals of Memphis and the Illuminati and the revival of Egyptian Masonry which inspired Mozart's The Magic Flute.

Hard cover with jacket. 114 pages.   M629 $7.50

FREEMASONRY, the Scottish Rite, and the public good.

Like Grand Commander Albert Pike before him, Ill∴ **HALL DID NOT TEACH A NEW DOCTRINE** but was an ambassador of an ageless tradition of wisdom that enriches us to this day....The world is a far better place because of Manly Palmer Hall, and **WE ARE BETTER PERSONS FOR HAVING KNOWN HIM** and his work.[74]

Praise for Lucifer also comes from the Brotherhoods. In the *Adelphi Quarterly* we are told: "The **FREEMASONS WERE FORMED AS A SCHOOL OF THE LUCIFERIAN BROTHERHOOD** at the time of the building of the Temple of Solomon...."[75] This newsletter goes on to mention that it was Lucifer who is:

> ...the symbol of mankind's emancipation and independence. He freed us from the doldrums and gave us the opportunity to challenge ourselves and grow and develop civilization, and He forced us into having to gain knowledge.[76]

So, according to this article, it was Lucifer who emancipated mankind and gave us freedom!

In fact, according to Masonic writer, Lynn Perkins, the fall of mankind was something **GOOD.** It was not a "fall" but a betterment of our situation.[77] He boldly declares that man "**rose** to Divine Status by partaking of the **'fruit of the tree of knowledge of good and evil.'**" [Emphasis in the original][78] He adds that the advice the serpent gave to Eve was "wiser than the recorded command of God that would have, if obeyed, confined Adam and Eve and their descendants to the status of animals forever...."[79]

Knowing of Pike's admiration for Lucifer, we shouldn't be astonished to find out that Pike created a Palladium Rite which "was a secret rite that openly worshiped Lucifer and practiced blatant occultism."[80] This rite was to be kept secret at all costs and only a chosen few were selected.[81] The Palladium, we are told:

> ...would be an international alliance of key Masons. It would bring in the Grand Lodges, the Grand Orient, the 97 degrees of Memphiz-Mitzraim (the Ancient and Primitive Rite) and the Scottish Rite. The name, Palladium, was taken from a Masonic order founded in 1720 which died out, only to re-emerge in Charleston under Pike.[82]

Domenico Margiotta, a 33° Mason, reveals this about the Palladium Rite:

> Palladism is necessarily a Luciferian rite. Its religion is Manichaean neo-gnosticism, teaching that the divinity is dual and that **LUCIFER IS THE EQUAL OF ADONAY,** with **LUCIFER THE GOD OF LIGHT** and Goodness struggling for humanity against Adonay the God of Darkness and Evil....Albert Pike had only specified and unveiled the dogmas of the high grades of all other masonries, for in no matter what rite, the **GREAT ARCHITECT OF THE UNIVERSE IS NOT THE GOD WORSHIPPED BY THE CHRISTIANS.**[83]

Did you notice that Margiotta admits that the Great Architect of the Universe (GAOTU), who is worshiped by Masons, **IS NOT** the God worshiped by the Christians? Yet, those Masons in the lower degrees of Masonry are never told that the GAOTU is not the God of the Christians. They are told that the GAOTU is the God of each individual's own choosing. Living in America, most Masons just **ASSUME** this refers to the Christian's God, never realizing nor suspecting that the GAOTU is Lucifer! Since many people do not really know what the Bible or Masonry teaches, they proudly go on saying they are a Christian but multitudes of them are blinded from the teachings of Masonry and the true Word of God.

PIKE: APOSTLE OF LUCIFER

Margiotta also commented:

To recruit adepts, they planned to use some members of the other rites, but in the beginning they meant to rely principally on those among the initiates of Ancient and Accepted Scottish Rites who were already addicted to occultism....

Thus it was particularly the initiates of the thirty-third degree Scottish Rites, who, owing to their extensive internal ramifications, were privileged to recruit adepts for Palladism....

One will better understand these precautions knowing that Palladism is essentially a Luciferian rite."[84]

William Josiah Sutton reports:

Very few Masons know that Albert Pike, this highest authority of Freemasonry, the Prince Adept, Mystic, Poet, and Scholar of Freemasonry, was himself also the head of the Palladist, another Secret Society which **OPENLY WORSHIPPED LUCIFER** and was bent on destroying Christianity, replacing it with the worship of Lucifer himself.

Albert **PIKE,** the head of the Freemasons, **WAS ALSO AN APOSTLE OF LUCIFER!**[85]

PIKE ADVOCATES MASONRY OF ADOPTION

"Pike, the Sovereign Pontiff of Lucifer, was the president of the Supreme Dogmatic Directory."[86] In fact, by 1889:

> Pike simultaneously occupied the positions of Grand Master of the Central Directory of Washington, D.C. (the head of D.C. Masonry), Grand Commander of the Supreme Council of Charleston (head of American Masonry), and Sovereign Pontiff of Universal Freemasonry (head of world Masonry).[87]

It's no wonder then, that occultist and 33° Mason, Arthur Edward Waite, tells us that **PIKE WAS CALLED THE "PONTIFF OF LUCIFERIAN FREEMASON-RY."**[88] It is important to remember that **PIKE WAS A FRIEND OF ROB MORRIS, THE FOUNDER OF THE EASTERN STAR!!**[89] In fact, **PIKE WAS A BIG ADVOCATE OF MASONRY FOR WOMEN.** Albert Mackey, another 33° Mason, explains:

> Albert Pike, who took great interest in this Masonry of Adoption and made a translation of the ritual into English with some elaboration dictated by his profound knowledge of symbolism and philosophy, points out the reason that in his judgment existed for the conferring of degrees upon the women of a Freemason's family. He says in the preface to his ritual of the Masonry of Adoption:

"Our mothers, sisters, wives and daughters cannot, it is true, be admitted to share with us the grand mysteries of Freemasonry, but there is no reason why there should not be also a Masonry for them, which may not merely enable them to make themselves known to Masons, and so to obtain assistance and protection; but by means of which, acting in concert through the tie of association and mutual obligation, they may co-operate in the great labors of Masonry by assisting in and, in some respects, directing their charities, and toiling in the cause of human progress."...

The Order of the Eastern Star has become just such an organization, strong enough to take an active and powerful co-operative concern in the beneficent labors of Freemasons for the care of the indigent and the afflicted. While entirely different and distinct from the Masonry of Adoption, being indeed of American and not French development, all the expectations so ably expressed by Brother Pike have in no other fraternal association been so admirably fulfilled as in the Order of the Eastern Star.[90]

If, according to Mackey, the Eastern Star fulfilled "all the expectations so ably expressed by Brother Pike,"[91] then there must be something very sinister about the Eastern Star! Even though the Eastern Star has posed as a Christian organization, we know that Pike certainly would not have been pleased with any such organization. Why? Simply because Pike, as I've already mentioned, was an admirer of Lucifer and steeped in occultism and mythology.[92] Such a person hates true Christianity. Pike, of course, was no exception.

PIKE'S "HYMNS"

In his book, *Pike's Poems,* he wrote numerous "hymns" to **PAGAN** gods.[93] Some of these gods were Hera, Poseidon, Aphrodite, Demeter, Apollon, Ares, Hermes, Hypnos, and Flora, among others. Let's view some of this poetry.

To Hera he wrote:

"Mother of Gods! devoutly **WE INCLINE OUR WILLING KNEES BEFORE THY HOLY SHRINE**
Before thine altars the obsequious kneel
We, prostrate at thy feet...."[94]

To Poseidon he entreated:

"Oh, come! our lofty altars for thee stand...."[95]

The hymn to Aphrodite states:

"Our altars burn for thee...."[96]

To Apollon he pleaded:

"Answer our hymn, and come to us, Most High!...
Oh, thou, whose name
Is hymned by all, let us to dare to claim
Thy holy presence here!
Hear us, bright God, and lend a gracious ear!...
Oh! bright Apollon, hear, and grant relief
To us who cry to thee!
And let us, ere we die, thy glory see![97]

To Ares he declared:

"WE BOW IN ADORATION AT THY SHRINE,

Dark-bearded God, majestic and divine!"[98]

Pike, when writing the poem to Hupnos (or Hypnos), the god of sleep, proclaimed:

"With drooping eyelids, head that ever nods!...
Thou, who dost sleep...."[99]

This hymn clearly shows to us that Pike is not referring to the God of the Christians, for my Bible testifies: "He that keepeth thee **WILL NOT SLUMBER.** Behold, He that keepeth Israel shall neither slumber nor sleep" (Psalm 121:3-4). If your god sleeps, then you have a different God than the God of the Bible!

Seeing that Pike reveres numerous gods, it's not hard to comprehend that Lucifer would be included in his pantheon. Some of his praise for Lucifer has already been noted. William Guy Carr, Retired Commander of the Royal Canadian Navy, comments: "There is plenty of documentary evidence to prove that Pike, like Weishaupt, was head of the Luciferian Priesthood in his day."[100]

Elsewhere Carr writes:

While Pike was Sovereign Pontiff of Universal Freemasonry, and Head of the Illuminati during the 1870's he revised and modernized the ritual of the **BLACK MASS** celebrated to emphasise the Luciferian and Satanic victory achieved in the Garden of Eden, and over Christ to end his mission on earth. The celebrant of the Black Mass plays the part of Satan. He introduces a Virgin Priestess to the joys of sexual intercourse and makes known to her the mystery of procreation. Pike's version also includes a paradox on the betrayal, and crucifixion of Christ. The desecration of a Host consecrated by a Roman Catholic Priest is part of this abomination. **LUCIFER IS WORSHIPPED AS "THE GIVER OF THE TRUE LIGHT"**; the fountain of All wisdom; and as the greatest of all Supernatural Beings. Satan is worshipped as Lucifer's Prime Minister....a Black Mass is usually followed by a Bacchanalian orgy. Those who attend are supplied with sex-stimulating drugs and beverages. They worship the body and indulge in sexual excesses, and perversions, of all kinds, Priestesses are provided for the occasion.[101]

Des Griffin, author of *The Fourth Reich of the Rich,* agrees that Pike "was an avowed worshipper of Satan by name,"[102] and he adds that he "practiced necromancy and all forms of sorcery."[103] Pike was also associated with the Theosophical Society and with Helena Petrovna Blavatsky, an occultist, who's been called "the Mother of the New Age Movement."[104] We read:

On October 20, 1875, a society was founded in New York, said to be for **"SPIRITUALIST INVESTIGATIONS"**; Olcott was President, Felt and Dr. Seth Pancoast Vice-presidents, and Mme. Blavatsky Secretary. Among other members were William Q. Judge, Charles Sotheran, one of the high dignitaries of American Masonry, also for a short time General **ALBERT PIKE,** Grand Master of the Scottish Rite for the Southern Jurisdiction U.S.A....[105]

PIKE: FOUNDER OF KU KLUX KLAN

Not only did Pike have a background of occultic practices, but he was also instrumental in the founding of the Ku Klux Klan![106] Carl Raschke reveals:

Pike was one of the original architects of the
Ku Klux Klan....The white robes, cross burnings,
conical hats, and use of such titles as "grand
dragon" and "imperial wizard" derives from the
strange lore developed by Levi.[107]

Pike himself was appointed the Grand Dragon.[108]
Anton Chaitkin reveals that "the Klan and the Scottish
Rite [Masonry] were one and the same enterprise...."[109]
Most Masons and Eastern Stars should be aware
that their ranks include very few (if any) black men
and women. In fact, many lodges still forbid blacks
to join. I believe part of this hatred and prejudice
to blacks can be partially traced back to Pike. In
Pike's book *Irano-Aryan Faith and Doctrine As
Contained in the Zend-Avesta,* he claims the Negroes
are the lowest race. He even maintained:

...that the existence of the Negro proved that
both the Creation account of Genesis and Darwin's
theory of evolution were false because the white
man could not have come from the same source
as the black man![110]

Pike emphasized: "I took my obligation to white
men, not Negroes. When I have to accept Negroes
as brethren or leave Freemasonry, I shall leave it."[111]
The Bible tells us that "Adam called his wife's
name Eve; because she was the mother of all living"
(Genesis 3:20), and God "hath made of one blood
all nations of men for to dwell on all the face of the
earth" (Acts 17:26). With God "there is no respect
of persons" (Romans 2:11, II Chronicles 19:7; Colossians
3:25). Of course, it is obvious that Pike doesn't
believe the Bible. In a book written by Rex R. Hutchens,
33° Mason, and Donald W. Monson, 32° Mason,
entitled *The Bible in Albert Pike's Morals and Dogma,*

we find that Pike even "occasionally adjusted the translation [of the Bible] by direct references to Greek and Hebrew as he (or his sources) understood them."[112]

DIVINE OR HUMAN?

Pike, writing of "Him who taught in Galilee"[113] (obviously referring to Jesus), alleges:

> Divine or human, inspired or only a reforming Essene, it must be agreed that His teachings are far nobler, far purer, far less alloyed with error and imperfection, far less of the earth earthly, than those of Socrates, Plato, Seneca, or Mahomet, or any other of the great moralists and Reformers of the world.[114]

This statement may **SOUND** pious, but it has flaws. Pike refers to Jesus as "Divine **OR** human," "inspired **OR** only a reforming Essene." He goes on to say that Christ's teachings are "far less alloyed [mixed] with error and imperfection" than other reformers. Christ's teachings have **NO** errors in them, but Pike believes they do. This, of course, is a natural conclusion if one denies the divinity of Christ, which Pike does. In *Morals and Dogma,* he notes: "...Jesus of Nazareth was but a **MAN LIKE US**...His history but the **UNREAL** revival of an older **LEGEND.**"[115] Since Pike does not believe that Christ is divine and perfect, then he cannot possibly believe His teachings were inspired and without error. It takes a divine and pure being to have flawless teachings. Jesus was the one and only person who could have faultless precepts, but Pike refuses to accept this. Rejecting Christ as the only hope for mankind, Pike turned to the occult. It is reported that he even had an image of Baphomet in his Lodge at Charleston (which was recently destroyed in the fall of 1989 by Hurricane Hugo).[116] As previously mentioned, Baphomet was drawn by the occultist Eliphas Levi. Pike was a disciple of Levi's and plagiarized portions of his writings, so it's not surprising to see that Pike would also use the drawing of Baphomet. Baphomet is an important figure in **SATANISM,** as well.[117] David Carrico remarks:

> Certainly the greatest contribution that Eliphas Levi made to Satanism was his engraving of the Baphomet....
>
> At almost every Satanic ritual where sacrifice and praise is offered to Satan, the influence of the **FREEMASON ELIPHAS LEVI** can be felt.[118]

BAPHOMET AND SATANISM

Anton LaVey acknowledges the importance of Baphomet in Satanic rituals and instructs where it should be placed. He states:

> Person performing ritual stands facing the altar and symbol of Baphomet throughout ritual....
>
> Amulet bearing the sigil [an occultic device used in magic and astrology] of Baphomet or the traditional pentagram of Satan are worn by all participants....
>
> **BAPHOMET REPRESENTS THE POWERS OF DARKNESS** combined with the generative **FERTILITY** of the goat. In its "pure" form the pentagram is shown encompassing the figure of a man in the five points of the star—three points up, two pointing down—symbolizing man's spiritual nature. In Satanism the pentagram is also used, but since Satanism represents the carnal instincts of man, or the opposite of the spiritual nature,

the **PENTAGRAM IS INVERTED** to perfectly accommodate the head of the god—its horns, representing duality, thrust upwards in defiance; the other three points inverted, or the **TRINITY DENIED.** The Hebraic figures around the outer circle of the symbol which stem from the magical teachings of the Kabala, spell out "Leviathan," the serpent of the watery abyss, and identified with Satan. These figures correspond to the five points of the inverted star.

The symbol of Baphomet is placed on the wall above the altar....

The sword is held by the priest and is used to point towards the symbol of Baphomet during the **INVOCATION TO SATAN.**[119]

LaVey's daughter, Zeena, describes her Satanic baptism like this:

As I sat wearing the red robe my mother made that morning, I toyed with the Baphomet amulet dangling around my neck (this image of the Satanic goat was handcrafted for me by the pioneering survivalist Kurt Saxon, a founding member of the Church of Satan)....

Since that night I understood what it means to be a Satanic Witch, a woman who makes full use of her feminine wiles. Throughout my life I would replay the words intoned during my baptism:...

And so we dedicate your life to love, to passion, to indulgence, and to Satan and the way of darkness, fane. Hail Zeena! Hail Satan! [Emphasis in the original][120]

It's **THIS** symbol, the **PENTAGRAM WITH TWO POINTS UP (OR BAPHOMET), THAT IS REPRESENTED IN THE EASTERN STAR LODGES!** Anton LaVey also writes:

The symbol of **BAPHOMET** was used by the Knights Templar to **REPRESENT SATAN.** Through the ages this symbol has been called by many different names. Among these are: The Goat of Mendes, The Goat of a Thousand Young, The Black Goat, The Judas Goat, and perhaps most appropriately, The Scapegoat.[121]

Other names are: Goat's Head Star and the Star of Mendes.[122]

KNIGHTS TEMPLAR AND MASONRY

Interestingly, the Knights Templar, a group that existed during the twelfth, thirteenth, and early part of the fourteenth centuries,[123] had numerous charges laid against them. Some of these charges were:

"1. Denial of Christ and defiling of the cross.

2. Adoration of an idol.

3. A perverted Sacrament performed.

4. Ritual murders.

5. The wearing of a cord of heretical significance.

6. The ritual kiss.

7. Alteration in the ceremony of the Mass and an unorthodox form of absolution.

8. Immorality.

9. Treachery to other sections of the Christian forces."[124]

In a book entitled *The Guilt of the Templars,* we are told that "the Knights Templars' confessions show them to have been basically a **HOMOSEXUAL** warrior order, like the Japanese samurai."[125] Other charges were that the Knights Templar participated in **BLACK MAGIC**[126] and **PEDERASTY** (anal intercourse, usually with a boy).[127] They practiced **"PHALLICISM OR SEX-WORSHIP AND SATANISM"**[128] and venerated "'The Baphomet,' the idol of the Luciferians. The crime of **SODOMY** was a rite of Templar initiation."[129] There was also a "ritual kiss" which involved a series of four kisses, the last one being a kiss on the anus or on the private parts.[130]

The demise of the Knights Templar came in 1314 when the last Grand Master, Jacques DeMolay, was burned at the stake.[131] This group, however, was not completely obliterated. According to Pike, "the Templars survived under a deep shroud of secrecy, and it was not long before they began taking their revenge—one that would extend some 400 years into the future."[132] In fact, many writers contend that **MASONRY IS THE CONTINUATION OF THE KNIGHTS TEMPLARS.**[133]

Former Grand Sovereign Commander, Henry C. Clausen, brags: "Masonry long has used the great inspirational story of Jacques DeMolay to illustrate its truths."[134] There is even a Masonic affiliated organization for young boys called the Order of DeMolay, taking its name from the immoral **PERVERT, JACQUES DEMOLAY! Of** course, **MASONS REVERE HIM.** In a Masonic book, *Questions and Answers,* we find: "The Masonic Order of Knights Templar claims descent from the older Order and **DE MOLAY IS HELD IN HIGH REGARD AS A MAN WHOSE LIFE WAS AN EXAMPLE FIT TO BE FOLLOWED."**[135] Do you want **YOUR** children following the example of homosexuality, blasphemy, murder, etc.? (Mason Albert Pike, by the way, was also a homosexual.[136]) Even the ritual or obscene kiss of the Templars has been carried over into the Masonic ritual, only it is in a **DISGUISED** form! Masonic writer, J. S. M. Ward, reveals that the lesson of the twenty-first degree:

> ...is humility, and, the more to impress this lesson on the initiate, he is compelled to kiss the pommel of the sword of the Knight Commander. This "kiss of humility" is reminiscent of the so-called "ritual kiss" of the Templars, which also was intended to humble the pride of the novice.[137]

As also mentioned, another charge against the Knights Templar was that they worshiped the idol Baphomet, the god of lust.[138] Occultist and Mason, Eliphas Levi, shows the connection between Baphomet and the ritual or obscene kiss:

> Baphomet is analogous to the dark God of Rabbi Simeon. He is the dark side of the divine face. This is why, during initiation ceremonies, the member elect must kiss the hind-face of **BAPHOMET,** or, to give him a more vulgar name, the **Devil.** Now, in the symbolism of the two faces, the hind-face of **GOD IS THE DEVIL**

and hind-face of the Devil is the hieroglyphic face of God.

WHY THE NAME OF FREEMASONS? FREE FROM WHAT? FROM THE FEAR OF GOD? YES, doubtless, for when one fears God, one is looking at him from behind."[139]

Gary Kah mentions that the:

...Knights Templars, as it turned out, had been masters of deception, experts in duplicity, appearing to serve Christ on the surface while worshipping Lucifer within their inner rites.[140]

RIDING THE GOAT

What is intriguing is that when a person joins the Masonic Lodge, there is a lot of joking about the new candidate "riding the goat."[141]

This cartoon appeared in the September 1991 issue of <u>The Scottish Rite Journal</u>.

Fertility was symbolized by the egg; the serpent; the organs of generation—then wholly a mystery—and in Egypt especially, by the bull.

Later nations substituted the goat. And we are not at all free from this as so clearly indicated by the fact that being accepted into initiatory orders is referred to as "riding the goat."[142]

Former Satanist and Mason, William Schnoebelen, writes:

That is interesting when one recalls Albert Pike's teaching about the he-goat of the witches' sabbat, and the way witches in the Middle Ages demonstrated their allegiance to Satan. They had to consent to sexual intercourse with "the goat," (usually a high priest rigged up with a goat's head, but occasionally a real demonic which looked goat-like). Or they had to perform the so-called osculum infamum (obscene kiss) which involved kissing the goat's backside to show their fealty [loyalty] to Satan.[143]

In Pike's book, *Morals and Dogma,* we find that the Knights Templar were set up as an organization designed to **TRICK THE PUBLIC** and the lower level initiates:

The Templars, like all other Secret Orders and Associations, had **TWO DOCTRINES,** one **CONCEALED** and reserved for the Masters...the other public....Thus they **DECEIVED THE ADVERSARIES WHOM THEY SOUGHT TO SUPPLANT.**[144]

Of course, this type of deception and deceit continues even today in both Masonry and the Eastern Star.

MASONIC SECRECY

Concerning Baphomet, how do the higher level Masons feel about this **GOD OF LUST?** Kenneth R. H. Mackenzie, a **MASONIC** author and "a leading British **OCCULTIST"** who was "excessively **INVOLVED WITH MAGIC AND SPIRITUALISM,"**[145] writing in his *Royal Masonic Cyclopaedia,* remarks:

> It has been suggested that Baphomet is none other than the Ancient of Days or Creator. More cannot be said here without improperly revealing what we are bound to **HIDE, CONCEAL, AND NEVER REVEAL.**[146]

You can see that this sensual god, Baphomet, is considered to be "none other than the Ancient of Days," meaning God. Eliphas Levi even blasphemously insinuates that Baphomet is the Holy Ghost![147] So, instead of Baphomet being something that the Masons would spurn, they adore him, but since they know that many people would be offended by this image, they have to conceal him under another form. As mentioned earlier, Masonic author, Lynn F. Perkins, states the following about the Masonic rituals:

> It should be carefully noted that the **PURPOSE OF THE RITUAL IS** just as much **TO CONCEAL** as to reveal the secret science that lies behind and within the outward and literal forms and symbols. The **TRUE WISDOM IS CONCEALED, HIDDEN,** not only from those who do not join the Masonic Order but also from those who "take" the degrees; and it will remain "hidden" until each Mason seeks revelation and finds the Truth for himself. There are no interpretations in the Ritual; they have to be sought elsewhere.[148]

Even the Eastern Star ritual book admits that the pentagram is "often called the Star of Bethlehem," but, **"ASIDE FROM THIS TIME-HONORED TRADITION**...there is a deep ethical and spiritual suggestiveness in this beautiful emblem which may be profitably considered from more than a **SINGLE** standpoint."[149] Notice that there is a "spiritual suggestiveness" ASIDE from the tradition of a star appearing at the birth of Jesus! In other words, there is an outward explanation and an inner or concealed meaning to the star used in the Eastern Star. Rob Morris has also acknowledged that this star corresponds to "the emblem on the Master's carpet"[150] in Masonry and we are told the "five-pointed star is an ancient and sacred symbol."[151] These are important admissions, once again showing the connection between Masonry, the Eastern Star, the occult, and Satanism. When they call the pentagram (or Baphomet) a "sacred symbol" they do not have reference to the God of the Christians. For example, Albert Pike claims that the "Deity of the Old Testament is everywhere represented as the direct author of Evil...."[152] Anton LaVey, in *The Satanic Bible,* boasts: "I dip my finger in the watery blood of your impotent mad redeemer, and write over his thorn-torn brow: The TRUE prince of evil—the king of the slaves!" [Emphasis in the original][153]

After telling us that the God of the Christians is the prince of evil, LaVey brags that Lucifer is "the bearer of light, the spirit of the air, the personification of enlightenment."[154] Another fascinating note is when the Satanic ritual is performed and the Princes of Hell are called forth from the four compass points, **LUCIFER, THE LIGHT-BEARER,** is the god called in from the **EAST.**[155] A book on witchcraft reminds us: "Lucifer is one of the multiple names of Satan. As **LUCIFER THE LIGHTBEARER** he has his home in the **EAST.**[156] Remember, the **MASONIC RITUAL HAS THE EAST AS REPRESENTING LIGHT AND THE EASTERN STAR RITUAL REQUIRES THAT THE PENTAGRAM FACE THE EAST** in a specific manner.[157] Are all these facts just "coincidences" or were they planned as such? After reading tens of thousands of pages of Masonic, Eastern Star, and witchcraft literature, I have no doubt whatsoever that each detail was intricately planned and carefully calculated to coincide with mythology, paganism, and witchcraft.

PENTAGRAM IS SACRED

For instance, in *History of the Star Points: Order of the Eastern Star* by John Kennedy Lacock, we were told the pentagram is a "sacred symbol."[158] Elsewhere the pentagram is listed as a symbol of the Deity or an item of protection.[159] A witchcraft organization, The Magic Door, run by the "Official Witch of Salem," Laurie Cabot,[160] agrees. They sell pentagram jewelry and advertise it as a "sacred symbol of protection and wisdom."[161] When Eliphas Levi invoked the apparition of Apollonius, we are informed that "his altar had a pentagram carved on it, and when a shrouded figure appeared before him, he placed one hand on the pentagram for protection."[162] A Masonic pamphlet denotes: "Five had the power to control evil spirits; the pentalpha [pentagram], therefore, became a magic amulet to protect the wearer against accident and disease."[163] In a New Age booklet, *For Full Moon Workers*, the same idea is found— this time with a warning:

> The concept of the pentagram as a symbol of
> the protection which is afforded by self discipline,

virtue and knowledge is one that unfolds with study and training.

It remains to say, before we get into the actual procedure of a full moon group meditation meeting, that the energies invoked during a full moon meeting are exceedingly powerful, and if the worker stays not within the protection of the pentagram, he lays himself open to various kinds of physical, emotional, psychical and mental trouble. We are dealing with fire, and our approach to the flame is one of sober common sense.[164]

Satanist Anton LaVey, however, sneers at those who think they are being protected from the powers of evil. He informs us:

White magic is supposedly utilized only for good or unselfish purposes, and black magic, we are told, is used only for selfish or "evil" reasons. Satanism draws no such dividing line. Magic is magic, be it used to help or hinder....

During white magical ceremonies, the practitioners stand within a pentagram to protect themselves from the "evil" forces which they call upon for help. To the Satanist, it seems a bit two-faced to call these forces for help, while at the same time protecting yourself from the very powers you have asked for assistance. The Satanist realizes that only by putting himself in league with these forces can he fully and unhypocritically utilize the Powers of Darkness to his best advantage.[165]

Can you see the connection between Satanism, witchcraft, the New Age movement, Masonry, and the Eastern Star? **ALL** of these groups use the pentagram and most claim its "protecting" power.

John Yarker, a Mason, declares: "The Masons, Rosicrucians, Templars, and Gnostics, all used the same class of symbols."[166]

So, then, when Masonic writer, Albert Mackey, states: "The star is a symbol of God,"[167] we no longer have to wonder **WHICH** God he is referring to since we have ample evidence that this Masonic "god" is Baphomet or Satan. Even Masonic writer, Manly Hall, "clearly identifies Baphomet with the satanic 'Goat of Mendes,' probably the best known representation of Lucifer in all occultism."[168]

ANOTHER MEANING

If you are an Eastern Star member or a Mason you will probably claim that **YOUR** Lodge teaches that the star is a symbol of the **TRUE** God, the God of the Christians. After all, the Eastern Star manual does mention that this star is the star of Bethlehem,[169] but as already noted they also inform us that there is **ANOTHER MEANING** in addition to this explanation.[170] Furthermore, we have ample proof from Masonic sources that what is taught in the Lodge is not what is actually meant. For example, Masonic author, George H. Steinmetz, shares the following:

> The symbols are *not* used in the commonly accepted meaning. It is "NOT BY EXACT RESEMBLANCE"; there *IS* a more recondite [occult or esoteric] interpretation, as we suspected; it is one of "SUGGESTIONS OR ASSOCIATION *IN THOUGHT*."

> There is a SECRET DOCTRINE in Freemasonry. That secret doctrine is concealed, rather than revealed, by the very lectures which, we are told,

offer a "rational explanation" of the ceremonies of initiation. If we were to accept these "rational explanations" as final, and seek no further, Freemasonry would be a farce. [Emphasis in the original][171]

Read those last two paragraphs again and let the message sink in!

Albert Pike also relates:

What is most worth knowing in Masonry is never very openly taught. The symbols are displayed, but they are mute. It is by hints only, and these the least noticeable and apparently insignificant, that the Initiate is put upon the track of the hidden Secret.

IT WAS NEVER INTENDED THAT THE MASS OF MASONS SHOULD KNOW THE MEANING OF THE BLUE DEGREES [the first three degrees of Masonry], and no pains were spared to **CONCEAL** their meaning.[172]

J. D. Buck, a Masonic writer, explains: "The most profound secrets of Masonry **ARE NOT** revealed in the Lodge at all. They belong only to the **FEW.**"[173] Another **MASONIC AUTHOR AND OCCULTIST,** Arthur Edward Waite, writes:

The Triangle, the Cross, the Pentagram, the so-called Star or Shield of Solomon are old portents indicating secret things. Behind their Masonic meanings are others of a deeper kind, and they can be read and understood in that light. The Word within the word, the Message at the back of the Symbol, the Second Sense of allegory: it is in the finding of these that we shall enter into the Secret Kingdom of RITES behind the

RITES, and into a living Masonry of which this at work among us is a vestige and a shadow. [Emphasis in the original][174]

SYMBOLS REPRESENT SOMETHING ELSE

A *Short Talk Bulletin* entitled "Symbolism" discloses:

It may be asserted in the broadest terms that the **FREEMASON WHO KNOWS NOTHING OF OUR SYMBOLISM KNOWS LITTLE OF FREEMASONRY.** He may be able to repeat every line of the ritual without an error, yet, if he does not understand the meaning of the ceremonies, the signs, the words, the emblems and figures, he is a **MASONIC IGNORAMUS.**[175]

Even a book on the Eastern Star admits:

A SYMBOL IS SOMETHING THAT REPRESENTS SOMETHING ELSE. A MASTERY OF THE SYMBOLISM of the Order is the **KEY TO THE UNDERSTANDING** of the precepts and principles which are **ALLEGORICALLY** and **FIGURATIVELY** presented.[176]

This book also explains:

The signet and chart are synonymous terms used to identify our special method of instruction. The tools of acquirement are symbolically represented and the **HIDDEN MEANINGS** are given as a **SYMBOLIC REPRESENTATION.** Through this instruction, each member is better enabled to see the full glory of His Shining Star.[177]

Masonic writer, J. S. M. Ward, even goes so far as to tell us:

The unknown Pantheistic deity hinted at in masonry is a matter of vital importance, both to those who desire to know what F.M. [Freemasonry] teaches, and also to those who hope by means of hints in our present ritual to rediscover something of our past history....

It [the Masonic Supreme Being] is distinctly Pantheistic rather than Monotheistic.... [Emphasis in the original][178]

Pantheism is a teaching which equates God with nature, which brings us back to Baphomet, for in a book entitled *Ancient Operative Masonry,* by S. R. Parchment, we are told that the Goat of Mendes (or Baphomet) is pantheistic and androgynous (meaning both male and female).[179] Yet another Masonic author, Albert G. Mackey, mentions that the "Supreme Deity was bisexual, or hermaphrodite, including in the essence of his being the male and female principles, the generative and prolific powers of nature."[180]

Remember Hermes? He "was also the original 'hermaphrodite,' the fusion of sexes in one person. Priests of Hermes wore artificial breasts and female garments."[181] This fits in real well with Baphomet, for Hermes, as well as Baphomet, are identical to Satan.[182]

EASTERN STAR'S REAL GOD

Parchment boasts that the Goat of Mendes "should remind Masons of the indefatigable struggle through which members of the Craft have passed."[183] He mentions that the Templars worshiped Baphomet and that:

...this symbol was meant to convey the divine wisdom of the Absolute [God]. The breasts of

394. The famous 'conjunction of opposites' was not symbolised only by the union of the sun and the moon or by the male and female principles; it was also illustrated by the 'androgyne', the unique being which united the masculine and feminine principles within itself.

The androgyne (or the hermaphrodite) symbolically watches over the beginning and end of every process concerned with magic and initiation.

194

this Pantheistic figure are female, representing Motherhood, to which the **RACE LOOKS FOR REDEMPTION**....Those who received initiation into the mysteries were given certain keys pertaining to both white and black magic which were portrayed by the right hand of Baphomet pointing upward to the bright disc of the waxing moon while the left pointed downward to Luna in darkness. That **MANY OF** the leading lights of **MASONRY WERE IN QUEST OF THE MAGICAL SECRETS NO STUDENT OF OCCULT SCIENCE WILL DENY....**[184]

Did you notice that Parchment claims that Baphomet is the one "to which the race looks for **REDEMPTION**"? Later on he explains that this androgynous Deity, Baphomet, is "the Great Architect of the Universe."[185] George Oliver, also a Mason, indicates that the "Great Architect of the universe is therefore symbolized in Freemasonry by the Blazing Star, as the herald of our salvation."[186] Eliphas Levi, the occultist and Mason, verifies that the:

> ...G which Freemasons place in the centre of the Burning Star signifies GNOSIS and GENERATION, the two sacred words of the ancient Kabbalah. It also signifies GRAND ARCHITECT,

for the Pentagram, from whatever side it may be looked at, always represents an A. By placing it in such a manner that two of its points are above and only one below, we may see the horns, ears, and beard of the hieratic god of Mendes [Baphomet], when it becomes the sign of infernal evocations.

The allegorical star of the Magi is nothing else...than the mysterious Pentagram.... [Emphasis in the original][187]

Since the Great Architect of the Universe is the god of Masonry, you can clearly see just **WHO** the Masonic and Eastern Star god is although he is concealed under symbolism in the lower levels of Masonry. Levi also informs us that the "G" stands for Venus and that Venus' symbol is a lingam (a symbol of the male private part)![188] Remember, Venus is another name for Lucifer[189] and, according to Rex R. Hutchens, 33° Mason, it is also representative of **"MASONIC LIGHT"**![190] The Bible warns about those who "swear by the name of the Lord, and make mention of the God of Israel, but not in truth, nor in righteousness" (Isaiah 48:1). This seems very applicable to the Eastern Star and Masonic organizations (as well as many other groups) for they mention the name of God but it is not mentioned in a truthful manner for they are concealing their pantheistic god of lust, under a name which will be acceptable to the majority of beguiled individuals.

Another Mason, Adam Weishaupt, bragged in a letter how he would subtly destroy Christianity by using deception and he even snickered at those who fell for his ploy. He wrote:

One would almost imagine, that this degree, as I have managed it, is genuine Christianity....I say, that Free Masonry is concealed Christianity....and as I explain things, no man need be ashamed of being a Christian. Indeed I afterwards throw away this name, and substitute Reason....You can't imagine what respect and curiosity my priest-degree has raised; and, which is wonderful, a famous Protestant divine, who is now of the Order, is persuaded that the religion contained in it is the true sense of Christianity. O MAN, MAN! TO WHAT MAY'ST THOU NOT BE PERSUADED? Who would imagine that I was to be the founder of a new religion? [Emphasis in the original][191]

Weishaupt also wrote:

I have contrived an explanation which has every advantage; is inviting to Christians of every communion; gradually frees them from religious prejudices [and] *cultivates the social virtues....My means are effectual, and irresistible. Our secret Association works in a way that nothing can withstand.* [Emphasis in the original][192]

WHO WOULD REMAIN?

William T. Still reports:

However, others in Weishaupt's Order wrote of their difficulties in seducing candidates away from Christianity. Philo (Baron von Knigge) had problems convincing some members of the Order that their goal was not to abolish Christianity:

"I have been at unwearied pains to remove the fears of some who imagine that our Superiors want to abolish Christianity....Were I to let them know that our General holds all Religion to be a lie, and uses even Deism...only to lead men by the nose."

Philo then candidly explained why initiates must have the true nature of the Order kept from them: "Should I mention our fundamental principles, so unquestionably dangerous to the world, who would remain?"[193]

In *Masonic Institutes* we are informed that Baron von Knigge also wrote:

I have put meaning to all these dark symbols, and have prepared both degrees, introducing beautiful ceremonies, which I have selected from among those of the ancient communions, combined with those of the Rosaic Masonry; and hence it will appear that we are the only true Christians. But all *this is only a cloak to prevent squeamish people from starting back.* [Emphasis in the original][194]

That question concerning "who would remain?" can easily be answered. Once one knows the deception, trickery, and devilishness of such an organization, the only ones who would remain are those who would be in complete agreement with the diabolical plans and who would acknowledge that Lucifer is their god.

Isn't it time that you come out from the Eastern Star, Masonry, and other kindred groups? The Bible warns: "Come out from among them, and be ye separate, saith the Lord, and touch not the unclean thing; and I will receive you" (II Corinthians 6:17). "Come out of her, My people, that ye be not partakers of her sins, and that ye receive not of her plagues" (Revelation 18:4).

7. SYMBOLISM OF THE EASTERN STAR

Many symbols are used in the Eastern Star. Mary Ann Slipper brags that the Eastern Star's "symbols, teachings and precepts are **ALL** found within the pages of the bible."[1] We've already looked at the pentagram in great detail, but I have never found **THAT** symbol mentioned in the Bible. There are some other Eastern Star symbols as well (such as the triangle, hexagram, and the broken column) that I have **NOT** been able to locate in the Scriptures, either. Even though some of these symbols are not in the Bible, they are very prominent in the Eastern Star work, so we will look at a few of them in more depth.

Every officer of the Eastern Star has a particular jewel or emblem representative of his or her office. The jewel for Martha is the broken column.[2] It signifies an "early death as in the case of Lazarus"[3] and "stands

MARTHA'S Jewels

for an unshakeable faith in Eternal Life through belief in the Word of Christ."[4] This explanation sounds logical, for those who are familiar with the Bible know that Lazarus died and was resurrected by Christ four days later. The Eastern Star members are told this meaning, but there just happens to be **ANOTHER, MORE SINISTER** meaning than the one presented to the candidates.

In *The Symbolism of the Eastern Star* by Mary Ann Slipper, we discover:

> A symbol is a figure of something intellectual, moral or spiritual, a visible object, **REPRE-SENTING** to the mind the semblance of **SOMETHING WHICH IS NOT SHOWN** but realized by association with it.[5]

Albert Mackey writes that a symbol is a "sensible image used to express an **OCCULT** but analogical signification."[6]

Turning to another Eastern Star book on symbolism we find under the heading "EMBLEM":

> An emblem is a figure or symbol which stands for something else.

> Every Eastern Star Officer is represented by a meaningful emblem.[7]

DUAL CONNOTATION

The insinuation here is that the emblem that is given to the officer has **ANOTHER MEANING** than the one presented to him or her in the ritual. For additional evidence of this, the book describes the word "SYMBOL" like this:

**A SYMBOL IS SOMETHING THAT REPRE-
SENTS SOMETHING ELSE.** A mastery of the
symbolism of the Order is the key to the
understanding of the precepts and principles which
are allegorically and figuratively presented.[8]

Furthermore, under "ESOTERIC" we discover this:

ESOTERIC things are taught only to a **CHOSEN
FEW.** In the specific application to lodge work,
it refers to those things which are transmitted
to the candidate for degrees during initiation.
The serious member who studiously applies himself
to the work of the Order by **SEARCHING FOR
THE SECRET, HIDDEN AND MYSTERIOUS
MEANING** of our symbolic teachings ever
increases his understanding of our **ESOTERIC**
concepts.[9]

By the way, the word "occult" is a synonym for
esoteric.[10] Another Eastern Star book affirms:

As we gather from the symbols used in our
ritualistic work, we see that a **STUDY OF HIDDEN
MEANING** is emphasized....

It will be seen that these symbols carry out the
HIDDEN MEANING of the lecture to which they
have been assigned....[11]

Slipper believes "that everyone who becomes a
member of the Order of the **EASTERN STAR SHOULD
BE FAMILIAR WITH THE ESOTERIC MEANING
OF EVERY SYMBOL** used in the work...."[12]
In other words, the person who wants to determine
the "secret, hidden and mysterious meaning" of the
Eastern Star symbols, will have to look into the occultic
teachings, for this book on symbolism reveals under

"OCCULTISM" that "Occultism refers to the study or belief in the **HIDDEN, SECRET, OR MYSTERIOUS SYMBOLISM."**[13]

In fact, Slipper emphasizes: "The symbols herein described are used by many **SECRET SOCIETIES** for the **SYMBOLS ARE AGES OLD,** and were so known and understood long before the building of the Pyramids."[14] She adds:

> Symbols **DEEPLY VEILED IN MYSTERY** and not understood, are but empty forms without any purpose or life. Reveal the **HIDDEN MEANINGS** and the symbols are **SPIRITUALLY** vitalized with eternal truth.

THE BROKEN COLUMN

Can we find the symbol of a broken column in paganism and if so, what does it represent? To learn the hidden meanings of some of these symbols we will be using numerous quotations from Masonic books. There should be no problem in doing so since a book on the Eastern Star makes the following comment:

> Masonry, the oldest of all secret orders which have survived the passing of the years, employs a most elaborate system of symbols in the ritualistic work.
>
> **SEVERAL OF THE SAME SYMBOLS HAVE BEEN BORROWED FOR USE IN THE ORDER OF THE EASTERN STAR...THE FIGURE OF THE SYMBOL SLIGHTLY CHANGED, BUT THE IDEA ASSOCIATED WITH THE SYMBOL KEPT INTACT.**[15]

Since a number of Eastern Star symbols have been adopted from the Masonic organization and since the idea of the emblem is the same as the Masonic symbol, the books on Masonry should give us a better perception of the hidden meaning. With this in mind, let's turn to the *Pocket Encyclopedia of Masonic Symbols,* and see what is said about the broken column: "A **BROKEN COLUMN** is a very old symbol; it **GOES BACK TO ANCIENT EGYPT** as do other parts of the Masonic Monument symbol, as almost universally used."[16] (Actually, most of the Masonic symbols have been taken from the Egyptians.[17]) Elsewhere we discover that **"COLUMNS WERE GODS."**[18] Another Masonic pamphlet claims: "Few emblems or symbols in Masonry include in their explanations so much of myth, legend and allegory as the Broken Column."[19] A more thorough explanation of this symbol can be found in a *Short Talk Bulletin,* entitled "The Broken Column," published by the Masonic Service Association for use in the Masonic Lodge. It states:

A **BROKEN COLUMN** denoted that a pillar of the state had fallen. In **EGYPTIAN MYTHOLOGY, ISIS IS SOMETIMES PICTURED WEEPING OVER THE BROKEN COLUMN** which conceals the body of her husband Osiris, while behind her stands Horus or Time pouring ambrosia on her hair. In Hasting's *Encyclopedia of Religion and Ethics,* Isis is said sometimes to be represented standing; in her right hand is a sistrum, in her left hand a small ewer and on her forehead is a lotus, emblem of resurrection. In the Dionysaic Mysteries, Dionysius is represented as slain; Rhea goes in search of the body. She finds it and causes it to be buried. She is sometimes represented as standing by a column holding in her hand a sprig of wheat, emblem of immortality; since, though it be placed in the ground and die, it springs up again into newness of life. She was

the wife of Kronus or Time, who may fittingly
be represented as standing behind her.[20]

Another Masonic book, *The Traditions, Origin
and Early History of Freemasonry,* by A. T. C. Pierson
agrees.[21] There is, however, a deeper meaning to
this symbol. Former Mason and Satanist, William
Schnoebelen, relates:

Isis was both virgin and mother, so the "beautiful
virgin" is Isis weeping. The broken column is
the missing member of Osiris [the phallus], the
acacia, an allusion to the eternal life preached
by the Egyptians as well as the fertility cults'
emphasis on vegetation. The urn is an evocation
of the canopic jars used in Egyptian funerals to
store the vital organs of mummies.

Finally, we have "Time," the god Saturn, a later form of the mysterious and evil god, Set. In astrology, Saturn is called the "greater malefic," or greater evil.[22]

WHO'S SATURN?

These different accounts have listed Horus, Kronus, and Saturn as the god standing behind Isis (or Rhea).[23] There is really no contradiction here, however,

since all of these gods were considered as a "god of time."[24] Kronus (also spelled Chronus, Chronos, Cronos, Cronus, and Kronos), from which we get our word "chronology,"[25] was the Greek name and Saturn was the Roman name of the same god.[26] Masonic writer, J. S. M. Ward, in his book *Freemasonry and the Ancient Gods,* tells us that Saturn "is the Satan, the *Tempter,* or rather Tester." [Emphasis in the original][27] Eliphas Levi claims: "Works of malediction and death" were "under the care of Saturn."[28] It's no wonder, then, that Saturn is called the "Lord of Death."[29] In fact, human sacrifices were even offered to him.[30]

Robert Macoy, a Mason who had a large part in the early organization of the Eastern Star, and friend of Rob Morris, reveals that some men believed:

> ...that Baal was the Saturn of Greece and Rome; and there was a great conformity between the rites and sacrifices offered to Saturn and what

the Scriptures relate of the sacrifices offered to Baal.[31]

Helen Petrovna Blavatsky, occultist and New Ager, also confirms that **SATURN IS BEL OR BAAL.**[32] The Bible condemned Baal worship on numerous occasions. Whenever the Israelites forsook the true God, they turned their worship to false gods, usually Baal. They went so far as to even burn their children as sacrifices to Baal: "They have built also the high places of Baal, to burn their sons with fire for burnt offerings unto Baal, which I commanded not, nor spake it, neither came it into my mind" (Jeremiah 19:5). Some other verses that deal with the abomination of Baal worship are: Judges 2:11, 13; 3:7; 8:33; 10:6, 10; I Samuel 7:4; 12:10; I Kings 18:18; 22:53; II Kings 17:16; 21:2-3; II Chronicles 17:3; 24:7; 28:2; 33:3; Jeremiah 11:13, 17; 23:13; 32:29, and 35. Yet, this is the god (under the name of **SATURN**) that is represented by the symbolism of the **BROKEN COLUMN** in the Eastern Star and Masonry!

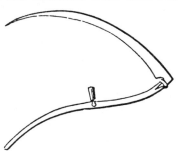

Another correlation between Saturn and the broken column symbolism is that the symbol for Saturn is a scythe.[33] The Masonic figure of the broken column shows the god with a scythe standing behind Isis. We find that "the scythe is also symbolic of the harvest—of renewed hopes for rebirth"[34] or **REINCARNATION.** This is quite fitting since the symbolism of the broken column represents Isis and

Osiris. Osiris had a "rebirth" due to **SPELLS** performed by Isis.[35] Isis was known as a powerful **SORCERESS**,[36] "the **GREAT ENCHANTRESS, the MISTRESS OF MAGIC, the SPEAKER OF SPELLS.**"[37] Not only was Isis a sorceress but she "has always been seen as the guiding light of the profession of **PROSTITUTION....**"[38] (Incidentally, a little extra note would be that Isis' name among the Syrians was Achot, meaning **"SISTER."**[39] Remember that Martha is known as the **"SISTER"** in the Eastern Star!)

Additionally, the acacia of Masonry and the fern or pine branch of the Eastern Star (for Martha) symbolizes eternal life or immortality.[40] The acacia, fern, and pine are all evergreens and thus can be interchanged without altering the symbolism.[41] In the *Pocket Encyclopedia of Masonic Symbols* we are told:

> In putting acacia at the Master's temporary grave, Freemasonry follows beliefs which go back to the captivity of the Jews in Egypt. Here acacia was supposed to have grown about and protected the chest into which **OSIRIS** had been tricked by his jealous brother, Typhon. Searching for her husband, Osiris, Isis discovered the tree in the home of an Egyptian king; for service she rendered the king, he gave her the tree and thus the body of her husband.[42]

This statement shows clearly that the **ACACIA IS ASSOCIATED WITH ISIS AND OSIRIS.** To show the relationship between Masonry and the Eastern Star once again, here is a quotation from an Eastern Star book referring to Martha:

> Never does Freemason cast the evergreen sprig into the open grave of his brother but the coming event is thus beautifully foreshadowed. The EMBLEM of the BROKEN SHAFT [broken column] betokens early death...." [Emphasis in the original][43]

Albert G. Mackey, 33° Mason, in his book *The Symbolism of Freemasonry,* explains that the mistletoe was "consecrated to the **POWERS OF DARKNESS**"[44] and then he reveals:

> In all of these ancient Mysteries, while the sacred plant was a **SYMBOL OF INITIATION,** the initiation itself was symbolic of the resurrection to a future life, and of the immortality of the soul. In this view, Freemasonry is to us now in the place of the ancient initiations, and the **ACACIA IS SUBSTITUTED** for the lotus, the erica, the ivy, the **MISTLETOE,** and the myrtle. The **LESSON** of wisdom **IS THE SAME;** the medium of imparting it is all that has been changed.[45]

By correlation, then, we find that the acacia of Masonry is dedicated to the powers of darkness since Masonry substitutes the acacia for the mistletoe![46]

SATURN IS HONORED

Returning to Saturn, we find an extra item of interest: Saturn is also represented by a goat's head![47] Does that remind you of the Goat of Mendes in the inverted pentagram? It should!

Additionally, **SATURN WAS** known as the god **SET.**[48] Remember Set, the "Egyptian god of evil,"[49] that was covered in detail earlier? In spite of the evilness of Saturn (or Set), Levi states that **SATURN IS "GOD THE FATHER"!**[50] I think it should be easy to see **WHO** is the God of the occultists and Masons. Of course, the average Mason (or Eastern Star member) has no idea whatsoever that Satan is the god represented in the Lodge, for this information is intentionally hidden from them until they seek out the hidden meanings, which they are encouraged to do.

In ancient mythology a festival was held in honor of Saturn which was called the Saturnalia.[51] "[T]emple **PROSTITUTION AND SEXUAL LICENSE...**was most prolific during the Roman Saturnalia."[52] This festival was also to celebrate the winter solstice,[53] which is still commemorated in witchcraft and Masonry today.[54] Saturn is also supposed to be called **NIMROD!**[55] Nimrod, I'm sure you will recall, was Noah's great-grandson (Genesis 10:8-9) and was called "a mighty hunter before the Lord." The word "before" in the Hebrew has several meanings, but one meaning is "against." By reading the entire context, you will notice that this is the correct explanation for this word. It was **NIMROD,** you see, who **BUILT THE TOWER OF BABEL IN DEFIANCE AND REBELLION AGAINST GOD** (Genesis 10:10; 11:2). Masons, however, are proud of this building for Arthur Edward Waite brags:

> As regards Masonry, **BABEL** of course **REPRESENTED A MASONIC ENTERPRISE** and early expositors reaped full benefit from the fact. They remembered that the people who were of "one language and one speech" journeyed from the East to the West, like those who have tried and proved as Master Masons. When they reached

an abiding-place in the land of Shinar, it is affirmed
that they dwelt therein as Noachidae, being the
first characteristic name of Masons. It was here
that they built their High Tower of Confusion....Out
of evil comes good, however, and (1) the confusion
of tongues gave rise to "the antient practice of
Masons conversing without the use of speech."[56]

Notice that according to Masonic testimony the
evil was not in the building of the tower, but in the
confusing of the languages. God confused the languages,
so it is implied that God caused the evil, but in
spite of this evil, Masons believe, good came because
they now converse by means of symbols.

Many other Masons agree that the Tower of Babel
endeavor was a Masonic enterprise. In the *Masonic*

Quiz Book, the question is asked "Who was **NIMROD?**" The answer is: "He was the son of Cush. In the Old Constitutions referred to as **ONE OF THE FOUNDERS OF MASONRY,** and in the Scriptures as the architect of many cities."[57] In the York manuscript we find: "At the making of the Tower of Babel there was Masonry first much esteemed of, and...**NIMROD WAS A MASON** himself and loved well Masons."[58]

John Yarker, another Masonic author, boasts: "It is well known that the **TOWER OF BABEL WAS ONE OF THE MOST ANCIENT TRADITIONS OF MASONRY....**"[59] William Adrian Brown adds this about the Tower of Babel: "In fact, this was about

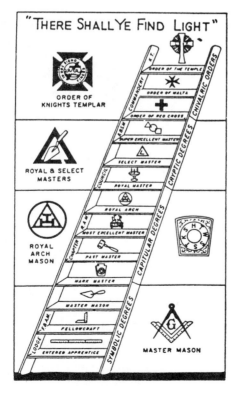

STRUCTURE OF THE
YORK RITE OF FREEMASONRY

the beginning of the **SONS OF LIGHT**."[60] Masons, by the way, are called the "Sons of Light," as can be attested to by numerous Masons.[61] H. L. Haywood, a Mason, reminds us that "...Masons, true Masons, are justly called the **'SONS OF LIGHT'**...."[62] Robert Hewitt Brown believes: "Long before the building of the Temple of King Solomon, masons were known as **'SONS OF LIGHT.'**"[63] There is a fascinating definition in the *Dictionary of Mysticism* for "Son of light": "**A PRACTITIONER OF WHITE MAGIC.**"[64] Interesting!

ALL IS NOT EXPLAINED

Former head of the Southern Jurisdiction of Masonry, Sovereign Grand Commander, Henry C. Clausen, has written:

> It must be apparent that the Blue Lodge or Symbolic Degrees [the first three Degrees of Masonry] cannot explain the whole of Masonry. They are the foundation....An Initiate may imagine he understands the ethics, symbols and enigmas, whereas a **TRUE EXPLANATION** of these **IS RESERVED FOR THE MORE ADEPT.**[65]

Furthermore, Albert Pike claims that Blue Masonry is ignorant of the real meaning of the **BROKEN COLUMN**. He states that it **IS A "REPRESENTATION OF ISIS,"**[66] but that the meaning was:

> ...known only to those who were initiated into the Mysteries. All the incidents were astronomical, with a meaning still deeper lying behind *that* explanation, and so hidden by a double veil. [Emphasis in the original][67]

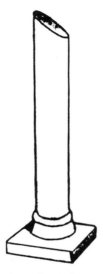

Here Pike admits that there was an even deeper secret than the description of Isis. Could this "secret" that Pike did not reveal be that the **SYMBOL HAS A SEXUAL CONNOTATION** to it (since the broken column does represent the generative male organ)? Albert Mackey, a high level Mason, of whom we are told never "read into a Masonic symbol a meaning which is not actually there,"[68] specifies:

> The **PHALLUS** was an imitation of the male generative organ. It was represented usually by a **COLUMN,** which was surrounded by a circle at its base, intended for the *cteis,* or female generative organ. [Italics in the original; Bold and caps added][69]

Another book, *Masonry and Its Symbols in the Light of "Thinking and Destiny,"* concurs that this "relates to sex power."[70]

Or, could this "secret" that Pike did not specify be that **SATAN** was being worshiped? Could this "secret" be that Saturn (Satan) is recognized as "God the Father,"[71] as Levi has claimed? Whatever the additional hidden meaning is, we know that the symbolism of the broken column is not any emblem that a Christian should display or wear proudly for it represents Satan under the guise of a pagan god.

THE TRIANGLE

The triangle is frequently used as a symbol in the Eastern Star.[72] Each of the offices held by Adah, Ruth, Esther, Martha, and Electa have the triangle as their jewel or badge of office.[73] All five of these women use the triangle in their secret signs. For example, Adah and Ruth use the triangle once while Esther uses the triangle twice. Two triangles are used by Martha and crossed triangles are utilized by Electa.[74] When a new Eastern Star Chapter is established,

EASTERN STAR

JEWELS OF OFFICERS

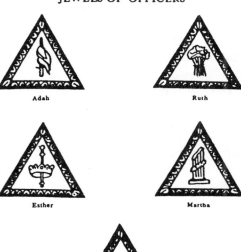

Adah

Ruth

Esther

Martha

Electa

the Officers-elect are to form an equilateral triangle around the Altar.[75] The Altar itself "is shaped in the form of a triangle. Traditionally, one angle is directed so that it points toward the East."[76] The pentagram itself is made up of triangles.[77] We are even told:

> There is always a **"REASON"** behind every movement in ritual ceremonies....Only when understanding and knowledge are obtained are the lessons and precepts of any Order of real benefit to its members.[78]

Since every movement has a specific meaning to it, let's see what the triangle represents and why the Eastern Star members use it with the point facing up and pointing toward the East.

There are different kinds of triangles—Obtuse, Isosceles, Scalene, Acute, Right Angle, and Equilateral Triangle. The right angle and equilateral triangles are used in Masonry and the equilateral triangle is utilized by the Eastern Star. The equilateral triangle is a triangle that is of equal length on all sides.[79] A triangle, with one point down, represents the deity. In fact, this type of triangle is called the "Deity's Triangle." It is also called the "Water Triangle."[80] With one point up, called the "Earthly Triangle," "Pyramid Triangle," or the "Fire Triangle,"[81] this emblem symbolizes "the PERFECT or DIVINE MAN." [Emphasis in the original][82]

DIVINITY OF MAN

The Eastern Star uses the triangle with one point up for their badges, which would signify that man is divine. However, this is unscriptural, for man is not divine. The teaching that man is divine or that man is a god, is a declaration that originated a very long time ago. Come with me as we view a beautiful, young woman, who was innocent and perfect, walking in a most fabulous garden. Picture this garden arrayed with brilliant flowers, luscious fruit hanging from the exquisite trees, the melodious strains of birds singing, the serene animals lying near by, the aroma of roses and other flowers filling the air. In the midst of this spectacular scene, the young, innocent woman hears a voice. She quickly turns to see who's talking only to find the most subtile of all beasts in the garden, asking "Yea, hath God said, Ye shall not eat of every tree of the garden?"

The woman, unafraid of any beast, begins to commune with the serpent.

> We may eat of the fruit of the trees of the garden: But of the fruit of the tree which is in the midst of the garden, God hath said, Ye shall not eat of it, neither shall ye touch it, lest ye die. And the serpent said unto the woman, Ye shall not surely die: For God doth know that in the day ye eat thereof, then your eyes shall be opened, and **YE SHALL BE AS GODS,** knowing good and evil (Genesis 3:1-5).

After this little conversation, the woman starts to look at the forbidden tree and notices that "the tree was good for food, and that it was pleasant to the eyes, and a tree to be desired to make one wise" so "she took of the fruit thereof, and did eat, and gave also unto her husband with her; and he did eat. And the eyes of them both were opened..." (Genesis 3:6-7a).

Satan, through enticement and lies, had just deceived the first man and woman by promising them godhood! He told Eve that she would know both good and evil. Satan's offer to know **BOTH** good and evil presented an option that was previously unknown to her. She had never known evil and, therefore, the lure of learning about something new and different must have intrigued her. Up to this point she had only known good, truth, perfection, health, and beauty. Now, because of the attraction of the unknown offered through Satan's deception, she would learn of evil, death, sorrow, defilement, pain, and separation from God. The very moment Adam and Eve partook of the forbidden fruit they died spiritually and were driven from the beautiful garden of Eden. That very day they experienced death to innocence, death to perfection, death to the joys they had known, and eventually they experienced a physical death even passing this physical death on to all mankind for "in Adam all die" (I Corinthians 15:22).

The day the serpent lied to Eve and put a doubt in her mind trouble began, but we see that the serpent (Satan) is still very much alive and is subtly continuing his tactics of lying and deception. This untruth told by Satan that we can be as gods can still be found echoed by his followers today. Anton Lavey, founder of the Church of Satan, declares: "Every man is a god if he chooses to recognize himself as one."[83] Another well-known and openly avowed Satanist, Michael Aquino, states that "we are our own gods!"[84] Of course, you can expect Satan's followers to teach and promote his falsehoods. You can even count on his demonic cohorts to reiterate this lie as can be seen by the theme of one spirit guide, Ramtha, who speaks through J.Z. Knight: "...we are like gods, part of God, yet unconscious of this identity."[85] Another demonic spirit guide, Mafu, channeled by Penny Torres, exclaims: "Those entities [like Hitler, etc.] whom you judge bad...of course, they are not, they are God."[86]

MASONRY, SATANISM, AND THE NEW AGE

Masonry, like Satanism and the New Age movement, promotes the teaching that the **MASON IS A DIVINE BEING.** In the third degree there is a very dramatic presentation where the candidate enacts a death and resurrection ceremony. When the Master Mason is raised from the "dead" he "is no longer an ordinary man, but a **DIVINIZED** man,"[87] says Wilmshurst. He also states that "He is now lord of himself; the true Master-Mason...."[88] Masonic writer, J. D. Buck, informs us:

Humanity...is the only Personal God....

Humanity, therefore, means *every human being ever born, in any age, or to be born in coming ages, on this Planet....*

It is far more important that **MEN SHOULD STRIVE TO BECOME CHRISTS** than that they should believe that Jesus was Christ. [Italics in the original; Bold and caps added][89]

Arthur Edward Waite writes that "the Master-Builder of the THIRD DEGREE does actually rise as Christ...." [Emphasis in the original][90]

In a book written by a 32° Mason, Charles H. Vail, entitled *The Ancient Mysteries and Modern Masonry,* we find:

The consummation of all this was to **MAKE THE INITIATE A GOD,** either by union with a Divine Being without or by the realization of the Divine Self within....

MAN IS LIKE GOD IN THAT HE BECOMES A GOD.[91]

Manly P. Hall, 33° Mason, boasts: **"MAN IS A GOD IN THE MAKING...."**[92] George H. Steinmetz, another Masonic writer, brags:

"Be still—and know—that I am God."..."THAT *I* AM GOD"—the final recognition of the All in All, the unity of the Self with the Cosmos—the cognition of the DIVINITY OF THE SELF! [Emphasis in the original][93]

Joseph Fort Newton, a well-known Mason, claims that the Third Degree of Masonry testifies "to the profoundest insight of the human soul—that God becomes man that man may become God."[94]

This theme of godhood or the divinity of man can be found in book after book written by Masons.[95] This subject would also have to be the object of the Eastern Star since no one can become an Eastern Star member without having a close relative who has received the third degree of Masonry. It is that degree which is claimed to make a Mason a **"DIVINIZED MAN."**[96] In the *Worthy Matrons' Hand Book* for the Eastern Star there is a song entitled "Star of the East." The last four lines are:

"And then the Obligation
Which lifts us above the clod—
The oath of **INITIATION**
That **CREATES US SONS OF GOD.**"[97]

In other words, the Eastern Star initiation makes the initiate a son of God! Mary Ann Slipper even reveals that by following the Star in the East, the Eastern Star members become Masters of themselves.[98]

Of course, there is more to discover about the symbol of the triangle. In addition to the triangle with one point up representing the divine aspect in man, we find that it also symbolizes deity. While many Masons and Eastern Stars believe that the deity portrayed by the triangle is the Trinity of the Christians, this is simply not the case. In one *Short Talk Bulletin,* "The Significant Numbers," a lecture meant to be read in the Masonic lodges, we are informed:

> It may be here emphasized that while some religions have found truth in a trinitarian godhead—for instance the "Father, Son and Holy Ghost" of many Christian sects—there is **NO TRINITARIAN MEANING TO THE MASONIC EMPHASIS ON THREE,** unless the reader desires to consider *any* reference to three as trinitarian! Freemasonry has but one Supreme Power which it denominates as the Great Architect of the Universe. While the triangle is His symbol and the number three the "symbol of the symbol" it is not from trinitarian implication but from a practice of antiquity so old that no man may say when first the triangle was a "word" for Deity.[99]

SHIVA THE DESTROYER

The triangle does not represent the Christian Trinity, but since it does symbolize a particular deity, just **WHO** could this deity be? In *Signs and Symbols of Primordial Man,* written by Albert Churchward, a Mason, we find that this **TRIANGLE** with the one point facing upward, was the **SYMBOL FOR SET** (or Sut)![100] In India, the triangle is "the caste mark of the followers of **SHIVA**...who wear it on their forehead."[101] Another Masonic writer, J. S. M. Ward, adds:

> With the point upwards the **EQUILATERAL TRIANGLE STANDS FOR SHIVA THE DESTROYER,** and signifies the flame which rises upwards from the funeral pyre toward Heaven. This symbol is familiar to us [the Masons] in several degrees, notably the Thirtieth degree.[102]

There's no contradiction here, for Set is the Egyptian devil and Shiva is the Indian god of destruction. Both names, **SET AND SHIVA,** are also listed in *The Satanic Bible* as another name for **SATAN!**[103] Furthermore, Helena Petrovna Blavatsky affirms: "Now, we have but to remember that Siva [Shiva] and the Palestinian Baal, or Moloch, and Saturn are identical...."[104] So, then, when the Masons and Eastern Stars tell us that the triangle represents the deity, we now know **WHICH** deity is being worshiped by the symbolism of the triangle.

Another clue as to which deity is being worshiped may be found in Alice Bailey's book, *Discipleship in the New Age.* She claims: "It might be said symbolically that 'the point of the triangle is based in the courts of Heaven (Shamballa) and from that point two streams of power pour forth....'"[105] Shamballa is the mythological place where the "Lord of the World," Sanat Kumara or Shiva (who is actually Satan), is supposed to live![106] Bailey is looking forward to the time when:

> ...there can be the inauguration of a new phase of activity in Shamballa. This will enable the Lord of the Word to become the ruler of a Sacred Planet, which, up to date, has not been the case.[107]

Interestingly, Bailey reminds us that Masonry emanates from Shamballa.[108] Lynn Perkins, a Masonic author, also agrees. He mentions that Shamballa "has a bearing on the ancient origins of Freemasonry and upon its future in the coming Aquarian Age...."[109] He adds:

> Shambhala,—the legendary and mystical home of the Great Masters of the Wisdom...out of which Ancient and Modern **FREEMASONRY** sprang...is the site of "the Great White Lodge" of Initiate Masters, which, as a Brotherhood of Mystics and **OCCULTISTS,** is a prototype, an original model, of which every Masonic Lodge is a more or less perfect physical and spiritual replica....That **MASONS OF TODAY ARE NOT AWARE OF THE EXISTENCE AND SIGNIFICANCE OF THE ESOTERIC TRADITION,** that encompasses the whole purpose and Destiny of every living Soul, is no proof that it does not exist.[110]

Let's return to the symbolism of the triangle. In *The Second Mile,* a book on the Eastern Star, we are told:

> In ancient times, resting on its point, this triangle was considered an emblem of a good kind, merciful God, and was called the "Water Triangle." The equilateral triangle resting on its base represented a just and **ANGRY** God, and was called the "Fire Triangle."[111]

In other words, the Eastern Star members are being told that the triangle they use represents an "angry God." This, of course, would fit the description of Shiva and Set! Again we see that when a symbol was chosen for the Eastern Star from two available choices, the worse designation was selected in each case. Remember that the pentagram has a "good" and an evil connotation, but Morris intentionally picked the evil arrangement with two points up, depicting the Goat of Mendes (a portrayal of Satan). The triangle also has a "good" and a bad implication, but, once again, the perverse option was preferred by Morris. Are you beginning to see that this organization was purposely designed with an evil intent?

In the *Interpretation of Freemasonry* by Martin L. Wagner, we see another explanation of the triangle:

> The triangle occupied a prominent place in the religious symbolism of every great nation of antiquity. It was a **RELIGIOUS SYMBOL** ages **BEFORE THE CHRISTIAN ERA.** In some of these ancient cults it represented spirit, the **MALE ACTIVE PRINCIPLE** or force, and matter, the **PASSIVE FEMALE ELEMENT,** and the individual or correlative principle which partakes of both and binds them together in one new entity. This evidently is its meaning in the Kabalah. In other cults it was a symbol of the yoni (vagina), the female principle in nature. **IT IS THIS PHALLIC SYMBOLIZATION THAT STILL REMAINS IN FREEMASONRY.**[112]

Cecil F. McQuaig makes this observation:

> The five points of the star, or the five triangles with their bases turned toward the pentagon, the Cabalistic sign of a man, symbolize once again the **PHALLIC** secret doctrine of Freemasonry. The upper point of the triangle thus representing the female generative organ, while the two angles

downward represent the thighs of the woman from between which every human being comes into the world.[113]

THE HEXAGRAM

When the two triangles (the "Water Triangle" and the "Fire Triangle") are joined together into one symbol, it forms a six pointed star known as a double triangle, hexagram, Solomon's Seal, Star of David, Crest of Solomon, star of the microcosm and the Shield of David, among other names. It is even called the "talisman of Saturn."[114] Slipper remarks:

The six pointed star is of ancient religious significance and is known as KING SOLOMON'S SEAL. Robert Morris has said that he borrowed the plan of the O.E.S. [Order of the Eastern Star] Signet from King Solomon's Seal. This six pointed star is used in masonic work and is also found in other well known secret orders. [Emphasis in the original][115]

The Second Mile, an Eastern Star book, reveals that the "six pointed star is a very ancient symbol, and one of the most powerful."[116] It sure is a powerful symbol—to witches, sorcerers, and magicians![117] "The hexagram is used in magic, witchcraft, occultism and

the casting of zodiacal horoscopes internationally and by all races."[118] "It was considered to possess mysterious powers,"[119] says *A Concise Cyclopaedia of Freemasonry.* E. A. Wallis Budge states:

> Those who believed in the physical significance of the Hexagram taught that communication between the living and the dead was possible, and adopted the dogma of REINCARNATION. [Emphasis in the original][120]

Gary Jennings, in *Black Magic, White Magic,* writes that this sign was used as a:

> ...stand-by for **MAGICIANS AND ALCHEMISTS.** The **SORCERERS** believed it represented the footprint of a special kind of **DEMON** called a trud and used it in ceremonies both to **CALL UP DEMONS** and to keep them away.[121]

HEXAGRAM AND DEMONS

Former Satanist, Bill Schnoebelen, reminds us: "To the sorcerer, the hexagram is a powerful tool to invoke Satan...."[122] Another author mentions that the hexagram "must be present to **CALL A DEMON FORTH** during a ceremonial rite. The word hex, meaning to place a curse on someone, comes from this emblem."[123] Could the calling forth of demons be what is meant by the following statement which appears in the book *The Symbolism of the Eastern Star?* "**...ALL THE SYMBOLS** we use in the O.E.S. speak of the **POWER BEHIND THE VISIBLE UNIVERSE—THE TREMENDOUS REALITY OF THE UNSEEN.**"[124]

A book entitled *Witchcraft, Magic and Alchemy,* links the hexagram to spiritualism.[125] Interestingly, this hexagram:

> ...certainly has three sixes. It contains a six, within a six, within a six: 666. (Count the sides of each triangle facing the clockwise direction, the sides facing the counterclockwise direction, and the third six—the sides of the inner hexagon.)[126]

666

It is fascinating to note that alchemists (magicians) "used the symbol to depict the union of fire and water."[127] Remember that the book, *Symbolism of the Eastern Star,* also calls these triangles the "Fire Triangle" and the "Water Triangle."[128] This is important for it shows that the terminology used by the Eastern Star and the magicians correlates. It also proves that the person who wrote the book on Eastern Star symbology must have had at least some knowledge of occultism.

TRIANGLE OF BATTLE

Another interesting notation is that in the pentagram arrangement, the Star Point apexes of Adah, Electa, and Esther form what is known as the "Triangle of Battle."[129] Slipper reveals:

> The Central Star is so placed that the Points Red and Blue face the East. This combination of color is significant symbolically. Red and Blue in combination symbolizes power and mentality. These two colors unite life with executive ability and placed together in service their language spells: Ruling Power.[130]

Shirley Plessner writes: "An **ESOTERIC** value is attached to the use of the number five in the star rays and their colors, secret words and mottoes, degrees and lessons, and in the symbols."[131] She adds elsewhere:

> The combination of the five star point colors is referred to as The Mystic Colors. A proper blending of the symbolic attributes which these colors represent creates a power which may be used to bless and benefit all of humanity.[132]

So, it is obvious that the layout of the star and the placement of the colors are very important.

Perhaps a witchcraft book, *What Witches Do*, will provide some insight as to the emphasis of these particular colors. Witch Stewart Farrar admits: "A first-degree witch must have his own **WHITE, RED AND BLUE** cords of initiation; the significance of their colours is one of the things I must not publish."[133] We can see that these colors are very important in witchcraft—so important that he claims he is not at liberty to divulge their meaning, yet these are the very **SAME** colors that the Eastern Star specifically points out as being significant!

When the witch is to be initiated into the Second Degree, we are told he or she:

> ...is bound and blindfolded as before, a **BLUE** cord round the knees being added to the **RED** cord round the wrists and neck, and the **WHITE** cord round the ankle, which are used in the First Degree.[134]

Again, these **SAME** colors are employed.

Just what could these colors mean? You may be surprised, but Masonic author, J. S. M. Ward, in *Freemasonry and the Ancient Gods*, fills us in:

> The colour of **BRAHMA IS "RED** as blood,"
> of **VISHNU "BLUE** as the heavens and sea,"

and **SHIVA "WHITE** with the ashes of the dead who are ever burned in His honour."...

Before leaving it, let us, however, note that Trimurti [the Hindu Trinity] is likewise of triple hue. Brahma is red, Shiva—white, Vishnu—blue.[135]

We are also told that the:

...color of the **LORD OF LUST IS RED,** the color of desire. The Tantras explain that the lord of lust should be worshiped seated with his consort on a bed made of the five evil spirits....[136]

In one book on color symbolism we find that **RED REPRESENTS MAN** and **BLUE REPRESENTS WOMAN.**[137] Once again we see the male-female connection. White represents innocence[138] and is therefore probably the offspring of the male (blue) and female (red) union.

Stewart Farrar claims that he cannot publish the significance of the red, white, and blue, but former witch, Bill Schnoebelen, explains this meaning. He said that when Atlantis supposedly sank, three magical traditions poured out of it and these three rays were red, white, and blue. The red ray represents power, the blue ray is wisdom, and the white ray symbolizes love. By the time a witch becomes a Master Witch, he is supposed to have mastered all three of these traditions.[139]

Another former witch, David Meyer, writes this about the "Triangle of Battle":

The **RED, BLUE AND WHITE** colors are very significant in their triangle of battle. I know that in the **OCCULT** there is a hierarchy of power as follows: Lucifer, then Beelzebub, then the seven princes, Rege, Medit, Set, Pan, Larz, Bacchus and Nemo. In the upper three levels of witchcraft Lucifer is represented by a white light. Rege (pronounced ree-JA) is the principality of the occult and appears as a blue light. Larz is the principality of sexual lust and appears as a red light. Thus, the triangle of battle is the combined triumviral [coalition of three sharing power] power of Lucifer and his two most powerful generals or princes, occultism and lust, which the witches say is a force that can be harnessed for good or used as evil. This **COLOR CODING IS A SACRED SECRET IN THE OCCULT WORLD** which is why Stewart Farrar would not comment. Every initiated witch must be involved with astrology and other occult practices and must participate in the "Great Rite" which is ritual sexual intercourse invoking the forces of the universe and drawing down the moon.[140]

Once again we see the occultic and sexual connotations that are prevalent in the Eastern Star right down to even the choice of a specific color combination. Is this just a "coincidence" or was it planned this way?

Associated with the "Triangle of Battle" within the pentagram is another interesting note. "Its angles are composed of the points of Adah, Electa and Esther. Each of these points represent the story of a **BATTLE.**"[141] Ed Decker points out that the number **FIVE:**

...is associated with the planet Mars and the ancient **GOD OF WAR,** called variously Aries, Horus or Mars....This is because Mars is the *fifth* planet on the magical diagram, the Tree of Life.... [Italics in the original; Bold and caps added][142]

Remember Horus? Under his name of Mars we learn more about this deity. Eliphas Levi calls Mars "the **EXTERMINATING** angel"[143] and "[w]orks of wrath and chastisement"[144] are consecrated to him. What kind of battle will take place under Mars' rule? This question is answered by J. S. M. Ward when he remarks:

> The plain man, who never studied the ancient wisdom, and laughs at the message of the stars, can see the writing on the wall; but those who are grounded in the ancient wisdom and the cosmic lore know full well that this *is* the age of Mars, the Destroyer. In days of old the Christ came when the point of the vernal equinox was in the new sign Pisces, and that sign ushered in the new dispensation and our modern world.

> To-day Pisces is falling from his high estate, and a new sign draws nigh. It is Aquarius, the sign of the perfected man. Under his rule we may look to see a great awakening of the spiritual in man, an uplifting of man towards the Godhead in place of the descent of the Godhead into man. This means **A NEW DISPENSATION, A NEW TYPE OF RELIGIOUS OUTLOOK**....We are moving towards a better, a more spiritual world, but **BEFORE US LIE DARKNESS, DIFFICULTIES, AND DANGER,** it may even be the Valley of the Shadow of **DEATH,** for Mars still has his work to do ere the moon shines forth and proclaims the time of change, and is succeeded by the sun in all his glory, and the reign of the new era is established. Mars, the Destroyer....whom will he slay and whom spare? [Italics in the original; Bold and caps added][145]

YIN AND YANG

There is another meaning of the hexagram. One Masonic author states:

> In one instance we have the interlaced triangles, one black, the other white, the white triangle has its point up; the black triangle points down....The interlaced black and white triangles represent the forces of darkness and light, error and truth, ignorance and wisdom and good and evil; when properly placed they represent balance and harmony.[146]

Another Masonic pamphlet affirms that these **TRIANGLES** "are symbolic of good and evil, day and night, the Chinese **YANG AND YIN,** etc."[147]

Yin and yang are considered to be opposites. Yin represents eternity, dark, feminine, left side of the body, etc. Yang is its opposite and represents history, light, masculine, right side of the body, etc.[148] A book, *Black Magic, White Magic,* explains the Yin-Yang like this:

> Another ancient magical sign called the yin-and-yang first appeared sometime before the 3rd century B.C. in China. This emblem became a favorite of **SORCERERS** and mystics throughout the Orient because it, too, embodies so many possible meanings.[149]

One well-known witch, Sybil Leek, who is called the "mistress of the occult," proclaims that the Yin-Yang theory is:

> ...an idea that inspired such things as Chinese boxing, breath control [used in yoga, meditation, etc.], the use of special herbs, and some rather erotic sexual exercises designed to nourish the Yang with the Yin.[150]

SEXUAL UNION

The last meaning that we will look at concerning the hexagram has to do with sexual union and reproduction. The triangle pointing downward "is a female symbol corresponding to the yoni"[151] and the "upward-pointing triangle is the male, the lingam...."[152] When the two triangles are interlaced, "it represents the union of the active and passive forces in nature; it represents the male and female elements."[153]

Albert Pike, in describing the arrangement of the lights in the forming of a triangle, remarks:

> These three great lights also represent the great mystery of the three principles, of creation, dissolution or destruction, and **REPRODUCTION** or regeneration, consecrated by all creeds in their numerous Trinities.[154]

These gods would be Brahma, Shiva, and Vishnu. Notice, too, that regeneration or sexual union is represented by the triangular design.

New Ager, Barbara Walker, even claims that the **TRIANGLE IS A SYMBOL OF THE MOTHER GODDESS.**[155] She also reveals the sexual overtones of the triangle. Walker writes:

It was known as the Kali Yantra...or sign of the vulva. In Egypt the triangle was the hieroglyphic sign for "woman" and it carried the same meaning among the gypsies, who brought it from their original home in Hindustan (India). In the Greek sacred alphabet, the *delta* or triangle stood for the Holy Door, vulva of the All-Mother Demeter ("Mother Delta").[156]

Another author explains:

The **SYMBOL OF THE OBSCENE RITES IS the Delta, or TRIANGLE** (the large pornography collection at the Library of Congress is called the Delta collection; each card in the catalogue listing a book in this collection has the symbolic triangle in the upper lefthand corner). The Delta represents the triune circles of eternity, the Hebrew Yod. The double Delta, or six pointed symbol of Judaism, represents the mail (sic) triangle supreme over the female triangle below and penetrating her.[157]

Alain Danielou, in *The Gods of India,* tells us:

The two complementary principles, the *linga* [symbol of the male generative organ] and the *yoni* [symbol of the female generative organ], are graphically represented by the fiery triangle with upward apex and the watery triangle with downward apex. When the triangles penetrate one another to form the hexagon, this is taken to show the state of manifestation.[158]

Once again, another Eastern Star symbol leads us back to the same place we were before. Symbol after symbol represents a pagan deity (usually from Egypt or India), as well as having a sexual connotation attached to it. Remember that most all of these revealing statements are coming to us **DIRECTLY FROM**

MASONIC SOURCES THEMSELVES. If Masons and Eastern Star members would read the literature promoted by the Masonic leadership, I don't think they would have any question about the occultism, paganism, and sexual implications and innuendoes that are being disguised by seemingly "innocent" symbols.

The sexual overtones even surface in the most unusual and unexpected places. For instance, in the February 1993 issue of *The Scottish Rite Journal*, it was bragged up that in:

> ...recognition of Freemasonry's historic tie to Baylor University, the Scottish Rite of Freemasonry, Southern Jurisdiction, has contributed over the years more than $100,000 to Baylor's J. M. Dawson Chair of Separation of Church and State.[159]

This same issue boasts: "Thus down the trail of the friendly years, Baylor and Masonry have walked hand in hand...."[160] Is it any wonder, then, that Baylor University, a Southern Baptist institute in Texas with **TIES TO THE MASONIC FRATERNITY,** has now "decided to allow **NUDE** models in the school's art studios this fall"?[161]

8. MORE EASTERN STAR SYMBOLISM

The square is a symbol that is used in the Eastern Star rituals. In *Symbolism of the Eastern Star* by Mary Ann Slipper we find:

> The square is of importance in all ritualistic work and holds that place in all rituals. All fraternal societies use the square, and insist upon making square corners in floor work....

> The square should be carefully observed in all floor work. It is of great significance. So well drilled are fraternalists in the making of "square corners" that it is done automatically with scarcely a thought to the "reason why."

> There is always a **"REASON"** behind every movement in ritual ceremonies and every member should try to know and understand, and be able to give an intelligent reason for doing thus and so.[1]

Since the square is so vitally important to the ritual work, and since there is a reason behind the movement, and since Slipper claims that every Eastern Star member should be able to give an answer as to why the square is used, let's see what is represented by the square.

First of all, the *Pocket Encyclopedia of Masonic Symbols* notifies us: "The square, in Masonry, may have—does have—more than one interpretation."[2]

One meaning of the square is that it portrays the material universe or the earth.[3] In the Egyptian Mysteries we discover that the initiate, after being given a password, passed through a door which:

...was an equilateral triangle a symbol typical of Heaven. The square on which he trod as he passed through was a symbol typical of Earth; the whole entrance symbolised passing from Earth to Heaven.[4]

Masonic author, J. D. Buck, writing in *Mystic Masonry,* also explains the Masonic significance of the triangle and the square:

The triangle in the square symbolizes potential Being before **EVOLUTION:** Man in the Garden of Eden. The square in the triangle symbolizes regeneration; the purification of the lower earthly nature so that it may "ascend to the Father"; return to Paradise. This is symbolized by the careful position of the compass and square in relation to the Holy Bible, while the three Greater lights, and three Lesser lights again make a double triangle; one greater because above, one lesser because below, which every Mason will understand.[5]

There is a remarkable correlation between the Egyptian Mysteries, Masonry, and the Eastern Star for Slipper reveals:

When turning square corners in floor work it is well to remember that this is acknowledging in action the great truth of being. The square not only means the acknowledgement of that Power

but also our belief in the finished work of the
Master Builder, who some day will summon each
one into that Great Temple not made with hands,
eternal in the heavens.[6]

In other words, the square used in the Eastern
Star floor work represents passing from earth to heaven.
Also of interest is that both J. D. Buck and Harold
Waldwin Percival mention that the Masonic Square
and Compass is just another form of the six pointed
star,[7] which we have already covered in detail.

There are a few problems, however, with the
Eastern Star portrayal. First of all, the god represented
by the Eastern Stars and Masons is not the God
who is referred to in the Bible. Slipper, in referring
to God, states:

That invisible power which all know does exist,
but understood by many different names, such
as God, Spirit, Supreme Being, Intelligence, Mind,
Energy, Nature and so forth.[8]

God is not Nature, nor Energy, nor Intelligence,
nor Mind. Additionally, in previous chapters we already
saw that the gods they worshiped carried names like
Set, Saturn, Thoth, Horus, Hermes, Shiva, etc. All
these gods represent Satan, as has been abundantly
proven earlier.

Second, there seems to be a teaching of universalism
in the representation of the square when it is stated
that some day "the Master Builder...will summon
each one into that Great Temple...."[9] Universalism
is a teaching which claims that all people will go to
heaven regardless of how they have lived their lives.
Again, this is an unscriptural belief, for we find in
Matthew 7:21: "Not every one that saith unto me,
Lord, Lord, shall enter into the kingdom of heaven;

but he that doeth the will of my Father which is in heaven." We also are told: "He that believeth on the Son hath everlasting life: and he that believeth not the Son shall not see life; but the wrath of God abideth on him" (John 3:36). There are many other verses that reiterate that there will be a separation between the righteous and the evil doers, such as in John 5:28-29:

> Marvel not at this: for the hour is coming, in the which all that are in the graves shall hear His voice, And shall come forth; they that have done good, unto the resurrection of life; and they that have done evil, unto the resurrection of damnation.

THE GODS

Another meaning of the square can be found in a quote taken from *A Defence of Masonry,* where we are told:

> The Pythagoreans...particularly held that a Square was a very proper Emblem of the Divine Essence. The Gods, they say, who are the Authors of every thing established in Wisdom, Strength and Beauty, are not improperly represented by the Figure of a Square.[10]

So, the square represents a god or gods. Just which god is it? We don't have to wonder for long,

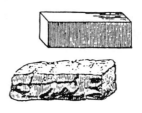

for a number of Masons have already revealed some of these gods to us. For instance, in *The Symbolism of Freemasonry* by Albert G. Mackey, 33° Mason, we see that the "Thebans worshipped Bacchus under the form of a rude, **SQUARE** stone."[11] He also explains that "Mercury, or Hermes, was always represented by a cubical stone, because he was the type of truth...."[12] In a footnote, he elaborates:

> In the most primitive times, all the gods appear to have been represented by cubical blocks of stone; and Pausanias says that he saw thirty of these stones in the city of Pharae, which represented as many deities.[13]

Masonic author, Albert Churchward, in *Signs and Symbols of Primordial Man*, writes:

> The Square is also very clearly depicted, symbolically, in the Egyptian *Ritual* and is plainly **SHOWN IN "THE BOOK OF THE DEAD,"** with three figures seated on it—two represented by the figure of Maat or Mati—Truth, Justice, Law, etc., the third figure being **OSIRIS,** seated on the **SQUARE** in the Judgment Hall. The Egyptian name is Neka.

> This Square you find depicted in many of the ancient temples and in the Great Pyramid, as two seats, one for Osiris and one for Maat—**IT IS THE MASONIC SQUARE.**[14]

In a poem referring to Jove, we find: "Jove is a circle, triangle, and square...."[15] Joseph Fort Newton, also a Mason, claims:

> Mercury, Apollo, Neptune, and Hercules were worshiped under the form of a **SQUARE** stone,

while a large black stone was the emblem of
Buddha among the Hindoos, of Manah Theus-
Ceres in Arabia, and of Odin in Scandinavia.[16]

Ptah and Osiris, both Egyptian gods, are also
listed as being connected to a square.[17]
It is fascinating to learn that the:

...Square, Rule, Plumb-line, the perfect Ashlar,
the two Pillars, the Circle within the parallel
lines, the Point within the Circle, the Compasses,
the Winding Staircase, the numbers Three, Five,
Seven, Nine, the double Triangle—these and other
such symbols were used alike by Hebrew Kabbalists
and Rosicrucian Mystics.[18]

"Geometrical figures, as lines, angles, **SQUARES,**
and perpendiculars, were ranked amongst the symbols
of **DRUIDISM.**"[19] In a later chapter the Cabala will
be covered in more detail, but briefly, the Cabala is
a book of **MAGIC.**[20] As far as the **DRUIDS** are
concerned, Masonic author, William Hutchinson,
acknowledges that "our mode of teaching the principles
of our profession [MASONRY] IS DERIVED FROM
THE DRUIDS...[and] our chief emblems originally
[came] from Egypt...."[21]

MASONS ARE PRESENT-DAY DRUIDS

He also brags "that we [Masonry] retain more of
the ceremonials and doctrines of the **DRUIDS** than
is to be found in the whole world besides...."[22] The
DRUIDS WERE OCCULTIC PRIESTS who worshiped
many gods, practiced **ASTROLOGY,** and offered
HUMAN SACRIFICES. So, by Masonic testimony,
Masonry is founded on the principles of magic and
occultism! You can also see from where the Masonic
and the Eastern Star symbols have been adopted!

Albert Churchward, a Mason, even writes about Masons as **"OUR PRESENT DRUIDS"!**[23] Even *The Short Talk Bulletin,* entitled "From Whence Came We?" boldly answers that Masonry's influence came from "primitive **MAGIC,** from ancient religions, from mysticism, symbolry, the **OCCULT,** architecture, history, Pagan rite and Christian observance...."[24]

It's no wonder, then, that Colin Wilson in his book, *The Occult,* writes that MASONRY **"BECAME THE HOME OF OCCULTISTS, ALCHEMISTS, ASTROLOGERS** and so on."[25] Arthur Edward Waite brags that "since Masonry appeared on the historical plane, **OCCULTISTS** and even mystics have tended towards it, [and] that it has **RECEIVED THEM ALL AMIABLY....**"[26] Manly Palmer Hall boasts:

> The Masonic order is not a mere social organization, but is composed of all those who have banded themselves together to learn and apply the principles of **MYSTICISM** and the **OCCULT** rites.[27]

Lest you think that these are statements made from a few bizarre, weird, uninformed Masons, let me reassure you that such is not the case. Hall had the honor of writing the foreword to Henry C. Clausen's book *Your Amazing Mystic Powers.* Clausen, by the way, was the Sovereign Grand Commander of the Southern Jurisdiction of Masonry—the highest position one can hold in Masonry! Yet, in spite of the prevalence of occultists in Masonry, the Eastern Star woman is told that they are "in social connection with the purest and best men in every section of the country."[28]

There is one final interpretation of the square that we will investigate. The lodge member is told in the first degree that the square is "to square our actions; the compasses, to circumscribe and keep us within bounds with all mankind, but more especially with a brother Mason."[29] This, however, is a **DISGUISED** meaning. Former Satanist, Mason, and witch, William Schnoebelen, explains what the real significance of the square is:

> Masonry exalts sexuality to the level of deity, but in a disguised, allegorical fashion....the square and compasses and other Masonic symbols are veiled references to the human reproductive organs—talismans designed to increase sexual desires....

> They [the square and compasses] symbolize the human reproductive organs, locked in coitus (when displayed together).[30]

Jim Shaw, former 33° Mason, also reveals the meaning of the symbolism of the square and compasses. He states:

> The square represents the female (passive) generative principle, the earth, and the baser, sensual nature; and the Compass represents the male (active) generative principle, the sun/heavens, and the higher, spiritual nature. The Compass, arranged above the Square symbolizes the (male) Sun, impregnating the passive (female) Earth with its life-producing rays. The true meanings, then are two-fold: the earthly (human) representations are of the man and his phallus, and the woman with her receptive cteis (vagina). The cosmic meaning is that of the active Sun (deity, the Sun-

god) from above, imparting life into the passive
Earth (deity, the earth/fertility goddess) below
and producing new life.[31]

So, once again, the symbols used by the Masons
and the Eastern Star members are representative of
a pagan god and carry a sexual connotation. Schnoebelen
mentions that "the square is the symbol of the lingam
(or god force in Witchcraft), and the compasses are
the symbol of the female organs, called the yoni or
shakti (goddess force) by occultists."[32] The connection
between Masonry, the Eastern Star, and witchcraft
should one more time be made conclusively clear.

You may wonder why I have spent so much time
correlating the symbolism of the Eastern Star to that
of the Masons. As I've mentioned before, Slipper,
in her book *Symbolism of the Eastern Star*, relates:

Masonry, the oldest of all secret orders which
have survived the passing of the years, employs
a most elaborate system of symbols in the ritualistic
work.

**SEVERAL OF THE SAME SYMBOLS HAVE
BEEN BORROWED FOR USE IN THE ORDER
OF THE EASTERN STAR**...the figure of the
symbol slightly changed, but **THE IDEA
ASSOCIATED WITH THE SYMBOL KEPT
INTACT.**[33]

This is important, for this shows us that the symbols
used in the Eastern Star rituals have the **SAME IDEA**
as the symbols used by the Masons. In fact, the
jewel of the Eastern Star Patron is the "Square and
Compasses within the Star."[34] We find: "Every Eastern
Star Officer is represented by a **MEANINGFUL**
emblem."[35] So, then, there was much thought that

went into selecting the jewel for each officer and the meaning of the symbol was known. In the *Adoptive Rite Ritual,* arranged by Robert Macoy, a Mason and friend of Rob Morris, the Worthy Patron is told:

> Your badge, the Square and Compasses within the Star, is an emblem of the **RELATIONSHIP EXISTING BETWEEN THE MASONIC FRATERNITY AND THE ORDER OF THE EASTERN STAR,** and admonishes you to be ever mindful of your obligations to both.[36]

Seeing the Masonic connection, we will look at yet another one of the symbols used in the Eastern Star: the Circle.

THE CIRCLE

Sarah H. Terry claims: "All symbols we use are made up of straight lines or circles. The floor work is only a means, not an end. The symbols point to the light, which shows the individual the way."[37] Terry additionally encourages us to search out the explanation of the symbols:

> It is a well known fact that certain lines or circles have a **DISTINCT MEANING** of their own. To find the **HIDDEN MEANING** of these lines should be the desire of every member of the Eastern Star.[38]

As we continue to discover the meanings of these symbols, we will also be able to detect what "way" is being pointed out for the Eastern Star members to follow.

The circle is the symbol of the universe.[39] Terry maintains that the circle "is derived from the **SUN**."[40] J. S. M. Ward, in *Freemasonry and the Ancient Gods,* explains that the circle also symbolizes God: "The circle indicates Infinity and, in particular, God the Infinite and Unknown, the study of whom is the object of their researches."[41] We have already seen who the god of Masonry is, so it is evident which god the circle represents.

One particular symbol that is prevalent in Masonry utilizes the circle but a point is added inside the circle. It is called the "point within the circle." Harold Waldwin Percival in his Masonic book entitled *Masonry and Its Symbols in the Light of "Thinking and Destiny,"* tells us: "The point and the circle are the same, the point is the infinitesimally small circle and the circle is the point fully expressed."[42] Since the point and the circle are the same, let's look at what Masons tell us about this specific symbol.

WORSHIP OF THE PHALLUS

First of all, notice that "the square and compasses are **RELATED** to the 'point within the circle.'"[43] This is quite some admission, for in the *Masonic Quiz Book* we find that this symbol "is from the Egyptian and is a symbolic sign for the **SUN** and the god **OSIRIS**."[44] Albert Mackey, 33° Mason, brags:

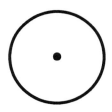

The point within the circle is an interesting and important symbol in Freemasonry, but it has been debased in the interpretation of it in the modern lectures that the sooner that interpretation is forgotten by the Masonic student, the better will it be. The **SYMBOL IS REALLY A BEAUTIFUL BUT SOMEWHAT ABSTRUSE ALLUSION TO THE OLD SUN-WORSHIP,** and introduces us for the first time to that modification of it, known among the ancients as the **WORSHIP OF THE PHALLUS.**[45]

In *The Gods of India* by Alain Danielou it is specified that he "who spends his life without honoring the phallus is verily unfortunate, sinful, and ill-fated."[46]

In another of Mackey's works, *The Symbolism of Freemasonry,* he writes:

> The Phallus was a sculptured representation of the *membrum virile,* or male organ of generation, and the worship of it is said to have originated in Egypt...The Phallus, therefore, was very universally venerated among the ancients....[47]

Mackey was a **HIGHLY RESPECTED MASON** and is still looked up to today by many "higher" level Masons. In one *Short Talk Bulletin* entitled "Albert Gallatin Mackey," lodge members were told: "Never did he read into a Masonic symbol a meaning which is not actually there."[48] We then have every reason to accept his interpretation that the point within a circle actually represents the phallus.

The point within a circle has been employed in some rather unique ways. For instance, one Masonic book states: "The sign of the infamous Mafia or Cosa Nostra is not the 'black hand,' as many believe, but the familiar dot within a circle."[49] We are further informed that:

Because the true purposes of Illuminism were so shocking, Weishaupt constantly encouraged the **SECRETIVE** nature of the order. No member was ever allowed himself to be identified as an Illuminati. The words Illuminism or Illuminati were never to be used in correspondence, but were to be replaced by the astrological symbol for the sun, a circle with a dot in the middle.[50]

Weishaupt, I'm sure you will recall, was a Mason. George Oliver states:

With this reference the Point within a Circle was an emblem of great importance amongst the British **DRUIDS.** Their temples were circular, many of them with a single stone erected in the centre; their solemn processions were all arranged in the same form; their weapons of war—the circular shield with a central boss, the spear with a hollow globe at its end, etc.—all partaking of this general principle; and without a circle it was thought impossible to obtain the favour of the gods. The rites of **DIVINATION** could not be securely and successfully performed unless the operator were protected within the consecrated periphery of a magical circle.[51]

Albert Churchward, a Mason, says:

The **POINT WITHIN A CIRCLE IS ONE OF THE HIEROGLYPHIC SIGNS OF THE SUN-GOD, RA,** but it is not merely an image of the solar disc. For one thing **IT IS A MASONIC SYMBOL,** and H.A. Giles, the Chinese scholar, who is himself a Mason, tells us it is held to represent the One Supreme Power, whatever that power may be, the Great Architect of the Universe, recognised alike by ourselves and our brother Masons of every religious denomination....[52]

The point within the circle represents other gods in other mythologies. For example, J. S. M. Ward points out that the "parm, or dot, is the mark of the Supreme Being."[53] Referring to one sculpture, he adds:

> On His forehead He bears the mark of a P. within a C. [point within a circle] which signifies that the sculptor considered that **SHIVA** represents the nearest god to the Supreme Being that finite minds can comprehend.[54]

Arthur Edward Waite claims that "He...was still named Horus at the point within the circle."[55] Masonic author, George H. Steinmetz, maintains: "The **POINT WITHIN A CIRCLE** is an ancient Egyptian sign for the **SUN** and **OSIRIS**."[56] Mason A. T. C. Pierson contends:

> In the **DRUIDICAL** rites the **POINT WITHIN THE CIRCLE** and the cube were emblems of **ODIN, THE SUPREME GOD,** the author of every thing that existeth, the Eternal, the Ancient, the Living and Awful Being, the searcher into concealed things, the being that never changeth.[57]

John Yarker, 33° Mason, indicates that "Captain Conder points out that the point within a circle, was their phonetic symbol for *An,* or God...." [Emphasis in the original][58]

Like all the other symbols which we have looked at, we find that the circle and the point within the circle refer to a pagan god. Also, like the previous symbols, the point within the circle has a sexual connotation. A lengthy excerpt from the *Short Talk Bulletin* entitled "Point Within a Circle," states:

We find it connected with **SUN WORSHIP,** the most ancient of religions....Of its presence in many of the religions of the East, Wilford says (*Asiatic Researches*):

"It was believed in India that at the general deluge everything was involved in the common destruction except the male and female principles or **ORGANS OF GENERATION,** which were destined to produce a new race and to repeople the earth when the waters had subsided from its surface. The female principle, symbolized by the moon, assumed the form of a lunette, or crescent, while the male principle, symbolized by the sun, assumed the form of the lingam (or Phallus) and placed himself erect in the center of the lunette, like the mast of a ship. The two principles in this united form floated on the surface of the waters during the period of their prevalence on the earth, and thus became the progenitors of a new race of men."

This is the more curious and interesting when a second ancient meaning of the symbol is considered—that the point represents the sun and the circle the universe. Indeed, this meaning is both modern and ancient, for a dot in a small circle is the astronomical symbol for the sun, and the derivation of this astronomical symbol marks its **MASONIC CONNECTION.** The Indian interpretation makes the **POINT THE MALE PRINCIPLE, THE CIRCLE THE FEMALE;** the point became the sun and the circle the solar system which ancient peoples thought was the universe because the sun is the vivifying, the life-giving principle, for all that lives.[59]

Many other authors agree with this interpretation. Albert Pike writes:

These two Divinities [Isis and Osiris], the Active and Passive Principles of the Universe, were commonly symbolized by the generative parts of man and woman....The Indian lingam was the union of both, as were the boat and mast and the point within a circle: all of which expressed the same philosophical idea as to the Union of the two great Causes of Nature, which concur, one actively and the other passively, in the generation of all beings....[60]

In *The Traditions, Origin and Early History of Freemasonry* by Pierson we find:

One further notice of the use of this figure [the point within the circle] as a symbol of Deity by the ancients. All nations recognized as an object of worship a great Supreme Deity by whom all that was, was made. Another idea was that nothing possessing life could be created without the junction of the **ACTIVE AND PASSIVE GENERATIVE POWERS.** And as God created all life, he must necessarily possess within himself each of those powers, and hence the **PHALLIC WORSHIP,** so common among the ancient nations, the symbol of which is found in this connection in the monuments of antiquity everywhere.[61]

ONE EMBARRASSED MASON

Rev. George Oliver, also a Mason, embarrassingly admits that the point within the circle:

...bore a more immediate relation to the **GENERATIVE PRINCIPLE** of nature, symbolized by the union of the sexes. I am ashamed to stain my page with the discussion which this part of my subject necessarily introduces; but it cannot be wholly avoided, as the **POINT WITHIN A**

CIRCLE, with an unequivocal ALLUSION TO THE PHALLIC WORSHIP, was the principal object of devotion with every people in the world. In India, the adytum, or most holy place in the temples of the deity, always contained the Linga or Phallus, which had a prominent situation assigned to it, amongst the innumerable emblems with which the walls were covered. In Egypt, the same practice was observed....The places of initiation in Chaldea were precisely of the same nature....In Greece, the Phallus was an universal amulet. It was thought to prevent every species of calamity; and was, accordingly, hung at the doors of houses, offices, and workshops. It was visible in every situation, and was even suspended from the necks of children, to preserve them from the effects of fascination. "The same indecencies," says Faber, "were practised in the rites of the Cabiric Ceres, as in those of Bacchus, OSIRIS, and Maha-Deva. Her deluded votaries vied with each other in a studied OBSCENITY OF LANGUAGE, and her nocturnal ORGIES were contaminated with the grossest LASCIVIOUSNESS." And Diodorus the Sicilian says that SUCH LANGUAGE was used under the impression that it WAS PLEASING AND ACCEPTABLE TO THE GODDESS. Even the Israelites themselves were not entirely free from the contamination of such abominable practices; for the Linga of the Hindus, the Phallus and the Priapus of the Greeks and Romans, and the Baal-Peor of the idolatrous Israelites, was one and the same monstrous emblem, which was equally represented by *a point within a circle*. [Italics in the original; Bold and caps added][62]

Notice that obscenity was pleasing to the goddess. This obviously cannot refer to the God of the Bible for in Ephesians 4:29 we find: "Let no corrupt communication proceed out of your mouth" and Colossians 3:8 admonishes us to "put off all these;

anger, wrath, malice, blasphemy, filthy communication out of your mouth."

Albert Mackey also recognized the real meaning of the point within the circle. He elaborates:

> This union of the phallus and the cteis, which is well represented by the *point within a circle,* was intended by the ancients as a type of the prolific powers of nature, which they worshiped under the united form of the active or male principle, and the passive or female principle. Impressed with this idea of the union of these two principles, they made the older of their deities hermaphrodite, and supposed Jupiter, or the Supreme God, to have within himself both sexes, or, as one of their poets expresses it, "to have been created a male and an unpolluted virgin."

> Now, this hermaphrodism of the Supreme Divinity was again supposed to be represented by the sun, which was the male generative energy, and by nature or the universe, which was the female prolific principle. And this union was symbolized in different ways, but principally by the *point*

within the circle, the point indicating the sun, and the circle the universe of nature, warmed into life by his prolific rays. [Emphasis in the original][63]

Remember that the Goat of Mendes, Baphomet, is a god that represents both sexes, so we end up going back to the symbol of the pentagram—the very symbol that is prominently displayed in the Eastern Star!

POWERFUL OCCULT SYMBOL

From *The Question of Freemasonry,* we learn: "The inverted five-pointed star within a circle is the highest form of satanic expression, representing Baphomet, the God of Mendes, or the embodiment of Lucifer as god."[64] Texe Marrs informs us that an:

...especially powerful occult symbol is formed whenever the circle is used to contain another occultic symbol within. For example, the *pentagram* is formed by enclosing the five-pointed star within the circle.... [Emphasis in the original][65]

Does the Eastern Star ritual employ the five pointed star within a circle? Of course, it does. Sarah Terry tells us:

The circle used in the winding of the labyrinth, and the final march around the star, embraces first the single virtue, then all these virtues bound together, a symbol of the five cardinal virtues that should go to make up a well-rounded life.[66]

In *History of the Order of the Eastern Star* we find: "The Labyrinth, or 'Maze' was made to conform to the idea of a **FIVE POINTED STAR, WITHIN A COMPLETE CIRCLE.**"[67]

Witch Laurie Cabot explains:

The **CIRCLE AROUND THE PENTAGRAM** represents the totality of all intelligence. It is the **SIGN FOR THE GOD AND GODDESS,** the fullness of cosmic intelligence. The circle pulls in light and directs it toward the center along its many radii. Each time I see a pentacle I am reminded of the encircling power of the All that surrounds and protects us, assuring us that each human being is at the center of divine life. Our Divine Mother encloses each of us in her womb. No matter where we are, what we do, in her we live and move and have our being.[68]

What a misrepresentation of Scripture! The Bible tells us that it is in God (not the Goddess or Mother Earth) in whom "we live, and move, and have our being" (Acts 17:28).

How is the circle drawn around the pentagram in the Eastern Star ritual? Jean M'Kee Kenaston describes this for us in detail, using the **ORIGINAL** names of the Eastern Star officers (see chapter 10 for more information about the original titles of the officers):

Heleon takes his seat at a point opposite the door and about two paces from the wall behind him. A small round table is placed before him at a distance of about one half the breadth of the room. The Bible is laid upon it....A cord is then stretched from his seat to the center of the table, and a circle made with that length of

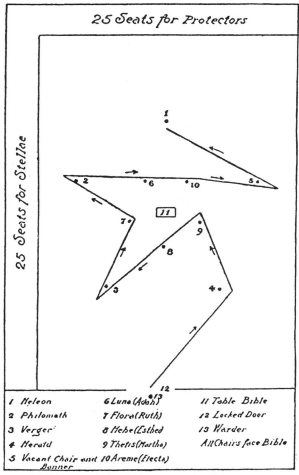

25 Seats for Protectors

25 Seats for Stellae

1	Heleon	6	Luna (Adah)	11	Table Bible
2	Philomath	7	Flora (Ruth)	12	Locked Door
3	Verger	8	Hebe (Esther)	13	Warder
4	Herald	9	Thetis (Martha)		All Chairs face Bible
5	Vacant Chair and Banner	10	Areme (Electa)		

cord so as to ascertain with exactness the stations of the other four Pillars. The five, when seated, represent five points of a Star, the Bible being the center....

The stations of the Correspondents are exactly ascertained as follows: Hebe takes her seat facing Heleon on the opposite side of the Bible and at half his distance from it. The cord is now stretched from her seat to the center of the table and a

202 HIDDEN SECRETS OF THE EASTERN STAR

circle made with that length of cord. Around
that circle their seats are placed, so that, when
seated, they represent five points of a Star contained
within the former one and having the same center.[69]

Now, how do the **WITCHES** cast their circle?
Laurie Cabot portrays her method for us:

To cast the traditional nine-foot circle take a
cord four and a half feet long and secure one
end of it in the center of the space where you
want to cast your circle. When you stand at the
free end of it and use it as a compass, you can
outline a perfect nine-foot circle.[70]

Do you see a correlation between the two methods?!
Just another "coincidence"?

CONJURATION OF DEMONS

According to the *Dictionary of Mysticism,* a magic
circle is drawn "around a person or object as protection
from danger. When calling up spirits for consultation,
the black magician usually stands inside a magic circle
for safety."[71] In *A Pictorial History of Magic and
the Supernatural* we find:

Wherever it appears the magic circle is a protective
girdle against evil spirits. In the practice of **MAGIC**
no invocation should be made outside the circle,
which can be completely drawn out or merely
indicated by using a wand. Once he was surrounded
by the circle the magician had nothing to fear
from any spirits who, if they had pursued him
into it, would have found themselves at his mercy.[72]

Yet, in *Treasury of Witchcraft,* we are told that
the circle is drawn on the ground "to enforce demons

to appear."[73] No wonder, then, that the circle is "one of the most powerful of all occult symbols"[74] and that it "serves to contain and concentrate the magical energy necessary to summon the appropriate powers or spirits."[75]

Starhawk, another witch, remarks:

The "Guardians of the Watchtowers" are energy forms, the *raiths* or spirits of the four elements. They bring the elemental energy of earth, air, fire, and water into the circle, to augment our human power. The vortex of power created when we invoke the four directions guards the circle from intrusions, and draws in the higher powers of the Goddess and God.[76]

By the way, the four elements play a very important part in the Eastern Star, so this will be covered in a later chapter.

THE LABYRINTH

Remember, too, we've already been told that the **LABYRINTH** "was made to conform to the idea of a **FIVE POINTED STAR, WITHIN A COMPLETE CIRCLE.**"[77] Albert Pike mentions that a **LABYRINTH** "**WAS BUILT IN HONOR OF THE SUN....**"[78] What is a labyrinth? J. E. Cirlot reveals that it is an:

...architectonic structure, apparently aimless, and of a pattern so complex that, once inside, it is impossible or very difficult to escape....Some are believed to have been conceived with the purpose of **LURING DEVILS INTO THEM** so that they might never escape. It is to be supposed, therefore, that, for the Primitive, the maze had a certain fascination comparable with the **ABYSS,** the whirlpool and other phenomena.[79]

Eastern Star writer, Shirley Plessner, also admits: "A labyrinth is a series of intricate passages through which it is difficult to find one's way."[80] Willis D. Engle, one of the early organizers of the Eastern Star, notes that this labyrinth is of "particular significance, weaving out, as it does, a complete double star."[81] As previously mentioned, Eastern Star author, Mary Ann Slipper, stated that there "is **ALWAYS A 'REASON'** behind every movement in ritual ceremonies...."[82] Starhawk agrees: **"EACH MOVEMENT IN A RITUAL HAS MEANING."**[83] Are you beginning to understand the correlation between the Eastern Star and witchcraft? In fact, a witchcraft organization, the Covenant of the Goddess, reveals that the **LABYRINTH IS ONE OF THE SYMBOLS OF THE GODDESS.**[84] This statement should become more important after reading chapter 10!

CORN, WINE, AND OIL

When a Eastern Star hall is dedicated, the symbols used are corn, wine, and oil.[85] These are the same symbols of consecration that Masons use for their dedications,[86] so we will see what the Masons tell us about them. Albert Mackey remarks that the "adoption of these symbols is supported by the highest antiquity."[87] In *Freemasonry: Its Hidden Meaning,* a Masonic book by George H. Steinmetz, he writes:

> The ancients who worshiped the Sun as a god, or as a symbol of God, considered all things yellow, golden color, of the sun, as pertaining to it; hence gold, brass and corn or grain, because of their color, were deemed sacred....

> In *Oriental Philosophy* Francis Grant refers to the ancient symbolical reference to wine, thus:

"God was at once the Wine of life and the Wine Bearer."...

In the ancient ceremony of crowning a king, his head was anointed with oil by the officiating priest. This oil was contained in a flask, fashioned from the horn of a bull or ram, and carried in the priest's girdle. The Jew, of course, considered the one so anointed as ordained by Jehovah; the Pagan priest ordained in the name of Taurus or Aries, depending on the horn from which the oil was poured.

Here, then, is the true wage of the Fellow-craft [the second degree in Masonry]: the corn which nourished his physical body, provided by the all-wise beneficence of his Creator, truly a "gift from God"; oil, the refresher of his physical body, that which "makes his face to shine." More mystically interpreted, the ointment which sets him apart from others, which makes him the "appointed" of God. And finally, wine, which, as [Francis] Grant says, is "not the wine of men, but the ecstatic inflow of a religious mystic experience"—the summation of his labors, the award for the arduous ascent of the three, five and seven steps of the winding stairs.[88]

Harry L. Haywood reveals in *Symbolic Masonry*:

In Greece, the priest, or the priest leading the worshippers, would walk three times around the altar, always keeping it to the right, sprinkling it all the while with meal and holy water....Being so often used in connection with the rites whereby a person or an object was "purified," circum-ambulation became, after a time, the Roman equivalent of purification. Also "among the Hindoos," says Mackey, "the same rite of Circumambulation has always been practised," in illustration of which he cites the early morning ceremonies of a Brahmin priest who first adores the sun then walks towards the west by way of the south saying, "I follow the course of the sun." Mackey likewise refers to the **DRUIDS** as having performed the same rite, and to the fact that even in recent years it has been a custom in the remoter portions of Ireland.....It will be interesting, further, to note that the Greeks accompanied the journey with a sacred chant, divided into three parts, the *strophe,* and *antistrophe,* and the *epode,* on which Mackey makes a significant comment: "The analogy between the chanting of an ode by the ancients and the recitation of a passage of Scripture in the Masonic Circumambulation will be at once apparent."[89]

SCRIPTURES USED AS A CHANT

I might add, the Eastern Star members should also recognize that Scripture is quoted during their dedication ceremony,[90] but as should be obvious, this Scripture recitation is only done as a form of a chant, rather than for the purpose of honoring God's Word.

Haywood also explains:

Before the influence of civilisation banished many barbarous usages from the rites of men it was no uncommon custom to bury a living human being under the cornerstone. This was at first, probably, intended to mollify the gods of the ground on which the building stood, and later a recognition of those sacrifice always required of men when they would build....As time went on effigies or statues were used in lieu of human beings, and this was in time refined away into the custom of placing metals, jewels, and other

valuables in the cornerstone, even as we Masons
now use Corn, Wine, and Oil.[91]

Another reason for the Masonic use of corn, wine,
and oil is that primitive people **OFFERED FOOD
TO THEIR GODS.** Haywood states: "This explains
why it was that the Greeks and Romans, in their
early periods, so often brought to their altars gifts
of corn, oil and wine."[92] To make sure we don't
miss the point, he adds:

> The same people also were accustomed to offer
> similar gifts to the gods when they undertook
> the erection of a building. Thinking to appease
> the gods for taking possession of the soil they
> would place fruits and grains in the bottom of
> the foundation pits....

> The **MASONIC** reader will understand from this
> **OUR CUSTOM OF USING CORN, WINE AND
> OIL** in the dedication of Masonic buildings.[93]

Looking further into the Masonic use of these
symbols, we find another fascinating explanation.
Harold Waldwin Percival proclaims: "The wages and
jewels he receives for his work as a Fellow Craft
are certain **PSYCHIC AND MENTAL POWERS,**
symbolized by corn, wine and oil...."[94]

Did you catch that? The corn, wine, and oil are
symbols of "**PSYCHIC** and mental powers." Once
again, the occultism in Masonry and the Eastern Star
raises its ugly head.

CORN, WINE, AND OIL FOR BAAL

The Bible, being a very practical book, addresses
this very issue of corn, wine, and oil. In Hosea 2:8

we find God speaking: "For she did not know that I gave her corn, and wine, and oil, and multiplied her silver and gold, which they **PREPARED FOR BAAL.**" How appropriate! The nation of Israel had been blessed by God and He had increased their material wealth, yet instead of thanking Him for His blessings, they turned around and offered their surplus to pagan idols. In the book of Amos the Lord says:

> I hate, I despise your feast days, and I will not smell in your solemn assemblies. Though ye offer Me burnt offerings and your meat offerings, I will not accept them...Take thou away from me the noise of thy songs; for I will not hear the melody of thy viols. But let judgment run down as waters, and righteousness as a mighty stream. Have ye offered unto Me sacrifices and offerings in the wilderness forty years, O house of Israel? But ye have borne the tabernacle of your Moloch and Chiun your images, the star of your god, which ye made to yourselves (Amos 5:21-26; Acts 7:43).

The references to Chiun, Remphan (found in Acts 7:43), and the phrase "star of your god" are intriguing. "Chiun is sometimes called Kaiwan, or spelled Khiun, and means *star*. The **STAR OF SATURN** was a god....The word Remphan also means the **STAR SATURN.**" [Italics in the original; Bold and caps added][95] Remember Saturn—the god who is equated with Satan?[96] What star is being referred to here? The pentagram—the five-pointed star used in Masonry, the Eastern Star, witchcraft, and Satanism![97] No wonder God was angry with the Israelites for worshiping this god and using his symbol. Do you think God is pleased with those who try to worship this god and his symbol today (even if under a disguise)?

The Bible clearly reveals to us that there is only one true God (Deuteronomy 4:35, 39; I King 8:60; Isaiah 45:5, 14, 18, 21-22; 46:9; 47:8, 10; Joel 2:27). However, during the time the Israelites wandered in the wilderness, they offered sacrifices to God but at the same time they were also worshiping pagan gods (idols). This type of "worship" is not acceptable to God. He proclaims: "I am the LORD: that is My name: and My glory will I not give to another, neither My praise to graven images" (Isaiah 42:8). In the days of the apostle Paul, the Gentiles were doing the same thing. Paul wrote:

> But I say, that the things which the Gentiles sacrifice, they sacrifice to devils, and not to God: and I would not that ye should have fellowship with devils. Ye cannot drink the cup of the Lord, and the cup of devils: ye cannot be partakers of the Lord's table, and of the table of devils (I Corinthians 10:20-21; See also: Deuteronomy 32:17 and Leviticus 17:7).

Dear Mason and Eastern Star participant, the next time you offer corn, wine, and oil in your dedications, remember that this is only another **DISGUISE FOR THE OCCULT** and **WORSHIP OF FALSE GODS** and what you are doing is not pleasing to God.

9. GAVEL, CLASPED HANDS, AND VEIL

The jewel or emblem of the Matron and of the District Deputy is the "Gavel within the Star."[1] We must remember that an "emblem is a figure or symbol which **STANDS FOR SOMETHING ELSE.**"[2] Of what, then, is the gavel symbolic? Shirley Plessner, in *Symbolism of the Eastern Star,* says: "It symbolizes the power and authority of the East."[3] The Masonic authority also comes from the East and the god represented there is **LUCIFER** (in a disguised form, of course)! Please remember that when the Satanic ritual is performed and the Princes of Hell are called forth from the four compass points, Lucifer, the Light-bearer, is the god called in from the **EAST.**[4] Additionally, in *The Treasury of Witchcraft,* it is revealed that Lucifer, the lightbearer, "has his home in the **EAST.**"[5] Remember, too, what the phrase "We have seen His star in the **EAST** and have come to worship Him" symbolizes. Of course, Masonic and Eastern Star sources don't leave us in the dark concerning the symbolism of the **GAVEL.**

Sarah H. Terry, in her Eastern Star book, *The Second Mile,* explains: "In ancient times the **GAVEL** referred to the **HAMMER OF THE GOD THOR.** In the hands of the one chosen to rule the Chapter it is an emblem of power."[6] Thor, of course, is another **PAGAN** god—a god of fertility.[7] He is part of the Scandinavian Trinity.[8] This is the **SAME** god that we have met before—only under a different name.

Masonic writer, Charles H. Vail, reveals that the gods were:

> ...known by different names in different countries—
> **OSIRIS-HORUS** in Egypt, Ormazd-Mithra in Persia,
> Zeus-Hermes in Greece, Jupiter-Ammon in Rome,
> **THOR-BALDER** in Britain and Scandinavia.[9]

Remember, too, that **THOR IS ANOTHER NAME FOR SIRIUS—THE BLAZING STAR USED IN THE EASTERN STAR!**[10] In fact, in *The Mysteries of Osiris or Ancient Egyptian Initiation,* we find that Thor is "God, or the *Savior.*" [Emphasis in the original][11]

Pike gives us some additional names for Thor. He explains: **"THOR WAS THE SUN, THE EGYPTIAN OSIRIS** and Kneph, the Phoenician **BEL OR BAAL."**[12] Bel (or Baal) was said to be the "lord of the air"[13] as well as a sun-god.[14] **BAAL IS ALSO A SYNONYM FOR THE DEVIL.**[15] Baal "had the body of a spider and **THREE HEADS**—those of a man, a toad and a cat."[16] By the way, at times Baphomet has been described as having "a head with **THREE FACES."**[17] This god Baal, under the name of Thor, is called "the Prince of the Power of the Air."[18] Baal worship is condemned by the Bible (I Kings 16:30-33, 22:53; II Kings 17:16, etc.), and in Ephesians 2:2 we find that Satan is called the "prince of the power of the air." Not only does Satan have the same title as is given to the god Thor, but we should notice that the word "Thor" means "thunder."[19] Thor "was the god of lightning and thunder in Norse mythology."[20] This is a significant statement for Satanists use the symbol called a "Satanic S," which resembles a lightning bolt. In Luke 10:18 Jesus says: "I beheld Satan as lightning fall from heaven." A Satanic rock group called KISS ("the name stands for 'Knights in Satan's

Service'"[21]) has a song on one of their albums entitled "God of Thunder." This song boasts:

> I was raised by the demons
> Trained to reign as the one
> God of Thunder and Rock and Roll
> The sound you're under
> Will slowly rob you of your virgin soul.
> I'm the Lord of the Wasteland
> A modern day man of steel
> I gather darkness to please me,
> I command you to kneel
> Before the god of thunder
> The god of rock and roll.[22]

This god is obviously Satan. Is it any wonder that the Bible further informs us that this "prince of the power of the air" is "the spirit that now worketh in the children of **DISOBEDIENCE**" (Ephesians 2:2)?

No wonder Elijah, when referring to Baal worship, asked the Israelites: "How long halt ye between two opinions? if the Lord be God, follow Him: but if Baal, then follow him" (I Kings 18:21).

By now, it should come as no surprise that the gavel or hammer of Thor also has a sexual connotation—like all of the previous Eastern Star symbols already covered. Again, we refer to Masonic sources for proof of this. J. S. M. Ward remarks:

> Thus we see that the **HAMMER, OR GAVEL,** and the tau were originally the same, and this is a natural evolution of symbols, for the tau cross is evolved from the **PHALLUS,** and that is the **SYMBOL OF GOD** the Creator....[23]

This reference shows us that the gavel, the hammer, and the tau cross were all the same and therefore, the meanings would be the same.

GAVEL ON MASON'S APRON

Ward continues:

> But this is not the only place where the tau cross occurs. The gabels, or gavels, are all T crosses and combine in one symbol the hammer, the sign of rule, and the T cross, the symbol of the male or creative side of the Deity; and, lest there should be any mistake, the T is placed on the apron of the Master of the Lodge, though placed [upside down], so as to give also the symbol of the square, and also to emphasise its **PHALLIC** meaning.[24]

Concerning the Tau cross, Mason A. T. C. Pierson writes:

> The Tau, or handled cross, was also a staff and a sacred symbol. The same idea was conveyed equally by the cypress sceptre of Jupiter, the trident of Neptune, the thyrsus of Bacchus, the

club of Hercules, the **CADUCEUS OF MERCURY,**
the mace of Thor, the staff of the Brahmins, the
Druid's wand, and the Persian crosier.[25]

The sexual connotation of the caduceus has already
been briefly discussed, so what was said about the
caduceus can be correlated to the Tau cross and to
the gavel with precisely the same meaning. Of course,
Ward tries to rationalize about the phallic symbolism.
He asserts:

Phallic worship, so called, appears to be exceedingly
ancient, and probably was the earliest of all; but
the **PHALLUS WAS ALWAYS A SYMBOL OF
GOD,** and though no doubt there were abuses,
yet we are not justified in assuming that they
were particularly flagrant in early times any more
than they are to-day in India, where the lingam
is venerated by millions of perfectly moral people,
taking the strictest views we have to-day of what
is meant by sexual morality.[26]

Linking a number of symbols together and showing
their relationship to one another, Masonic scholar,
J. D. Buck, purports:

The perfect equilibrium of spirit and matter is
symbolized by the six-pointed star, which is again
only another form of the Square and Compass,
each now having a base-line from which to form
a triangle. Inclose the star in a circle, which
symbolizes Infinity, and you symbolize the harmony,
or at-one-ment of the Spirit that descended, and

the body, now purified, with Divinity, or the Over-Soul. Place within the Star thus inclosed the Egyptian emblem of Life [the ankh], and we symbolize *Immortality,* as the result of regeneration. Transform the circle into a serpent and it now symbolizes Wisdom, as the crown or result of equilibrium; and is also a double glyph of the return of matter to its source in spirit. Separate the tongue and tail of the serpent by a *Thor's Hammer,* or *Svastica* [swastika], inclosed within a circle, and it symbolizes regeneration through conquest of animal sense, precisely as taught in the Lodge, under the spiritual meaning of the symbol of the Compass." [Emphasis in the original][27]

THERE IS NO RELIGION HIGHER THAN TRUTH

There is ample proof from Masonic and Eastern Star sources that symbol after symbol being used in the Lodge represents their "god" (Lucifer or Satan) and the worship of the phallus. This is shameful and any decent and morally upright person would not want to be involved in such degradation and perversion. Sadly, most people in these organizations have no idea that this is what has been portrayed.

CLASPED HANDS

There were several signets designed for use in the Eastern Star. Shirley Plessner explains:

> The signet and chart are synonymous terms used to identify our special method of instruction. The tools of acquirement are symbolically represented and the **HIDDEN MEANINGS** are given as a **SYMBOLIC REPRESENTATION.** Through this instruction, each member is better enabled to see the full glory of His Shining Star.[28]

The signet, then, contains emblems with hidden meanings and these emblems have a **"SYMBOLIC** representation." In other words, the emblems that

MORRIS SIGNET.

are found on the signet **DO NOT ACTUALLY** mean what is normally imagined but rather they **MEAN SOMETHING ELSE** altogether.

The first signet prepared for the Eastern Star was painted by the oldest daughter of Dr. Rob Morris.[29] In the *Manual of the Eastern Star Degree* by Morris (1860), the initiates were told:

> The names of the five characters, Jephthah's Daughter, Ruth, Esther, Martha, and Electa are seen in the different points and the histories of these made up the Degree. Each of these has an emblem opposite to it. They are the Sword, the Sheaf, the Crown and Scepter, the Monument [Broken Column] and the Clasped Hands.[30]

The broken column has already been discussed. Let's now turn our attention to the Clasped Hands, but before we do, let's notice what Morris wrote in *The Mosaic Book*. He proclaims:

> The **ARCANA, SECRETS, OR ESOTERIC** portions of every Rite—and especially those of the York Rite, by far the most popular in America—have been so profoundly **HIDDEN** under the sacred veil of obligation, that the most penetrating eye will fail to discover any of them in the American Adoptive Rite [Eastern Star].[31]

Do you understand what he is implying? He claims that the secrecy is so great and so well hidden in the York Rite that even the "most penetrating eye will fail to discover" any of the secrets in the Adoptive Rite, meaning the Eastern Star! Of course, with a great deal of study, it is possible to discover these hidden, disguised, and concealed meanings.

ALTAR TO FIDES

What, then, does the symbol of the clasped or joined hands represent? Well, this emblem was a Pythagorean symbol.[32] (Remember the **MAGICIAN** Pythagoras whom the Masons highly revere?) Many Masonic sources reveal that the clasped hands are a "symbol of fidelity,"[33] but they don't stop with that explanation. For example, Albert G. Mackey, 33° Mason, confesses:

The *right hand* has in all ages been deemed an emblem of fidelity, and our ancient brethren worshiped **DEITY UNDER THE NAME OF FIDES** or Fidelity, which was sometimes represented by **TWO RIGHT HANDS JOINED,** and something by two human figures, holding each other by the right hands....

Numa was the first who erected an altar to **FIDES,** under which name the **GODDESS OF OATHS** and honesty was worshiped. Obligations taken in her name were considered as more inviolable than any others. [Italics in the original; Bold and caps added][34]

Oh, so here again the Eastern Star symbol represents a **PAGAN GOD**—this time it is Fides. Mackey isn't the only Mason who admits this, either. Daniel Sickles declares:

The right hand in all ages has been deemed an emblem of fidelity and the Ancients worshipped Deity under the name *Fides* [gave high honor to the virtue of fidelity and recognized it as one of the highest attributes of the Godhead and the true Occult Fraternities of today do likewise— R. Swinburne Clymer] or Fidelity, which was sometimes represented by two right hands joined and sometimes by two human figures holding each other by the right hand. [Emphasis in the original][35]

In fact, the very first degree of the Masonic ritual contains the following question and answer:

Q. Why were you caused to rest your right hand on the Holy Bible, square, and compasses?

A. Because the right hand was supposed by our ancient brethren to be the seat of fidelity, and so they worshipped Deity under the name of *Fides,* which was supposed to be represented by the right hands joined, and by two human figures holding each other by the right hand; the right hand, therefore, we masonically use to signify in the strongest manner possible the sincerity of our intentions in the business in which we are engaged. [Emphasis in the original][36]

How can a Christian worship Fides and at the same time worship the God who commanded: "Thou shalt have **NO** other gods before Me" (Exodus 20:3)? Another of God's precepts is: "Make **NO MENTION** of the name of other gods, neither let it be heard out of thy mouth" (Exodus 23:13).

THE VEIL

The emblem of Adah is the sword and veil.[37] The veil is also used when a person is initiated into the Eastern Star. A thin white veil is thrown over the individual's head and face.[38] This is somewhat reminiscent of the hoodwink that is used in the Masonic

initiation, although the Masonic blindfold completely blocks everything from view whereas the veil used in the Eastern Star is only a thin one. The meaning being represented, however, is the same for both organizations.

The room in which the Eastern Star candidate is, is supposed to be semi-dark until after the veil is lifted.[39] The Patron then addresses the initiate with these words:

In removing the veil from your eyes, my sister, we bring you into the full light of the beauty of our chapter room. In the ancient ceremonies of initiation the veil was used as a symbol to teach the candidate that as he advanced in knowledge, he was enlightened by the spirit of education. That he was led from the darkness of ignorance

into the marvelous light of truth, and we desire
that the glory of the bright Eastern Star shall be
clearly seen by you with no veil to dim its lustre.[40]

It is after the veil is lifted, that the candidate is
conducted around the star points "for further
enlightenment."[41] In *A Dictionary of Symbols* we
find that "the veil signifies the **CONCEALMENT**
of certain aspects of truth or of the deity."[42]

WALK IN DARKNESS

To show the similarities between Masonry's and
the Eastern Star's use of the veil/hoodwink, I'll quote
from *Pocket Encyclopedia of Masonic Symbols:*

> **BLINDFOLDING A CANDIDATE** in any rite
> is not for practical but for **SPIRITUAL** reasons.
> The temporary blinding is a **SYMBOL OF
> PRESENT DARKNESS,** which will be displaced
> by light when and if the initiate succeeds in
> penetrating the mysteries before him.[43]

Masonic author, Harry L. Haywood, claims:

> Being in Masonic ignorance, a seeker after light,
> and a representative of the natural untaught man,
> it is fitting that the candidate be made to walk
> in darkness by wearing the hoodwink which Mackey
> has well described as "a symbol of **SECRECY,
> SILENCE, DARKNESS,** in which the mysteries
> of our art should be preserved from the unhallowed
> gaze of the profane." The use of the blindfold
> goes far back among **SECRET SOCIETIES,** even
> to the **ANCIENT MYSTERIES,** in which the
> candidate was usually made to enter the sanctuary
> with eyes covered. The Cathari, whom Innocent
> III tried so hard to annihilate, and who were at

bottom Christian mystics, were accustomed to call those seeking initiation into their mysteries "hoodwinked slaves," implying that the eyes of the soul were still blind in ignorance and lust. Our own use of the device is in harmony with these old customs and ideas. The purpose of the hoodwink is not to *conceal* something from the candidate, for it has another significance: it symbolises the fact that the candidate *is yet in darkness,* like the babe lying in its mother's womb. Being in darkness the candidate is expected to prepare his inmost mind for those revelations that will be made to him after the hoodwink is removed. [Italics in the original; Bold and caps added][44]

FROM DARKNESS TO LIGHT

Joseph Fort Newton, a very well-known and respected Masonic author, attests: "By the same sign, **INITIATION** is our **BIRTH FROM THE DARKNESS** of prenatal gloom **INTO THE LIGHT OF MORAL AND SPIRITUAL FAITH...."**[45] Can you see a few problems here for a Christian man or woman? For one thing, a Christian has **ALREADY** "passed from death unto life" (John 5:24; I John 3:14). We are no longer in **DARKNESS.** Jesus declared: I am the light of the world: he that followeth Me shall not walk in **DARKNESS,** but shall have the light of life" (John 8:12). Peter tells us that since we "are a chosen generation, a royal priesthood, an holy nation, a peculiar people," we "should shew forth the praises of Him who hath called [us] **OUT OF DARKNESS** into His marvellous light" (I Peter 2:9). Paul reveals that Christ "hath delivered us from the power of darkness, and hath translated us into the kingdom of His dear Son" (Colossians 1:13). In fact, Paul's mission was to preach the gospel and to "open their eyes, and to turn them from darkness to light, and from the power of Satan unto God" (Acts 26:18). Other verses that deal with the theme that, as God's children, we no longer walk in darkness can be found in: I John 1:5-6; John 12:35, 46; and I Thessalonians 5:4.

Here, then, is the dilemma. When a Christian enters the lodge room and partakes of the initiation ceremony, even though he or she is no longer in darkness, the veil represents darkness. In fact, the lodge takes the place of Christ for it claims that through the initiation the candidate passes from "the darkness of ignorance into the marvelous light of truth."[46] Compare this statement with I Peter 2:9! Not only does the lodge try to take Christ's place, but it also tries to negate the salvation experience the Christian candidate has previously had by insisting that the person enters the lodge room in the state of darkness. Granted, many candidates do actually enter in a state of darkness because they have never been born again, but for a Christian this is a disgrace because the lodge claims to dispel the darkness that only Christ can banish. In the Masonic book by Harold Waldwin Percival, we are told: "A hoodwink or blind is put over his eyes, so that he feels he is in darkness, without light, and cannot find his way. Then the thing he most desires is light."[47] The Christian already has the light and has found the way.

Notice also that it is stated that the eyes of the soul were still blind in ignorance and lust.[48] As a Christian, we are no longer in spiritual ignorance and in Acts 17:30 we find this solemn admonition: "And the times of this ignorance God winked at; but now commandeth all men every where to repent." Referring to the phrase "still blind in...lust,"[49] Peter wrote: "As obedient children, not fashioning yourselves according to the former lusts in your ignorance: But as He which hath called you is holy, so be ye holy in all manner of conversation" (I Peter 1:14-15). What Paul wrote to the Romans could be very applicable to the founders of Masonry and the Eastern Star: "For they being ignorant of God's righteousness, and going about to establish their own righteousness, have not submitted themselves unto the righteousness of God" (Romans 10:3; See also: Ephesians 4:18).

MASONRY TRIES TO USURP CHRISTIANITY

In *The Ahiman Rezon,* the Masonic monitor published by the Grand Lodge of South Carolina, we find the following mentioned about the new candidate:

> There he stands without our portals, on the threshold of this new Masonic life, in **DARKNESS, HELPLESSNESS, AND IGNORANCE.** Having been **WANDERING AMID THE ERRORS** and covered over with the pollutions of the outer and profane world, he comes inquiringly to our doors, **SEEKING THE NEW BIRTH,** and asking a withdrawal of the veil which conceals divine truth from his uninitiated sight.[50]

Here we discover that the candidate has "been wandering amid the **ERRORS** and covered over with the pollutions of the outer and profane world."[51] Obviously, for a Christian, this statement insinuates that Christianity is in error and the initiate must be cleansed from his previous involvement with his religion. Furthermore, the new candidate comes to Masonry "seeking the new birth."[52] Only through Christ Jesus can the new birth or salvation be obtained, but once again Masonry tries to usurp Christianity and the Bible and claims that through Masonry the new birth can be acquired. What Paul wrote to the Ephesians seems appropriate as a revelation for us:

Having the understanding darkened, being alienated from the life of God through the ignorance that is in them, because of the blindness of their heart: Who being past feeling have given themselves over unto lasciviousness, to work all uncleanness with greediness. But ye have not so learned Christ (Ephesians 4:18-20).

Another problem with the symbolism of the veil is, as Haywood mentions, that the "use of the blindfold goes far back among secret societies, even to the Ancient Mysteries...."[53] The Ancient Mysteries were found in many pagan societies like Egypt, Babylon, and India. It is the teachings of the Ancient Mysteries that we have been covering in detail with the symbolism throughout this book, so you can see that these mysteries were decadent, degenerate, and corrupt, including sexual orgies, and animal and human sacrifices, yet this is where the symbolism for the veiling of the candidate is taken from.

BACK TO PAGANISM

In *Signs and Symbols of Primordial Man* Masonic author, Albert Churchward, reveals more about the veil:

The 17th and 18th chapters of the *Ritual* must be interesting to those of the 18°, because here we find that the blind Horus, or Horus in the dark, or blindness or invisibility, had the veil of darkness (a net) over his head, so that he was unable to see, and had to pass through difficulties, danger and darkness, after which he was presented to the great circle of Chiefs or Princes, the veil being removed by Thoth, who restored him to light, life, health and strength, and all the glorious company of Princes, in which he was given a place.[54]

Remember Thoth? He was the Egyptian god who had great **MAGIC** powers,[55] taught people the **OCCULT** arts,[56] and was the originator of **ALCHEMY.**[57] Thoth was also one of the other names given for the Eastern Star known as **SIRIUS.**[58] New Ager and occultist, Helen Petrovna Blavatsky, even links **THOTH AND SATAN TOGETHER.**[59] In spite of these facts, it is Thoth who is credited with restoring the candidate to light! Can you see that the light that is referred to is not the light of God's Word? Once again, the symbolism employed by the Eastern Star takes us back to **PAGANISM!**

Even though it may be hard for the average Mason or Eastern Star member to discern what is being represented in the lodge, it is not impossible to discover (with a lot of study and research) what is being portrayed. The facts, although not necessarily readily available, are accessible and it is plain to see the **DECEPTION** that was deviously and deceitfully designed and orchestrated. Do you want to be a member of such an organization? The Bible asks:

> What agreement hath the temple of God with idols? for ye are the temple of the living God; as God hath said, I will dwell in them, and walk in them; and I will be their God, and they shall be My people. Wherefore **COME OUT FROM AMONG THEM, AND BE YE SEPARATE,** saith the Lord, and touch not the unclean thing; and I will receive you (II Corinthians 6:16-17).

"Come out of her, My people, that ye be not partakers of her sins, and that ye receive not of her plagues" (Revelation 18:4).

10. EASTERN STAR GODDESSES

For those Eastern Star members who may still be unconvinced about the paganism in their organization, perhaps this chapter will be enlightening to them.

Rob Morris, founder of the Eastern Star, boasted about its origins. He wrote:

> About the first of February, 1850, I was laid up for two weeks with a sharp attack of rheumatism, and it was this period which I gave to the work in hand. By the aid of my papers and the memory of Mrs. Morris, I recall even the trivial occurrences connected with the work, how I hesitated for a theme, how I dallied over a name, how I wrought face to face with the clock that I might keep my drama within due limits of time, etc. The name was first settled upon—*The Eastern Star*. Next the number of points, five, to correspond with the emblem on the Master's carpet. This is the pentagon, "The signet of King Solomon," and eminently proper to Adoptive Masonry....
>
> The colors, the emblems, the floral wreaths, the esotery proper to these five heroines, were easy of invention. They seemed to fall ready-made into my hands. The only piece of mechanism difficult to fit into the construction was the cabalistic motto, but this occurred to me in ample time for use....
>
> The selections were:
>
> 1. Jephthah's Daughter, as illustrating respect to the binding force of a vow.
>
> 2. Ruth, as illustrating devotion to religious principles.

3. Esther, as illustrating fidelity to kindred and friends.

4. Martha, as illustrating undeviating faith in the hour of trial.

5. Electa, as illustrating patience and submission under wrong.

These are all Masonic virtues, and they have nowhere in history more brilliant exemplars than in the five characters presented in the lectures of the Eastern Star.[1]

Doesn't that sound so pious and religious? Morris continues:

It is a fitting comment upon these statements that in all the changes that the Eastern Star has experienced at so many hands for thirty-four years [1884], **NO CHANGE IN THE NAMES,** histories or essential lessons has been proposed.[2]

Really? This is just another example of so-called "Masonic honesty." The names of the officers had changed—and Morris knew it! (This isn't the first outright lie that we've caught Morris in, either. Remember his lie about St. John instituting the degree of Electa while at the same time claiming that he himself originated all the degrees?)

NAMES CHANGED

Henry Wilson Coil, 33° Mason, comments:

In 1855, **MORRIS REVISED THE RITUAL** and printed it under the name, *The Mosaic Book,* and purported to create a *Supreme Constellation* *of the American Adoptive Rite,* of which he was "Most Enlightened Grand Luminary."[3]

Turning to *The Mosaic Book,* **WRITTEN BY** Rob Morris, we find the following names of the officers: Heleon, Philomath, Verger, Herald, Luna, Flora, Hebe, Thetis (or Thesis), Areme, and Warder.[4] Do these names look the same to you as Adah, Ruth, Esther, Martha, and Electa? Of course not! The simple fact is, the **NAMES WERE CHANGED!**

12   HISTORY OF ORDER

Brothers: Helion, the first and chief Pillar; president of the council; personator of Jephthah—symbol, Lion.

Philomath, the second Pillar; lieutenant to Helion; personator of Boaz—symbol, Coiled Snake.

Verger, the third Pillar; personator of Ahasuerus; treasurer—symbol, Raven.

Herald, the fourth Pillar; personator of St. John; secretary—symbol, Eagle.

Warder, fifth Pillar; keeper of portals—symbol, Dove.

Sisters: Luna, the first or chief Correspondent; personator of Adah—symbol, Violets.

Flora, the second Correspondent; personator of Ruth—symbol, Sunflower.

Hebe, the third Correspondent; personator of Esther—symbol, Lilies.

Thesis, the fourth Correspondent; personator of Martha—symbol, Pine branch with cones.

Areme, the fifth Correspondent; personator of Electa—symbol, Roses.

Emblems found on the border of the Charters and used in the Mosaic book were:

The five stars in a blue circle represented the Constellations.

The gavel represented the five Pillars.

The heart represented the five Correspondents.

The perfect ashler represented the landmarks.

The sun, the Luminaries represented "the governing officers of the Supreme Constellation".

The ring and the memorial, "the semi-annual passport communicated by the V. E. Grand Secretary to the Subordinate Constellations was for traveling purposes only.

There was a form of initiation, or lecture, in which the candidate was instructed into the lessons, secrets, etc., of the work. The whole ceremony was brief, but intricate, and closed with an admonition to the candidate to cultivate the

Page 12 taken from <u>History of the Order of the Eastern Star</u>, *published in 1989 by the General Grand Chapter.*

A book entitled *History of the Order of the Eastern Star,* which was published in 1989 by the General Grand Chapter of the Eastern Star, pointedly mentioned that in:

...1860, Dr. Morris set about organizing under a different title or name....

The **TITLES OF THE OFFICERS WERE CHANGED,** lectures or charges were taken from Bible stories and **GIVEN BIBLE NAMES,** but many of the principal **IDEAS REMAINED UNCHANGED....**This proved to be popular, and many Master Masons were authorized to communicate the degrees. The lectures remained in five charges, **UNDER DIFFERENT NAMES,** but the **CABALISTIC MOTTO,** and **CABALISTIC WORD REMAINED THE SAME.**[5]

PAGANISM UNDER GUISE OF CHRISTIANITY

This fact is reiterated a few pages later:

All superfluities were abandoned and sylvan titles eliminated and plain Bible characters used by the office bearers who gave each part.

NAMES AND TITLES OF OFFICERS WERE CHANGED.... The Labyrinth, or "Maze" was made to conform to the idea of a five pointed star, within a complete circle. Squares and triangles were introduced into the floor work, and other ideas before unknown or overlooked were developed....Symbols and colors remained the same, except that the sunflower as used for Ruth, was changed to the yellow jessamine. **TWO OF THE SIGNS HAVE UNDERGONE SOME CHANGES,**

BUT THE CABALISTIC WORD, MOTTO AND SYMBOLIC MEANING AS FIRST GIVEN in the Mosaic Book and Manual REMAIN UNCHANGED.[6]

CHAPTER III.

Families of the Eastern Star.

The Supreme Constellation appeared to have been a self-styled organization with no authority, and soon fell into decay. Upon its disruption all the large amount of supplies remained in the hands of its Supreme Grand Secretary, Robert Macoy of New York, and in 1860, Dr. Morris set about organizing under a different title or name, and organizations were styled "Families of the Eastern Star." Charters of the old form were issued thus showing that the two systems were identical in spirit, the second having taken the place of the first.

The titles of the officers were changed, lectures or charges were taken from Bible stories and given Bible names, but many of the principal ideas remained unchanged. This proved to be popular, and many Master Masons were authorized to communicate the degrees. The lectures remained in five charges, under different names, but the Cabalistic Motto, and Cabalistic word remained the same.

Up to this time many rituals had been written. Robert Macoy, of New York, who was manager of the Macoy Publishing Co., and very rhetorical in writing had promulgated many ideas along the lines of Adrogynous Masonry. These rituals were constantly undergoing revision. When supplies for an organization were ordered a ritual would be sent and the next time a different ritual, until there was no stability in the work.

From 1850 to 1855 Dr. Morris was very active in communicating degrees and appointing Master Masons to communicate them. These degrees were communicated to many in the South and West. In 1855 he published a ritual called "The Mosaic Book". The States and Territories were districted.

Page 14 taken from <u>History of the Order of the Eastern Star</u>, *published in 1989 by the General Grand Chapter.*

Fascinating! Notice that the symbols, colors, Cabalistic Motto, Cabalistic word, and the **SYMBOLIC MEANING HAVE REMAINED THE SAME,** but the **NAMES WERE CHANGED TO BIBLE NAMES.** As one book, *The Mysteries of Osiris or Ancient Egyptian Initiation,* states: "Names change; principles never."[7] In other words, the Eastern Star is not, and never has been, Bible-based! It is only using the names of Bible characters to continue its paganism under a guise. In fact, we are told: "The reading of Scripture text between the points was originated by the Patrons of Queen Esther Chapter, Indianapolis, Ind., and inserted in the Ritual in 1878."[8] This was 28 years after the founding of the Eastern Star!

Even the word "sylvan" hints at paganism, for it means "forest" or "woods." It was in such undetected places as these that the pagans worshiped their gods with animal and human sacrifices and where they engaged in their sexual orgies. Remember that Pan, whom we have already mentioned, is the god of nature "and is usually represented with horns...and with legs covered with hair (denoting the vitality of base forces, earth, shrubs and the instincts)."[9]

In *A General History of the Order of the Eastern Star* by Willis D. Engle, we are told:

> One of the principal causes of dissatisfaction was the **NUMEROUS CHANGES MADE IN THE RITUAL.** That in use in 1874 was revised and materially altered in 1875, so that previous editions were useless when the later was used, and, in 1876, he [Robert Macoy] issued another differing still more from previous ones; even the different editions of the syllabus gave radically different directions as to the manner of giving the signs, so that...[when] the chapters which were using the 1875 ritual applied to the Masonic Publishing Company for additional copies of it, they were

informed that it was out of print, and that copies of it could not be purchased.[10]

In fact, Macoy "took complete control of affairs and by raising Charter fees and other means, soon amassed quite a fortune for himself."[11]

WHY were the names changed? Could it be to DISGUISE the fact that the five women were originally the names of goddesses? Yes, that's right! Are you aware that Luna, Flora, Hebe, and Areme are names of goddesses and that Thetis is the name of a sea goddess (or nymph) in mythology?

ADAH WAS LUNA

Adah was originally known as Luna.[12] Who was Luna? According to Pearl Cleveland Wilson, Luna, in:

...Roman mythology, [is] the goddess of the moon. A minor deity, Luna was connected chiefly with calendar reckoning. She is said to have been worshiped by the Romans from the time of Romulus, the legendary founder of Rome. In Rome there were three temples to her. Luna was sometimes associated with the Roman goddess Diana. Her Greek counterpart was Selene, an early moon goddess. The latin word *luna* means moon.[13]

Notice that Luna is sometimes associated with Diana and Selene. In the book, *Mythology,* we discover that Diana (also called Artemis):

...was the Moon, called Phoebe and Selene (Luna in Latin)....

In the later poets, Artemis is identified with Hecate. She is "the goddess with three forms," Selene in the sky, Artemis on earth, Hecate in the lower

Triple Goddess

world and in the world above when it is wrapped in darkness. Hecate was the Goddess of the Dark of the Moon, the black nights when the moon is hidden. She was associated with the deeds of darkness, the Goddess of the Crossways, which were held to be ghostly places of evil magic.[14]

Laurie Cabot, a witch, states: "At death Hecate was said to meet the departed souls and lead them to the Underworld....And so Hecate became known as the Queen of the Witches...."[15] This brings to mind that the star used in the Eastern Star represents Hermes, who also was the conductor of the dead to the underworld.[16]

Hecate was the "name by which Diana was known in the infernal regions. In heaven her name was Luna."[17] It's no wonder that Hecate is called the "Queen of the Witches" since she taught **SORCERY** and **WITCHCRAFT**,[18] but why would this be one of the goddesses chosen for the Eastern Star under the name of Luna? Could it be that the person who selected these names was well-versed in mythology and witchcraft? Diana's symbol, by the way, is a **CRESCENT AND**

CRESCENT MOON & STAR (Diana)

The crescent moon and star are used by both witches and the Eastern Star.

STAR, which is a **FERTILITY** emblem and a **SYMBOL OF WITCHCRAFT.**[19]

VIRGIN OR LESBIAN?

We also discover that Diana is the patron saint of the **FEMINISTS AND LESBIANS.**[20] She shunned men and:

> ...devoted herself to hunting, always accompanied by a band of young women, who, like herself, abjured marriage. She is depicted with a quiver and attended by dogs. Her most famous temple was at Ephesus, and was one of the seven wonders of the world.[21]

Do you recall that this is the goddess who represented Adah, Jephthah's daughter? Remember that Adah was a young girl who was committed to perpetual virginity in order to fulfill the vow her father had spoken (see Judges 11:37-40).

Notice that Diana's most famous temple was at Ephesus.

> In Ephesus and elsewhere, the cult of Diana encouraged **SEXUAL LICENSE AND SACRED PROMISCUITY.** The idolatrous statue of Diana depicted her with a multitude of breasts, signifying her sensual nature.[22]

Do you realize that this very **GODDESS** and her temple of worship were spoken of in the Bible? The Apostle Paul was ministering in Asia when an uproar took place. Demetrius, a silversmith, made shrines for Diana and thus acquired a tremendous amount of profit by doing so, but Paul's preaching was persuading the people that idols were nothing compared to the true God (see Acts 19:26 and I Corinthians 8:1-6). Demetrius, therefore:

> ...called together...the workmen of like occupation, and said, Sirs, ye know that by this craft we have our wealth. Moreover ye see and hear, that not alone at Ephesus, but almost throughout all Asia, this Paul hath persuaded and turned away much people, saying that they be no gods, which are made with hands: So that not only this our craft is in danger to be set at nought; but also that the temple of the great goddess Diana should be despised, and her magnificence should be destroyed, whom all Asia and the world worshippeth. And when they heard these sayings, they were full of wrath, and cried out, saying, Great is Diana of the Ephesians. And the whole city was filled with confusion (Acts 19:25-29).

In fact, for two hours the people chanted "Great is Diana of the Ephesians" (Acts 19:34). Of course, this was pagan worship and idolatry which is condemned in the Scriptures, but in spite of this, the Eastern Star reverted to paganism when they chose **GODDESSES** to represent the **ORIGINAL** officers.

As mentioned, Luna (also called Diana, Hecate, Selene, and Artemis) is a moon goddess. Another moon goddess is Io.[23] In Greek mythology:

> ...the violet sprang for Io, a priestess of Juno's temple, with whom Jupiter was almost caught in one of his flirtations. Not having time to conceal

her, he changed her into a white heifer; but grass not being good enough for so delicate a creature, the god created the violet as her special food.[24]

Would you like to guess what flower was selected for Adah (who was at one time called Luna) in the Eastern Star? That's right! It's the violet.[25]

Aleister Crowley, both a Mason and Satanist, mentions that "Luna is blue...."[26] What color was chosen for Luna who is now called Adah? Blue, of course! Is this just an amazing set of coincidences or was there extensive preparation involved in laying out the plans for this organization and the ritual which followed?

ESTHER WAS HEBE

The goddess originally mentioned in the Eastern Star for Esther was Hebe.[27] We are told that in Greek mythology Hebe is:

...the goddess of youth and the daughter of Zeus and Hera. Hebe was for a time the cupbearer of the gods, distributing nectar and ambrosia at their feasts, but she was later replaced in this office by the young Trojan prince Ganymede. On Mount Olympus, the home of the gods, she was in charge

of domestic matters, such as preparing the chariot for Hera whenever Hera wished to leave Olympus. She also served as a handmaiden to her brother Ares. When Heracles, or Hercules, became one of the gods, Hebe married him. They had two children, Alexiares and Anicetus. The Romans worshiped Hebe as Juventas and believed, as did the later Greeks, that she had the power to bestow eternal youth.[28]

RUTH WAS FLORA

Flora was the goddess who had represented Ruth.[29] Flora, also known as Chloris, was the goddess of springtime and flowers in Roman mythology.[30] This is one of the goddesses to whom Albert Pike wrote a poem.[31]

The Romans held an annual festival in honor of Flora, called the Floralia, which "was celebrated with merriment and licentiousness."[32]

We are also told in both the Floral and the Dionysian processions, naked girls in a half-drunken frenzy danced around an immense painted phallus carried on the end of a pole. It is related that Cato the Younger being present at one of these festivals, there was hesitation in starting the orgies because of his celebrated modesty and gravity, so he was obliged to retire....

In Greece and Rome the orgies of the Dionysia were similar to those of the Floralia. Of them Buret says, in *Syphilis in Ancient and Prehistoric Times,* "At a signal from the Aediles the courtesans sprang into the circus, undressed themselves until they were naked, and assumed lascivious attitudes, amid the plaudits of a delirious people, where to the sounds of trumpets, naked men jumped into the arena, and an awful melee of prostitution was publically (sic) accomplished amid the transports of the multitude."[33]

Of course, this isn't surprising since the symbols that have been used by the Eastern Star and Masons are of a sexual and licentiousness nature.

Why was Flora chosen to represent Ruth? Could it be that this particular goddess was selected because of occultism? You see, in the occult the four (or sometimes five) elements play a prominent role. The color yellow symbolizes the earth element and Ruth's color is yellow.[34] How appropriate, then, for her to be depicted by a goddess of flowers and springtime. The emblem for Ruth is a sheaf or sheaves of barley.[35] "Generally speaking, all sheafs (sic), bunches and sprays stand for **PSYCHIC FORCES**...."[36] Remember, we do know that the sheaf is not actually representing

a sheaf for Shirley Plessner reminds us: "An emblem is a figure or symbol which stands for **SOMETHING ELSE.**"[37]

MARTHA WAS THETIS

Martha was originally called Thetis (or Thesis).[38] In Greek mythology she was a sea goddess whose son's name was Achilles.[39] You're probably familiar with the story of Achilles. He was the mighty Greek warrior during the Trojan War. "During infancy Thetis plunged him into the Styx, so making every part of his body invulnerable except the heel by which she held him."[40] The Styx:

> ...was a dark and dreary river in Greek and Roman mythology. Dead souls had to be carried across it by Charon, a boatman, in order to reach the Lower World [hell]. The gods took their most sacred oaths by the river Styx.[41]

Interestingly, we find the river Styx mentioned in Masonry. In *What? When? Where? Why? Who? in Freemasonry* we are told:

> Ancient peoples were convinced that some boat, ship, canoe, ark or raft, carried the souls of dead men across a mythical body of water to another land; the story of Charon, ferryman on the River Styx, beyond which were the Elysian fields, is

familiar to all. Hence, the ark as a means of safety from storm and stress in Masonic symbolism is but a continuation of a mythology hoary with age....Both anchor and ark are ancient symbols of safety and a passage from this life to another. Freemasonry but adapts to her purposes what has been common to many beliefs in many ages.[42]

THE SEA GODDESS

Why would a sea goddess be used to represent Martha when Martha's story has nothing to do with the ocean? Is it possible that a sea goddess was necessary to reflect the element water? The color dedicated to Martha is green and green is the color used to symbolize the water element. In the Egyptian creation story, green is assigned to water since water played a part in their creation.[43] Green also symbolized victory and was used in the funeral ritual.[44] Remember, the story of Martha does involve a funeral—the death

Rainbow Isis

244   HIDDEN SECRETS OF THE EASTERN STAR

of Lazarus. It also symbolizes victory since Lazarus was raised from the dead. As previously mentioned, the story of Martha and Lazarus actually seems to parallel the story of Isis and Osiris. Aleister Crowley discloses: "The pure earth, known to the ancient Egyptians in that Equinox of the Gods over which Isis presided, was green."[45]

John Algeo, the president of the Theosophical Society in America,[46] recently wrote an article about *The Wonderful Wizard of Oz,* and its author, Frank Baum, also a member of the Theosophical Society,[47] who was "well read in the occult sciences."[48] (Incidentally, Baum also wrote a play entitled *The Uplift of Lucifer, or Raising Hell.*[49]) Referring to the Emerald City Algeo explains: "Emerald or **GREEN** is the color of harmony, of balance; it is midway in the color spectrum; it is the color of the **FOURTH** or harmonizing ray."[50] Isn't it amazing to notice that Martha's color, green, just happens to also be the **FOURTH** point of the star?[51] Additionally, Algeo points out:

We can overcome death and illusion only in the world of death and illusion. We must pass through the valley of the shadow of death to come to the land of eternal light. So Dorothy must go to

the uttermost West, encounter the wicked Witch
of death, and over come her—with water, the
symbol of life.[52]

Again we see the correlation between the color
(green), the element (water), and death—all used in
the Eastern Star story of Martha.

The Eastern Star ritual tells us that Martha's flower
is the pine cone (or fern).[53] In *A Dictionary of Symbols*
we find that "the pine is a symbol of immortality."[54]
That fits quite well with Martha since there is a
death and resurrection connotation. However, pine
cones are also "regarded as symbols of fertility."[55]
"Among the Greeks, Babylonians, and others, the
phallus was a symbol of the resurrection because of
its ability to come to life and erect itself."[56] Of course,
this, too, fits into the story of Martha (under the
legend of Isis and Osiris).

What is also intriguing is that the pine tree is
"sacred to the sea god."[57] Ah, is this just another
reason why Martha was at one time identified as
Thetis, the sea goddess? Isis, by the way, is also
referred to as the "Star of the Sea"![58] Did Morris
choose each goddess with the different elements and
specific colors in mind or are these just mere
"coincidences"? You be the judge.

ELECTA WAS AREME

So far we've covered the goddesses Luna (Adah),
Hebe (Esther), Flora (Ruth), and Thetis (Martha).
There remains one more—the impersonator of Electa
who was called Areme. First of all, let's look at
Electa's symbol which is the lion.[59] Earlier I quoted
from Masonic sources that clearly showed us that
the lion **DOES NOT** represent Christ but actually
refers to the lion that raised **OSIRIS** from the dead.[60]

With this in mind, it was interesting to discover that the lion was also the symbol of Ishtar (also known as Isis), the goddess of love.[61] (Osiris was the pagan god who committed incest with his sister, Isis, which resulted in the birth of Horus.) Could there be a correlation between the symbol of the goddess of love (the lion), and Electa's symbol (also a lion) and her pass which is "Love one another"?[62] Incidentally, the lion "was emblematical of the Sun."[63]

Now, who was Areme? In all likelihood, you have never even heard of this name, much less know anything about her. Scores upon scores of reference materials were examined only to find **NO MENTION** of her name at all. Book after book on mythology, as well as dictionaries, encyclopedias, occult books, and numerous other sources were checked. The results were the same: no mention of Areme.

Knowing that the other four names previously used in the Eastern Star were names of goddesses, I was quite sure that Areme would also be a goddess, yet no one seemed to know anything about this name. Was there a particular reason why this name was so elusive? After much more research, a phone call, and several letters, the pieces of the puzzle seemed to start to fall into place.

In conversation with a former witch (who was also a Satanist and Mason), I was informed that in witchcraft there is a **SECRET GODDESS WHOSE NAME IS ONLY KNOWN TO THE INITIATES.**[64] The witchcraft group to which he belonged did not have Areme as their secret goddess, but different traditions have different goddesses. He also told me that the color associated with this goddess is usually red or white. Surprisingly (or perhaps not so surprisingly!) Areme's color just happens to be red. I started wondering, Could the Eastern Star actually have a **SECRET GODDESS** like the witches do? Was Rob Morris aware of this? Could this be why there was no reference to Areme? Even the well-known witch, Starhawk, referred to "the **SECRET NAME** of the Goddess" in her book *The Spiral Dance: A Rebirth of the Ancient Religion of the Great Goddess.*[65]

AN EGYPTIAN GODDESS

Shortly after this conversation I received a letter from another former witch. He wrote that Areme "was an **OBSCURE** Egyptian goddess."[66] At least my suspicion that Areme was a goddess was finally confirmed. If Areme was a secret name known only to initiates, obviously there would be very little or no information about her available.

So, then, all five names that Rob Morris had **ORIGINALLY** used were the names of **GODDESSES,** although each of these goddesses impersonated a **BIBLE CHARACTER.** It is also interesting that the goddesses Morris had chosen were taken from **THREE** different countries. Luna and Flora were Roman goddesses, Hebe and Thetis were Greek goddesses, and Areme was an Egyptian goddess. The number **THREE** is very important in Masonry and, of course, in witchcraft.[67]

Albert Pike claims: "This continual reproduction of the number **THREE** is not accidental, not without a profound meaning: and we shall find the same repeated in all the Ancient philosophies."[68] Could this be why **THREE** nations were represented by these goddesses (and not one, two, four, or five)? Or again, is this just a "coincidence" that just happened? Flowers were very important in paganism as well.

> The **GREEKS ASSIGNED A FLOWER OR FLOWERS TO EACH DEITY** in their pantheon and believed that, by inhaling the scent of a plant sacred to a god or goddess, they could share in the attributes of that particular deity....The Romans shared this belief.[69]

It just so happens that each of the Eastern Star "Bible" characters also is assigned a particular flower. In *Burial Service for the Order of the Eastern Star,* we find: "In the ceremonies of our Order, **FLOWERS BEAR AN IMPORTANT PART."**[70] Fruit is also carried in a vessel.[71] Notice that the Greeks and Romans were involved in this practice and that four out of the five Eastern Star goddesses were Greek and Roman! Incidentally, flowers and fruit are also offered in the Transcendental Meditation initiation rite.[72]

ORDER OF THE AMARANTH

One other degree that is offered to Eastern Star members is the Amaranth degree. It was prepared by Robert Macoy and "was intended by him to be used as the third and highest degree of Adoptive Rite."[73] Jean M'Kee Kenaston explains:

> The illustration used upon the first page of the ritual shows the all-seeing eye of progress at the top, with graduated degrees typifying the road to progress with the Eastern Star upon the first step, Queen of the South as the second step, and Amaranth upon the third and top step.[74]

What is interesting about this degree is that the:

...word amaranth is derived from the Greek word meaning unwithering and is chiefly used in poetry, and applied to certain plants which, from not soon fading, typify immortality....

In ancient Greece the amaranth was sacred to Ephesian Artemis. It was supposed to have special healing properties, and as a symbol of immortality was used to decorate images of the gods and tombs.[75]

Remember, Artemis is the same goddess as Diana which we just covered. Once again we can see the **GODDESS CONNECTION!**

It is also important to make a brief mention of the all-seeing eye. This eye is another Masonic symbol, a representation of **OSIRIS.**[76] Pike clearly reveals that the all-seeing eye is "the emblem of Osiris, the Creator."[77] He also maintains that Osiris' "power was symbolized by an Eye over a Sceptre. The Sun was termed by the Greeks the Eye of Jupiter, and the Eye of the World; and **HIS [OSIRIS']** is the All-Seeing Eye in our Lodges."[78]

These names of gods and goddesses are still in use in Masonry. For example, the collars worn for

the 25° sport the names of Osiris, Ahura, Isis, and Ceres, along with the fertility symbols of the crescent moon and the bull. So, remember the next time you, a family member, or a friend attends a Masonic or Eastern Star meeting and impersonates one of the "Bible" women that behind this facade stands a **GODDESS!** As previously mentioned, in the book *History of the Order of the Eastern Star,* we are reminded:

> The **TITLES OF THE OFFICERS WERE CHANGED,** lectures or charges were taken from Bible stories and **GIVEN BIBLE NAMES,** but many of the principal **IDEAS REMAINED UNCHANGED....**

> Two of the signs have undergone some changes, but the Cabalistic word, Motto and symbolic meaning as first given in the Mosaic Book and Manual remain unchanged.[79]

KNIGHT OF THE BRAZEN SERPENT
TWENTY-FIFTH DEGREE

Taken from <u>A Bridge to Light</u> *by Rex Hutchens, published in 1988 by the unanimous approval of the Committee on Rituals and Ceremonial Forms of the Supreme Council of Scottish Rite Masonry.*

11. WHAT IS THE CABALISTIC MOTTO?

The Cabalistic Motto is an important part of the Eastern Star, but before we look at their motto, let's see what the Cabala is. The Cabala (also spelled Cabbala, Cabbalah, Kabala, Kabbala, Kabbalah, Kabalah, Kaballa, Quabalah, Qabala, etc.), according to one occult magazine:

> ...is a very powerful system, and Pagans should take advantage of it. Witches do, after all, steal (er, borrow) anything that works, regardless of the tradition....It may well bring Pagans closer their (sic) Gods.[1]

A description for the book, *A Kabbalah for the Modern World*, by Migene Gonzalez-Wippler, urges: "This book needs to be in the library of every **OCCULTIST, PAGAN, KABBALIST, MYSTIC** and person involved in the **NEW AGE**. The Kabbalah is the basic form of Western mysticism."[2]

Another occult catalog indicates:

> The Qabalah, whose disciplines includes the **OCCULT** sciences of **ASTROLOGY AND TAROT,** forms the basis of the Western Mystery Tradition. It is a system of mystical knowledge and **SPIRITUAL** development in the same way that **YOGA** is the mystical system of the East. The **TREE OF LIFE**—a diagram consisting of ten circles connected by twenty-two "paths" is the heart of Qabalistic teaching.[3]

In an article entitled "Jung and the Qabalah," we are told:

> The Qabalah is one of the most ancient Western philosophical systems. **IT FORMS MUCH OF**

The Tree of Life

**THE INNER FOUNDATIONS UPON WHICH
ASTROLOGY, TAROT, ALCHEMY, NUMER-
OLOGY, MYTHOLOGY AND CEREMONIAL
MAGIC ARE BASED.**[4]

According to *Webster's Dictionary,* the Cabala
is "a medieval and modern system of Jewish **THEOS-
OPHY,** mysticism, and **THAUMATURGY** marked
by belief in creation through emanation and a cipher
method of interpreting Scripture" and "a traditional,
ESOTERIC, OCCULT, OR SECRET matter."[5]
**REINCARNATION, MAGICAL POWER OF WORDS
AND SIGNS, THE POWER OF AMULETS,
DIVINATION, CONJURATIONS OF SPIRITS, AS
WELL AS OTHER OCCULTIC PRACTICES, PLAY
AN IMPORTANT ROLE IN THE CABALA AND**

CABALISTIC TEACHINGS.[6] The book, *Magical Arts,* claims:

> Like most of the occult systems within the European tradition of high magic, the **CABALA INCLUDED SPELLS** designed to induce an unseen population of spirits to carry out the magician's wishes.[7]

In fact, in the *Dictionary of Mysticism,* we are told that the **CABALA "IS AN ESSENTIAL ELEMENT IN MOST SCHOOLS OF OCCULTISM."**[8]

CABALA RELATED TO OCCULTISM

Surely this isn't the same Cabala that the Eastern Stars refer to, is it? Let's turn to Eastern Star author, Mary Ann Slipper, for the answer. She writes:

> **CABALISTIC IS RELATED TO OCCULTISM,** the science of the secrets of nature. Kabalah was a secret system of the Jewish rabbis to interpret the **HIDDEN MEANING** of the Pentateuch. We use the word to **COVER OUR HIDDEN MEANINGS AND SECRETS.** To the uninitiated the Kabalah would seem to be full of meaningless jargon, but this is a necessity to **CONCEAL THE SECRETS** from the profane.[9]

Notice that Slipper brags that the Eastern Star uses the word Cabala "to cover [the] hidden meanings and secrets" and then adds that "this is a necessity" in order to "conceal the secrets from the profane," who are, of course, those who are not members of the Eastern Star. Joseph Leon Blau remarks that, according to the Cabalistic theory:

> Every letter in the Scriptures contains a revelation beyond its literal significance. This superrevelation

has nothing to do with the meaning of the passage under consideration. It depends on such factors as the size, shape, and decoration of the letters of the sacred text in the sacred language.[10]

In Revelation and elsewhere we are warned that we are not to add to, nor take away from, God's Word (Revelation 22:18-19; Deuteronomy 4:2; Proverbs 30:6). Peter also cautions us that the Scriptures can be wrested (or twisted) and doing so will only lead to destruction (II Peter 3:16). Therefore, it is a very unwise practice to manipulate the Scriptures as do the Cabalists.

THEOSOPHY: A MYSTIC CULT

Since the Cabala is a "system of Jewish theosophy," let's see what theosophy is. Theosophy is, according to the *Masonic Quiz Book,* a **"MYSTIC CULT."**[11] It is also a religious system that stresses **OCCULT** practices and theories such as **CLAIRVOYANCE, TELEPATHY,**[12] **EVOLUTION, KARMA, REINCARNATION,**[13] **MYSTICISM, AND SPIRITUALISM.**[14] It is also claimed to be a **"TECHNIQUE FOR ACHIEVING SALVATION"**[15] and "used for the invocation of the angels."[16] Again, the Bible admonishes us:

Let no man beguile you of your reward in a voluntary humility and worshipping of angels, intruding into those things which he hath not seen, vainly puffed up by his fleshly mind, And not holding the Head [Christ] (Colossians 2:18-19a).

The Theosophical Society was founded on October 20, 1875, by the medium[17] and occultist Madame Helena Petrovna Blavatsky.[18] "According to *The*

Theosophical Glossary (by H. P. Blavatsky), 'its avowed object was at first the specific investigation of psychic or so-called "spiritualistic" phenomena....'"[19]

The Theosophical Society's publication was called *Lucifer,*[20] and Albert Pike, a Mason, was one of its members for a while.[21]

It is interesting to note that Madame Blavatsky, "an open Satanist,"[22] and founder of the Theosophical Society, as well as Annie Besant and Alice Bailey, her successors, were all involved with Masonry.[23] While it is often denied that women have belonged to Masonry, there was a movement of men and women called Co-Masonry which did form an alliance with the Grand Orient Freemasonry of France.[24] An offshoot of the Theosophical Society is the Lucis Trust,[25] which was one time known as the Lucifer Publishing Company.[26] Alice Bailey, the head of Lucis Trust, had a husband, Foster Bailey, who was also a 32° Mason.[27] It's no wonder, then, that the **SAME** doctrines and beliefs can be found in the Cabala, Theosophy, the New Age movement, Witchcraft, Masonry, and the Eastern Star, for they all have the **SAME** source.

PIKE BLASPHEMES

For instance, in the Cabala, "the Sun represents that angel of light...."[28] Who is the "angel of light"? II Corinthians 11:14 answers that question for us: "Satan [who is also Lucifer] himself is transformed into an angel of light." Blavatsky remarked: "...Lucifer or Luciferius is the name. Lucifer is divine and terrestrial Light, 'the Holy Ghost' and 'Satan' at one and the same time."[29] In other words, Blavatsky claims that Lucifer is the Holy Ghost **AND** Satan, but she is not the only one who has called Lucifer the Holy Ghost. Masonic author, Albert Pike, insulted and blasphemed the Holy Ghost when he recorded that

Angels of Light??? Notice the hooves!!! (Taken from <u>Beyond the Pillars</u>, *a book which is only to be purchased by a "Master Mason in good standing, through the Secretary of his lodge.")*

"the body of the Holy Spirit, the universal Agent, [is] the Serpent devouring its own tail."[30] In fact, in the 28th degree of the Masonic lecture, the Masons being initiated are told the **IDENTICAL** thing![31]

Eliphas Levi, a Mason, stated this about Lucifer: "The intellectual Lucifer is the spirit of intelligence and love; it is the paraclete, it is the Holy Spirit...."[32] The word "paraclete" means "advocate" or an "intercessor." St. John penned: "If any man sin, we have an advocate [paraclete] with the Father, Jesus Christ the righteous" (I John 2:1). Christ is our mediator:

"For there is one God, and one mediator between God and men, the man Christ Jesus" (I Timothy 2:5). Masonry tries to steal the title of Jesus Christ and apply it to Lucifer (Satan), but this is no surprise for Lucifer has boasted:

> I WILL ascend into heaven, I WILL exalt my throne above the stars of God: I WILL sit also upon the mount of the congregation, in the sides of the north: I WILL ascend above the heights of the clouds; I WILL BE LIKE THE MOST HIGH" (Isaiah 14:13-14).

Satan's boast, however, rings hollow since God reveals: "[T]hou shalt be brought down to hell, to the sides of the pit" (Isaiah 14:15).

The prophet Jeremiah proclaimed that the prophets prophesied lies in the Lord's name. God said that they were "prophets of the deceit of their own heart; Which think to cause My people to forget My name..." (Jeremiah 23:26-27). God continues:

> [B]ehold, I am against the prophets...that STEAL MY WORDS....Behold, I am against the prophets...that use their tongues, and say, He saith....Behold, I am against them that...cause My people to err by their lies, and by their lightness; yet I sent them not, nor commanded them: therefore, they shall not profit this people at all, said the Lord (Jeremiah 23:30-32).

Another prophet of God, Isaiah, gave this warning:

> Woe unto them that CALL EVIL GOOD, AND GOOD EVIL; THAT PUT DARKNESS FOR LIGHT, AND LIGHT FOR DARKNESS; that put bitter for sweet, and sweet for bitter! Woe unto them that are wise in their own eyes, and

prudent in their own sight!...Which justify the wicked for reward, and take away the righteousness of the righteous from him (Isaiah 5:20-21, 23).

Isn't this exactly what Masonry and the Eastern Star have done? They have called Lucifer the Holy Spirit and have relegated the God of the Old Testament to a place of evil. Masonic author, Albert Churchward, even tells us that it was El Shaddai (a Hebrew word for the Almighty God) who fell from heaven![33]

CABALA USED FOR CONJURING LUCIFER

Webster's definition for the word "Cabala" also mentioned that the Cabala is a system of thaumaturgy. Thaumaturgy (or theurgy) is so-called white magic,[34] an "occult art, often involving rites and incantations, for controlling divine and beneficent spirits."[35] In fact, the Cabala has "chants and incantations" which even include "the formula for summing up Lucifer...."[36]

One well-known thaumaturgist and necromancer was Cagliostro, an Illuminati member and **MASON.**[37] Below is an excerpt about what took place in the **MASONIC** meetings under Cagliostro's guidance:

The magus's voice was oddly vivacious as he proceeded to question his audience about the rite they had come to witness. That night in 1783, the initiated brethren of the **MASONIC** temple would determine whether one of their members should be elevated to master **MAGICIAN.** To do so, they would consult the spirit of a wise man from another time. Their magus was Count Allessandro di Cagliostro....He would direct the Masons in **CONJURING THE SPIRIT....**

THE OCCASION WAS JUST ONE OF SCORES OF SUCH MAGICAL CEREMONIES STAGED BY CAGLIOSTRO IN MASONIC TEMPLES throughout Europe during the latter half of the eighteenth century.[38]

Cagliostro came to be celebrated as the most powerful **MAGICIAN** of his day. He built his reputation as a magical healer and a formidable diviner of the future....Like other masters of ceremonial magic, he attributed his skills to secrets inherited from an ancient body of **OCCULT** knowledge.[39]

[He] was sometimes known to give commands to the forces over which the tutelary powers had granted him the power of ascendancy. And in so doing, the magician was working according to the rule of the mystic alchemists and thaumaturgists who commanded the angels to intervene, **CONJURED UP THE DEVIL,** or called God to their aid in the course of traditionally preserved ceremonial rites.[40]

By his sermons, his laying on of hands, his invocations to the **GREAT ARCHITECT OF THE UNIVERSE,** with his eyes lowered on the Bible, Cagliostro well knew how to inflame hearts and to conduct himself as a hierophant. Through apparitions, voices, seances of clairvoyance and predictions of the future, he showed himself to be a perfect thaumaturge.[41]

WHITE MAGIC IS DANGEROUS

In *The Mysteries of Magic: A Digest of the Writings of Eliphas Levi,* in the table of contents, we find the heading **"THAUMATURGICAL** Experience of Eliphas Levi." This "white magic" includes the following items:

I. Evocation of Apollonius of Tyana

II. Ghosts in Paris—The Magician and the Medium— Eliphas Levi and the Sect of Eugene Vintras

III. The Magician and the Sorcerer—Secret History of the Assassination of the Archbishop of Paris[42]

Remember that **LEVI WAS ALSO A MASON.** S. R. Parchment in his book, *Ancient Operative Masonry*, reveals this about thaumaturgy:

> On this aspect of the theurgic art volumes could be written; but since the writer as a chela [disciple] of the Operative School of Phree Messens [Freemasons] is interested only in the promulgation of the philosophy of *high magic*, he deems it unnecessary to go further into the diabolical side of magic, which would only stimulate the emotions of perverted souls, and might be instrumental in leading others into the clutches of the black magicians, from whose embrace few are able to extricate themselves. [Emphasis in the original][43]

It is quite obvious that this "white magic" is extremely dangerous, yet this type of magic is part of what is embodied in the Cabalistic doctrine.

Arthur Edward Waite, another **MASON AND OCCULTIST,**[44] wrote a large book entitled *The Holy Kabbalah*. He acknowledges: "It must be admitted that the term Kabbalah was applied early in its history to some forms of mediaeval **MAGICAL** practice."[45] He also plainly stated that the Cabala "is described

most adequately as a system of **THEOSOPHY.**"[46]
Later he adds that:

> ...there was a so-called Practical and Thaumaturgical
> Kabbalah which not only belongs to Magic but
> has helped to create its forbidden arts in the
> West....We owe our mediaeval **WITCHCRAFT**
> chiefly to this source; we owe also our mediaeval
> **DEMONOLOGY....**[47]

"There is no doubt that Ceremonial Magic in the
West owes its typical processes and its peculiar
complexion to Kabbalism...."[48]

MASONRY AND THE CABALA

Other Masons have written favorably about the
Cabala. F. De P. Castells brags that his book, *The
Genuine Secrets in Freemasonry Prior to A.D. 1717,*
gives "the final and crowning proof of our thesis
that **FREEMASONRY IS KABBALISM IN ANOTHER
GARB.**"[49] Pike boasts that "Masonry is a search
after Light. That search leads us directly back, as
you see, to the **KABALAH.**"[50] He then states: "The
**KABALAH IS THE KEY OF THE OCCULT
SCIENCES....**"[51]

Paul Foster Case was a Mason and Golden Dawn
member.[52] He is "known to students of **OCCULTISM**
as the outstanding authority of **TAROT, QABALAH,
ALCHEMY** and related subjects of the Western
OCCULT Tradition."[53] In his book, *The Masonic
Letter G,* he explains "that Masonry cannot be fully
appreciated or understood without knowledge of the
Qabalist Tree of Life and its insight into the true
nature of man and of the Cosmos."[54]

Albert Mackey, a 33° Mason, mentions that:

...some acquaintance with [the Sephiroth of the Kabalah—Rex R. Hutchens], therefore, seems to be necessary to the Freemason who desires to penetrate into the more abstruse arcana of his Order.[55]

TREE OF LIFE

The Sephiroth are ten attributes, manifestations, or emanations of the Cabalistic supreme essence of God who is called En-Soph (also spelled En-Sof, Ein-Soph, Ein-Sof; Ayn Sof; Eiyn Sof; Ain Soph, Ainsoph, Aur en soph, etc.).[56] The names of the 10 emanations (which may vary from group to group) are: Crown, Wisdom, Understanding, Mercy, Severity, Beauty, Victory, Glory, Foundation, and Kingdom. These ten manifestations are drawn in a diagram called the Tree of Life.

[It] consists of ten circles, connected by twenty-two lines. The circles represent ten aspects or phases of the Divine Emanation. They are numbered from 1 to 10, and are called Sephiroth, or Numerations. The twenty-two lines which link these ten circles to one another are said to represent the letters of the Hebrew alphabet, and the forces corresponding to those letters. The whole Tree, with its ten numbers and twenty-two letters, represents the thirty-two paths of wisdom.[57]

When Adam and Eve ate of the Tree of the Knowledge of Good and Evil, God put them out of the Garden of Eden so that they would not partake of the Tree of Life, yet this is the Tree that the Cabalists use for their drawings. They believe that

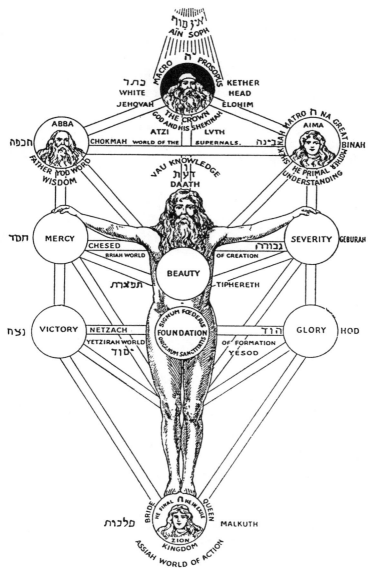

THE SACRED TREE OF THE SEPHIROTH

by advancing through the different stages of this
Tree of Life, an individual can partake of godhood.[58]

You should also recall Baphomet, the Goat of
Mendes, who is represented by the inverted pentagram.
We are told that the pentagram on his forehead represents
"Light and the Cabala, the Tree of Life...."[59]

In light of what has been previously covered, it
is no surprise to learn that there is also a sexual
connotation connected to the Cabalistic Tree of Life.
Masonic author, A. E. Waite, reveals:

> [I]t follows that Wisdom and Understanding,
> otherwise, CHOKMAH and BINAH, the second
> and third SEPHIROTH in the Tree of Life, are
> in a state of union, which is obvious by the nature
> of things; and it is shewn elsewhere in the ZOHAR
> that this union or marriage produces a Son, who
> in fact is Divine Knowledge. [Emphasis in the
> original][60]

SEX IS THE CENTRAL ROOT

The Zohar (meaning "Book of Splendor"[61]) is a
Cabalistic book of "esoteric interpretations of Scripture
combine[d] with mysticism, magic, and astrology."[62]
Waite adds:

> The doctrine of sex in the ZOHAR is...a Key
> general to the House of Doctrine: all other teaching
> in the great Theosophical Miscellany may be said
> to encompass it....It is the central root which I
> have mentioned, and from this root the Tree of
> Knowledge grows. [Emphasis in the original][63]

Did you notice that the "doctrine of sex" is so
important to the Cabala that it is considered to be
the "central root"?

Moshe Idel, in his book, *Kabbalah,* concurs: "One of the striking characteristics of Kabbalistic theosophy is the strong role played by erotic and sexual motifs; they recur repeatedly in Kabbalistic works...."[64]

We've already covered a number of symbols used in the Eastern Star ritual and have noted their sexual connotations. As previously mentioned, the jewel worn by the Worthy Patron in the Eastern Star is a Square and Compass.[65] This badge, "an emblem of the relationship existing between the Masonic fraternity and the Order of the Eastern Star,"[66] symbolizes "the human reproductive organs, locked in coitus...."[67] Seeing the connection between the Cabala, Masonry, and sex, it's no surprise to find Masonic author, Rex R. Hutchens, claiming: "The point here is simply that the Square and Compasses of the Symbolic Lodge may be interpreted in a Kabalistic way...."[68]

Where did the Cabala originate? Christian D. Ginsburg relates:

The Kabbalah was first taught by God himself to a select company of angels, who formed a theosophic school in Paradise. After the fall the angels most graciously communicated this heavenly doctrine to the disobedient child of earth, to furnish the protoplasts with the means of returning to their pristine nobility and felicity. From Adam it passed over to Noah, and then to Abraham, the friend of God, who emigrated with it to Egypt, where the patriarch allowed a portion of this mysterious doctrine to ooze out.[69]

Interesting! The only angel the Bible mentions who was around Adam and Eve when they fell was Lucifer, the serpent. It is evidently Lucifer, then, who is credited with teaching the Cabala to mankind!

In spite of the **OCCULTISM AND SEXUAL IMPLICATIONS OF THE CABALA,** Rob Morris, the founder of the Eastern Star, had a **CABALISTIC MOTTO** that he wanted to work into his organization. This is part of Morris' own account:

> The colors, the emblems, the floral wreaths, the esotery proper to these five heroines, were easy of invention. They seemed to fall ready-made into my hands. The only piece of mechanism difficult to fit into the construction was the cabalistic motto, but this occurred to me in ample time for use.[70]

You can see that Morris was determined to use the Cabalistic Motto—even though he had encountered difficulty in trying to incorporate it into the Eastern Star ritual.

F.A.T.A.L.

What is the Cabalistic Motto? In the *Greenwood Encyclopedia of American Institutions* we find:

> The emblem of the OES [Order of the Eastern Star] is the five-pointed star with a pentagon in the star's center. The pentagon in turn has an altar with an open Bible in its center. Within the borders of the pentagon are the letters F.A.T.A.L. These letters stand for a Cabalistic message: "Fairest Among Thousands, Altogether Lovely." Moreover, juxtaposing these five letters spells FATAL, which is intended to remind each initiate that "it would be fatal to the character of any lady" were she to divulge OES secrets....[71]

Below is the "Recognition Test," which is how an Eastern Star woman is examined to see if she is a member.

Q. Are you a member of the Order of the Eastern Star?

A. We have seen His star in the East.

Q. For what came you here?

A. And are come to worship Him.

Q. Have you the **CABBALISTIC WORD?**

A. I have.

Q. Will you give it to me?

A. I will, with your assistance.

Q. Begin.

A. No, you begin.

Q. Begin you.

A. F.

Q. A.

A. T.

Q. A.

A. L. Fatal.

Q. Has that word any significance?

A. It has, two. First, that it would be fatal to the character of any lady for truth, who should disclose the secrets of these degrees unlawfully. Second, each of the letters of this word stands for one or more words, which words make the **CABBALISTIC MOTTO.**

Q. Have you the **CABBALISTIC MOTTO?**
A. I have.
Q. Will you give it to me?
A. I will, with your assistance.
Q. Begin.
A. No, you begin.
Q. Begin you.
A. Fairest.
Q. Among.
A. Thousands.
Q. Altogether.
A. Lovely, Fairest among thousands, altogether lovely."[72]

Each of the five women represented by the star points in the Eastern Star is given the title of "Fairest Among Thousands, Altogether Lovely."[73] (Originally, it was "Fairest Among Ten Thousand, and Altogether Lovely."[74]) The printed lecture, which has replaced the Cabalistic Motto with asterisks, is given as follows:

JEPHTHAH'S DAUGHTER, because she devoted her life to preserve her father from eternal infamy, was the *******

RUTH, because she forsook home, friends, and all things, in a heathen land, to seek out the people of God, was the *******

ESTHER, because she offered her crown and life to preserve her people, was *******

MARTHA, because amidst all the despair of death and the woe of desolation, she preserved her faith in the Word of God, was the *******

ELECTA, because in her martyrdom for Christ's sake she hesitated not to sacrifice all things that love can prize or friendship cherish, was the *******[75]

REPLACING CHRIST

The phrase, "Fairest among thousands, altogether lovely" is a description that has been applied to Christ by the ancient writers.[76] Nevertheless, the Eastern Star bestows this title upon their initiates. You see, this is putting the Eastern Star member in the place of Christ by attributing this expression to each individual. Of course, this is not the only place where this is done. Each of the five star points also has a specific emblem that helps to compose each degree:

1. The Open Bible is appropriate to Jephthah's Daughter as the symbol of obedience to the word of God.

2. The Bunch of Lilies is appropriate to Ruth, as the Lily of the Valley.

3. The Sun is appropriate to Esther, as the effulgent sun is that symbol of crowned majesty.

4. The Lamb is appropriate to Martha, as the symbol of innocence, faith and humility.

5. The Lion is appropriate to Electa, as the symbol of the courage and strength which sustained her during her severe trials.[77]

Once again, symbols and phrases that have been applied to Christ have now been assigned to the Eastern Star ladies. Christ is the "Word of God." Revelation 19:13 states this about Christ: "His name is called The Word of God." In the Song of Solomon we find: "I am the rose of Sharon, and the lily of the valleys" (Song of Solomon 2:1). Malachi 4:2 reveals: "But unto you that fear my name shall the Sun of righteousness arise with healing in His wings...." Many verses refer to Christ as "the Lamb of God." For example, John exclaimed: "Behold the Lamb of God, which taketh away the sin of the world" (John 1:29). See also: John 1:36; Revelation 5:6; 7:17; 14:10; 15:3; 19:9; 21:22; and 22:1, 3. In Revelation 5:5 we see that Christ is referred to as the "Lion of the tribe of Juda." So, although many of these woman are innocent and unaware of what has taken place, they have taken upon themselves names that belong to Christ **ALONE**. Even in the book, *History of the Order of the Eastern Star,* it is admitted that these titles belong to Christ.[78]

A General History of the Order of the Eastern Star, written by Willis D. Engle, one of the early workers in the organization, also shows that these are not just random symbols but that they refer to Christ. He writes:

> **THEY ALL ALLUDE TO CHRIST,** Who is the light and key to the Eastern Star, and Who is the Word of God; the Lily of the Valley; The Sun of Righteousness; the Lamb of God; and the Lion of the Tribe of Judah.[79]

With references to Christ, the Eastern Star looks like a good, religious, and even a Christian, organization, but as we have previously noted, this guise is only a cover-up. If most women knew what was actually going on behind the scenes of the Eastern Star, they would never have joined, so to keep up the facade, this organization is presented as a wholesome, outstanding, and distinguished order for ladies.

DEADLY 13

Is there a more sinister meaning to the word "FATAL" than meets the eye? One day I decided to add up the letters numerologically and was amazed to discover that they totaled 13. In numerology, the word "FATAL" would be figured like this:

F = 6
A = 1
T = 2
A = 1
L = 3
   13 (Total of 6 + 1 + 2 + 1 + 3)[80]

Arthur Lyons remarks:

Since 13 is the number following the perfect cycle of 12, it is symbolic of death or the unknown. In cartomancy, the ace of spades, the thirteenth card in the suit, is in many cases a symbol of death.[81]

Even the word "FATAL" means "deadly" or "lethal." Dick Sutphen, a New Ager, comments:

Thirteen has had negative connotations for many, being feared as an unlucky omen or the symbol of death. Indeed, it does represent death, but not in the ordinary sense—death is merely a change of form. The thirteen used so significantly in American heraldry signifies the change, the **DEATH,**

Arcanum Number XIII

Death

Transformation of the Body

TO THE OLD WAYS and the **BEGINNING OF THE NEW ORDER** of the Ages.[82]

Notice that the number 13 represents "death to the old ways and the beginning of the New Order of the Ages"! It's no wonder, then, that the Scottish Rite Masonry's magazine was called *The New Age*. We are also informed that the "number 13 has great significance in Masonic symbolism...."[83]

DEATH AND RESURRECTION

Furthermore, in the Tarot deck, the thirteenth card is called "Death" or the "Skeleton Reaper."[84]

In the Waite pack, a skeleton in armour rides a white horse and carries a banner with a white rose signifying life. On the horizon beyond him is the gateway of immortality. Most other packs show a skeleton with a scythe, but the Death card does not necessarily stand for physical death—rather, for the death of the old self followed by rebirth, renewal. Most occult fraternities' initiation rituals include a symbolic death and rebirth; (as does the Wiccan second degree with its story of the Descent of the Goddess and her conquest of Death) so card 13 may also be said to symbolize Initiation.[85]

Needless to say, Masonry, as an occult fraternity, also includes a symbolic death and resurrection ritual in the third degree.

Returning to the Cabala, we find that it is also "a **TECHNIQUE FOR ACHIEVING SALVATION.**"[86] The Eastern Star, too, is a means for achieving salvation. One of the ceremonies that appeared in the July 1913 issue of the *National-Mizpah Eastern Star Magazine,* had the following poem:

"With letters **CABALISTIC**—
Representing a beauteous whole—...
With a radiance pure and bright,
Shines forth our Eastern Star.

A Star, a Square, an Angle—
A Principle, deep and true—
A march, mid labyrinth tangle
With colors of symbolic hue,
And then the Obligation
Which lifts us above the clod—
The **OATH OF INITIATION**
That **CREATES US SONS OF GOD.**"[87]

If you noticed the poem carefully, you can see that it is the oath of initiation that supposedly makes us a son of God. There is no mention of having our sins forgiven, there is no mention of the atonement that Christ made for us on the cross, there is no mention of confession to God for the sins we've committed. No! According to this poem, it is through the Eastern Star oath that we become a child of God. Yes, we can see the correlation between the

Cabala and the Eastern Star but there is no connection between the Word of God and the Eastern Star. Christ is mentioned just enough to make people believe that this organization is a Christian group, but He is not mentioned in a way that would lead people to the cross for salvation through His sacrifice on Calvary.

Of course, the teaching of a way of salvation other than through Christ is typical of the Masonic lodge. They teach that salvation is obtained through good works. Swinburne Clymer candidly admits in *The Mysticism of Masonry:*

> **MASONRY DOES NOT TEACH SALVATION BY FAITH NOR THE VICARIOUS ATONEMENT.** Go through its degrees, study the history as taught by its recognized authorities and you cannot find that it ever countenances these doctrines.[88]

He then gives a quotation that the so-called "Father of Light" gave to his disciple: "[T]he time is coming and now is, when they may no longer foolishly say, 'this man will save me, or that man will take my sins upon himself.'"[89]

MASONRY'S PLAN OF SALVATION

A. T. C. Pierson, another Mason, claims that **MASONRY "MUST ULTIMATELY BE THE SOLE RELIGION** of the human race, because it is the only religion in which the plan of salvation is clearly developed."[90] Masonic writer, J. D. Buck, proclaims:

> Every soul must "work out its own salvation".... Salvation by faith and the vicarious atonement were not taught, as now interpreted, by Jesus, nor are these doctrines taught in the exoteric Scriptures. They are later and ignorant perversions

of the original doctrines. In the Early Church, as in the Secret Doctrine, there was not one Christ for the whole world, but a potential Christ in every man.[91]

Lynn Perkins, another Mason, states:

Masonry teaches that redemption and salvation are both the power and the responsibility of the individual Mason. Saviors like Hiram Abiff can and do show the way, but men must always follow and demonstrate, each for himself, his **POWER TO SAVE HIMSELF,** to build his own spiritual fabric in his own time and way. **EVERY MAN** in essence **IS HIS OWN SAVIOR AND REDEEMER; FOR IF HE DOES NOT SAVE HIMSELF, HE WILL NOT BE SAVED.**[92]

In *Clausen's Commentaries on Morals and Dogma,* written by 33° Mason, Henry C. Clausen, who was the head of the Southern Jurisdiction of Masonry, we find: "This taught the plain lesson of **PERSONAL REDEMPTION THROUGH INDIVIDUAL VIRTUE.**"[93] Yet another Masonic writer, Forrest D. Haggard, contends: "The salvation of the individual is the end goal in most Organized Religions and men enter to 'save themselves.' Masonry is certainly based upon this principle."[94] Many other examples of this Masonic teaching of salvation by an individual's works could be given, but it should be clear that the doctrine of salvation by faith in Christ alone has been cast aside for the "filthy rags" of our own righteousness (see Isaiah 64:6). Romans 10:3 plainly shows that "they being ignorant of God's righteousness, and going about to establish their own righteousness, have not submitted themselves unto the righteousness of God."

12. IS DEATH A VICTOR?

When a member of the Eastern Star dies, the Eastern Star may perform a service for the deceased upon request to do so.[1] A closer look at this ritual uncovers some interesting points that need to be considered.

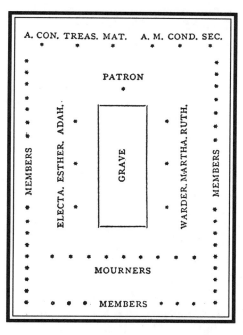

First of all, we are told that the "members of the Chapter will form a **SQUARE** round the grave...."[2] J. S. M. Ward, a Masonic author, relates that "[b]y itself the Square represents matter, and hence our bodies."[3] The burial ritual says basically the same thing: "We are often told that in the world of matter all bodies are subject to the laws of mutual attraction and repulsion."[4] There is a deeper meaning, however, to the symbolism of the square, for in the *Pocket Encyclopedia of Masonic Symbols*, we find: "The

SQUARE, IN MASONRY, may have—does have—more than one interpretation."[5] The *Pocket Masonic Dictionary* asserts that the oblong square is the "[r]itualistic term for form of lodge."[6]

AMENTA IS HELL

Albert Churchward, a Masonic author, explains the symbolism of the square like this:

> Take the oblong **SQUARE** first (a **MASONIC** term). The form of Lodges is oblong **SQUARE**....This was the Heaven of Atum [an Egyptian god] based or founded on the four quarters of the **SOLSTICES,** and the **EQUINOXES** which followed the making of Amenta.[7]

Elsewhere he states: "Our [the Masonic] Lodge likens Amenta."[8] Earlier in this book, he informed us that **AMENTA IS THE EGYPTIAN UNDERWORLD OR HELL,**[9] and here he is comparing the **MASONIC LODGE** to **AMENTA!** Amazing, isn't it?! Churchward also discloses a little bit more about Amenta and one of its residents. He mentions that **ABADDON** is the Hebrew name for the Egyptian **SERPENT** Abut-Unti which lived in the **ABYSS.** In fact, according to an Egyptian ritual, Abaddon is the "beast that was taken and cast alive in the lake of fire, or in the red lake, the pool of the damned in the fiery pit of the 'recess' in Amenta."[10] Isn't this fascinating? Amenta has a "lake of fire" and contains the "damned," yet we are told that the **MASONIC LODGE REPRESENTS THIS PLACE!!** Furthermore, **ABADDON,** the beast that is cast into this lake of fire, just happens to be a **SACRED NAME** in the 17th degree of Masonry (the Knights of the East and West).[11]

The Bible also refers to Abaddon. Revelation 9:11 informs us that the **DEMONS IN HELL "HAD A KING OVER THEM,** which is the angel of the bottomless pit, **WHOSE NAME** in the Hebrew tongue **IS ABADDON...."** Abaddon is the king over the demons, yet the Masons believe that Abaddon is a "sacred word" and brag that their Lodge is likened unto Abaddon's abode!

So, a **SQUARE** is formed around the deceased Eastern Star's grave. Does this square, like the Masonic square, also represent hell?

During the service the Patron intones: "Our beloved Sister has fallen in life's battle, acknowledged the supremacy of death, **YIELDED TO A VICTOR,** whom none can resist, and entered upon the **SLEEP THAT KNOWS NO WAKING."**[12] In an Eastern Star book entitled *The Ladies' Friend,* there is a discussion of an ancient Adoptive Degree of Masonry called the Mason's Daughter. During this lecture, the women are told that the Masons:

> ...are taught to look forward with hope and confidence to the opening scenes of eternity, to look upon death without fear or trembling, and **WELCOME THE GRIM TYRANT AS A KIND MESSENGER** sent by our Supreme Grand Master to conduct us to that Grand Lodge above where the Great Architect of the Universe presides.[13]

Let's pause and look at these last few sentences more closely. Notice that death is called **"A VICTOR"** in the burial service and that death should be **WELCOMED "AS A KIND MESSENGER."** What does the Bible teach about death? Good question! The answer can be found in I Corinthians 15:26 where we read: "The last **ENEMY** that shall be destroyed is death." Death, then, is not a "kind messenger" or a "victor" but our enemy. Contrary to Scripture, in

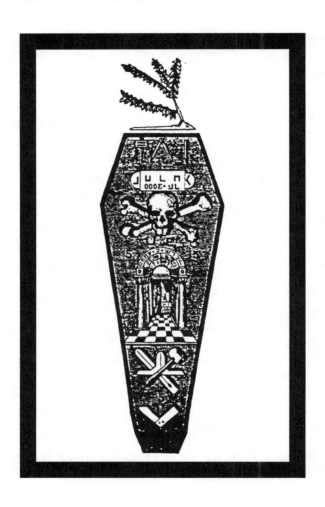

Symbolism of the Eastern Star, we find: **"DEATH IS A FRIEND** of ours...."[14]

DEATH IS NOT THE END

Another false teaching presented in this speech is that death is a "sleep that knows no waking." According to the Bible, there will be a waking from the sleep of death. Daniel 12:2 states: "[M]any of them that sleep in the dust of the earth shall awake, some to everlasting life, and some to everlasting contempt." John also explains that:

...the hour is coming, in the which all that are in the graves shall hear His voice, And shall come forth; they that have done good, unto the resurrection of life; and they that have done evil, unto the resurrection of damnation (John 5:28-29).

Death is not the end. "And death and hell were cast into the lake of fire. This is the second death. And whosoever was not found written in the book of life was cast into the lake of fire" (Revelation 20:14-15).

The lecture remarks about the "supremacy of death." The word "supremacy" implies "superiority over all others" or "supreme authority or power." Death, however, is not supreme for death itself shall be destroyed when Christ comes to reign over His kingdom (I Corinthians 15:24-28).

In spite of this lecture stating that death is a "sleep that knows no waking," the Eastern Star also teaches that "there is no death." In the memorial service, Adah, Martha, and Electa all state: "There is no death!"[15] Apollonius of Tyana also believed:

...that birth and death are only in appearance; that which separates itself from the *one* substance (the *one* Divine essence), and is caught up by matter, seems to be born; that, again, which releases itself from the bonds of matter, and is reunited with the one Divine Essence, seems to die. [Emphasis in the original][16]

Do you remember who Apollonius of Tyana was? He was the **OCCULTIST AND MAGICIAN** Eliphas

Levi claims to have called up from the dead.[17] Perhaps that is why when Adah, as she deposits her blue flower on the grave, says:

> Some believe that the **SOULS OF OUR DEPARTED FRIENDS RETURN AT TIMES,** when yearning is strong within them, and bring us consolation from heavenly sources; others, that our Divine Father makes them His messengers to save us from despair in those moments when our hearts sink within us.[18]

This is the teaching of **SPIRIT COMMUNICATION** or **COMMUNICATION WITH THE DEAD.** Eliphas Levi states: "For spiritists, in fact, there is no death."[19] Again, this is a practice strictly forbidden by God's Word. Deuteronomy 18:10-12 tells us:

> There shall not be found among you any one that maketh his son or his daughter to pass through the fire, or that useth divination, or an observer of times, or an enchanter, or a witch, Or a charmer, or **A CONSULTER WITH FAMILIAR SPIRITS,** or a wizard, or a **NECROMANCER.** For **ALL** that do these things are an **ABOMINATION** unto the Lord: and because of these abominations the Lord thy God doth drive them out from before thee.

Of course, Masonry, as well as the occultists, teach this **SAME** theory.[20] Joseph Fort Newton, a well-known Masonic author, claims:

> There is no death in nature; there is only living and living again. The earliest form of life is a tiny cell which does not die, but divides and multiplies life. When forms of life become more complex some cells become useless, and must be removed. Then death comes, not to hurt, but

to clear away the rubbish, that the stream of life may flow on....

There would be no life, if there were no death, for **DEATH IS THE FRIEND OF LIFE** and supports it. We live to die and die to live, like all things else. **DEATH IS THE MIRY ROAD BACK TO LIFE AGAIN,** and only by dying daily do we live at all. Nothing in nature dies or is lost, death being the dark room in which life changes its robes and marches on. Were it not for death, the stream of life would be clogged and stagnant, and there would be no advance. Such seems to be the meaning and **MINISTRY OF DEATH,** and it is not only benign, but full of hope.[21]

This is the belief in **REINCARNATION** which is being promoted here.

SALVATION THROUGH CHRIST—NOT WORKS

Another problem encountered in the burial service is that it is insinuated that all Eastern Star members go to heaven—although they may have never even professed to be a Christian. A **"SALVATION BY WORKS"** theory can be detected in one ritual which states: "As she in her life exemplified the virtues of those chosen servants of God—the lovely heroines of the Order—so surely shall be her reward."[22] Another ritual book mentions that the deceased "has passed into the fulness of immortal life and now abides in the mercy and care of our Heavenly Father."[23] Yet another book, the *Order of the Eastern Star,* by F. A. Bell, indicates that all are saved:

> She is ready for that Divine summons, "Come ye blessed of my Father, receive the kingdom prepared for you from the beginning of the world."

> Our sister walked among us in constancy and with courage....She has finished her course in faith, and she has laid hold on eternal life. Before our Altar she studied with us the high principles of our order, and "hast professed a good profession before many witnesses." In her life she exemplified the noble virtues taught in our Order....

> Having served God with constancy on earth she will be united hereafter with the blessed company of His saints.[24]

There is no mention here of a person ever accepting Christ as her personal Savior. The only item necessary for her to obtain eternal life seems to be that she "studied with us [the Eastern Star] the high principles of our order...." In fact, the lecture even adds: "Who can doubt that her spirit, freed, may have an opportunity to practice these teachings in a grander and fuller sense."[25] This, of course, insinuates the possibility that the Eastern Star member may be able to have the privilege of continuing the Eastern Star teachings in her afterlife.

Masonry, too, seems to teach that every Mason is admitted to heaven regardless of the kind of life he lived while on earth. In one *Short Talk Bulletin* we find:

> ...**MASONRY SYMBOLICALLY INITIATES US INTO THE ETERNAL LIFE** here and now, makes us citizens of eternity in time....Here is the deepest secret Masonry has to teach—that we are immortal here and now; that death is nothing to the soul; that eternity is today.[26]

In other words, according to this lecture, the **MASONIC INITIATION IS WHAT GIVES ETERNAL LIFE!**

WHO ARE THE UNSAINTED COWANS?

George Oliver, a Masonic scholar, explains:

> The general resurrection has been embodied in the third degree of Masonry; and the reward of duty is pointed out in our glorious Symbol. That is the great harvest when the wheat and the tares, the worthy Mason and the unsainted cowan shall be gathered together for final separation.[27]

Notice that the Mason's reward is heaven but that the cowans (those **OUTSIDE** of Masonry) will be separated in the harvest. Oliver continues:

> The Great Architect of the Universe being thus seated on the Cloudy Canopy...and amidst the most profound silence the Books will be opened where the actions of all mankind have been registered by the finger of God. And from their evidence the whole human race will be separated into **TWO DISTINCT CLASSES;** viz., the **FAITHFUL BROTHER** will occupy the one, and the **OBTRUSIVE COWAN** the other. The former will be approved, and placed in the north-east, on the right-hand side of the Judge, as successful candidates for his mercy;...while the latter will be placed on his left hand as candidates rejected.

> The Judge will then proceed to pass sentence on both which can never be reversed. He will declare his approbation of those good and worthy brethren who stand at his right hand; applauding their Faith, their Hope, and their Charity; and give them immediate possession of that holy place

which is veiled in clouds and darkness beyond the summit of the Ladder. And he will declare the reason why they are thus distinguished. It is because they have accomplished those moral and religious duties which are recommended in the Lectures of **MASONRY....**"Come ye blessed of my Father, enter into the joy of your Lord!"

While this is going on, what are the feelings of the **IRRECLAIMABLE COWANS** who have been placed on the left hand...? TGAOTU [The Grand Architect of the Universe], therefore, after condemning their falsehood, their profanity, and their unrepented sins, pronounced the final sentence which consigns them to everlasting punishment.

He then graciously proceeds to justify the sentence. It is because they have been reprobate and profane— atheists and unbelievers....And therefore he consigns them to that place of darkness and despair prepared for the devil and his angels; while his faithful followers are transferred by the angelic host, who are in attendance for that very purpose, from their exalted situation in the north-east, to the Grand Lodge above, where they will exist for ever in perfect charity and perfect happiness.[28]

While this may sound somewhat like evangelical, Christian teaching, you must understand that it is not. First of all, the two groups into which these people will be separated are the "worthy Masons" and the "unsainted cowans" or the "profane." It is now necessary to analyze just what is meant by the "cowans" and the "profane." We are not left in the dark as Masons are quick to tell us that the cowan is an outsider. For instance, Arthur E. Powell, in *The Magic of Freemasonry,* explains:

The Tyling of the Lodge—the first, constant and last care of every Freemason—affords a sense of security and of privacy, keeping off the prying or critical eyes of the world of **COWANS WITHOUT,** and giving a Mason the opportunity of "letting go" the reins of restraint, and of being his real self, that Higher Self which he is afraid of shewing, freely and frankly, anywhere but within the sacred precincts of the Temple, where men trust him and call him Brother. For in the name of Brother there is high **MAGIC.**[29]

In *Duncan's Ritual of Freemasonry,* we are told that the Masons "assemble in a room well **GUARDED FROM ALL COWANS** and eavesdroppers...."[30] J. S. M. Ward, in *Freemasonry and the Ancient Gods,* explains how he "endeavored to avoid anything [in his book] which would tell a **COWAN** what our signs actually are...."[31] Albert Churchward relates that the ancient brethren met "on the highest hill or lowest vale or any other secret place, the better to **GUARD AGAINST COWANS AND ENEMIES....**"[32] In one *Short Talk Bulletin,* we are informed that "[o]nly by strict adherence to these principles can Masons be sure that **NO COWAN OR EAVESDROPPER SITS IN THEIR LODGES.**"[33] Many other Masonic sources agree,[34] so it is easy to see that the **COWAN IS SOMEONE WHO IS OUTSIDE THE MASONIC FRATERNITY.**

Likewise, the "profane" are those who are not Masons. Carl H. Claudy, in his Masonic book, *Masonic Harvest,* writes: "In the Masonic sense a 'profane' is one not initiated."[35] Clearly, then, the separation that Oliver believes takes place will be a **SEPARATION BETWEEN THE MASONS AND THE NON-MASONS,** with the Masons being rewarded with heaven and the non-Masons being lost.

Another erroneous teaching can be found in an opening ceremony listed in Bell's *Order of the Eastern Star*, where an "Opening Ode" contains these words:

> Keep in view the Lodge supernal,
> Life is love enthroned in heaven,
> Where the true light never wavers,
> And our mortal sins forgiven."[36]

This song gives the impression that our mortal sins will be forgiven in heaven, giving us a second chance after death for forgiveness. The Bible, however, tells us: "It is appointed unto men once to die, but after this the judgment" (Hebrews 9:27).

In the memorial service that is held for all those who have died in the past year, there is a blanket statement that all the "friends whom we mourn live in unspoken bliss" and are "amid the beauties of Paradise."[37] In the prayer of the burial service are these words: "Thou hast decreed that we all shall die and come to dust. Thou hast also decreed that we shall rise from death to everlasting life."[38] Again, it is inferred that all those who die will be raised to everlasting life, but the Bible clearly makes a distinction between those who have received Christ as Lord and Savior and those who have not. It is on this basis, and this basis alone, that a person can ever hope to enter heaven. Revelation 21:27 explains:

> And there shall in no wise enter into it [heaven] any thing that defileth, neither whatsoever worketh abomination, or maketh a lie: but they which are written in the Lamb's book of life.

13. SECRECY AND THE EASTERN STAR

Is the Eastern Star a secret society? *The Authorized Standard Ritual of the Order of the Eastern Star of New York,* a book published by the Grand Chapter of the Order of the Eastern Star, gives us the answer: "It is a **SECRET** organization with signs and passwords peculiar to itself, which are held sacred by the members."[1] These secrets cannot be bestowed until after the initiation fee has been paid by the candidate.[2] During the initiation itself, the candidate is asked by the Conductress: "Are you prepared to undergo the necessary trials and assume our obligation of **SECRECY?**"[3]

Before any of the secrets are conveyed to the new member, the Patron informs the initiate:

The Order of the Eastern Star inculcates practical lessons, designed to impress upon all who unite with it, the important duties we owe to one another....By means of **SECRET SIGNS AND PASSWORDS,** which we possess, we are enabled to recognize one another wherever we may meet. We are willing to put you in possession of these secret signs and passwords that you too may be recognized as a member of the Order....It consists of a series of solemn pledges which you must give to this Chapter and by which you will bind yourself, not only to preserve the most sacred **SECRECY** respecting the work of the Order, but also to the faithful performance of the duties which devolve upon you as a member of the Order. It will be necessary for you to assume this obligation before you can participate in our labors or enjoy our privileges. With this knowledge of our aims and the requirements of the Order, are you now willing to assume the Covenant of Adoption?[4]

PERPETUAL COVENANT

This **COVENANT OF SECRECY IS A PERPETUAL AGREEMENT,** according to the Eastern Star. One of the landmarks states: "A covenant of **SECRECY,** voluntarily assumed, is perpetual; from the force of such obligation there is no release."[5] The candidate must swear to this obligation, but she is not told exactly what she is to uphold. She is forced to pledge and bind herself to secrecy even though she has no idea what type of oath she is promising to keep. The same, of course, is true in Masonry. The Mason is told by the Worshipful Master:

> ...before you can be permitted to advance any farther in Masonry, it becomes my duty to inform you, that you must take upon yourself a solemn oath or obligation, appertaining to this degree, which I, as Master of this Lodge, assure you will not materially interfere with the duty that you owe to your God, yourself, family, country, or neighbor. Are you willing to take such an oath?[6]

The Mason's obligation then includes the following:

> ...I will always hail, **EVER CONCEAL, AND NEVER REVEAL,** any of the arts, parts, or points of the hidden mysteries of Ancient Free Masonry, which may have been, or hereafter shall be, **AT THIS TIME, OR ANY FUTURE PERIOD,** communicated to me....[7]

This is an unfair oath for anyone to have to swear to, for he does not know what will be communicated to him in the future degrees. The Mason, taking the oath of the 3°, **PROMISES TO CONCEAL ALL CRIMES COMMITTED BY A FELLOW MASON** except those of treason and murder.[8] By the 7° of Masonry, the candidate has to promise that he:

> ...will assist a Companion Royal Arch Mason when I see him engaged in any difficulty, and will espouse his cause so far as to extricate him from the same, **WHETHER HE BE RIGHT OR WRONG.**[9]

In the 13° the oath is taken to the effect that **ALL CRIMES ARE TO BE CONCEALED, INCLUDING MURDER AND TREASON.**[10]

This, of course, means that if a Mason has committed murder and the judge is also a Mason, the judge is obligated by his Masonic oath to set the murderer free, even if it results in placing the blame on an innocent person! In fact, this command is given in one handbook:

> **YOU MUST CONCEAL ALL THE CRIMES OF YOUR BROTHER MASONS...AND SHOULD YOU BE SUMMONED AS A WITNESS AGAINST A BROTHER MASON BE ALWAYS SURE TO SHIELD HIM....IT MAY BE PERJURY TO DO THIS, IT IS TRUE, BUT YOU'RE KEEPING YOUR OBLIGATIONS.**[11]

Although the Eastern Star members do not take such blatant and perjurious oaths, it must be remembered that **NO WOMAN** can become a member of this organization **UNLESS** one of their close male relatives has taken some of these oaths! It must also be noted that the Eastern Star "has come to be looked upon as a 'strong right arm of Masonry.'"[12] The women are reminded a number of times throughout the Eastern Star ritual that they are **CONNECTED TO MASONRY.**[13] It is through the granting of the Eastern Star degrees, that the **"LADIES ARE ADOPTED INTO THE MASONIC COMMUNION,"**[14] so even though the women may not swear to such **ILLEGAL** obligations, they are promoting and endorsing such oaths by association with Masonry (although most likely ignorantly and unknowingly so).

A LEGAL OATH?

Is such an oath as this a legal contract? Can such a contract be legally binding? According to *Law and Banking,* we find: "In studying contracts, we observed that if one is induced to enter into a contract by fraud, he may rightfully refuse to perform."[15] We also note: "Agreements that disrupt or subvert the workings of government are, of course, illegal and unenforceable."[16] Legally, then, a person who has taken such an oath should not be required to abide by it since it would be subversive to our criminal system.

Is this a Scriptural contract? Let's see what the Bible teaches. We find in Leviticus that if an individual would sin through ignorance and if the sin would later be brought to his attention, when he knew that he had committed sin, he was required to bring a sacrifice to atone for his sins (Leviticus 4:2-31). Since Jesus is now our sacrifice, when we realize that we have done something that we should not have done, we are to "confess our sins [and] He is faithful and just to forgive us our sins, and to cleanse us from all unrighteousness" (I John 1:9). So, the Eastern Star and Masonic oaths are contrary to the legal and Scriptural aspects, therefore they are not binding upon the person who has realized the wrong of such an obligation. Furthermore, the Bible tells us that we are not to swear at all (Matthew 5:34-37).

We also find that the children of Israel provoked the Lord often with their idolatry. How did they do it? Secretly, of course:

> And the children of Israel did **SECRETLY** those things that were not right against the Lord their God, and they built them high places in all their cities, from the tower of the watchmen to the fenced city (II Kings 17:9).

Secrecy of this nature is not pleasing to God. Also, if the Eastern Star and Masonic organizations are such wonderful, religious groups which promote moral precepts and Biblical truths, why would there be a need for such secrecy? The answer is, there wouldn't be such a need! If the Eastern Star members only portray the five women from the Bible why can no one enter the Lodge room and see the drama? The Bible, after all, is an open book and if these five degrees are taken from the Bible, why not share such Biblical knowledge with anyone who would be interested in learning more about God's Word?

The members may say that they don't want anyone else learning the secret grips and passwords so that an outsider (or "profane" person) would not impose on the group and request help. This, however, is not a good enough reason, for they are not only to keep the grips and passwords secret, but they are to keep the ceremony itself secret as well.[17] Any truly moral organization in a free society would not have to meet in secret and keep their ceremonies secret.

Actually, there is a **REASON** for the passwords. Masonic writer, J. S. M. Ward, explains the following about Masonic passwords:

> Why passwords at all? Here we wander into a strange field, no less than that of old world **MAGIC,**

I think. The candidate entered the Entered Apprentice Lodge from the outside world. Prior to his entry, the Lodge has been opened by a peculiar ceremony—a ceremony which in the technical language of **MAGIC AND THE OCCULT,** raises the vibrations of those present...they...are raised to a higher key and force is generated....All I need say further is that such passwords are universal in the great mystery rites, ancient and modern.[18]

PAGANISM CONTINUES

Additionally, to make sure that their **SECRECY** is well-protected, the Eastern Stars, as do the Masons, have a guard with a sword stationed outside the Lodge room door.[19] The guard may be a woman but a man is preferred. The badge of office for the guard is the "Cross-swords within the Star."[20] During the "Opening Ceremonies" the following exchange takes place:

W. M. [Worthy Matron]—Where is our Sentinel stationed?

A. M. [Associate Matron]—Outside the closed door.

W. M.—What are his duties? and explain his badge of office.

A. M.—To protect the Chapter against the introduction of improper persons. His badge of office, the Cross-swords within the Star, emblems of protection, admonishes him that upon his watchful care depends our security against interruption, without which the solemnity of our

If the Sentinel is a lady, she will wear the five-colored sash, but should the Sentinel be a gentleman, the five-colored collar is proper.

proceedings would be destroyed and all **SECRECY** lost.[21]

You see, this type of **SECRECY WAS PRACTICED IN THE ANCIENT MYSTERIES—THE PAGAN AND OCCULTIC OBSERVANCES OF THE HEATHEN.** Secrecy was enforced in order to cover up their wicked rituals because they knew that if the public had been made aware of what was going on, there would have been repercussions. The Egyptians even worshiped a **GOD OF SECRECY AND SILENCE** whose name was Harpocrates (or Harpokrates).[22] "In early youth he was frequently called 'the infant Horus'— Harpakhrad—or Harpokrates."[23] Horus, you should recall, was the offspring of Isis and Osiris.

[Harpocrates] was painted naked, and in the figure of a boy, crowned with an Egyptian mitre...he held in his left hand a horn of plenty, whilst a finger of his right hand was upon his lip, thereby commanding silence.[24]

Altars were reared to him and then wreathed in flowers.[25]

No wonder Masonic and Eastern Star members need secrecy—especially with such blasphemy as presented in a poem that J. S. M. Ward penned. Ward founded the Masonic Study Society and authored *The Entered Apprentice's Handbook*.[26] On page 1 of this book we find:

"Bacchus died and rose again,
On the Golden Syrian Plain;
Osiris rose from out his grave;
And thereby mankind did save;
Adonis likewise shed his blood
By the yellow Syrian flood,
Zoroaster brought to birth
Mithra from his cave of earth
And we to-day in Christian Lands
We with them can join hands."[27]

TAKE HEED!

Books containing the Eastern Star ritual are not to seen by other individuals, either. In *The Eastern Star: The Evolution from a Rite to an Order*, written by Mason Harold Van Buren Voorhis, we are informed: "The work contains no analyses of rituals or liturgies of the degrees of the Eastern Star. Such studies are not for general distribution."[28] Another book contained this warning:

TAKE HEED!...

We commit this volume to your care under the covenant-seal of secrecy. It must not be *lent, sold,* or wilfully *mislaid*. It must not be *copied* in whole or in part.

Copies placed in charge of Heleon [the personator of Jephthah], are for the use of the Pillars and Correspondents of this Constellation, and for no other persons; and upon its dissolution or the forfeiture of its Charter, they are to be immediately returned—carefully enveloped and sealed—to the Grand Secretary [as named on the title page—Jean M'Kee Kenaston]. *Vide! Audi! Tace!* (See! Hear! Keep silent.) [Emphasis in the original][29]

Elsewhere the following lengthy caution is given:

TAKE HEED!

Brother.

We commit this volume to your care under the covenant-seal of secrecy. It must not be *lent, sold*, or wilfully *mislaid*. It must not be *copied* in whole or in part.

Copies placed in charge of Heleon, are for the use of the Pillars and Correspondents of this Constellation, and for no other persons; and upon its dissolution or the forfeiture of its Charter, they are to be immediately returned — carefully enveloped and sealed — to the Grand Secretary [as named on the title page]. *Vide! Audi! Tace!* (See! Hear! Keep silent.)

Excerpt from <u>History of the Order of the Eastern Star</u> *by Jean M'Kee Kenaston.*

The...Books are delivered to Heleon under the following pledges:

1. That they are not to be sold, lent, or wilfully mislaid, that no portion of them is to be copied; and when not in use, that they are to be **KEPT UNDER LOCK AND KEY.**

Heleon will distribute those sent to him to the proper officers respectively, under the same binding pledges, who will be permitted to use them only for the purposes designated. **NONE** but Pillars and Correspondents and their legal successors **CAN HAVE ACCESS TO THEM.**

3. Pillars and Correspondents receiving them will commit their respective portions to memory as soon as possible.

4. THE FACT OF THE EXISTENCE OF SUCH BOOKS IS NOT TO BE MADE KNOWN TO THE PUBLIC.

5. Upon the dissolution of the Constellation or forfeiture of the Charter, they are to be carefully enveloped, sealed, and returned to the V.E. [Very Enlightened] Grand Secretary of the Supreme Constellation, as named on the title page.

6. They are always to be considered to be the property of the Supreme Constellation, to be returned when called for.[30]

It is obvious that secrecy means a great deal to the leaders of the Eastern Star—so much so that the public is not to know that these books even exist!

One of the Landmarks states: "The modes of recognition, which are the peculiar secrets of the

Order, cannot be changed, without destroying the foundation of the system."[31] However, as William Meyer points out:

> The Eastern Star ritual which contains all the modes of recognition and secret work is sold by the Macoy Publishing and Masonic Supply Co., and permits anyone who desires to know these "peculiar secrets," to obtain same for the price of $1.25, without paying for expensive initiation.[32]

He adds:

> These secrets are published by several Masonic publishing houses and copies of the rituals can be found in the Library of Congress. The promise of secrecy is on the side of the initiate only and not on the side of the lodge publishing house which sells the so-called secrets to *anyone* who has the price to pay for the ritual. Eastern Star members promise to keep secret what the Masonic publishing house publishes for all the world to read. [Emphasis in the original.][33]

I'm not saying that these "secrets" are easy to obtain. They are not—unless you know where to go for them. I wrote to the Eastern Star headquarters in Washington D.C., for information and they politely told me that individuals who do not belong to the lodge cannot purchase their literature. In fact, they would not sell me anything unless I provided them with proof of membership.[34] On rare occasions, one may be able to locate a book on the Eastern Star in a local library, but there are even some restrictions in some cases. One person said she found 2 or 3 books in one library but was forbidden to take out the books or to copy any information from them. In fact, she was only allowed to look at the books for 30 minutes!

On occasion, some Masonic and occult books may be found in a "rare books room" in some obscure place behind lock and key. For instance, at the Pennsylvania State University Library there is such a room. Here the person must fill out a card listing the book(s) being requested, along with his or her address. While looking at the book, the person is under supervision and cannot leave the room with the book or even take the book to the copier.

One such book in this room was from 33° Mason, Manly Palmer Hall, entitled *An Encyclopedic Outline of Masonic, Hermetic, Qabbalistic and Rosicrucian*

Conjuration of a demon: Baphomet can be seen in the upper left-hand corner and a skull in the upper right-hand corner. Also notice the magic circle within the square on which the magician stands. The demon that was summoned up stands within a magic circle as well. It is this book which is highly recommended and sold through a Masonic publishing house!

Symbolical Philosophy: Being an Interpretation of the Secret Teachings Concealed Within the Rituals, Allegories and Mysteries of All Ages. A chapter in this book is called "Ceremonial Magic and Sorcery." It includes a picture of Baphomet and there is also a mention about Eliphas Levi "invok[ing] the spirit of Apollonius of Tyana...."[36] This book, by the way, was also listed as a **MASONIC** book in *The Scottish Rite Journal*.[37] It is also promoted and sold through Macoy Publishing and Masonic Supply Company![38] In fact, Hall's one book, *The Lost Keys of Freemasonry*, which mentions Lucifer, was **PUBLISHED** by Macoy Publishing![39]

Some of these secret books are written in code so that if an uninitiated person would see it, it would be difficult to decipher. One Eastern Star book I

117

EASTERN STAR.

7T 20s 3o 1J 2D 8i 3m 28b 3t 1a 1v 4h 28b 33t 3o 7i 18c 14b 7t 21t 16a ℂ, 16a 3r 6i 28s 29a 26t 21c 7t 2f, 6a 19m 13l 7t 1v 7o 4h; 2r 6i 1a 5s ℓ 29a 6b, 13l 6i 7a 29a 6b, 2r 6i 1a ℓ 23t, 16a 6a 1a 20m 5p 16t 6i 8o 7t 26t 7t 1b 3o 7t 6n 16h 6i 11f 2i 7t —7T 3p 8i "9A 25m 2d." 7T 20s 19R 8i 3m 28b 16h 7t 3h, 9c, 2i 24f 7t 20b, 7t 5e 12p 8a 7t 24s; 6s, 22c 26a 7u 7t 24b, 7t 5l 25a 5o 7t 10o, 36s 1a 7m 6t 7t 9c 3h 17w 4b 4a 21f 12b 7t 18s; 13t, 32t 7t 18e 8u. 7T 8i "13W 8i 12t?" 7T 20s 3o 12E 8m 28b 13p 7t 15r 2h, 2p 11d, 7u

7t 7h; 6s, 11p 6i 7u 7t 5l 17s; 13t, 16t 6i 9o 2i 24f 3o 7t 10p; 7t 2h 9w 18t 9o 2i 24f 3o 7t 10p 16s 4b 4a 8l 20w 7t 18e. 7T 3p 8i "7W 18w 14t?" 7T 20s 3o 8M 8i 3m 28b 13p 7t 21t 16a 17f 27t 2i 36s 1a 7m 29a 26t 18f 1a 30t; 6s, 2r 7t 30t 20t 19f 1a 9l 3a 7t 2f; 13t, 32t 7t 18e 8u 16a 10l 15t 7t 30t. 7T 3p 8i "11B 14t 12t?" 7T 20s 3o 6E 8i 3m 28b 23c 7t 26a 7u 7t 24b, 7t 5l 25a 5o 7t 10o, 7t 15p 3o 7t 13f 11r 7u 7t 18s; 6s, 32t 7t 18e 8u. 7T 3p 8i "11L 6o 19a."

7T 14f 16b 5o 4p 3l 27a 10f 20w 7t 15f 23w: 12f, "7t 7m 3o 9h 4d":5s 15b, "7t 7m 3o 9h 33s 11e 6b 19B 26t 19s 12h 7t 17e 3o 9h 6g":11t 15b. "7t 7m 3o 9h 5m 9h-21a 26t 7t 1k 2i 7b 3o 9h 6p:" 22f 15b, "7t 7m 2i 10w 13s 17m 9h 3S 5o 13h 14r 26t 13B 6a 7t 4d 3o 9h 27b:" 9f 15b, "7t 7m 3o 9h 4d 10w 3w 6t 3o 7t 22c." 7T 12c 18b 8i 24a 26t 1J 2D 16a 10a 26t 7t 6c 18h 3o 7t

saw entitled *The Ladies' Friend,* had page after page
of the following code:

> 7T 20s 3o 1J 2D 8i 3m 28b 3t 1a 1v 7o 4h 28b
> 33t 3o 7i 18c 14b 7t 21t 16a 17f, 16a 3r 6i
> 28s 29a 26t 21c 7t 2f, 6a 1a 19m 131 7t 1v 7o
> 4h; 2r 6i 1a 5s 23t 29a 6b, 131 6i 7a 29a 6b, 2r
> 6i 1a 11t 23t, 16a 6a 1a 20m 5p 16t 6i 8o 7t 7h
> 26t 7t 1b 3o 7t 6n 16h 6i 11f 2i 7t 3h.—7T 3p
> 8i "9A 25m 2d." 7T 20s 3o 19R 8i 3m 28b 16h
> 7t 3h, 9c, 2i 24f 3o 7t 20b, 7t 5e 12p 8a 7t
> 24s....[40]

The first eleven words of the above code are:
"The sign of Jephthah's Daughter is made by taking
a veil...." If you take notice, the letter following
each number in the code is the first letter of each
word when translated.

WHAT'S THE BIG SECRET?

Some ritual books that can be purchased have
asterisks in place of the actual passwords. So, although
you may have an idea of what the ritual is about,
you are not provided with the passwords.

However, for those of you who are curious as to
what the passwords are, I'll share them with you.
The pass for Adah is "Alas, my daughter."[41] Ruth's
pass is "Who is this?"[42] For Esther, the pass is "What
wilt thou?"[43] Martha's pass is "Believest thou this?"[44]
Finally, the pass for Electa is "Love one another."[45]
All of these phrases can be found in the Bible (see
Judges 11:35; Ruth 3:9, paraphrased; Esther 5:3; John
11:26; and II John 1:5), so why the big deal of
secrecy?

Apparently, the big secret, then, is not really the
passwords or the drama of the five women since at
least some of this is found in the Bible and can be

checked out by anyone. The secret must lie deeper than this.

If the Eastern Star is truly based on the Bible, then they would obey the Bible. For example, in Isaiah 45:19 God says: **"I HAVE NOT SPOKEN IN SECRET...**I the Lord speak righteousness, I declare things that are right." (See also Isaiah 48:16.) Jesus Himself said: "I spake openly to the world; I ever taught in the synagogue, and in the temple, whither the Jews always resort; and **IN SECRET HAVE I SAID NOTHING"** (John 18:20). Jeremiah 23:24 asks: "Can any hide himself in secret places that I shall not see him? saith the Lord. Do not I fill heaven and earth? saith the Lord." Deuteronomy 27:15 explains:

> Cursed be the man that maketh any graven or molten image, an abomination unto the Lord, the work of the hands of the craftsman, and putteth it in a secret place. And all the people shall answer and say, Amen.

Don't the Eastern Star members make a pentagram and put it in their secret place in the lodge room? This is an abomination to God. Ephesians 5:11-13 plainly tells us:

> Have no fellowship with the unfruitful works of darkness, but rather reprove them. For it is a shame even to speak of those things which are done of them in secret. But all things that are reproved are made manifest by the light: for whatsoever doth make manifest is light.

Jesus inquired: "Why call ye Me, Lord, Lord, and do not the things which I say?" (Luke 6:46).

The Eastern Star members can brag all they want to about their organization being based on the Bible,

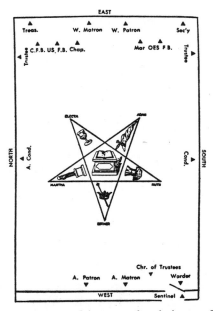

but while they are making such claims, they are not obeying the Bible, showing that they "profess that they know God; but in works they deny Him, being abominable, and disobedient, and unto every good work reprobate" (Titus 1:16).

These may be strong statements and I realize that **MOST INDIVIDUALS WHO BELONG TO THE EASTERN STAR HAVE NO IDEA ABOUT THE OCCULTIC AND PAGAN NATURE OF THEIR ORGANIZATION,** but I challenge each one of them to search their own literature. See what Masonry teaches in their own books. After all, the Eastern Star is connected to the Masonic organization and they were formed to support the Masons in their aims and goals.[46]

Is the Eastern Star a secret society, then? Obviously, in some respects they are. Is it a Christian organization? Of course not!

14. THE FOUR ELEMENTS

What are the four elements and what do they have to do with the Eastern Star? The four elements are earth, air, fire, and water.[1] To these four elements, there is sometimes added a fifth one which is ether or spirit.[2] As mentioned earlier, in witchcraft "the five points of the Pentagram represent the five Elements of Nature—Earth, Air, Fire, Water, and Spirit—with the top point corresponding to Spirit, the unifying element."[3]

In some cases the five elements are water, fire, wood, metal, and earth.[4] In occult vocabulary the fifth element is known as "Azoth."[5] Albert Pike, in *Morals and Dogma,* refers to Azoth on several occasions.[6] In fact, Pike even has a picture of Azoth in his book on page 839. John Yarker, a Mason, shares the explanation of this figure:

> [I]t represents a winged-globe on which is a triangle inside a square, upon which reposes a dragon; on the latter stands a human figure with two heads, and two hands; surrounding the heads, one of

which is male and the other female, are the sun, moon, and five stars; the hand on the male side holds a compass, that on the other a square. The symbolism here clearly alludes to the dual **SEXUAL** nature of all metals.[7]

One symbol that is used to represent the four elements is the Tetragrammaton (or Tetragram).[8] According to the *Dictionary of Mysticism,* the Tetragram "has been used for **CONJURING THE ELEMENTARY SPIRITS.**"[9] Laurie Cabot, a witch, uses the Tetragrammaton as a **TALISMAN** for protection.[10] The Tetragrammaton is an "equilateral triangle inscribed with the Hebrew letters for the fourfold name of God."[11] Manly Palmer Hall, a 33° Mason and occultist, remarks:

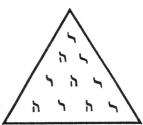

The four letters can be combined in 72 combinations, resulting in what is called the **SHEMHAMFORESH,** which represents, in turn, the laws, powers, and energies of Nature by which the perfection of man is achieved.[12]

WHAT IS SHEMHAMFORESH?

Interestingly, the word "Shemhamforesh" is used in Satanism. In *The Satanic Bible* are some instructions to be followed before beginning a ritual: "Whenever the words 'Shemhamforash!' and 'Hail Satan!' are spoken by the person acting as priest, the other participants will repeat the words after him."[13]

Of course, **WITCHES** aren't the only ones who use the Tetragrammaton. **MASONS ALSO USE THIS SYMBOL.** In fact the Master's jewel of the 4th degree is a small equilateral triangle with the Tetragrammaton characters appearing on the reverse side.[14] The "first letter of the Ineffable Name of Deity, called the Tetragrammaton (Yahweh)" is also "found within the triangle on the 14th Degree ring."[15] Many other Masonic authors refer to this symbol.[16]

MORE SEXUAL CONNOTATIONS

Typical of so many other Masonic symbols, the Tetragrammaton also has a sexual connotation. Masonic author, Albert Mackey, claims that:

> ...the Ineffable Name of God in Hebrew, being read cabalistically, includes within itself the male and female principle, the generative and prolific energy of creation; and here we have, again, the widely-spread symbolism of the phallus and the cteis, the lingam and the yoni, or their equivalent, the point within a circle, and another pregnant proof of the connection between Freemasonry and the ancient Mysteries.[17]

Charles Vail, also a Mason, agrees that the Tetragrammaton contains the "personal pronouns He and She, the male and female, representing the two great principles of nature...."[18]

Mackey goes even further by contending that the Tetragrammaton:

> ...is supposed to denote the hermaphroditic essence of Jehovah, as containing within himself the male and the female principle,—the generative and the prolific energy of creation.[19]

Albert Pike mentions that the Tetragrammaton "is the *Azot* [Azoth] of the Alchemists....[20] Pike also reveals:

> The Hermaphroditic figure [of Azoth] is the Symbol of the double nature anciently assigned to the Deity, as Generator and Producer, as BRAHM and MAYA among the Aryans, Osiris and Isis among the Egyptians. As the Sun was male, so the Moon was female; and Isis was both the sister and the wife of Osiris. The Compass, therefore, is the Hermetic Symbol of the Creative Deity, and the Square of the productive Earth or Universe. [emphasis in the original][21]

Once again we can see how the symbolism contains **HIDDEN REFERENCES TO REPRODUCTION** as well as expressing the idea of a hermaphroditic or androgynous god. This is an important disclosure for, if you remember, Baphomet, among other pagan gods, was supposed to be an androgynous god—a god bearing the features of both male and female. You should also remember that Baphomet is represented by the inverted pentagram which is the symbol used in the Eastern Star.

BAPHOMET AND THE FOUR ELEMENTS

The four elements also play a prominent role in witchcraft. Margot Adler, a witch, announces: "Craft ritual usually starts with casting and creating this magical space and ritually purifying it with the ancient elements: fire, water, earth, and air."[22] In a brochure from Nuit Unlimited Imports, a witchcraft organization, we find that the drawing of Baphomet by the occultist Eliphas Levi contains all kinds of occult symbolism. It states:

> Symbols were included relating directly to ceremonial magic and identified with **BAPHOMET**. Much of the same symbols carry forward as on the **DEVIL CARD** in the Thoth deck of Crowley.[23]

As the explanation for some of the symbols are given, it is intriguing to notice that the symbolism of the four elements is included in this drawing.[24] For example, the scales on the body represent the "emotional side of man, the **WATER ELEMENT**."[25] The feathers symbolize "that which is mercurial and volatile. The **FIRE ELEMENT**."[26] The cloven hooves depict the "animal nature of man, the concept that we may not have fully evolved out the (sic) beast kingdom. The **ELEMENT OF EARTH.**[27] Finally, the wings symbolize "Man's struggle to rise above his environment. The **AIR ELEMENT.**[28] So, the scales, feathers, cloven hooves, and wings on Baphomet represent the four elements.

Concerning the Devil card in the Tarot deck we find:

> It takes the form of Baphomet (of the Knights Templars) portrayed as having the head and feet of a he-goat and the bosom and arms of a woman. Like the Greek sphinx, it incorporates the **FOUR ELEMENTS:** its black legs correspond to the earth and to the spirits of the nether world; the green scales on its flanks allude to water, the undines, and dissolution; its blue wings to sylphs and also to bats (because the wings are membranous); and the red head is related to fire and salamanders. The aim of the devil is regression or stagnation in what is fragmentary, inferior, diverse and discontinuous. Finally, this Tarot mystery-card is related to the instincts and to desire in all its passionate forms, the magic arts, disorder and perversion.[29]

This card is number 15 in the deck. Is it just a coincidence that $1 + 5 = 6$? Incidentally, Eastern Star writer, Sarah H. Terry, in *The Second Mile,* states that six is evil.[30]

On Baphomet's head is a five pointed star. This is to represent "the power of spirit dominating the elements."[31] Another item of interest on Baphomet is the caduceus. As previously mentioned, the caduceus itself:

> ...signifies the integration of the four elements, the wand corresponding to earth, the wings to air, the serpents to fire and water (by analogy

with the undulating movement of waves and flames).[32]

Since Baphomet represents Satan,[33] as well as the four elements,[34] it is no surprise to find that *The Satanic Bible* is divided into four categories—each category representing one of the four elements:

Fire—Book of Satan
Air—Book of Lucifer
Earth—Book of Belial
Water—Book of Leviathan.[35]

In occultist Helena Petrovna Blavatsky's book, *Isis Unveiled,* we find that Proclus "held that the four elements are all filled with *daemons* [demons]...." [Emphasis in the original][36]

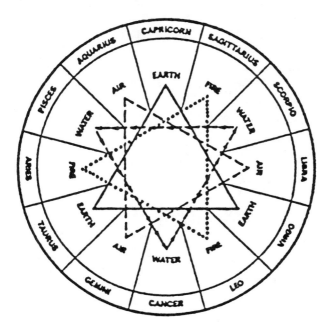

STAR OF THE MAGI

Eliphas Levi reveals that the:

...Pentagram expresses the mind's domination over the elements and it is by this sign that we bind the demons of the air, the spirits of fire, the spectres of water, and the ghosts of earth. It is the Star of the Magi, the burning star of the Gnostic schools the sign of intellectual omnipotence and autocracy.[37]

Perhaps this is why Pike gives the following instructions:

Another Jewel is necessary for you, and in certain undertakings cannot be dispensed with. It is what is termed the Kabalistic pantacle [PENTAGRAM]....This carries with it the power of **COMMANDING THE SPIRITS** of the elements. **IT IS NECESSARY FOR YOU TO KNOW HOW TO USE IT....**[38]

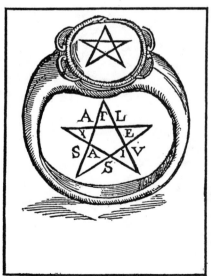

THE PYTHAGOREAN SIGNET RING.
The number five was peculiarly associated by the Pythagor with the art of healing, and the pentagram, or five-pointed was to them the symbol of health. The above figure represe magical ring set with a talismanic gem bearing the pentalph star formed by five different positions of the Greek Alpha. On subject Albert Mackey writes: "The disciples of Pythagoras, were indeed its real inventors, placed within each of its int angles one of the letters of the Greek word ΤΓΕΙΑ, or the L one SALUS, both of which signify health; and thus it was t the talisman of health. They placed it at the beginning of epistles as a greeting to invoke a secure health to their corresp ent. But its use was not confined to the disciples of Pythage As a talisman, it was employed all over the East as a chas resist evil spirits."

From Cartari's *Imagini degli Dei degli Antichi.*

What does all this have to do with the Eastern Star? It's really simple. Levi claims that the "Star of the Magi," which is used in the Eastern Star, is actually the pentagram. He further states that when the Pentagram is placed:

> ...in such a manner that two of its points are above and only one below, we may see the horns, ears, and beard of the hieratic god of Mendes [or Baphomet], when it becomes the **SIGN OF INFERNAL EVOCATIONS.**[39]

He should know since he was the artist who drew Baphomet!

Even in astral projection (when a person leaves his body), the four elements can be activated. In *Psychic Voyages* we read:

> In Astral Projection, the person sends up a "ray" of himself into the scene...."If you will," writes the instructor, you will be able to pass through Water, Earth, Air, and Fire. The traveler should converse with forms and persons he meets in this other world and "test them by Divine names and forces."[40]

THE GOAT OF THE SABBATH

The Eastern Star member will probably be quick to object saying that the pentagram is **ONLY** a representation of a human being. Sarah Terry proclaims: "From writers of the mysteries of the Orient we find that the pentagon represents the human body— the four points the limbs and the single point the head."[41] Elaborating further she says that "it is a symbol of man, with his arms outstretched, feet outstretched...."[42] There just happens to be a problem

Man the microco
(after Agrippa
of Nettesheim).

with this explanation, however, for she has just described
the pentagram with one point up and the symbol of
the Eastern Star is a pentagram with two points up
(unless she is talking about a person standing on his
head). In fact, Eliphas Levi addresses this very subject.
He writes:

> The **PENTAGRAM WITH TWO HORNS IN THE
> ASCENDANT REPRESENTS SATAN,** or the goat
> of the Sabbath....**IT IS THE FIGURE OF A
> HUMAN BODY** with the four members and a
> point representing the head; a human figure **HEAD
> DOWNWARD NATURALLY REPRESENTS THE
> DEMON,** that is, intellectual subversion, disorder
> and folly.[43]

It is intriguing to note that during the "drawing down of the moon" in witchcraft, the High Priestess "assumes the 'Goddess position'—feet astride and arms outstretched making a Pentagram of her own body—and recites the Charge."[44]

W. L. Wilmshurst, a Masonic author, agrees that "the five-pointed star (or pentagram) is also a symbol of man, and expresses a variety of truths concerning him." He continues:

> In the rituals in the *Book of the Dead* the candidate is described as a "keeper of five"; Operative fellow-craft Masons worked in batches of five, and a Speculative fellow-craft Lodge to-day consists of five brethren; all these allusions having a deeper significance than can be explained here, but bearing upon the present state of human evolutional development.[45]

Terry is not the only Eastern Star person to give the explanation that the pentagram represents a human being. In *The Symbolism of the Order of the Eastern Star*, written by Mary Ann Slipper, we find:

> Each human being upon earth may be likened unto a five-rayed star—A living, breathing, active star. It has been pointed out that the number five rules in the human body, and we, who are named stars, may reasonably lay a direct claim to being such upon the material as well as upon other planes. This is the symbol of the human star;— The head has five rays; as two eyes, two ears, and one nose.[46]

Of course, witches and other occultists are quick to agree.[47] Sybil Leek, a witch, pens:

> The five-pointed star represents man himself, his physical body and the parts of that body rules by the numbers of certain angels.

The topmost point of the pentagram represents the head of man....[48]

Elsewhere Slipper adds:

Upon the floor of the Chapter Room, or upon the Signet, our Star means to all students of the Order:

HUMANITY—the Body of all mankind.
The White Ray is the HEAD.
The Yellow Ray and the Green Ray are the HANDS.
The Blue and the Red rays are the FEET.[49]

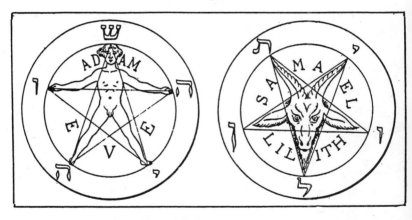

Slipper has just described in detail a star with a person's head (the white point or Esther) pointing downward! Remember that Levi claims that "a human figure **HEAD DOWNWARD NATURALLY REPRESENTS THE DEMON....**"

In *A Treatise on White Magic*, a book written by the occultist, Alice Bailey (who was also a Mason[50] and whose husband was a Mason), we find basically the same thing. She comments:

The sum total called man is roughly divided into five parts some of greater importance than others, but all completing that living organism we call a human being.

a. The head.
b. The upper torso, or that part which lies above the diaphragm.
c. The lower torso, or that part lying below the diaphragm.
d. The arms.
e. The legs.[51]

This all may sound innocent enough, but we must remember that Bailey is writing from an occultic perspective. Notice even the title of her book refers to "white magic." Later in this book Bailey explains about the kundalini being raised. Kundalini is the name of a goddess[52] and is represented as a serpent coiled at the base of the spine.[53] It is claimed that this serpent is asleep and must be awakened and

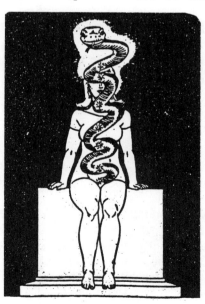

reunited with Shiva who is represented by the third eye.[54] This awakening can be accomplished by practicing Tantra (or sexual) yoga. Matthew Fox asserts:

> The aim of yoga is to rouse this serpent power, to lift *her* head and bring her up the channel of the spine to the...crown of the head. *She* is the symbol of transformation...as she moves up through the human body....

> Befriending this (serpent) creature can add to our own process of transformation....Each of us must reclaim the power of the serpent...we can befriend the serpent to help us choose life and good. [Emphasis and ellipses in the original][55]

Through intercourse, it was believed, man could "form a direct link with divinity, for, by partaking in a sacred act, man inevitably becomes sacred."[56]

> The ultimate intention is that Kundalini shall ascend permanently to the top of the skull, where a transcendental sexual union takes place.

> The postures that awaken Kundalini are frequently sexual....The Tantric obtains his energy through sexual intercourse....[57]

With this in mind, it is fascinating to read Bailey's explanation:

> There has been much loose talk about the raising of the kundalini fire and much misapprehension in the matter. Let me assure you that it is most difficult to raise, and can only be done by a definite act of the will and through the intense mental focussing and concentrated attention of the man, seated on the throne of consciousness

in the head. The Masonic tradition has the teaching
clearly held in its beautiful ritual of the raising
of the great Master-Mason.[58]

What Alice Bailey has just told us is that when
the Master Mason (the name of the third Masonic
degree) is "raised," he is enacting the awakening of
kundalini or the serpent power! In the *Truth Journal*
we are informed: "Some fraternal Orders, such as
Freemasons, have record of it [kundalini] and symbolize
its influences by the degrees of initiation conferred
upon its members."[59] We are even blasphemously
told that this kundalini is supposed to be the Holy
Spirit.[60]

Actually, this awakening of the kundalini can be
found in numerous Masonic books. For example, Manly
P. Hall notes that "Hiram Abiff is symbolic of the
Spirit Fire of the Kundalini of Hindu mysticism."[61]
Some other Masons who have mentioned this are:
Charles W. Leadbeater (who was also an occultist),[62]
R. Swinburne Clymer,[63] and Arthur H. Ward,[64] among
others.

Remember, this **KUNDALINI POWER BEING
AWAKENED HAS TO BE ENACTED BY EVERY
MASTER MASON SO THAT HE OR ONE OF HIS
FEMALE RELATIVES MAY HAVE THE
"PRIVILEGE" OF BECOMING AN EASTERN STAR
MEMBER!**

THE GROUP WITHOUT A BIBLE

Bailey also refers to bhakti yoga or the "yoga of
devotion"[65] as well. She claims that during the time
of Atlantis this yoga "was initiated for the training
of the aspirants of that time."[66] Once again she ties
in the Masonic order: "The remnants of this Atlantean
group remain with us in the modern **MASONIC**

movements, and the work of the Hierarchy was thus perpetuated in sign and symbol."[67] She adds:

> Today, in the world, another great moment of crisis has arrived....a group of men and women who will supersede eventually the previous hierarchical effort. They will supersede all churches, all groups, and all organisations and will eventually constitute that oligarchy of elect souls who will govern and guide the world....
>
> They are of all races; they speak all languages; they embrace all religions, all sciences and all philosophies. Their characteristics are synthesis, inclusiveness, intellectuality and fine mental development. They own to no creed, save the creed of Brotherhood, based on the one Life. They recognise no authority, save that of their own souls, and no Master save the group they seek to serve, and humanity whom they deeply love. They have no barriers set up around themselves, but are governed by a wide tolerance, and a sane mentality and sense of proportion....It does not matter if their terminologies differ, their interpretations of symbols and scriptures vary, or their words are few or many. They see their group members in all fields—political, scientific, religious, and economic—and give to them the sign of recognition and the hand of a brother.[68]

This sure does sound like Masonry! Did you notice several things that this group exhibits?

They "will govern and guide the world."

"They will supersede all churches...."

"[T]hey embrace all religions...."

"Their characteristics are...inclusiveness...."

Their only creed is Brotherhood.

"They recognise no authority...and no Master save
      the group...."
They are governed by tolerance.
Later Bailey states:

It is a group therefore without a terminology or
Bible of any kind; it has no creed nor any dogmatic
formulations of truth. The motivating impulse
of each and all is love of God as it works out in
love for one's fellow man. They know the true
meaning of brotherhood, without distinction of
race. Their lives are lives of **WILLING
SERVICE....**[69]

This quotation is especially interesting since Mary
Ann Slipper tells us the following about the "human
star" pentagram:

The five "rays" of the human star when totalled,
      spell **SERVE.**
That is our mission upon earth—service.[70]

What an amazing "coincidence"!

HOW TO BECOME A CHRIST

Another pious statement concerning the pentagram
comes from Eastern Star author Sarah Terry. She
writes: "The pentagon may also be considered as
outlining the five stages of man—Birth, Life, Death,
Resurrection and Ascension."[71] Jean M'Kee Kenaston
says that the Star alludes to the Birth, Death, Resurrection
and Ascension of the Lord Jesus Christ."[72] However,
according to Masonic author, Charles H. Vail, this
process is what makes each person a Christ![73] In
the Mysteries a:

...candidate was received by the initiating Hierophant at the proper time and place, usually a secluded chamber in a temple or pyramid, and laid on the stone floor with arms outstretched; sometimes on a wooden cross, which was hollowed out to support the human figure. He was then touched with the thyrsus, the "spear of the crucifixion," on the heart; he then passed into a deep trance. The body was placed in a sarcophagus of stone, a vault or tomb beneath the floor of the Hall of Initiation, and carefully guarded. Meantime, while the body was dead and buried, he himself was fully alive in the invisible world (Hades), and undergoing what was called the tests of earth, water, fire and air. He then put on his perfected Bliss Body, which was now fully organized as a vehicle of consciousness. After the third day the cross, bearing the body, was lifted up and carried out into the air on the east side of the pyramid or temple and placed on a sloping surface ready to greet the rising sun. At the moment the first rays touched the face, the perfected Initiate, the Horus or Christ, rose from the dead, resuscitated the body, and glorified it by his resurrected body, no longer a natural man but a spiritual man, having overcome death and hell.[74]

Alice Bailey, an occultist, says basically the same thing. Even her book title, *From Bethlehem to Calvary: The Initiations of Jesus*, gives this away.

The word **"HIEROPHANT"** was used in the above quotation. It was the "ancient title of higher adepts and teachers of the classical mysteries. Currently used by **OCCULTISTS** as a title of initiators into **ESOTERIC** knowledge."[75] Albert Mackey points out that **HIEROPHANT** of the Mysteries **IS NOW CALLED THE MASTER OF THE LODGE IN MASONRY.**[76]

PENTAGRAM AND THE MICROCOSM

Another explanation that an Eastern Star person may give concerning the pentagram to make it look innocent, is that it is a symbol of the microcosm. However, even this description has occultic overtones for New Agers, magicians, occultists, witches, Satanists, and Masons all use this **SAME** definition.[77] In the *Dictionary of Mysticism* we find:

> **Microcosm:** Literally, *the small universe*—the term used by **THEOSOPHISTS AND OCCULTISTS** for man, regarded as a replica of the macrocosm (the *great universe*), because it contains all the elements, qualities and potencies of the latter.[78]

A few examples showing that occultists claim that the pentagram is a symbol of the microcosm follow. An organization called the Continental Association of Satan's Hope (CASH) advertises that a **"POWERFUL SATANIC PENTAGRAM CAN NOW BE YOURS ABSOLUTELY FREE!"** [Emphasis in the original][79] It goes on to explain:

> *You will find the Satanic Pentagram invaluable and indispensable as you attempt to draw from the infernal power of our lord Satan! This extremely powerful amulet is the sign of the microcosm and is the summation of all the occult forces! In other words, there is no amulet or talisman more powerful or even close to as powerful as the Satanic Pentagram!* [Emphasis in the original][80]

Across the bottom of this ad are the words in large letters: "HAIL SATAN!"[81]

Laurie Cabot remarks:

The star is always drawn with one continuous stroke, with one point upright, and to me it represents the continuous outline of the human body: the head at the top, the two arms, the legs, the mystic center where all points cross. It is a symbol of the human body that goes back millennia, and it resonates to something old and sacred in our souls. Even people who know little about Witchcraft feel this when they look at Leonardo da Vinci's famous representation of the Microcosmic Man that shows the muscular male body, arms and legs outstretched, standing as a five-pointed figure in the perfect circle. It looks as if he could lift off the page and soar. Instinctively we know that this proud, self-confident, almost defiant stance is at the heart of what it means to be human.[82]

THE BURNING STAR

Eliphas Levi reveals:

The star of the microcosm, or the **MAGIC PENTAGRAM,** that star wherein the human figure was represented by Agrippa, with the head in the ascending point and the four members in the four other points—the Burning **STAR, WHICH, WHEN INVERTED, IS THE HIEROGLYPHIC SIGN OF THE GOAT OF BLACK MAGIC,** whose head can then be sketched in the star with the two horns above, the ears on the right and left, and the beard below, sign of antagonism and blind fatality, the goat of lewdness assaulting heaven with its horns, a sign execrated even in the Sabbath by initiates of a superior order.[83]

In *The Occult* by Colin Wilson, we are informed:

In magic, the principle is altogether more complicated. Man is the "microcosm," whose symbol is a five-pointed star (or pentacle)....The occultists of the Middle Ages and the Reformation saw man and the universe connected by thousands of invisible bonds.[84]

Charles H. Vail, a Mason, notes:

The Blazing Star or Pentagram also represents the human body,—the five points representing the four limbs and head. It is thus called the sign of the Microcosm. All the Mysteries of Magic were said to be summed up in this symbol. Paracelsus pronounces it the greatest and most potent of all signs.[85]

PENTAGRAM USED TO EVOKE DEMONS

There are many other instances that could be given, but one more should suffice. Spence indicates:

The Pentagram, the sign of the Microcosm, was held to be the most powerful means of **CONJURATION** (to practice magic, sorcery, to evoke demons and tempests) in any rite....[86]

We have seen that the pentagram is associated with the microcosm as well as the four elements. Eastern Star author, Shirley Plessner, maintains:

Four is said to be the number of the world. The four sides of the square, the four major points of direction, and the four seasons are used symbolically in our work. The symbolic four figures prominently in our work.[87]

Notice, first of all, that the number four is associated with "the four major points of direction." In mythology we find that Horus had four sons and each one guarded one of the four cardinal points.[88] Masonic writer, Sir Wallis Budge, in his book, *Egyptian Magic,* explains:

> The four children of Horus, or the gods of the four cardinal points, were called Mestha, Hapi, Tuamutef, and Qebhsennuf, and with them were associated the goddesses Isis, Nephthys, Neith, and Serqet respectively. Mestha was man-headed, and represented the south, and protected the stomach and large intestines; Hapi was dog-headed, and represented the north, and protected the small intestines; Tuamutef was jackal-headed, and represented the east, and protected the lungs and the heart; and Qebhsennuf was hawk-headed, and represented the west, and protected the liver and the gall-bladder.[89]

Second, notice that Plessner claims "the four seasons are used" in the Eastern Star work. According to Albert Pike, Horus was "the author of the Seasons, and the God of Time...."[90] Plessner adds:

> Four of the five Star Point Heroines are used to symbolize the seasons. In this comparison, a whole year is used to represent the span of a lifetime. The spring or youth of life is symbolized by Adah. The summer of life, with its abundance and growth is symbolized by Ruth. The autumn, or the harvest time of the year, is symbolized by Electa who represents the period of full maturity in life. The winter of life is symbolized by Martha because at the end of the year, or lifetime, one must rely on faith in eternal life in order to be able to face the unproductive, barren days of the wintertime of this earthly life.[91]

THE UNKNOWN DEITY

Notice that since there are only four seasons only four of the Eastern Star women were mentioned. That leaves one other woman with no season attached to her. With this in mind, it was fascinating to read in Helena Petrovna Blavatsky's work the following:

The heads [of Phanes, a pagan god with the heads of a man, hawk, eagle, and bull] relate to the **ZODIAC,** and typify the **FOUR SEASONS** of the year, for the *mundane* serpent is the *mundane* year, while the serpent itself is the symbol of Kneph, the hidden or *unrevealed* deity.... [Italics in the original; Bold and caps added][92]

The **UNREVEALED** deity? Do you remember that there just happens to be a goddess in the Eastern Star represented by Areme that seems to be an **UNKNOWN DEITY?** Is this just another "coincidence" again?

A further revelation about the seasons can be found in *The Satanic Bible*. Anton LaVey declares:

The **SOLSTICES** and **EQUINOXES** are also celebrated as holidays, as they herald the first day of the **SEASONS.** The difference between a solstice and an equinox is a semantic one defining the relationship between the sun, moon, and the fixed stars. The solstice applies to summer and winter; the equinox refers to autumn and spring. The summer solstice is in June, and the winter solstice is in December. The autumn equinox is in September, and the spring equinox is in March.[93]

Masonry, by the way, commemorates the equinoxes and they celebrate the solstices in the form of the two St. Johns.[94] One *Short Talk Bulletin* reports:

THE CRAFT OF THE WISE
WITCHES' HOLIDAY
WHEEL OF THE YEAR

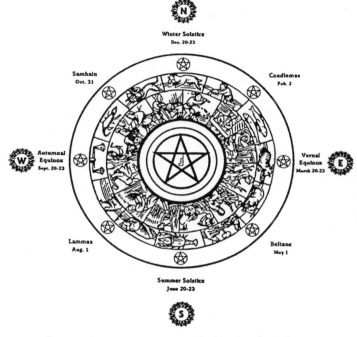

Every ending is a beginning and for Witches this is Law.
Where they enter in, from there they must withdraw.

Through the countless years, in a thousand religions, cults, mysteries, in a hundred climes and lands, priests and people celebrated the solstices. We know it not only from history and the records of ancient peoples, often cut upon stone, but from myths and legends; the story of Ceres and her search for her daughter Prosperpine, the allegory of Isis, Osiris and Horus....

Feasts and festival days of a hoary antiquity were not lightly to be given up, even by those who put their faith upon a Cross. It was of no use for the early Church to ban a pagan festival. Old habit was too strong, old ideas too powerful. Hence clever and thoughtful men in the early days of Christianity turned the pagan festivals to Christian usage, and the old celebrations of summer and winter solstice became the Sts. Johns' Days of the Middle Ages.[95]

COLOR THERAPY

In addition to the number four being important in the Eastern Star, Slipper notes: "Sound, color, form and number are the avenues along which life of the ages expresses itself. There can be no sound apart from color."[96] Alice Bailey, a New Ager, asserts: "The Mysteries [which includes Masonry] will restore colour and music as they essentially are to the world...."[97] In the *Rosicrucian Manual* we find:

Color therapy is a subject that has been long considered by the **OCCULTISTS.** It is held that color affects the human emotions and plays a definite part in relationship to health, moods, and our reactions. However, color therapy was heralded by the mundane scientists as an **OCCULT SUPERSTITION!**[98]

Another interesting remark about the use of color comes from the well-known witch, Sybil Leek. She asserts:

In this century there has been a great increase in color awareness. This is no coincidence; many persons use **COLOR** who may not even know of **ITS LINK WITH OCCULTISM,** that each color has its own number and therefore a vibratory force....The number and vibrations of color connect everything on and in the earth—air, fire and water,

332   HIDDEN SECRETS OF THE EASTERN STAR

all the elements of the world—with the cosmic rays and ultimately with the Supreme Being.[99]

It comes as no surprise, then, that each of the four elements are also assigned colors. These colors vary depending on the group. Laurie Cabot writes: "Traditions vary as to which elements, colors, animals, or spirits guard the four directions and which symbols or talismans should be used to represent them."[100] One set of colors, however, is blue, yellow, green, and red—the **SAME COLORS** as used by the Eastern Star in their inverted pentagram.[101] In fact, one pamphlet states:

> Not only is the star inverted, but the colorful attributes of the 5 points are even the correct colors for the four magical elements, air (blue), earth (yellow), water (green) and fire (red); plus the fifth point, the bottom, represents **"akasha,"** the spiritual power of the "astral plane" which is the fusion of all the other "rays" of the star into white. [Emphasis in the original][102]

Stewart Farrar, a witch, in his book, *What Witches Do,* reveals:

> By the time he is ready for the second degree, a **WITCH** is supposed to have grasped the meaning and magical application of the elements, so for this the **CORDS ARE RED (FIRE), YELLOW (EARTH), BLUE (AIR), AND GREEN (WATER).**[103]

It certainly seems quite evident that the founder of the Eastern Star had a **THOROUGH** knowledge of **MAGIC!**

Plessner has noted that the four seasons are also represented in the Eastern Star work.[104] Masonic writer,

George Oliver, mentions in his book that La Pluche claims:

> Isis used to clothe herself in such dresses as were agreeable to the different seasons of the years. To announce the beginning of spring, which overspreads and enamels the earth with flowers and verdure, she wore carpets of different colours, etc.[105]

Isis, I'm sure you will recall, is an Egyptian goddess who seems to be represented by Eastern Star symbolism such as the broken column.

Another Egyptian divinity, Phtha, is depicted with a sceptre in his hand. Frederic Portal explains:

> This sceptre is painted of the four colors attributed to the four elements—the red, denoting fire; blue, air; green, water; and the brown-yellow, or russet, sand or earth.[106]

Again we can see a correlation between paganism and the Eastern Star—even including the colors which have been chosen. The choice of these colors was most likely intentionally chosen for Plessner, under the item, "Mystic Colors," discloses:

> The combination of the five star point colors is referred to as The Mystic Colors. A proper blending of the symbolic attributes which these colors represent creates a power which may be used to bless and benefit all of humanity.[107]

Any occultist will most likely tell you that certain colors have certain meanings and power. Many times specific colors are chosen for particular ceremonies and spells. For instance, Laurie Cabot, the "Official

Witch of Salem,"[108] writes: "We choose the colors of our candles according to a table of correspondences to bring in the correct planetary influences."[109] Witchcraft practitioner, Scott Cunningham, concurs:

> Colors are also used for their specific vibrations....If I was (sic) especially interested in herb magic...I might wear a green robe to help key my rituals into Earth energies. Specific robes can also be made and worn by the industrious for certain spells or cycles of spells....[110]

Mary Ann Slipper also is aware of the significance of colors. She proclaims:

> The use of colors in mythology is largely symbolical for the purpose of expressing some simple fact or mood....

> All fraternal Orders have drawn largely upon **COLORS** to interpret and illustrate **HIDDEN MEANINGS.**[111]

Hidden meanings? Of course! In other words, what I've been presenting here is not way off base since the Eastern Star writers have already given us veiled hints that there are meanings that are deeper than what they have disclosed.

PLANTS ARE SACRED TO THE GODDESS

Not only does each Eastern Star character have a specific color, she also has a specific flower assigned to her. Manly Palmer Hall writes:

> Albert G. Mackey calls attention to the fact that each of the ancient Mysteries had its own peculiar plant sacred to the gods or goddesses in whose

honor the rituals were celebrated. These sacred plants were later adopted as the symbols of the various degrees in which they were used.[112]

For example, an evergreen marks the grave of the dead sun god.[113] This would correlate to the degree of Martha whose flower is the fern or pine cone and symbolizes immortality.[114]

At one time the flower for Ruth was the sunflower but has now been changed to the yellow jessamine.[115] The sunflower, however, was "given high rank among sacred plants"[116] because it was "venerated as being sacred to Divinity."[117] Violets, the flower of Adah, was the flower of Io, a moon goddess. Remember, Adah's original name was Luna—a **MOON** goddess.

Esther's flower is the lily.[118] This flower was the emblem of many goddesses such as Diana, Juno, and Lilith.[119]

> The Greeks and Romans regarded it, as we do, as a symbol of purity....Among older nations, it typed virginity and innocence, like most of the white flowers; hence the lilies on our altars at Easter—relics of a sun worship begun in Egypt— will sometimes have their anthers removed, that the lilies may remain virgin.[120]

The rose is the flower for Electa. Like the lily, the rose was the emblem of numerous goddesses, one of whom was Venus. Since **VENUS IS THE GODDESS OF LOVE,**[121] a rose:

> ...was given to the diners at banquets as a reminder that love affairs, told when spirits were high and tongues adventurous, were not to be babbled over the cups, or under other circumstances and in other places. Hence arose the use of the rose as a symbol of secrecy....[122]

"The red rose...was for life—**LOVE**—the blood of broken hearts...."[123] Does that remind you of Electa in any way? Her pass, by the way, is **"LOVE** one another."[124]

GEMS AND MAGICAL POWERS

In addition to the specific color and flower, each Eastern Star woman has a gem associated with her. The other officers in the Eastern Star are also designated a particular gem. Dr. Dennis Cuddy, a scholar and researcher, informs us: "Colors represented in the rainbow and in crystals or **GEMS ARE ALSO IMPORTANT IN THE OCCULT** and represent various energies."[125]

The gems for the Eastern Star women are:

PERSON	GEM	ASSOCIATED MEANING
Adah	Sapphire	Obedient Loyalty
Ruth	Topaz	Humble fulfillment of duty
Esther	Diamond	Purity
Martha	Emerald	Eternal Life
Electa	Ruby	Sacrifice[126]

The meanings of these gems sound innocent enough, but Shirley Plessner adds: **"ADDITIONAL ASSOCIATED MEANINGS for ALL** of these jewels may be found in any standard book of the history and tradition of gems and jewels."[127] In other words, there are additional meanings that are not presented to the Eastern Star members. So, let's see what other books tell us about gems.

Turning to the book, *Power of the Witch*, by Laurie Cabot, we find:

Many Witches wear crystals as jewelry, along with other gemstones that have magical powers. Jewelry is a way to have magic on your body without anyone knowing it but you and others who are wise in the ways of the Craft. In general, Witch jewelry is worn because it directs energies to various parts of the body.[128]

She adds: "Every Witch has an altar on which are placed a pentacle, candles, sacred stones, a wand, an athame, incense and burner, and other sacred and personal objects."[129] One book advertised on the back of a **MASONIC** book by Alex Horne is entitled *Precious Stones: Their Occult Power and Hidden Significance*.[130] Some other books that are recommended on this cover are: *A History of Magic, Witchcraft and Occultism; The Magical Ritual of the Sanctum Regnum; Inner Traditions of Magic;* and *Seasonal Occult Rituals*.[131]

Arthur Edward Waite, a Mason and occultist, reveals:

Talismans may be made either of the seven kabbalistic metals—gold, silver, iron, copper, fixed mercury, brass, and lead—or of precious stones, such as carbuncles, crystals, diamonds, emeralds, agates, sapphires, and onyxes.[132]

In one of Eliphas Levi's books, we are told that a "description is given of the correct robes, perfumes and jewels to be used in magical work for each day of the week."[133] It is clear to see that particular gems (or stones) are important in witchcraft, Masonry, and the Eastern Star.

S. R. Parchment, in his book, *Ancient Operative Masonry,* notes:

In each kingdom there are special mediums through which the elementary spirits of nature readily manifest. Thus, if birthstones are properly treated by a true Magus, the classes of nature spirits which are vibrating in unison with these gems may become the ready servants of those who wear them. However, it should be strictly understood that the wearing of such gems is but a crutch for those who have not discovered the secret by which they may manufacture the true philosopher's stone—esoterically known as the "emerald tables of Hermes"; in the plant kingdom certain shrubs have the same magical power.[134]

NOT ARBITRARILY ADOPTED

I think the best explanation that can be given comes from Albert Mackey who wrote a book with Rob Morris, the founder of the Eastern Star. In answering the question, "What is Freemasonry?," he responds:

Hence then, the rites and ceremonies of Masonry— its secret modes of initiation—its traditions and legends—its jewels and emblems, are not unmeaning composition, arbitrarily adopted to suit the taste or fancy of their inventors, but are the means judiciously and wisely intended, by a method which has the sanction, and is recommended by the experience of the remotest antiquity, to communicate the light and knowledge of divine truth.

And this divine truth consists not in erratic speculations on questions of polemic theology— not in the inculcation of sectarian and contracted views of religious faith—but in the inquiry into the true nature of God and the human soul. These are the inspiring and elevating topics which it is the design of Masonry to discuss—these are the doctrines which it seeks to investigate.[135]

Notice that Mackey declares that the jewels, emblems, rites, and ceremonies were not "arbitrarily adopted" but were "judiciously and wisely intended." Charles H. Vail, another Mason, readily agrees:

We have seen that Masonry is modeled on the Ancient Mysteries, and derives its important symbols and legends from that source. Is this a mere coincidence? Was there meant to be only a similarity in outward form? We cannot so believe; the analogy is far too close. The men who formulated the ritual very well knew what they were doing. We believe that the secret vaults contain jewels not yet discovered, and it should be the work of every true Mason to search diligently for "More Light." To discover the full meaning of the glyphs and allegories is to revive the Ancient Wisdom, the Secret Doctrine of Antiquity, the real Lost Word. That such Wisdom once existed will not be denied by any intelligent Mason, for the whole superstructure of the Order is based upon the traditions of its existence....

We have seen that the **MASTERS OF OLD WERE TRUE OCCULTISTS**—Masters of Divine Science. **MASONRY HAS PRESERVED** for us the names that indicate **THE REALITY OF OCCULT KNOWLEDGE AND POWER** in the Perfect and Sublime Master, Prince Adept, Sublime Prince of the Royal Secret, etc....This would be in line with the ancient tradition—a recovery of the real Lost Word, the key to the Science of Knowledge. Every Mason should labor assiduously for the realization of this ideal. Let us not be content with the mere rudiments of our philosophy.... **INTELLIGENT MASONS ARE BEGINNING TO REALIZE THAT THERE IS SOMETHING MORE IN OUR SYMBOLS AND LEGENDS, AND THEY**

ARE SEEKING THEIR INNER AND ULTIMATE MEANING....

So mote it be.[136]

The ending of Vail's statement is the exact phrase used by occultists: "So mote it be." In fact, these words can also be found in Eastern Star manuals,[137] although it is not seen nearly as frequently as in Masonry. Starhawk, a witch, explains: "'So mote it be' means 'So must it be' and is **TRADITIONAL FOR ENDING A SPELL** or magical working in the Craft."[138]

If Masonry was so carefully crafted, would not the Eastern Star ritual likewise be well-planned? I believe that the same thing Vail said about Masonry can be applied to the Eastern Star:

IS THIS A MERE COINCIDENCE? WAS THERE MEANT TO BE ONLY A SIMILARITY IN OUTWARD FORM? WE CANNOT SO BELIEVE; THE ANALOGY IS FAR TOO CLOSE. THE MEN WHO FORMULATED THE RITUAL VERY WELL KNEW WHAT THEY WERE DOING.[139]

15. A LOOK AT THE RAINBOW GIRLS

The Rainbow Girls is a group that was organized on April 6, 1922, by W. Mark Sexson.[1] Sexson was a 33° Mason for a number of years before founding the Rainbow Girls.[2]

On February 14, 1928, he was elected to the highest office and given the highest rank attainable in Freemasonry, that of Most Worshipful Grand Master of a sovereign Masonic Grand Jurisdiction.[3]

He was also initiated into the Eastern Star.[4]

The story of how the Rainbow Girls came to be is found in the ritual book of the Rainbow Girls:

One evening in the spring of 1922, Mr. Sexson had been asked to make an address before South McAlester Chapter No. 149. As the DeMolay had come under his close study and observation during his masonic activities, he became more and more conscious of the fact that an Order for girls setting forth some of the truths of Masonry would be necessary. He made a stirring appeal for such an organization in his address and the Worthy Matron, Mrs. Sarah Church, immediately replied, "We would start it if we had someone to write the ceremony of Initiation." Mr. Sexson said, "I will write the Ritual." The next day, he wrote the Ritual, giving it the name, Order of the Rainbow for Girls. He dictated it to the Church stenographer, Mrs. Helen Ambrose, in the study of the First Christian Church of which he was then minister. He asked the regular officers of South McAlester Chapter No. 149, O.E.S. [Order of the Eastern Star], to exemplify the work and furnish them with typewritten copies of the Ritual.

On April 6, 1922, the degrees were exemplified for the first time on a class of one hundred seventy-one girls in the auditorium of the Scottish Rite Temple, McAlester, Oklahoma.[5]

Did you notice that Sexton's desire was to start an organization for girls that would set "forth some of the truths of **MASONRY**"? This was the purpose for the Rainbow Girls. Since Masonry is an occult organization, this should give us some reason for concern.

As in Masonry and the Eastern Star, there are secret signs and passwords[6] and an oath of **SECRECY** is required.[7] Faith states:

...I receive you under the sign of **SECRECY**....Ever be reminded that our deliberations must be **HIDDEN FROM THE PROFANE.** What you see and hear in this Assembly room is **SECRET.**[8]

There is a Confidential Observer stationed inside the door and an Outer Observer stationed outside the door. The Outer Observer is told that:

...the responsibility that rests upon you is indeed grave. The **SECRECY** of our deliberations depends entirely upon your watchfulness. The **SECRET** portals of our Assembly are yours to guard and if you do not know those who seek admission you will see to it that some one vouches for them. The security of the Assembly in all its deliberations is centered in the confidence and trust that has been placed in your hands.[9]

Due to the secretive nature of this group, a Rainbow Girl whose parents are not Mason or Eastern Star members, cannot even have her parents attend her initiation ceremony.[10] Why would there be so much

secrecy if this group actually promoted the great
ideals they claim to endorse?

Membership in the Rainbow Girls is limited to
girls between the ages of twelve and twenty[11] "who
are the daughters of Masonic or Eastern Star families
or friends of such girls."[12]

> Assemblies must be sponsored by the O.E.S. [Order
> of the Eastern Star] Chapters or regular lodges
> of Freemasonry—or societies or clubs whose
> membership consists entirely of members who
> are in good standing of either of the above.[13]

In other words, the **RAINBOW GIRLS IS
DEPENDENT UPON FREEMASONRY OR THE
EASTERN STAR IN ORDER TO OPERATE ITS
ORGANIZATION.**[14] In fact, we are informed: **"NONE**
is allowed to meet or function without the presence
of a Master Mason."[15] Although a girl is not required
to have a parent who is either a Mason or an Eastern
Star member, she does need to have a friend whose
parent or parents belong to the Masons or the Eastern
Star.[16]

SOUNDS INNOCENT, BUT...

The Rainbow Girls is listed as one of the **"ALLIED
MASONIC GROUPS."**[17] We also learn it is one of
a large number of "organizations which **DEPEND
ON MASONRY** for their membership."[18] Stephen
Brent Morris, a 33° Mason, states that the Rainbow
Girls is one of the **"MASONICALLY SPONSORED**
youth groups."[19] Yet another Masonic book, *What?
When? Where? Why? Who? in Freemasonry,* reveals:

> The Order of DeMolay, for boys; the Order of
> Rainbow and the Order of Job's Daughters for

344   HIDDEN SECRETS OF THE EASTERN STAR

girls, are the principal youth organizations with **CONNECTIONS WITH FREEMASONRY**....It is emphasized that none of these organizations is Masonic, but all are **CONNECTED WITH FREEMASONRY** through those who conduct them or through direct sponsorship by some Masonic body.[20]

There should be no question, then, that the Rainbow Girls has some ties to the Masonic fraternity.

The stated goal of the Rainbow Girls sounds innocuous enough. We are told, in the *Allied Masonic Groups and Rites,* that the purpose of this organization:

...is to teach young girls those broad fundamental principles of right living and right thinking for which all Masonic bodies stand. The ideals of Rainbow are high, and its work beautiful and impressive. Its aim is to supplement home training, school training, and church training, although not a substitute for these.[21]

[The] Order is based on the ninth chapter of Genesis and on the virtues of faith, hope, and charity. The seven colors of the rainbow symbolize life, religion, nature, immortality, fidelity, patriotism, and virtue. The Rainbow Girls may receive two degrees: the Initiatory and the Grand Cross of Color.[22]

The Worthy Associate Advisor asks each of the sisters (faith, hope, and charity) what their stations represent. The Sister of Faith explains her place near the altar with these words: "The Altar is the most sacred place in our Assembly Room. Upon it rests the Holy **BIBLE, SYMBOL OF WHITE LIGHT,** from which we derive strength to sustain us through life."[23] The other sisters explain their stations and then a prayer is offered. Who could find fault with

such an organization? Could there be any danger in such an innocent-sounding group? Let's continue and you'll be able to see for yourself!

Even though the Rainbow Girls sounds religious, there are numerous problems with this organization—although it is not nearly as evident as in the Masonic fraternity. First of all, when the prayer is offered, a blessing is invoked upon Masonry: "Bless, we pray Thee, the great Masonic Fraternity; bless the Order of the Eastern Star; bless our Masonic home...."[24] So, even though prayer is offered, it is asking for God's favor to be put upon an occult organization. Repeatedly the Masonic order is praised and held in high esteem. At one point the Worthy Advisor says:

> Members of the Masonic Fraternity and members of the Order of the Eastern Star, we are delighted to have you with us in our deliberations. It is because of the organization which you represent and because of the interest in the girlhood of our country that we have this Assembly. You are an inspiration and a help. We extend to you a cordial invitation to be present at all of our meetings.[25]

BIBLE IS SYMBOLICAL

Another problem is with the use (or abuse) of the Bible. In the Rainbow Girls, as in Masonry and the Eastern Star, the Bible is only a symbol.[26] For instance, the *Short Talk Bulletin,* entitled "The Nature of Symbols," reveals:

> The Bible on the Altar of a Masonic lodge is a symbol of the Volume of the Sacred Law; to a well-informed Mason it means *any* book of *any* religion which is revealed in printed characters on a page. In lodges in the Far East, the book on the Altar may be a Koran, the Vedas, the Talmud, the Analects of Confucius; perhaps even Egypt's Book of the Dead, if that is desired by an initiate. [Emphasis in the original][27]

Masonic author, Joseph Fort Newton, declares: "Like everything else in Masonry, the **BIBLE,** so rich in symbolism, **IS ITSELF A SYMBOL....**"[28] Oliver Day Street, another Mason, claims:

> There is nothing sacred or holy in the mere book. It is ordinary paper....(we must) frankly acknowledge the Bible to be **A SYMBOL ONLY.** Those Christian Masons who would enforce belief in the teachings of the Bible have simply mistaken the symbol for the thing itself.[29]

Even the *Masonic Record* of June 1926 warned: "...the Bible...can, therefore, have *no other place in our lodge than that of a symbol.*" [Emphasis in the original][30] G. Wingate Chase, in his *Digest of Masonic Law,* goes even further when he states: "In fact, Blue Lodge (that is, Craft) Masonry, *has nothing whatever to do with the Bible;* it is not founded upon the Bible. If it was it would not be Masonry." [Emphasis in the original][31] This view of the Scripture is commonplace in Masonry for Masons do not believe that the Bible is the inerrant Word of God or that it is infallible.[32] If the Bible is not infallible, of course, then any "holy" book would do upon the altar.

THE WHITE LIGHT

In the case of the Rainbow Girls, the Bible is called a "symbol of **WHITE LIGHT**."[33] That phrase is quite revealing! You see, in a book by the New Age occultist, Alice Bailey, entitled *A Treatise on White Magic*, we are told how to control the astral body. One way is by a "direct method of relaxation, concentration, stillness and flushing the entire personality with pure **WHITE LIGHT**."[34] The instructions are then given on how to "call down a stream of pure **WHITE LIGHT**."[35] Bailey's husband was a Mason and her writings are followed explicitly by many in the New Age movement. Of course, Bailey is far from the only one who advocates the use of the white light. Witches, occultists, and New Agers **ALL** use this phrase. For proof, here are just a few samples:

- Barbara Powell, a psychic, says:

Remember, as with all divination, relax and surround yourself with the **WHITE LIGHT** of protective energy. Then, allow your mind to flow into the earth patterns and accept the message you find there. Earth divination is one of the most harmonious forms of divination.[36]

- The Tara Center, a well-known New Age organization who is promoting the "New Age Christ," called Maitreya, explains:

Triangles work is easy. Mentally link up with the two other members; visualize a **TRIANGLE OF WHITE LIGHT** circulating above your heads; then say The Great Invocation aloud (whenever possible). See your **TRIANGLE** linked with all other triangles, transmission and meditation groups on the planet. See the **WHITE LIGHT** circulating among this network of focal points and pouring out to envelop the world, thus helping to form a channel for the downpouring of Light and Love into the body of humanity.

When you say: "From the centre where the Will of God is known," which is Shamballa, visualise a great sphere of **WHITE LIGHT.**[37]

I'm sure you will recall that Shamballa is the mythological place where the "Lord of the World," Sanat Kumara or Shiva (who is actually Satan), is supposed to live![38]

- Circle Network, a witchcraft organization, had an article on how to meditate in their magazine. Part of the instructions were: "Begin by visualizing a protective **WHITE LIGHT** around you."[39]

- Dennis Carpenter, a witch, advises: "Connect with the Divine as you know it. Imagine yourself surrounded with **WHITE LIGHT,** a protective sphere of light that will keep you safe throughout this meditation."[40]

- The Polleys, spiritist teachers, make mention of "enlightenment for those along the path of **WHITE LIGHT**" in their newsletter entitled *Voices from Spirit.*[41]

- Lazaris, a spirit guide (actually a demon), "suggests that he be visualized, simply, as a sphere of **WHITE LIGHT.**"[42]

- New Age channeler, Elizabeth Clare Prophet, held a conference where "the Ascended Masters of the Great White Brotherhood" were supposed to be contacted to speak "on America's destiny in the new age." The Great White Brotherhood was described as a "spiritual order of Western saints and Eastern masters. The word 'white' refers not to race but to the aura of **WHITE LIGHT** that surrounds these immortals."[43]

■   Corinne Heline, a New Age author, talks about "forming a mental image of oneself."[44] She adds: "A little practice will enable one to actually feel that in the presence and power of this **WHITE LIGHT** is the radiation of Divine Spirit, the Spirit that is master of all things."[45] Heline also states:

> A teacher once said: "The highest and deepest **OCCULT TEACHING** is that the **WHITE LIGHT** must never be used for the purpose of an attack or personal gain, but may be properly employed by anyone at any time for self-protection against adverse psychic influences, whoever may exert them. It is a spiritual armor and may be employed in a constructive way whenever a need may arise."[46]

■   In an article entitled "The Spirits Speak" by Timothy Green Beckley, he describes a trance channeler (a medium or psychic). How does she go into a trance?

> At the start of each channeling session, Diana [Minz] evokes the **WHITE LIGHT** so that only positive energy may come through. She also has the person who has come to her mentally create a blue ball of healing energy which encircles them adding to their overall feeling of wellbeing and creating a relaxed atmosphere.

> After entering the "silence"—during which **SHE LEAVES HER BODY AND ALLOWS AN "OUTSIDE" INFLUENCE TO TAKE CONTROL**—Diana's voice changes and an entity identified as Lady Diana begins to speak.[47]

Example after example could be given of such quotations about the "white light."[48] It is also interesting to note that *The White Light* is the name of a publication

of the **OCCULT** organization the Temple of Truth.[49]
It is billed as "The Magazine of Ceremonial Magick."[50]
The name of their bookstore is The Magick Circle.[51]

Is the use of the phrase "white light" in the Rainbow
Girls just a pious expression or was it intentionally
planned? Knowing that this organization was conceived
by a 33° Mason, I'm sure it was deliberately contrived.
Remember that former witch, David J. Meyer, reports:
"In the upper three levels of witchcraft **LUCIFER
IS REPRESENTED BY A WHITE LIGHT.**"[52]

PRINCIPLES OF OCCULTISM

In our last chapter we looked at Alice Bailey's
explanation that the awakening of the kundalini was
enacted in the death and resurrection ritual of a
Mason in the third degree.[53] It is therefore fascinating
to read what occultist and New Ager, Elizabeth Clare
Prophet, has to say. Describing her book, we find
that it:

> Includes a practical explanation of Hindu devotion
> to Mother as the "Goddess **KUNDALINI**"—**THE
> WHITE LIGHT** that rises through the spiritual
> centers of your being, activating **COSMIC
> CONSCIOUSNESS.** You can accomplish this
> acceleration of light through the daily rosary.[54]

Here we see that the Goddess **KUNDALINI IS
EQUATED WITH THE WHITE LIGHT!** Just another
"coincidence"? Masonic writer, Arthur H. Ward, in
Masonic Symbolism and the Mystic Way, notes: "When
later he [the Mason] is given **LIGHT,** it means really
that he is taught the principles of **OCCULTISM....**"[55]

The Rainbow Girls are told that their organization
is based on Genesis 9—the story of the rainbow.[56]
First of all, let's notice that the Worthy Associate

Advisor states that the rainbow symbolizes the "ancient promise of God to His people that He will never again destroy the world."[57] This, however, is not completely true. Turn to Genesis 9:11. God promised Noah:

> I will establish my covenant with you; neither shall all flesh be cut off any more by the waters of a flood; neither shall there any more be a flood to destroy the earth.

The promise was that the earth would never again be totally destroyed by **A FLOOD**. The earth, nevertheless, will be destroyed once again by fire (see II Peter 3:7, 10-13).

Since the **RAINBOW IS ONLY A SYMBOL,**[58] we have to look further for another explanation. One clue where to look is given in the Rainbow Girls' ritual where Charity relates:

> I will explain to you our traditional lesson. Ever since you were a little child you have heard the **ANCIENT TRADITION** that at the end of the rainbow is a Pot of Gold. Across the plains and over the mountains, where the end of that mystic symbol seemed to touch the bosom of Mother Earth, countless hundreds have gone in search of its hiding place. None have ever discovered the actual spot where the rainbow touches the

earth. It always vanishes as the searcher approaches, or its position changes, and it is seen farther on. Those who have sought the truth of this legend have grown weary and tired and have fainted along the journey. To us the Pot of Gold is none other than the heart of the American girl, deeply impressed in early life with its responsibilities. On the station before you is a vessel representing the traditional Pot of Gold and you are now entitled to know its contents.[59]

The rainbow, you see, is not really the rainbow mentioned in Genesis 9 but is a mythological rainbow with the pot of gold, which is mentioned frequently in the ceremony.[60]

We will check into some of the contents in the Rainbow Girls' "pot of gold," but first let's see what mythology and the **"ANCIENT TRADITION"** teach about the rainbow. Masonic author, George Oliver, discloses:

It is remarkable that in all the ancient systems of **MYTHOLOGY,** the Great Father, or the **MALE GENERATIVE PRINCIPLE** was uniformly symbolized by a **POINT WITHIN A CIRCLE.** This emblem was placed by the Scandinavian priests and poets on the central summit of a **RAINBOW,** which was fabled to be a bridge leading from earth to heaven; the emblem, therefore, represented Valhall (sic), or the supernal palace of the chief celestial deity....The palace thus elevated was no other than the celestial system, illuminated by a central Sun, whose representative on earth was Thor, a god depicted by Verstegan with a crowned head placed in the centre of twelve bright stars, expressive of the Sun's annual course through the Zodiacal Signs.[61]

THE DEVIL'S BRIDGE

Let's notice that the rainbow, like other Masonic symbolism, represents "the male generative principle"! Texe Marrs, a Christian researcher and expert on the New Age movement, writes:

> In the practice of voodoo black magic in Haiti and Africa today, the **RAINBOW IS DEPICTED AS AN EVENT CELEBRATING THE MARRIAGE OF A "RAINBOW GOD" TO THE "SERPENT GOD."**

> In the ancient Jewish **KABBALA**—now being revived by New Age teachers of today—mystical rabbis taught that the **RAINBOW SYMBOLIZED A SEXUAL RITE.** The bow of the rainbow was supposedly the phallus of the male god which descended into the kingdom of the womb, the queen or goddess. The union was said to create immense divine powers.[62]

The Scandinavian god, Thor, was just mentioned by Oliver. He was already covered in Chapter 9, but in Scandinavian mythology, there was a rainbow bridge called Bifrost.[63] This bridge was "also known as the 'devil's bridge'"[64] and was equated with the river Styx of the Egyptians,[65] which was the river that they believed flowed through hell.

Interestingly, a book written by Masonic author, Rex R. Hutchens, is called *A Bridge to Light*. It is a book promoting the teachings of Albert Pike's *Morals and Dogma* and printed by The Supreme Council of Scottish Rite Masonry. The "publication and distribution of this edition" was "UNANIMOUSLY APPROVE[D]" by the Committee on Rituals and Ceremonial Forms.[66] The book is labeled as **"UNDOUBTEDLY 'THE' BOOK FOR EVERY SCOTTISH RITE MASON.**

IT PROVIDES AN ATTRACTIVELY ILLUSTRATED CLEAR EXPLANATION OF OUR ORDER AND ITS DEGREES."[67] On the book's cover can be seen a **RAINBOW BRIDGE**. The description of this scene explains:

> The cover illustration is an Eastern scene to commemorate the tradition that the East was a source of wisdom. The young seekers of knowledge on the left are invited to cross over the bridge; that is, receive the teachings of the Scottish Rite, that they might stand in the light of knowledge, symbolized by the rainbow.[68]

In reference to the bridge, it is fascinating to study the word "pontiff" which is short for "pontifex." *The New Age,* the journal for The Supreme Council of Scottish Rite Masonry, tells us:

> The word "pontifex" itself is a compound of the two Latin words *"facere,"* "to make" and *"pons"* or *"pontis,"* "a bridge." The Romans thought of their priests as makers of a bridge between God and man, so they called such a priest "pontifex," "a bridge-builder." In this sense, therefore, and in no other, let us pontificate!...
>
> **IT IS NO MERE COINCIDENCE** that one of the degrees in our Rite is that of grand Pontiff, for Freemasonry has built its bridges well, and some of them are very long indeed.[69]

A Dictionary of Symbols adds that "the rainbow is a natural symbol of the pontificate."[70] I'm sure it's no coincidence, either, that Pike "used the term, Sublime **PONTIFF OF LUCIFER,** to describe himself."[71] After all, in "Masonic symbolism, the Rainbow appears as the sacred depiction of Lucifer, the Light Bearer, and it indicates his Brightness."[72]

The rainbow bridge (also called the antahkarana) is referred to frequently by the New Age movement and is found repeatedly in occult literature.[73] Dr. Dennis Cuddy, a Christian author, explains: "In the occult, the rainbow is a hypnotic device supposedly forming a bridge between the individual and the over-soul or Great Universal Mind. This 'Mind' is not God."[74] Of course, the mention of the rainbow bridge is also found in Masonic literature. Lynn F. Perkins, a Mason and author of *Masonry in the New Age*, reveals the following about the antahkarana:

> Masons, as "Builders of a Spiritual Fabric," should become familiar with this old Hindu term. It refers to the "Bridge" or "Pathway" that every human being is consciously or unconsciously building between his "lower self" and his "High-Self," between his imperfect self and his perfect self. The process of the "Builder" never ceases **FROM LIFE TO LIFE EITHER IN OR OUT OF A PHYSICAL BODY.** The "rough stone" ultimately becomes the "Perfect Ashlar."[75]

In passing, notice that Perkins is also promoting **REINCARNATION** by his remark about "life to life"! In the teachings of Tibetan Buddhism:

> ...the **RAINBOW SYMBOLIZES MAN'S** ultimate perfect state—**DIVINITY,** when he has achieved an inner unity of good and evil, shadow and light, and becomes one with the Great One.

In other words, **THE NEW AGE TEACHES THAT MAN'S PATH TO GODHOOD IS SYMBOLIZED BY THE "RAINBOW BRIDGE,"** which man crosses over by achieving higher consciousness. The reward at the other end of the rainbow: self-empowerment, immortality, divinity.[76]

LAMBSKIN APRON

Now let's look at some of the items found in the "pot of gold" during the Rainbow Girls ceremony. Knowing that the "Irish legend of the leprechaun with his pot of gold at the end of the rainbow sought to instill in man a covetous desire for treasures and prosperity on earth,"[77] it is interesting to have Charity explain to the initiate:

On the station before you is a vessel representing the traditional Pot of Gold and you are now entitled to know its contents....

It is filled with the treasures of life and we have accepted you into our Assembly with the hope that you will always regard them as truly sacred to you personally in your future life. The Pot of Gold has been hidden from the eyes of many, who have searched for it in the past. It is yours today if you will accept it.[78]

Inside of it is: The Holy Bible, American Flag, Declaration of Independence and Constitution of the United States, list of Presidents who were Master Masons, and a miniature Lambskin apron.[79]

While the Bible is a sacred book to all true Christians, the other items mentioned can hardly be equated on the same level as the Bible, yet the Rainbow Girl is told that all the items in this pot of gold are sacred.[80]

The main "treasure" in this pot seems to be the miniature apron. The initiate is told:

> Last, but by no means least, we find this miniature lambskin **APRON, IN THE CENTER OF WHICH IS A STAR.** I give it to you as your own. **IT IS A SACRED SYMBOL THAT BINDS.** To your father, if he were a Mason, the lambskin apron was sacred, and though you may never fully know its meaning, it will be dear to you because he loved it, and to him it was priceless. Keep it always....Keep in mind that the great Fraternity which has sponsored this Assembly has preserved them for you.[81]

The apron is so important that when a Rainbow Girl dies, there is special mention of this apron made at her funeral service and the apron is then put on her casket to be buried with her.[82] During the funeral service, Charity intones:

> I have this miniature lambskin apron in the center of which is a star. It is a symbol of the tie that binds. In this life she was never privileged to know its meaning; since all things may be made known in the life to come, I now lay this little apron on her casket. Let it be buried with her mortal body. May her memory ever be sacred in

> the hearts and lives of Masons, Eastern Stars and Rainbow girls (sic), that our union may be unbroken until true meaning of all secrets and symbols shall be revealed, who have kindly made our girls' fraternity possible.[83]

This ceremony admits that the secrets and symbols will not be fully revealed to the Rainbow Girl. One of those secrets may have been revealed by Masonic author, Harold Waldwin Percival, when he mentioned that the **"APRON AS A SQUARE** symbolizes the **FOUR ELEMENTS** of nature working in the fourfold body through its four systems and the four senses."[84] We've already seen how the four elements play a role in the Eastern Star, but why so much ado about a tiny apron? Let's turn to a few Masonic sources to see the rationale behind this symbol.

W. L. Wilmshurst, Masonic author, writes: "Brethren, I charge you to regard your apron as one of the most precious and speaking symbols our Order has to give you."[85]

When Adam and Eve sinned they sewed together an apron of fig leaves. We find, however, that God was not pleased with the aprons and He made them coats of skin to clothe them (Genesis 3:7, 21), but Arthur Edward Waite, another Mason, indicates that "in Craft **MASONRY** and its connection the **APRON IS THE ONLY PROPER AND POSSIBLE CLOTHING."**[86]

A newly initiated Mason is instructed that his white apron represents purity.[87] This apron, however, is only a symbol, so to find the real meaning behind this object, we return to mythology. Albert Pike notes that the god Jupiter Ammon's picture was painted with the sign of the Ram or Lamb.[88] He mentions that Jupiter Ammon is "the same as Osiris, Adoni, Adonis, Atys, and the other sun-gods...."[89] Masonic writer, William Hutchinson, also notes that Jupiter Ammon is "painted with horns"[90] and that he is the "same as **BAAL** or Moloch...[and] Adonis, whom some ancient authors call **OSIRIS.**"[91] His ceremonies "consisted in clothing the Initiate with the skin of a white lamb. And **IN THIS WE SEE THE ORIGIN OF THE APRON OF WHITE SHEEP-SKIN USED IN MASONRY.**"[92] So, the apron was used in connection with the ceremonies of Osiris and **THAT** is why the Masons use it, claims Pike!

APRON HAS ROOTS IN PAGANISM

Charles Vail, in his book, *The Ancient Mysteries and Modern Masonry,* also informs us that this apron has its roots in paganism. He writes:

In the Ancient Mysteries the investiture of the **APRON** formed an essential part of the ceremony of Initiation....The Essenes and **DRUIDS** invested their candidates with a White Robe, and the Scandinavians gave the candidate a White Shield. **IN ALL THESE CEREMONIES** whatever the material or form, **THE SYMBOLIC SIGNIFICANCE WAS ALWAYS THE SAME. THE WHITE APRON OF MASONRY WAS DERIVED FROM THESE ANCIENT CEREMONIES, AND IS ONE OF THE MOST SIGNIFICANT SYMBOLS IN OUR ORDER....**[93]

Many other Masons agree. For instance, John T. Lawrence, announces:

The apron is a very ancient symbol, and this mode of investiture is found even in the old **PAGAN** rites. The Essenians clothed their candidates with a white robe reaching to the ground and bordered with a blue fringe. Something answering to the apron is found in the Persian rites of Mithras. The sacred thread of the Brahmin may also be mentioned in this connection....[94]

William Adrian Brown even mentions that the "African **WITCH DOCTOR WEARS AN APRON** along with the rest of his dress."[95]

The apron has more symbolism to it than meets the eye. Brown adds: "In our Masonic education we have much to learn about this **APRON AND ITS TRUE MEANING WHICH CANNOT BE WRITTEN UPON THESE PAGES.**"[96] Of course, some Masons will go into more depth about the symbolism. W. L. Wilmshurst notes:

> The *Tau* displayed upon the Apron worn by those of Master rank is a form of the Cross, and also of the Hammer of **THOR,** of Scandinavian religion....

> The further important point should be noticed that the **APRON COVERS THE CREATIVE, GENERATIVE ORGANS** of the body; and it is especially to these that the significance of the *Tau* attaches. Spiritual self-building and the erection of the "superstructure" are dependent upon the supply of creative energy available from the generative nervous centre, the "power-house" of the human organism. [Italics in the original; Bold and caps added][97]

As with so many other Masonic symbols, the apron is also used in connection with a phallic symbol.

One more notation should suffice. Paul Foster Case, a **MASON WHO IS ALSO "KNOWN TO STUDENTS OF OCCULTISM** as the outstanding authority of Tarot, Qabalah, Alchemy and related subjects of the Western Occult Tradition,"[98] in his book, *The Masonic Letter G,* claims:

> To some modern minds this may seem to be indelicate, but even a slight acquaintance with the symbols of the **ANCIENT MYSTERIES FROM WHICH FREEMASONRY IS PROUD TO CLAIM DESCENT** will suffice to show that the hierophants of those days had no false modesty. It was patent to them that all nature declares the value and sacredness of that power which man degrades when he permits himself to become the slave of his senses. Hence Mackey says:

> "The phallus, therefore, as the symbol of the male generative principle, was very universally venerated among the ancients, and that too as a religious rite, without the slightest reference to any impure or lascivious application."

> Nor is the practical instruction of the **MASONIC LODGE** by any means free from reference to the same ancient idea of the importance of the **GENERATIVE POWER.** The apron which is the distinguishing badge of a Mason is worn so as to conceal this part of the body....

LUCIFER'S PRIESTHOOD

No wonder we are told:

THE APRON IS THE TOOL OF THE CEREMONIAL MAGICIAN AND A SYMBOL

OF LUCIFER'S PRIESTHOOD. It also functions as a sacrilegious parody of the veil in the temple of Solomon, in that **IT VEILS THE "MOST HOLY PLACE"—IN THIS CASE, THE MASON'S GENITAL REGION.**[100]

Even though the correlation to paganism is bad enough, there is something even more sinister about this apron. Masonry claims:

> The lambskin apron is the first gift a man received in Masonry and one of the first symbols which is explained to him. It is his first tangible evidence of becoming a Mason, and **IT WILL BE WITH HIM FROM THAT DAY FORWARD INTO ETERNITY....**

> No greater honor will he ever receive upon this earth than the honor to wear the white apron as it is intended to be worn.[101]

Arthur E. Powell, in *The Magic of Freemasonry,* brags:

> Philosophically regarded, the **FREEMASON'S APRON FULFILS PERFECTLY THE CLASSICAL DEFINITION OF A SACRAMENT—AN OUTWARD AND VISIBLE SIGN OF AN INWARD AND SPIRITUAL GRACE.**[102]

Notice that the candidate is told that this **APRON WILL FOLLOW HIM INTO ETERNITY.** This apron is also considered to be a sacrament!

WHITE THRONE JUDGMENT

When the candidate is invested with this apron, he is told that:

> ...when at last, after a life of faithful service your weary feet shall have come to the end of life's toilsome journey and from your nerveless grasp shall have dropped forever the working tools of life, may the record of your life be as pure and spotless as this fair emblem which I place in your hands tonight, and when your trembling soul shall stand, naked and alone, before the **GREAT WHITE THRONE,** there to receive judgement for the deeds done while here in the body, may it be your portion to hear from Him who sitteth as the Judge Supreme, the welcome words: Well done, thou good and faithful servant. Thou has been faithful over a few things, I will make thee rule over many things! Enter into the joy of thy Lord.[103]

Although this charge sounds wonderful and religious, there is a problem with it. First of all, who is the "Lord" in Masonry? As you should readily see by now, the Masonic God is really Lucifer, howbeit under the guise of other pagan deities. Another problem with this charge becomes apparent when you check the Bible. You see, the **GREAT WHITE THRONE JUDGMENT** is mentioned in Revelation 20:11-15. Turning to these verses, we discover that **ONLY WICKED PEOPLE APPEAR AT THIS JUDGMENT** and then they are cast into the lake of fire.[104]

Part of an Eastern Star poem reads:

"And when is past life's toilsome week,
Welcome the **HOME** that Masons seek!"[105]

Sadly, that final home is the lake of fire and the "Lord" is Satan. In fact, just a few pages after this poem we find these dreadful words: "A lady who makes us a pledge of honor, such as I require of you, **PLEDGES HER VERY SOUL....**"[106] How sad, but how true!

Another segment of the above poem tells us:

"And our emblems on the wall,
Point us to the Lodge in Heaven....
In the bonds of Mason's duty,
SEEK WE NOW THE MASON'S LIGHT."[107]

We've already seen that the light the Masons refer to is the **LIGHT OF LUCIFER.** As Eliphas Levi and Albert Pike have written: "LUCIFER, the *Light-Bearer!*...Lucifer, the Son of the Morning!" [Emphasis in the original][108] Helena Petrovna Blavatsky, both an occultist and Mason,[109] boasts:

...that Satan, or the red *Fiery* Dragon...and *Lucifer,* or "Light-bearer" is in us; it is our Mind—our temptor (sic) and Redeemer, our intelligent liberator and saviour from pure animalism. [Emphasis in the original][110]

Manly Palmer Hall, also a **MASON AND OCCULTIST, BELIEVES THAT THE MESSIAH IS "THE PLANET VENUS, OTHERWISE CALLED LUCIFER...."**[111] We also notice that in the writings of Lynn Perkins, a Mason, he claims: "The **PATH TO HEAVEN SEEMS TO BE BY THE WAY OF HELL** and intended that way by the Creation."[112] There's one problem with this view, however, and that is **THERE IS NO ESCAPE FROM HELL** (see Luke 16:26).

COME OUT FROM AMONG THEM!

There are some words of warning given in Isaiah which would be good for every Mason, Eastern Star, Rainbow Girl, and every other Masonically-affiliated member to think about.

> Woe to the rebellious children, saith the Lord, that take counsel, but not of Me; and that cover with a covering [their Masonic apron!], but not of My spirit, that they may add sin to sin: That walk to go down into Egypt [Egyptian mythology], and have not asked at My mouth; to strengthen themselves in the strength of Pharaoh, and to trust in the shadow of Egypt!...Now go, write it before them in a table, and note it in a book, that it may be for the time to come for ever and ever: That this is a rebellious people, lying children, children that will not hear the law of the Lord (Isaiah 30:1-2, 8-9).

Masons lie and intentionally deceive at the initiations. They also will not hear the law of the Lord, for God has specifically told us:

- "Be ye not unequally yoked together with unbelievers: for what fellowship hath righteousness with unrighteousness? and what communion hath light with darkness?" (II Corinthians 6:14).
- "Have no fellowship with the unfruitful works of darkness, but rather reprove them" (Ephesians 5:11).
- "Come out from among them, and be ye separate, saith the Lord, and touch not the unclean thing; and I will receive you" (II Corinthians 6:17).
- "Swear not at all" (Matthew 5:34; James 5:12).
- "These are the things that ye shall do; Speak ye every man the truth to his neighbour; execute the judgment of truth and peace in your gates: And

let none of you imagine evil in your hearts against his neighbour; and love no false oath: for all these are things that I hate, saith the Lord" (Zechariah 8:16-17).

READY-MADE MEMBERSHIP

Even though the youth groups such as the Rainbow Girls, Job's Daughters, and the DeMolays, seem like innocent organizations, we must remember that these associations are considered to be "feeder groups." The adolescents in these societies are being groomed for potential membership in Masonry and the Eastern Star when they reach adulthood. In fact, according to *The New Age,* a Masonic journal, we are told that about 50% of DeMolays join Masonry when they reach 21 years of age.[113] The August 1991 issue of *The Scottish Rite Journal* reveals:

DeMolays reach the age of membership at 21.
THIS IS NOT A COINCIDENCE; IT WAS INTENDED TO PROVIDE THEM WITH A GOAL—TO BE A MASON....

Masonry is the only organization in the world that has it own ready-made membership resources. We have only to bring these youths into our Lodges, Eastern Star Chapters, or other Masonic organizations.[114]

In the February 1992 issue we find:

Masonic sponsorship of the Order of DeMolay has been and will continue to be the key to success. In every pronouncement, every item of printed matter, publication, and even on shirts made for the DeMolay Chapters, we can see highlighted

SPONSORED BY THE FREEMASONS. [Emphasis in the original][115]

ADOPTIVE MASONRY

Bill Schnoebelen points out some of the dangers involved even in these youth groups: "They are technically called '**ADOPTIVE' MASONRY,** and the youth who joins **IS SPIRITUALLY ADOPTED INTO THE MASONIC FAMILY,** even though not actually a Mason."[116] He continues:

The SPIRIT of Freemasonry looms over every meeting of DeMolays or Rainbows! Whether he knows it or not, the Mason who is present brings with him a luciferian priesthood, which envelopes all who are involved in the meeting....

The same spiritual principality which presides over witchcraft also reigns over all Masonic youth orders! With Masonry being based on sexual fertility cults, the young person walks innocently into a spiritual minefield without warning or advance knowledge when joining a Masonic youth order. They stand in Satan's temples, surrounded by insipid ceremonials which give no warning about the danger lurking beneath them....

At the age when powerful hormones are running at full capacity, these young people are surrendering themselves unknowingly to a spirituality which is engineered to provoke lust!

The rites and symbols of Masonry are sexual in spirit. A young person who is receiving moral doctrine at home is having that teaching subtly undermined by submitting their spiritual priestcraft to the Master Mason who's in charge!

Masonry exalts sexuality to the level of deity, but in a disguised, allegorical fashion. As mentioned earlier, the square and compasses and other Masonic symbols are veiled references to the human reproductive organs—talismans designed to increase sexual desires.

While these orders teach pious principles on the surface, they are pouring fuel on the smoldering fires of teen emotions. [Emphasis in the original][117]

"KINDERGARTEN FOR SATANISM"

One former DeMolay member goes so far as to call the DeMolays a "kindergarten for Satanism," for he "believes it was a major stepping stone for him into occultism and witchcraft."[118] Unfortunately, I'm afraid this is all too true, since we've already seen what is actually being promoted in both the Eastern Star and Masonry.

If you are a member of any Masonic organization (including the Eastern Star, Rainbow Girls, Job's Daughters, etc.), and are also interested in following Christ, you have a decision to make. **EITHER** you can continue on in Masonically-affiliated groups and pay homage and worship to **LUCIFER OR** you must renounce your membership and follow Christ.

Be ye not **UNEQUALLY** yoked together with unbelievers: for what fellowship hath righteousness with unrighteousness? and what communion hath light with darkness? And what concord hath Christ with Belial? or what part hath he that believeth with an infidel? And what agreement hath the temple of God with idols?...Wherefore **COME OUT FROM AMONG THEM** and **BE YE SEPARATE,** saith the Lord, and **TOUCH NOT** the unclean thing; and I will receive you... (II Corinthians 6:14-17).

No man can serve **TWO** masters: for either he will hate the one, and love the other; or else he will hold to the one, and despise the other. Ye **CANNOT** serve God and mammon (Matthew 6:24).

"Thou shalt worship the Lord thy God, and Him **ONLY** shalt thou serve" (Matthew 4:10). "Have **NO FELLOWSHIP** with the unfruitful works of darkness, but rather **REPROVE** them" (Ephesians 5:11).

NO MORE EXCUSES

You may plead ignorance of what is taking place in the Lodge and no doubt most are innocent, especially in the lower degrees, but ignorance does not protect a person from consequences. If I take a walk in the woods and I'm unaware that a poisonous snake is in my path, will I be protected if it bites me? If I would drink poison from a bottle thinking I was taking medicine, I would still die (or become extremely sick) even though I was innocent of the fact. If I would go through a stop sign I did not see, I would still be arrested for breaking the law. Our actions have consequences—even though we may be uninformed about what we are doing.

What would be worse, however, is for someone to ignore a situation after the facts have been presented. If you warned me that a bottle of medicine was actually filled with poison instead, I would be foolish to ignore your counsel. This book has served as a warning. It is now up to you to make the final decision. Will **YOU** serve God or Lucifer? "Choose you **THIS DAY** whom ye will serve...but as for me and my house, we will serve the Lord" (Joshua 24:15).

To those who have not yet joined the Eastern Star or any other Masonic group, but are leaning that way, consider the consequences. Are you willing to pledge your allegiance to **LUCIFER?** Are you willing to partake in **PAGAN AND OCCULTIC** ceremonies with **SEXUAL** overtones? Do you feel comfortable taking an oath in violation of James 5:12 that tells us to **"SWEAR NOT,** neither by heaven, neither by the earth, neither by any other oath"? These are just a few of the items that need to be considered.

Perhaps you are not a member of any secret society and have no intention of joining any and you live a fairly decent life. Even though you may be a moral and honest person, if you have never invited Christ into your heart as your own **PERSONAL** Savior, you, too, need to repent. Maybe you are not committing a blatant sin, but the Bible tells us that **"ALL** have sinned and come short of the glory of God"** (Romans 3:23). The **"ALL"** includes both you and me, and "the wages of sin is [eternal] death; but the gift of God is eternal life through Jesus Christ our Lord" (Romans 6:23). God's gift to us is eternal life, but we must accept this gift to make the transaction valid. If I had a gift to give to you and you refused to accept it, that gift would do you no good. You must **RECEIVE** this gift for it to become effective.

SOME GOOD NEWS

Even though **ALL** of us are born in sin, the good news is that "Christ Jesus came into the world to save sinners" (I Timothy 1:15). If you have never accepted Christ as your **PERSONAL** Savior and would like to do so, the first step is to be born again. John 3:3 emphasizes: **"EXCEPT** a man be born **AGAIN,** he **CANNOT** see the kingdom of God." How can one be born **AGAIN?** We all know that we were born once, our physical birth, but can we enter into our mother's womb and be born the second time (see John 3:1-17)? No. The second birth comes by being born into the family of God. John 3:16:

> For God so **LOVED** the world [that includes **YOU!**] that He **GAVE** His only Begotten Son, that **WHOSOEVER** [that includes **YOU**] **BELIEVETH** [trusts, clings to, relies] on Him [God's Son, Jesus] should not perish [in hell], but have everlasting life.

All you need to do is sincerely believe with all your heart that Jesus is the Son of God and to be willing to turn from your sins, whatever they are—big or small. Ask Jesus to come into your heart and help you to live for Him, and He **WILL** do it. "He that covereth his sins shall not prosper: but whoso **CONFESSETH AND FORSAKETH** them shall have mercy" (Proverbs 28:13). John 6:37 promises: "Him that cometh to Me I will **IN NO WISE** cast out." Romans 10:9 states: "If thou shalt **CONFESS** with thy mouth the Lord Jesus, and shalt **BELIEVE** in thine heart that God hath raised Him from the dead, thou **SHALT** be saved [born again]."

If you would like to be born again, pray your own prayer or sincerely pray the following:

Dear Jesus, I realize that I am a sinner. I believe that You died for my sins. Please forgive me of my past sins and come into my heart. Save me for Your

sake, and help me to live for You. I ask this in Your name. Amen.

If you sincerely prayed and asked Jesus to forgive you of your sins, you will have the assurance that you are now a child of God. John 1:12 reveals: "But **AS MANY AS RECEIVED HIM,** to them gave He power to become the sons of God, even to them that **BELIEVE** on His name." Read your Bible **EVERY** day (start with the book of John), and find a Bible-believing church where you can worship God with other born again believers.

"Therefore being justified by faith, we have peace with God through our Lord Jesus Christ" (Romans 5:1), "and the peace of God, which passeth all understanding, shall keep your hearts and minds through Christ Jesus" (Philippians 4:7). "If the Son [Jesus Christ] therefore shall make you free, ye shall be free indeed" (John 8:36).

ENDNOTES

Chapter 1: A Brief History of the Eastern Star

1. *History of the Order of the Eastern Star* (n.p., 1989), p.37; See also: "Follow the Star: Together We Build a Better Life" (Washington, D.C.: General Grand Chapter Order of the Eastern Star, 1989), p.2; Mary Ann Slipper, *Symbolism of the Eastern Star* (n.p., 1927), p.136; F. A. Bell, *Bell's Eastern Star Ritual* (P. R. C. Publications, Inc., 1988 Revised Edition), p.19; John J. Robinson, *A Pilgrim's Path: One Man's Road to the Masonic Temple* (New York, New York: M. Evans and Company, Inc., 1993), p.18; *The Eastern Star Journal* (Summer Edition, 1993), Back Cover.

2. Harold Van Buren Voorhis, *The Eastern Star: The Evolution from a Rite to an Order* (Richmond, Virginia: Macoy Publishing and Masonic Supply Company, Inc., 1938), p.5-6; See also: Lucien V. Rule, *Pioneering in Masonry: The Life and Times of Rob Morris, Masonic Laureate, Together with Story of Clara Barton and the Eastern Star* (Louisville, Kentucky: Brandt and Connors Company, 1922), p.10, 137; David B. Dibrell, "Rob Morris: Founder of the Eastern Star," *The Scottish Rite Journal* (November 1992, Vol. 100, No. 11), p.13, 15; Charles A. Watts, *Worthy Matrons' Hand Book: Order of the Eastern Star*, (Washington, D.C.: General Grand Chapter, Order of the Eastern Star, 1988), p.30.

3. *History of the Order of the Eastern Star, op. cit.,* p.10.

4. Voorhis, *op. cit.,* p.7; See also: Jean M'Kee Kenaston, Compiler, *History of the Order of the Eastern Star* (Cedar Rapids, Iowa: The Torch Press, 1917), p.60; David B. Dibrell, "Rob Morris: Founder of the Eastern Star," *The Scottish Rite Journal* (November 1992, Vol. 100, No. 11), p.13; Lucien V. Rule, *Pioneering in Masonry: The Life and Times of Rob Morris, Masonic Laureate, Together with Story of Clara Barton and the Eastern Star* (Louisville, Kentucky: Brandt and Connors Company, 1922), p.103.

5. *Ibid,* p.9.

6. Jean M'Kee Kenaston, Compiler, *History of the Order of the Eastern Star* (Cedar Rapids, Iowa: The Torch Press, 1917), p.53.

7. *Ibid,* p.67; See also: Charles A. Watts, *Worthy Matrons' Hand Book: Order of the Eastern Star*, (Washington, D.C.: General Grand Chapter, Order of the Eastern Star, 1988), p.32; D. Duane Winters, *A Search for Light in a Place of Darkness: A Study of Freemasonry* (no other information available), p.60; Lucien V. Rule, *Pioneering in Masonry: The Life and Times of Rob Morris, Masonic Laureate, Together with Story of Clara Barton and the Eastern Star* (Louisville, Kentucky: Brandt and Connors Company, 1922), p.102, 138.

8. Charles A. Watts, *Worthy Matrons' Hand Book: Order of the Eastern Star*, (Washington, D.C.: General Grand Chapter, Order of the Eastern Star, 1988), p.31.

9. F. A. Bell, *Bell's Eastern Star Ritual* (P. R. C. Publications, Inc., 1988 Revised Edition), p.18.

10. Voorhis, *op. cit.,* p.10; See also: David B. Dibrell, "Rob Morris: Founder of the Eastern Star," *The Scottish Rite Journal* (November 1992, Vol. 100, No. 11), p.14.

11. Kenaston, *op. cit.,* p.60.

12. *Ibid.,* p.75, 60; See also: Watts, *op. cit.,* p.31; Voorhis, *op. cit.,* p.12.

13. *History of the Order of the Eastern Star, op. cit.,* p.18; See also: Lucien V. Rule, *Pioneering in Masonry: The Life and Times of Rob Morris, Masonic Laureate, Together with Story of Clara Barton and the Eastern Star* (Louisville, Kentucky: Brandt and Connors Company, 1922), p.177.

14. Lucien V. Rule, *Pioneering in Masonry: The Life and Times of Rob Morris, Masonic Laureate, Together with Story of Clara Barton and the Eastern Star* (Louisville, Kentucky: Brandt and Connors Company, 1922), p.139-140.

15. Voorhis, *op. cit.,* p.16.

16. *Ibid.,* p.18.

17. *Ibid.,* p.19, 21; See also: Rule, *op. cit.,* p.139.

18. *Ibid.,* p.28.

19. *Ibid.,* quoting Rob Morris, p.19.

20. *Ibid.,* quoting Rob Morris, p.21.

21. Willis D. Engle, *A General History of the Order of the Eastern Star* (Indianapolis, Indiana: Willis D. Engle, 1901), p.14.

22. Mary Ann Slipper, *Symbolism of the Eastern Star* (n.p., 1927), p.136.

23. Robert Macoy (Arranged by), *Adoptive Rite Ritual* (Virginia: Macoy Publishing and Masonic Supply Company, 1897), p.12-13; See also: Rule, *op. cit.,* p.102.

24. Voorhis, *op. cit.,* quoting Rob Morris, p.33.

25. D. Duane Winters, *A Search for Light in a Place of Darkness: A Study of Freemasonry* (no other information available), p.60; Henry Wilson Coil, *Coil's Masonic Encyclopedia* (New York, New York: Macoy Publishing and Masonic Supply Company, Inc., 1961), p.11; Rule, *op. cit.,* p.121, 139, 174, 175, 177.

26. Engle, *op. cit.,* p.25; See also: David B. Dibrell, "Rob Morris: Founder of the Eastern Star," *The Scottish Rite Journal* (November 1992, Vol. 100, No. 11), p.13.

27. Voorhis, *op. cit.,* p.41; Henry Wilson Coil, *Coil's Masonic Encyclopedia* (New York, New York: Macoy Publishing and Masonic Supply Company, Inc., 1961), p.11; David B. Dibrell, "Rob Morris: Founder of the Eastern Star," *The Scottish Rite Journal* (November 1992, Vol. 100, No. 11), p.13; Rule, *op. cit.,* p.177.

28. *History of the Order of the Eastern Star, op. cit.,* p.11.

29. Voorhis, *op. cit.,* p.11.

30. *Ibid.,* p.58, 60; David B. Dibrell, "Rob Morris: Founder of the Eastern Star," *The Scottish Rite Journal* (November 1992, Vol. 100, No. 11), p.14-15.

31. *Ibid.,* p.63.

32. *History of the Order of the Eastern Star, op. cit.,* p.25.

33. *Ibid.*

34. Engle, *op. cit.,* p.52.

35. *History of the Order of the Eastern Star, op. cit.,* p.27.

36. *Ibid.,* p.28.

37. *Ibid.,* p.31.

Chapter 2: The Masonic Connection

1. Alvin J. Schmidt and Nicholas Babchuk, Editors, *The Greenwood Encyclopedia of American Institutions: Fraternal Organizations* (Westport, Connecticut: Greenwood Press, 1980) p.97; See also: John J. Robinson, *A Pilgrim's Path: One Man's Road to the Masonic Temple* (New York: New York: M. Evans and Company, Inc., 1993), p.18.

2. *What? When? Where? Why? Who? in Freemasonry* (Silver Spring, Maryland: Masonic Service Association of the United States, 1956), p.28.

3. F. A. Bell, *Bell's Eastern Star Ritual* (P. R. C. Publications, Inc., 1988 Revised Edition), p.94; William J. Whalen, *Handbook of Secret Organizations* (Milwaukee, Wisconsin: The Bruce Publishing Company, 1966), p.29.

4. *Ibid.*; Albert G. Mackey, *The Symbolism of Freemasonry* (New York: Clark and Maynard, 1869), p.29; William J. Whalen, *Handbook of Secret Organizations* (Milwaukee, Wisconsin: The Bruce Publishing Company, 1966), p.27, 29; See also: John J. Robinson, *A Pilgrim's Path: One Man's Road to the Masonic Temple* (New York: New York: M. Evans and Company, Inc., 1993), p.18; Charles A. Watts, *Worthy Matrons' Hand Book: Order of the Eastern Star* (Washington, D.C.: General Grand Chapter, Order of the Eastern Star, 1988), p.17, 18.

5. Thomas Lowe, *Adoptive Masonry: Eastern Star Ritual* (Chicago, Illinois: Ezra A. Cook, 1913), p.20-21.

6. Bell, *op. cit.*; See also: *Ritual of the Order of the Eastern Star* (Washington, D.C.: General Grand Chapter Order of the Eastern Star, 1956), p.56, 77.

7. Lucien V. Rule, *The Life and Times of Rob Morris* (no other information available), p.11.

8. Sarah H. Terry, *The Second Mile* (Corpus Christi, Texas: Christian Triumph Press, 1935), p.63.

9. *The Authorized Standard Ritual of the Order of the Eastern Star of New York* (New York, Press of Andrew H. Kellogg Company, 1876; Twentieth Edition, 1916), p.22; Robert Macoy (Arranged by), *Adoptive Rite Ritual* (Virginia: Macoy Publishing and Masonic Supply Company, 1897), p.9; William J. Whalen, *Handbook of Secret Organizations* (Milwaukee, Wisconsin: The Bruce Publishing Company, 1966), p.26, 27; *What Is the Order of the Eastern Star?* (Newtonville, New York: HRT Ministries, Inc., n.d.), p.1; William Meyer, *The Order of the Eastern Star* (no other information available), p.1; Schmidt and Babchuk, *op. cit.*, p.99; "Follow the Star: Together We Build a Better Life" (Washington, D.C.: General Grand Chapter Order of the Eastern Star, 1989), p.3; *The Eastern Star Journal* (Summer Edition, 1993), Back Cover; John J. Robinson, *A Pilgrim's Path: One Man's Road to the Masonic Temple* (New York: New York: M. Evans and Company, Inc., 1993), p.18.

10. G. W. Brown, *The Ladies' Friend* (Ann Arbor, Michigan: Press of Dr. A. W. Chase, 1866), p.5.

11. *The Authorized Standard Ritual of the Order of the Eastern Star of New York*, *op. cit.*, p.15; Bell, *op. cit.*, p.39; William J. Whalen, *Handbook of Secret Organizations* (Milwaukee, Wisconsin: The Bruce Publishing Company, 1966), p.26; Robert Macoy (Arranged by), *Adoptive Rite Ritual* (Virginia: Macoy Publishing and Masonic Supply Company, 1897), p.14.

12. *What? When? Where? Why? Who? in Freemasonry, op. cit.*, p.28; D. Duane Winters, *A Search for Light in a Place of Darkness: A Study of Freemasonry* (no other information available), p.6; See also: Bell, *op. cit.*, p.39.

13. Schmidt and Babchuk, *op. cit.*, p.99.

14. Bell, *op. cit.*, p.53; Robert Macoy (Arranged by), *Adoptive Rite Ritual* (Virginia: Macoy Publishing and Masonic Supply Company, 1897), p.67.

15. *Ibid.*, p.64; William J. Whalen, *Handbook of Secret Organizations* (Milwaukee, Wisconsin: The Bruce Publishing Company, 1966), p.27.

16. Schmidt and Babchuk, *op. cit.*, p.97; See also: Rule, *The Life and Times of Rob Morris, op. cit.*, p.102.

17. Bell, *op. cit.*, p.18; *The F.A.T.A.L. Flaw* (Issaquah, Washington: Free the Masons Ministries, n.d.), p.2; See also: William Schnoebelen, *Masonry: Beyond the Light* (Chino, California: Chick Publications, 1991), p.104; Albert G. Mackey, *Encyclopedia of Freemasonry*, Vol. 1 (Chicago, Illinois: The Masonic History Company, 1909), p.302; Robert Macoy (Arranged by), *Adoptive Rite Ritual* (Virginia: Macoy Publishing and Masonic Supply Company, 1897), p.9; Albert G. Mackey, *An Encyclopedia of Freemasonry and Its Kindred Science* (Chicago, Illinois: The Masonic History Company, 1924), p.29.

18. Robert Macoy (Arranged by), *Adoptive Rite Ritual* (Virginia: Macoy Publishing and Masonic Supply Company, 1897), p.9.

19. Malcolm Duncan, *Duncan's Ritual of Freemasonry* (New York: David McKay Company, Inc., n.d., 3rd Edition), p.105.

20. Jabez Richardson, *Richardson's Monitor of Free-Masonry* (n.p., 1860), p.31; John J. Robinson, *Born in Blood: The Lost Secrets of Freemasonry* (New York, New York: M. Evans and Company, 1989), p.221 and many other sources.

21. Edmond Ronayne, quoting A. T. C. Pierson, *The Master's Carpet (Mah-Hah-Bone)* (n.p., 1879), p.235; See also: A. T. C. Pierson, *The Traditions, Origin and Early History of Freemasonry* (New York: Masonic Publishing Company, 1865), p.240.

22. Bell, *op. cit.*, p.9; See also: *The Authorized Standard Ritual of the Order of the Eastern Star of New York, op. cit.*, p.121-122.

23. Duncan, *op. cit.*, p.34-35; Richardson, *op. cit.*, p.10; Charles G. Finney, *The Character, Claims and Practical Workings of Freemasonry* (Chicago, Illinois: National Christian Association, 1938), p.44.

24. *Ibid.*, p.65-66; Richardson, *op. cit.*, p.21.

25. *Ibid.*, p.96; Richardson, *op. cit.*, p.30.

26. David L. Carrico, quoting Lynn F. Perkins, *The Pentagram, Freemasonry and the Goat* (Evansville, Illinois: Followers of Jesus Christ, 1992), p.17.

27. Bell, *op. cit.*, p.18-19.

28. Lowe, *op. cit.*, p.19-20; See also: Jean M'Kee Kenaston, Compiler, *History of the Order of the Eastern Star* (Cedar Rapids, Iowa: The Torch Press, 1917), p.582-584; Brown, *op. cit.*, p.7-8; William J. Whalen, *Handbook of Secret Organizations* (Milwaukee, Wisconsin: The Bruce Publishing Company, 1966), p.25.

29. Statement from a personal letter dated November 17, 1991, quoting from *Freemasonry and American Culture 1880-1930* by Lynn Dumenil.; See also:

D. Duane Winters, *A Search for Light in a Place of Darkness: A Study of Freemasonry* (no other information available), p.61.

30. Jean M'Kee Kenaston, Compiler, *History of the Order of the Eastern Star* (Cedar Rapids, Iowa: The Torch Press, 1917), p.95.

31. *Ibid.*, quoting Rob Morris, p.75.

32. Lucien V. Rule, *Pioneering in Masonry: The Life and Times of Rob Morris, Masonic Poet Laureate, Together with Story of Clara Barton and the Eastern Star* (Louisville, Kentucky: Brandt and Connors Company, 1922), p.123.

33. Kenaston, *op. cit.*, p.601.

34. *History of the Order of the Eastern Star* (General Grand Chapter in the U. S. A., 1989), p.19.

35. *Ritual National Imperial Court of the Daughters of Isis North and South America* (Chicago, Illinois: Ezra A. Cook Publications, Inc., n.d.), Back Cover.

36. Bell, *op. cit.*, p.20.

Chapter 3: The Eastern Star and Christianity

1. Willis D. Engle, *A General History of the Order of the Eastern Star* (Indianapolis, Indiana: Willis D. Engle, 1901), p.119.

2. *Ibid.*

3. *Ibid.*, p.120.

4. *Ibid.*

5. Robert Macoy (Arranged by), *Adoptive Rite Ritual* (Virginia: Macoy Publishing and Masonic Supply Company, 1897), p.13; See also: *The Eastern Star Journal* (Summer Edition, 1993), Back Cover; Mary Ann Slipper, *The Symbolism of the Eastern Star* (n.p., 1927), p.5.

6. "Follow the Star: Together We Build a Better Life" (Washington, D.C.: General Grand Chapter Order of the Eastern Star, 1989), p.3-4; See also: Charles A. Watts, *Worthy Matrons' Hand Book: Order of the Eastern Star* (Washington, D.C.: General Grand Chapter, Order of the Eastern Star, 1988), p.16; Shirley Plessner, *Symbolism of the Eastern Star* (Cleveland, Ohio: Gilbert Publishing Company, 1956), p.ix.

7. George Oliver, quoting Rob Morris in *The Historical Landmarks and Other Evidences of Freemasonry, Explained* (Vol. I & II) (New York: John W. Leonard and Company, 1855), p.109.

8. Lucien V. Rule, *Pioneering in Masonry: The Life and Times of Rob Morris, Masonic Poet Laureate, Together with Story of Clara Barton and the Eastern Star* (Louisville, Kentucky: Brandt and Connors Company, 1922), p.109.

9. *Ibid.*

10. *Ibid.*, p.110.

11. Macoy, *op. cit.*, p.16; F. A. Bell, *Bell's Eastern Star Ritual* (P. R. C. Publications, Inc., 1988 Revised Edition), p.21.

12. Ruth Adams, *One Little Candle* (Richmond, Virginia: Macoy Publishing and Masonic Company, Inc., 1966), p.102, 126; Sarah H. Terry, *The Second Mile* (Corpus Christi, Texas: Christian Triumph Press, 1935), p.7.

13. Macoy, *op. cit.*, Inserted syllabus.

14. *Ibid.*, p.86.

15. Jean M'Kee Kenaston, Compiler, *History of the Order of the Eastern Star* (Cedar Rapids, Iowa: The Torch Press, 1917), p.544-545.

16. Sarah H. Terry, *The Second Mile* (Corpus Christi, Texas: Christian Triumph Press, 1935), p.11; See also: Rex R. Hutchens and Donald W. Monson, *The Bible in Albert Pike's Morals and Dogma* (Washington, D.C.: Supreme Council, 33rd Degree, 1992), p.165.

17. Adam Clarke, *Clarke's Commentary, Volume II—Joshua to Esther* (Nashville, Tennessee: Abindgon-Cokesbury Press, n.d.), p.151. See also: *The Old Testament According to the Authorised Version Historical Books—Joshua to Esther,* by Various Authors (London: Society for Promoting Christian Knowledge, 1887), unnumbered page; Finis Jennings Dake, *Dake's Annotated Reference Bible* (Lawrenceville, Georgia: Dake Bible Sales, Inc. 1979), p.282; Thomas Lowe, *Adoptive Masonry: Eastern Star Ritual* (Chicago, Illinois: Ezra A. Cook, 1913), p.32-35; Shirley Plessner, *Symbolism of the Eastern Star* (Cleveland, Ohio: Gilbert Publishing Company, 1956), p.10-12, 15-17, etc.

18. William Meyer, *The Order of the Eastern Star* (no other information available), p.7.

19. Kenaston, *op. cit.*, p.548; G. W. Brown, *The Ladies' Friend* (Ann Arbor, Michigan: Press of Dr. A. W. Chase, 1866), p.33.

20. Juliette T. Burton, *The Five Jewels of the Orient* (New York City, New York: Macoy Publishing and Masonic Supply Company, 1928), p.102.

21. Kenaston, *op. cit.*, p.553; G. W. Brown, *The Ladies' Friend* (Ann Arbor, Michigan: Press of Dr. A. W. Chase, 1866), p.48.

22. Macoy, *op. cit.*, p.108; F. A. Bell, *Bell's Eastern Star Ritual* (P. R. C. Publications, Inc., 1988 Revised Edition), p.81; Thomas Lowe, *Adoptive Masonry: Eastern Star Ritual* (Chicago, Illinois: Ezra A. Cook, 1913), p.44; Kenaston, *op. cit.*, p.594-595.

23. *Ibid.*, p.108-109; F. A. Bell, *Bell's Eastern Star Ritual* (P. R. C. Publications, Inc., 1988 Revised Edition), p.81-82; Thomas Lowe, *Adoptive Masonry: Eastern Star Ritual* (Chicago, Illinois: Ezra A. Cook, 1913), p.44; Kenaston, *op. cit.*, p.595.

24. *Ibid.*, p.109; F. A. Bell, *Bell's Eastern Star Ritual* (P. R. C. Publications, Inc., 1988 Revised Edition), p.81-82; Thomas Lowe, *Adoptive Masonry: Eastern Star Ritual* (Chicago, Illinois: Ezra A. Cook, 1913), p.44; Kenaston, *op. cit.*, p.554.

25. Kenaston, *op. cit.*, p.556.

26. *Ibid.*, p.537.

27. Macoy, *op.cit.*, p.109-110; F. A. Bell, *Bell's Eastern Star Ritual* (P. R. C. Publications, Inc., 1988 Revised Edition), p.81-82; Thomas Lowe, *Adoptive Masonry: Eastern Star Ritual* (Chicago, Illinois: Ezra A. Cook, 1913), p.44-45; Kenaston, *op. cit.*, p.556, 596; Robert Phillips, *A Little Light on the Heroines of the Order of the Eastern Star* (Goldwater, Michigan, n.p., 1910), p.35.

28. Thomas Lowe, *Adoptive Masonry: Eastern Star Ritual* (Chicago, Illinois: Ezra A. Cook, 1913), p.43; F. A. Bell, *Bell's Eastern Star Ritual* (P. R. C. Publications, Inc., 1988 Revised Edition), p.80; Robert Phillips, *A Little Light on the Heroines of the Order of the Eastern Star* (Goldwater, Michigan, n.p., 1910), p.34; Terry, *op. cit.*, p.25.

29. Kenaston, *op. cit.*, p.554; See also: *The Authorized Standard Ritual of the Order of the Eastern Star of New York* (New York, Press of Andrew H. Kellogg Company, 1876; Twentieth Edition, 1916), p.73.

30. *Ibid.*, p.545.

31. G. W. Brown, *The Ladies' Friend* (Ann Arbor, Michigan: Press of Dr. A. W. Chase, 1866), p.33.

32. *Ibid.*, p.61.

33. Macoy, *op. cit.*, p.16.

34. Rule, *op. cit.*, p.177.

35. Kenaston, *op. cit.*, p.538; See also: Brown, *op. cit.*, p.61; Rule, *op. cit.*, p.177.

36. F. A. Bell, *Bell's Eastern Star Ritual* (P. R. C. Publications, Inc., 1988 Revised Edition), p.90; Lowe, *op. cit.*, p.57; Macoy, *op. cit.*, p.116-118; Kenaston, *op. cit.*, p.599; *The Authorized Standard Ritual of the Order of the Eastern Star of New York* (New York, Press of Andrew H. Kellogg Company, 1876; Twentieth Edition, 1916), p.77; Brown, *op. cit.*, p.17.

37. Kenaston, *op. cit.*, p.563; See also: *The Authorized Standard Ritual of the Order of the Eastern Star of New York* (New York, Press of Andrew H. Kellogg Company, 1876; Twentieth Edition, 1916), p.77; Brown, *op. cit.*, p.62-63.

38. *Ibid.*, p.599.

39. Bell, *op. cit.*, p.91; Lowe, *op. cit.*, p.58.

40. Kenaston, *op. cit.*, p.565.

41. *Ibid.*, p.599.

42. *Ibid.*, p.565-566.

43. *Ibid.*, p.544.

44. *Ibid.*, p.565.

45. *Ibid.*, p.599.

46. *Ibid.*, p.565.

47. *Ibid.*, p.561-562.

48. *Ibid.*, p.544.

49. *Ibid.*, p.566.

50. *Ibid.*, p.17.

51. *Ibid.*, p.548; See also: Engle, *op. cit.*, p.91; Rule, *Pioneering in Masonry, op. cit.*, p.177.

52. *Ibid.*, p.649, 592; See also: Brown, *op. cit.*, p.40; Engle, *op. cit.*, p.91.

53. *Ibid.*, p.551; See also: Brown, *op. cit.*, p.41; Engle, *op. cit.*, p.91; Rule, *Pioneering in Masonry, op. cit.*, p.177.

54. *Ibid.*, p.593.

55. Frank Charles Thompson, Editor, *The New Chain-Reference Bible*, (Indianapolis, Indiana: B. B. Kirkbride Bible Company, Inc., 1957), p.261.

56. Edward Reese, Editor, *The Chronological Bible*, (Nashville, Tennessee: Regal Publishers, Inc., 1977), p.395.

57. *Ibid.,* p.399.

58. *Ibid.,* p.531.

59. Kenaston, *op. cit.,* p.397; Brown, *op. cit.,* p.55; Engle, *op. cit.,* p.91.

60. *Ibid.,* p.525.

61. *Ibid.,* p.70.

62. Macoy, *op. cit.,* p.140; Bell, *op. cit.,* p.173.

63. Bell, *op. cit.,* p.194-195; See also: Macoy, *op. cit.,* p.163-164.

64. Macoy, *op. cit.,* p.165-165; Meyer, *op. cit.,* p.15.

65. Meyer, quoting from the Masonic ritual, *op. cit.,* p.15

66. *Ibid.,* p.15-16.

67. Macoy, *op. cit.,* p.141, 142, 143, 157, 158; Bell, *op. cit.,* p.173, 191, 194.

68. *Ibid.,* p.157.

69. *Ibid.,* p.158.

Chapter 4: His Star in the East

1. Willis D. Engle, *A General History of the Order of the Eastern Star* (Indianapolis, Indiana: Willis D. Engle, 1901), p.137.

2. *Ritual of the Order of the Eastern Star* (Washington, D.C.: General Grand Chapter Order of the Eastern Star, 1956), p.81; John J. Robinson, *A Pilgrim's Path: One Man's Road to the Masonic Temple* (New York: New York: M. Evans and Company, Inc., 1993), p.82.

3. Robert Macoy (Arranged by), *Adoptive Rite Ritual* (Virginia: Macoy Publishing and Masonic Supply Company, 1897), p.293; See also: Thomas Albert Stafford, *Christian Symbolism in the Evangelical Churches* (Nashville, Tennessee: Abingdon Press, 1942), p.81; Arthur Edward Waite, *The Mysteries of Magic: A Digest of the Writings of Eliphas Levi* (Chicago, Illinois: De Laurence, Scott and Company, 1909), p.205.

4. *Ibid.*

5. Charles A. Watts, *Worthy Matrons' Hand Book: Order of the Eastern Star* (Washington, D.C.: General Grand Chapter, Order of the Eastern Star, 1988), p.26.

6. *The F.A.T.A.L. Flaw* (Issaquah, Washington: Free the Masons Ministries, n.d.), p.5; See also: D. Duane Winters, *A Search for Light in a Place of Darkness: A Study of Freemasonry* (no other information available), p.71.

7. Mary Ann Slipper, *The Symbolism of the Eastern Star* (n.p., 1927), p.9-10.

8. *The Scottish Rite Journal* (November 1993; Vol. 101, No. 11), p.57.

9. *Short Talk Bulletin,* "Blazing Star," Part 1 (March 1965; Vol. 43, No. 3), p.12.

10. *Ibid.*

11. *Ibid.,* p.7; See also: A. T. C. Pierson, *The Traditions, Origin and Early History of Freemasonry* (New York: Masonic Publishing Company, 1865), p.66-67; George Oliver, *Symbol of Glory Shewing the Object and End of Freemasonry* (New York: John W. Leonard and Company, American Masonic Agency, 1855), p.258; Albert Pike, *Morals and Dogma of the Ancient and Accepted Scottish*

Rite of Freemasonry (Richmond, Virginia: L. H. Jenkins, Inc., 1871), p.787; John T. Lawrence, *The Perfect Ashlar* (London: A. Lewis, 1912), p.200; Amaury De Riencourt, *The Eye of Shiva: Eastern Mysticism and Science* (New York, New York: William Morrow and Company, Inc., 1980), p.63.

12. Albert G. Mackey, *A Manual of the Lodge* (New York: Charles E. Merrill Company, 1870), p.50-51; *Short Talk Bulletin*, "Mosaic Pavement and Blazing Star" (April 1951; Vol. 29, No. 4; Reprinted April 1990), p.7.

13. George Oliver, *The Historical Landmarks and Other Evidences of Freemasonry, Explained* (Vol. I & II) (New York: John W. Leonard and Company, 1855), p.118; See also: George Oliver, *Symbol of Glory Shewing the Object and End of Freemasonry* (New York: John W. Leonard and Company, American Masonic Agency, 1855), p.255.

14. George Oliver, *Symbol of Glory Shewing the Object and End of Freemasonry* (New York: John W. Leonard and Company, American Masonic Agency, 1855), p.259; See also: *Short Talk Bulletin*, "Mosaic Pavement and Blazing Star" (April 1951; Vol. 29, No. 4; Reprinted April 1990), p.7, 8.

15. *Short Talk Bulletin*, "Mosaic Pavement and Blazing Star" (April 1951; Vol. 29, No. 4; Reprinted April 1990), p.7; *Short Talk Bulletin*, "Blazing Star," Part 1, *op. cit.*, p.5.

16. Oliver, *Symbol of Glory, op. cit.*, p.741, p.122.

17. Francois Ribadeau Dumas (Translated by Elisabeth Abbott), *Cagliostro: Scoundrel or Saint?* (New York: The Orion Press, 1967), p.46.

18. *Short Talk Bulletin*, "Blazing Star," Part 1, *op. cit.*, p.5; See also: *Short Talk Bulletin*, "Mosaic Pavement and Blazing Star," *op. cit.*, p.7.

19. Arthur Edward Waite, quoting Eliphas Levi, *The Mysteries of Magic: A Digest of the Writings of Eliphas Levi* (Chicago, Illinois: De Laurence, Scott and Company, 1909), p.76-77; See also: Helena Petrovna Blavatsky, *Isis Unveiled*, Vol. I: Science (New York, New York: Trow's Printing and Bookbinding Company, 1877), p.138.

20. J. S. M. Ward, *Freemasonry and the Ancient Gods* (London: Simpkin, Marshall, Hamilton, Kent and Company, Ltd., 1921), p.278; Oliver, *Symbol of Glory, op. cit.*, p.741, p.152; Oliver, *The Historical Landmarks, op. cit.*, p.122, 134-135.

21. Papa Jim, Inc. (1989 Catalog), p.48.

22. Oliver, *Symbol of Glory, op. cit.*, p.741, p.152-153; *Short Talk Bulletin*, "Mosaic Pavement and Blazing Star," *op. cit.*, p.7; Sir Wallis Budge, *Egyptian Magic* (Secaucus, New Jersey: University Books, Inc., n.d.), p.180.

23. Frank Gaynor, Editor, *Dictionary of Mysticism* (New York: Philosophical Library, 1953), p.4; See also: Waite, *The Mysteries of Magic, op. cit.*, p.216.

24. William Hutchinson (Revised by George Oliver), *The Spirit of Masonry*, (New York: Bell Publishing Company, 1982; Originally published in 1775), p.80.

25. J. E. Cirlot (Translated by Jack Sage), *A Dictionary of Symbols* (New York: Dorset Press, 1991 Edition), p.2; See also: Gaynor, *op. cit.*, p.4; Arthur Edward Waite, *The Secret Tradition in Freemasonry* (London: Rider and Company, 1937), p.136; Arthur Edward Waite, *Emblematic Freemasonry and the Evolution of Its Deeper Issues* (London: William Rider and Son, Ltd., 1925), p.83; Waite, *The Mysteries of Magic, op. cit.*, p.208; Papa Jim, Inc., *op. cit.*, p.48; Oliver, *Symbol of Glory, op. cit.*, p.741, p.152.

26. William O. Peterson, Editor, *Masonic Quiz Book: "Ask Me Another, Brother"* (Chicago, Illinois: Charles T. Powner Company, 1950), p.219; Editors of Time-Life Books, *Magical Arts* (Alexandria, Virginia: Time-Life Books, 1990), p.60.

27. For example, see: *Ibid.,* p.225; Lucien V. Rule, *Pioneering in Masonry: The Life and Times of Rob Morris, Masonic Poet Laureate, Together with Story of Clara Barton and the Eastern Star* (Louisville, Kentucky: Brandt and Connors Company, 1922), p.158, 161, etc.

28. Albert Pike, *Morals and Dogma of the Ancient and Accepted Scottish Rite of Freemasonry* (Richmond, Virginia: L. H. Jenkins, Inc., 1871), p.15.

29. *Ibid.,* p.506, 411, 430, 486; See also: Edmond Ronayne, quoting Albert Mackey, *The Master's Carpet (Mah-Hah-Bone)* (n.p., 1879), p.314; W. J. McCormick, *Christ, the Christian and Freemasonry* (Belfast, Ireland: Great Joy Publications, 1984), p.91; C. F. McQuaig, *The Masonic Report* (Norcross, Georgia: Answer Books and Tapes, 1976), p.48, 49; Alice A. Bailey, *From Bethlehem to Calvary: The Initiations of Jesus* (New York: Lucis Publishing Company, 1965), p.60, 63; *Short Talk Bulletin,* "Mosaic Pavement and Blazing Star," *op. cit.,* p.8.

30. *Ibid.,* p.13; See also: W. J. McCormick, *Christ, the Christian and Freemasonry* (Belfast, Ireland: Great Joy Publications, 1984), p.91.

31. *Ibid.,* p.15, 467; See also: *Sphaera Imaginatio* (1986, Issue #16), p.16; Albert Churchward, *Signs and Symbols of Primordial Man* (London: George Allen and Company, Ltd., 1913, Second Edition), p.206, 369; Geoffrey Parrinder, Editor, *World Religions: From Ancient History to the Present* (New York, New York: Facts on File, 1971), p.140; Veronica Ions, *Egyptian Mythology* (England: The Hamlyn Publishing Group, Ltd., 1965), p.21, 82; *Circle Network News* (Summer 1984; Vol. 6, No. 2), p.3; M. Esther Harding, *Woman's Mysteries: Ancient and Modern* (New York: G. P. Putnam's Sons for the C. G. Jung Foundation for Analytical Psychology, 1971 Edition), p.172.

32. *Circle Network News* (Summer 1984; Vol. 6, No. 2), p.3.

33. Alice A. Bailey, *From Bethlehem to Calvary: The Initiations of Jesus* (New York: Lucis Publishing Company, 1965), p.60; *Short Talk Bulletin,* "Mosaic Pavement and Blazing Star," *op. cit.,* p.7.

34. Albert Churchward, *Signs and Symbols of Primordial Man* (London: George Allen and Company, Ltd., 1913, Second Edition), p.421, 468.

35. Hugh A. Moran and David H. Kelley, *The Alphabet and the Ancient Calendar Signs* (Palo Alto, California: Daily Press, 1969, Second Edition), p.104.

36. Churchward, *op. cit.,* p.369.

37. Oliver, *The Historical Landmarks, op. cit.,* p.396; R. Swinburne Clymer, *The Mysteries of Osiris or Ancient Egyptian Initiation* (Quakertown, Pennsylvania: The Philosophical Publishing Company, 1951, Revised Edition), p.38.

38. Churchward, *op. cit.,* p.468.

39. Israel Regardie, *The Golden Dawn* (St. Paul, Minnesota: Llewellyn Publications, 1986), p.186, 188.

40. Churchward, *op. cit.,* p.469.

41. *Ibid.,* p.206.

42. Oliver, *The Historical Landmarks, op. cit.,* , p.396; R. Swinburne Clymer, *The Mysteries of Osiris or Ancient Egyptian Initiation* (Quakertown, Pennsylvania: The Philosophical Publishing Company, 1951, Revised Edition), p.38.

43. Churchward, *op. cit.,* , p.426, 469; R. Swinburne Clymer, *The Mysteries of Osiris or Ancient Egyptian Initiation* (Quakertown, Pennsylvania: The Philosophical Publishing Company, 1951, Revised Edition), p.38.

44. A. T. C. Pierson, *The Traditions, Origin and Early History of Freemasonry* (New York: Masonic Publishing Company, 1865), p.67.

45. Churchward, *op. cit.,* , p.206, 421.

46. R. Swinburne Clymer, *The Mysteries of Osiris or Ancient Egyptian Initiation* (Quakertown, Pennsylvania: The Philosophical Publishing Company, 1951, Revised Edition), p.38; Veronica Ions, *Egyptian Mythology* (England: The Hamlyn Publishing Group, Ltd., 1965), p.21.

47. Veronica Ions, *Egyptian Mythology* (England: The Hamlyn Publishing Group, Ltd., 1965), p.21.

48. Clymer, *The Mysteries of Osiris, op. cit.,* p.38.

49. Ed Decker, quoting Kenneth Grant, *The Question of Freemasonry Companion* (Issaquah, Washington: Saints Alive in Jesus, 1992), p.47; William Schnoebelen, *Masonry: Beyond the Light* (Chino, California: Chick Publications, 1991), p.101.

50. *Ibid.*

51. Edmond Ronayne, *The Master's Carpet (Mah-Hah-Bone)* (n.p., 1879), p.224.

52. Clymer, *The Mysteries of Osiris, op. cit.,* p.38.

53. Ronayne, *op. cit.*; Clymer, *The Mysteries of Osiris, op. cit.,* p.37.

54. *Ibid.*

55. *Ibid.,* p.135.

56. Churchward, *op. cit.,* p.369.

57. Clymer, *The Mysteries of Osiris, op. cit.,* p.135.

58. Oliver, *The Historical Landmarks, op. cit.,* p.396.

59. Clymer, *The Mysteries of Osiris, op. cit.,* p.38.

60. William T. Still, *New World Order: The Ancient Plan of Secret Societies* (Lafayette, Louisiana: Huntington House, Inc., 1990), p.25.

61. Clymer, *The Mysteries of Osiris, op. cit.,* p.37.

62. Robert Sessler, *To Be God of One World: The French Revolution Globalized* (Merlin, Oregon: Let There Be Light Publications, 1992), p.97.

63. *The F.A.T.A.L. Flaw, op. cit.,* p.5.

64. Pike, *op. cit.,* p.15; Pierson, *op. cit.,* p.67; Thomas Bulfinch, *Bulfinch's Mythology* (New York: Thomas Y. Crowell Company, Inc., 1970), p.907; *The World Book Encyclopedia,* 1961 Edition; Vol. 16, p.396.

65. William Schnoebelen, *Masonry: Beyond the Light* (Chino, California: Chick Publications, 1991), p.101; *Battle Cry* (March/April 1991), p.4; See also: William J. Schnoebelen, *Twice the Child of Hell* (Issaquah, Washington: Saints Alive in Jesus, n.d.), p.9; *The F.A.T.A.L. Flaw, op. cit.,* p.5; J. Edward Decker, *Freemasonry: Satan's Door to America?* (Issaquah, Washington: Free the Masons Ministries, n.d.), p.3.

66. Churchward, op. cit., , p.27, 196, 199, 347.

67. *Circle Network News* (Summer 1984), op. cit., p.3.

68. *Sphaera Imaginatio* (1986, Issue #16), p.17; See also: Geoffrey Parrinder, Editor, *World Religions: From Ancient History to the Present* (New York, New York: Facts on File, 1971), p.140; Ions, op. cit., p.21; M. Esther Harding, *Woman's Mysteries: Ancient and Modern* (New York: G. P. Putnam's Sons for the C. G. Jung Foundation for Analytical Psychology, 1971 Edition), p.172, 218; Mustaga El-Amin, *Freemasonry: Ancient Egypt and the Islamic Destiny* (Jersey City, New Jersey: New Mind Productions, 1988), p.93; Churchward, op. cit., p.369.

69. Texe Marrs, *Texe Marrs Book of New Age Cults and Religions* (Austin, Texas: Living Truth Publishers, 1990), p.299.

70. Joseph Campbell, *The Hero with a Thousand Faces* (Princeton, New Jersey: Princeton University Press, 1968, Second Edition), p.213.

71. *The World Book Encyclopedia*, 1961 Edition; Vol. 18, p.251; *Webster's Seventh New Collegiate Dictionary*, 1967, p.502.

72. Marrs, *Texe Marrs Book of New Age Cults*, op. cit., p.299.

73. *Ibid.*, p.186; David Spangler, "Finding Heaven on Earth, *New Age Journal* (January/February 1988; Vol. 4, Issue 1); *Is the Antichrist in the World Today?*, Interview with Constance Cumbey (Oklahoma City, Oklahoma: Southwest Radio Church, 1982); David Spangler, *Emergence: The Rebirth of the Sacred* (New York: Dell Publishing, 1984), p.32; "Earth and Spirit: The Spiritual Dimension of the Environmental Crisis," Chinook Learning Center, p.6; Texe Marrs, *Dark Secrets of the New Age: Satan's Plan for a One World Religion* (Westchester, Illinois: Crossway Books, 1987), p.37); Catalog from the Flower Essence Society, p.17; David Spangler, *Links with Space* (Marina Del Rey, California: DeVorss and Company, 1971), p.13; David Spangler, *Revelation: The Birth of a New Age* (Middleton, Wisconsin: The Lorian Press, 1976), p.11; Constance Cumbey, *The Hidden Dangers of the Rainbow: The New Age Movement and Our Coming Age of Barbarism* (Shreveport, Louisiana: Huntington House, Inc., Revised Edition, 1983), p.51.

74. David Spangler, *Reflections on the Christ* (Scotland: Findhorn Publications, 1977), p.43-44.

75. *Ibid.*, p.45.

76. *The Scottish Rite Journal* (May 1992; Vol. 100, No. 5), p.38.

77. "Freemason Section on Compuserve," *The Scottish Rite Journal* (August 1992; Vol. 100, No. 8), p.41.

78. *The Star-Spangled Banner* (Washington, D.C.: Supreme Council, 33rd Degree, Ancient and Accepted Scottish Rite of Freemasonry, Southern Jurisdiction, n.d.), p.1.

79. Henry C. Clausen, *Emergence of the Mystical* (Washington, D.C.: Supreme Council, 1981, Second Edition), p.19.

80. Lynn F. Perkins, *Masonry in the New Age* (Lakemont, Georgia: CSA Press, 1971), p.195.

81. Arthur Lyons, Jr., *The Second Coming: Satanism in America* (Dodd, Mead and Company, 1970), p.70.

82. *The World Book Encyclopedia*, 1961 Edition; Vol. 12, p.340; See also *Health* (February 1986), p.80; Percival George Woodcock, *Short Dictionary of Mythology* (Philosophical Library, 1953), p.94; *New Larousse Encyclopedia of Mythology* (Prometheus Press, 1972 Edition), p.238; *Perceptions* (Summer 1993, Vol. 1, Issue 2), p.20; Gaynor, *op. cit.*, p.77; Thomas Bulfinch, *Bulfinch's Mythology: The Age of Fable or Stories of Gods and Heroes* (Garden City, New York: Doubleday and Company, Inc., 1948), p.7; Edith Hamilton, *Mythology* (Boston, Massachusetts: Little, Brown and Company, 1942), p.34; Thomas Bulfinch, *The Age of Fable or the Beauties of Mythology* (New York: The Heritage Press, 1942), p.9; Joseph Campbell, *The Masks of God: Creative Mythology* (New York, New York: The Viking Press, 1968), p.203.

83. *Ibid.*; See also *Short Talk Bulletin*, "The Masonic Rod" (September 1957; Vol. 35, No. 9; Reprinted March 1986), p.6; Edith Hamilton, *Mythology* (Boston, Massachusetts: Little, Brown and Company, 1942), p.35; Percival George Woodcock, *Short Dictionary of Mythology* (Philosophical Library, 1953), p.94.

84. *New Larousse Encyclopedia of Mythology* (Prometheus Press, 1972 Edition), p.238.

85. Harry E. Wedeck, *Treasury of Witchcraft* (New York, New York: Philosophical Library, 1961), p.8.

86. *Ibid.*, p.188.

87. Albert E. Bedworth and David A. Bedworth, *Health for Human Effectiveness* (Englewood Cliffs, New Jersey: Prentice-Hall, Inc., 1982), p.6; See also Campbell, *The Hero with a Thousand Faces, op. cit.*, p.72.

88. Pike, *op. cit.*, p.506.

89. Catalog from Sounds True, Inside front cover; Edith Hamilton, *Mythology* (Boston, Massachusetts: Little, Brown and Company, 1942), p.44.

90. Cirlot, *op. cit.*, p.249; See also *Complete Occult Digest A to Z* (North Hollywood, California: International Imports, 1984), p.115; *What? When? Where? Why? Who? in Freemasonry* (Silver Spring, Maryland: Masonic Service Association of the United States, 1956), p.37; Anton Szandor LaVey, *The Satanic Bible* (New York: Avon Books, 1969), p.59, 145; Thomas Bulfinch, *Bulfinch's Mythology: The Age of Fable or Stories of Gods and Heroes* (Garden City, New York: Doubleday and Company, Inc., 1948), p.181; Thomas Bulfinch, *Bulfinch's Mythology* (New York: Thomas Y. Crowell Company, Inc., 1970), p.957.

91. Stewart Farrar, *What Witches Do: The Modern Coven Revealed* (Custer, Washington: Phoenix Publishing Company, 1983, Revised Edition), p.33.

92. Charles G. Berger, *Our Phallic Heritage* (New York, New York: Greenwich Book Publishers, Inc., 1966), p.32; See also Thomas Bulfinch, *Bulfinch's Mythology: The Age of Fable or Stories of Gods and Heroes* (Garden City, New York: Doubleday and Company, Inc., 1948), p.181.

93. Anton Szandor LaVey, *The Satanic Bible* (New York: Avon Books, 1969), p.59.

94. Robin Lane Fox, *Pagans and Christians* (New York: Alfred A. Knopf, Inc., 1986), p.32.

95. *Ibid.*, p.130.

96. Berger, *op. cit.*, p.45.

97. *Ibid.*, p.71.

98. *Ibid.*, p.82-83.

99. *Ibid.*, p.48.

100. Henry C. Clausen, *Messages for a Mission* (Supreme Council, 1977), p.6; See also Clymer, *The Mysteries of Osiris, op. cit.*, p.58.

101. David L. Carrico, quoting Janet and Stewart Farrar, *The Pentagram, Freemasonry and the Goat* (Evansville, Illinois: Followers of Jesus Christ, 1992), p.7.

102. J. P. Brooke-Little, *An Heraldic Alphabet* (New York: Arco Publishing Company, Inc., 1973), p.57; Gaynor, *op. cit.*, p.31; Percival George Woodcock, *Short Dictionary of Mythology* (Philosophical Library, 1953), p.29; Thomas Bulfinch, *Bulfinch's Mythology: The Age of Fable or Stories of Gods and Heroes* (Garden City, New York: Doubleday and Company, Inc., 1948), p.7; Thomas Bulfinch, *The Age of Fable or the Beauties of Mythology* (New York: The Heritage Press, 1942), p.9; Berger, *op. cit.*, p.204; Peterson, *op. cit.*, p.256.

103. Pike, *op. cit.*, p.502; Cirlot, *op. cit.*, p.35.

104. *Ibid.*, p.35, 36.

105. Pike, *op. cit.*, p.502.

106. Cirlot, *op. cit.*, p.35, 36.

107. David L. Carrico, *Lucifer—Eliphas Levi—Albert Pike and the Masonic Lodge* (Evansville, Indiana: Followers of Jesus Christ, 1991), p.18-22; J. D. Buck, *Mystic Masonry* (Illinois: Indo-American Book Company, 1913, Sixth Edition), p.xvi; Arthur Edward Waite, *The Holy Kabbalah* (London: Williams and Norgate Ltd., 1929), p. 553; Arthur Edward Waite, *The Secret Tradition in Freemasonry* (London: Rider and Company, 1937), p.619; Joseph Fort Newton, *The Builders: A Story and Study of Masonry* (Cedar Rapids, Iowa: The Torch Press, 1914), p.66; Arthur Edward Waite, *An Encyclopedia of Freemasonry and of Cognate Instituted Mysteries: Their Rites, Literature and History*, Vol. II (New York: Weathervane Books, 1970), p.278; Rex R. Hutchens and Donald W. Monson, *The Bible in Albert Pike's Morals and Dogma* (Washington, D.C.: Supreme Council, 33rd Degree, 1992), p.19, 29, 42, 45, 63, 71, 101, 102, 103, 159, 170, 172, 174, 177, 178, 181, 243, 244; Robert A. Morey, *The Origins and Teachings of Freemasonry* (Southbridge, Massachusetts: Crowne Publications, Inc., 1990), p.37, 38, 49, 75.

108. Lucien V. Rule, *Pioneering in Masonry: The Life and Times of Rob Morris, Masonic Poet Laureate, Together with Story of Clara Barton and the Eastern Star* (Louisville, Kentucky: Brandt and Connors Company, 1922), p.158.

109. Waite, *The Mysteries of Magic, op. cit.*, p.214.

110. *Short Talk Bulletin*, "The Masonic Rod" (September 1957; Vol. 35, No. 9; Reprinted March 1986), p.3-4.

111. Peterson, *op. cit.*, p.256.

112. Larry Kunk, *What Is the Secret Doctrine of the Masonic Lodge and How Does It Relate to Their Plan of Salvation?* (1992, Unpublished manuscript), p.17-18.

113. Manly Palmer Hall, *An Encyclopedic Outline of Masonic, Hermetic, Qabbalistic and Rosicrucian Symbolical Philosophy: Being an Interpretation of the Secret Teachings Concealed Within the Rituals, Allegories and Mysteries of All Ages* (San Francisco, California: H. S. Crocker Company, Inc., 1928), p.95; See also: Cirlot, *op. cit.*, p.82, 256; Berger, *op. cit.*, p.54.

114. Farrar, *op. cit.*, p.82; See also: Cirlot, *op. cit.*, p.82, 256.

115. J. L. Bracelin, *Gerald Gardner: Witch* (London: The Octagon Press, 1960), p.35.

116. Colin Wilson, *The Occult: A History* (New York, Random House, 1971), p.455.

117. *Ibid.*, p.456.

118. Ions, *op. cit.*, p.82.

119. To obtain a copy of *Hidden Secrets of Masonry*, send $3.95 plus $1.05 postage ($5.00 total) to Sharing, 212-S E. 7th St., Mt. Carmel, PA 17851-2211.

120. John Sebastian Marlow Ward, *The Sign Language of the Mysteries* (Land's End Press, 1969), p.63; Albert G. Mackey, *The Symbolism of Freemasonry* (New York: Clark and Maynard, 1869), p.164; Rex R. Hutchens, *A Bridge to Light* (Washington, D.C.: Supreme Council, 33° Ancient and Accepted Scottish Rite of Freemasonry, Southern Jurisdiction, 1988), p.175, 250; Thomas Bulfinch, *Bulfinch's Mythology: The Age of Fable or Stories of Gods and Heroes* (Garden City, New York: Doubleday and Company, Inc., 1948), p.7; *The World Book Encyclopedia*, 1961 Edition; Vol. 12, p.340; Gaynor, *op. cit.*, p.31, 77, 111; Thomas Bulfinch, *The Age of Fable or the Beauties of Mythology* (New York: The Heritage Press, 1942), p.9; John Yarker, *The Arcane Schools* (Belfast, Ireland: William Tait, 1909), p.36, 63; *Short Talk Bulletin*, "The Masonic Rod," *op. cit.*, p.6; Edith Hamilton, *Mythology* (Boston, Massachusetts: Little, Brown and Company, 1942), p.34; Percival George Woodcock, *Short Dictionary of Mythology* (Philosophical Library, 1953), p.68; Laurie Cabot with Tom Cowan, *Power of the Witch: The Earth, the Moon, and the Magical Path to Enlightenment* (New York, New York: Delacorte Press, 1989), p.150.

121. Bedworth and Bedworth, *op. cit.*, p.6; See also: *Chrysalis* (Autumn 1987, Vol. 2, Issue 3), p.253; Cirlot, *op. cit.*, p.207; Paul Hamlyn, *Greek Mythology* (London: Paul Hamlyn, Ltd., 1967), p.5, 52; Gaynor, *op. cit.*, p.77; Carl Jung, M.-L. Von Franz, Joseph L. Henderson, Jolande Jacobi, Aniela and Jaffe, *Man and His Symbols* (Garden City, New York: Doubleday and Company, Inc. 1964), p.156; Campbell, *The Hero with a Thousand Faces*, *op. cit.*, p.72; *New Larousse Encyclopedia of Mythology*, *op. cit.*, p.123; *Short Talk Bulletin*, "The Masonic Rod," *op. cit.*, p.6; Edith Hamilton, *Mythology* (Boston, Massachusetts: Little, Brown and Company, 1942), p.34; Geoffrey Parrinder, Editor, *World Religions: From Ancient History to the Present* (New York, New York: Facts on File, 1971), p.148; Peterson, *op. cit.*, p.256.

122. Paul Hamlyn, *Greek Mythology* (London: Paul Hamlyn, Ltd., 1967), p.52.

123. Garth Fowden, *The Egyptian Hermes: A Historical Approach to the Late Pagan Mind* (England: Cambridge University Press, 1986), p.161.

124. Texe Marrs, *Dark Secrets of the New Age: Satan's Plan for a One World Religion* (Westchester, Illinois: Crossway Books, 1987), p.93; Maurice Bessy, *A Pictorial History of Magic and the Supernatural* (New York: Hamlyn Publishing Group Limited, 1964), p.87.

125. W. J. McCormick, *Christ, the Christian and Freemasonry* (Belfast, Ireland: Great Joy Publications, 1984), p.25; See also: Perkins, *op. cit.*, p.327; Laurie Cabot with Tom Cowan, *Power of the Witch: The Earth, the Moon, and the Magical Path to Enlightenment* (New York, New York: Delacorte Press, 1989), p.150; John Maxson Stillman, *The Story of Alchemy and Early Chemistry* (New York, New York: Dover Publications, Inc., 1960), p.151.

126. Pike, op. cit., p.365; See also: John Maxson Stillman, The Story of Alchemy and Early Chemistry (New York, New York: Dover Publications, Inc., 1960), p.151.

127. Your Masonic Capital City (Silver Spring, Maryland: The Masonic Service Association of the United States, n.d.), p.37.

128. Pike, op. cit., p.79; See also: R. Swinburne Clymer, The Mysticism of Masonry (Quakertown, Pennsylvania: The Philosophical Publishing Company, 1924), p.68.

129. Alice A. Bailey, Reappearance of the Christ (New York: Lucis Publishing Company, 1948), p.104.

130. Your Masonic Capital City, op. cit.

131. E. M. Butler, The Myth of the Magus (New York: MacMillan Company, 1948), p.259.

132. David L. Carrico, Manly P. Hall: The Honored Masonic Author (Evansville, Indiana: Followers of Jesus Christ, 1992), p.12.

133. G. A. Riplinger, quoting Helena Petrovna Blavatsky, New Age Bible Versions (Munroe Falls, Ohio: A. V. Publications, 1993), p.400-401.

134. Carl Jung, M.-L. Von Franz, Joseph L. Henderson, Jolande Jacobi, and Aniela Jaffe, Man and His Symbols (Garden City, New York: Doubleday and Company, Inc. 1964), p.154, 156; See also: Gaynor, op. cit., p.77.

135. Hamlyn, op. cit., p.52; New Larousse Encyclopedia of Mythology, op. cit., p.124.

136. Joseph Campbell, The Masks of God: Creative Mythology (New York, New York: The Viking Press, 1968), p.204.

137. Albert G. Mackey, The Symbolism of Freemasonry (New York: Clark and Maynard, 1869), p.164, 294.

138. Churchward, op. cit., p.190; History of the Order of the Eastern Star (General Grand Chapter in the U. S. A., 1989), p.13.

139. Pike's Poems (Little Rock, Arkansas: Fred W. Allsopp, 1899), p.69-72.

140. Clausen, Messages for a Mission, op. cit., p.20; Rex R. Hutchens, Short Talk Bulletin, "Albert Pike—The Man Not the Myth" (June 1990; Vol. 68, No. 6), p.3; Robert A. Morey, The Origins and Teachings of Freemasonry (Southbridge, Massachusetts: Crowne Publications, Inc., 1990), p.28, 36; Ibid., p.26; What? When? Where? Why? Who? in Freemasonry (Silver Spring, Maryland: Masonic Service Association of the United States, 1956), p.58; Short Talk Bulletin, "Albert Pike" (July 1923; Vol. 1, No. 7; Reprinted December 1988), p.11; Perkins, op. cit., p.344; Arthur Edward Waite, The Holy Kabbalah (London: Williams and Norgate Ltd., 1929), p.552, 553; Samuel Harrison Baynard, Jr., History of the Supreme Council, 33rd Degree, Vol. II (Williamsport, Pennsylvania: Grit Publishing Company, 1938), p.71, 76-77.

141. History of the Order of the Eastern Star (General Grand Chapter in the U. S. A., 1989), p.18.

142. Rex R. Hutchens, A Bridge to Light (Washington, D.C.: Supreme Council, 33☐ Ancient and Accepted Scottish Rite of Freemasonry, Southern Jurisdiction, 1988), p.175, 250; New Larousse Encyclopedia of Mythology, op. cit., p.27; Campbell, The Masks of God, op. cit., p.151; Gaynor, op. cit., p.77; John Yarker, The Arcane Schools (Belfast, Ireland: William Tait, 1909), p.63; John Maxson Stillman, The Story of Alchemy and Early Chemistry (New York, New

York: Dover Publications, Inc., 1960), p.151; Pike, *op. cit.*, p.82, 502, 586; Hall, *An Encyclopedic Outline, op. cit.*, p. 36; Ions, *op. cit.*, p.86; Fowden, *op. cit.*, p.23; *An Invitation for a September Song*, n.p. listed; Perkins, *op. cit.*, p.327; Percival George Woodcock, *Short Dictionary of Mythology* (Philosophical Library, 1953), p.94, 144; Helena Petrovna Blavatsky, *Isis Unveiled*, Vol. I: Science (New York, New York: Trow's Printing and Bookbinding Company, 1877), p.554; M. Esther Harding, *Woman's Mysteries: Ancient and Modern* (New York: G. P. Putnam's Sons for the C. G. Jung Foundation for Analytical Psychology, 1971 Edition), p.171; Editors of Time-Life Books, *Magical Arts* (Alexandria, Virginia: Time-Life Books, 1990), p.61; Laurie Cabot with Tom Cowan, *Power of the Witch: The Earth, the Moon, and the Magical Path to Enlightenment* (New York, New York: Delacorte Press, 1989), p.150; *Mysteries of Mind Space & Time: The Unexplained* (Vol. 1) (Westport, Connecticut: H. S. Stuttman, Inc., 1992), p.41; McCormick, *op. cit.*, p.25.

143. LaVey, *op. cit.*, p.60; See also: Ions, *op. cit.*, p.85, 86; *The World Book Encyclopedia*, 1961 Edition; Vol. 17, p.206; Editors of Time-Life Books, *Magical Arts* (Alexandria, Virginia: Time-Life Books, 1990), p.52, 53; Gaynor, *op. cit.*, p.186; Fowden, *op. cit.*, p.22.

144. Ions, *op. cit.*, p.85, 75, 91; See also: Gaynor, *op. cit.*, p.87; *New Larousse Encyclopedia of Mythology, op. cit.*, p.19; E. A. Wallis Budge, *Amulets and Superstitions* (New York, New York: Dover Publications, Inc., 1978), p.xix.

145. Ions, *op. cit.*, p.86; Fowden, *op. cit.*, p.23.

146. George H. Steinmetz, *Freemasonry: Its Hidden Meaning* (New York: Macoy Publishing and Masonic Supply Company, 1948), p.35; See also: Arthur Edward Waite, *The Secret Tradition in Freemasonry* (London: Rider and Company, 1937), p.37, 146.

147. *Ibid.;* See also: George H. Steinmetz, *The Lost Word: Its Hidden Meaning* (New York: Macoy Publishing and Masonic Supply Company, 1953), p.134.

148. Ions, *op. cit.*, p.86; See also: Perkins, *op. cit.*, p.324.

149. Catalog from Abyss, p.39; See also: *The World Book Encyclopedia*, 1961 Edition; Vol. 17, p.206; Ions, *op. cit.*, p.85; *Necronomicon* (New York, New York: Avon Books, 1977), p.xix.

150. Cirlot, *op. cit.*, p.155.

151. Dave Hunt and T. A. McMahon, *The Seduction of Christianity: Spiritual Discernment in the Last Days* (Eugene, Oregon: Harvest House Publishers, 1985), p.140; Hutchens, *A Bridge to Light, op. cit.*, p.250; Sessler, *op. cit.*, p.132; Johanna Michaelsen, *Like Lambs to the Slaughter* (Eugene, Oregon: Harvest House Publishers, 1989), p.121; John Maxson Stillman, *The Story of Alchemy and Early Chemistry* (New York, New York: Dover Publications, Inc., 1960), p.151; *Mysteries of Mind Space & Time: The Unexplained* (Vol. 1) (Westport, Connecticut: H. S. Stuttman, Inc., 1992), p.41.

152. James S. Fritz, "Alchemy," *The World Book Encyclopedia*, 1961 Edition; Vol. 1, p.278; R. Swinburne Clymer, *The Mysticism of Masonry* (Quakertown, Pennsylvania: The Philosophical Publishing Company, 1924), p.177; David Carrico with Rick Doninger, *The Egyptian-Masonic-Satanic Connection* (Evansville, Indiana: Followers of Jesus Christ, 1991), p.98; *Necronomicon* (New York, New York: Avon Books, 1977), p.xxvii; Editors of Time-Life Books, *Magical Arts* (Alexandria, Virginia: Time-Life Books, 1990), p.61; Wedeck, *op. cit.*, Page following p.40, 219; *Mysteries of Mind Space & Time: The Unexplained* (Vol. 1) (Westport, Connecticut: H. S. Stuttman, Inc., 1992), p.27.

153. *Circle Network News* (Summer 1987; Vol. 9, No. 2), p.14.

154. Scott Cunningham, *Wicca: A Guide for the Solitary Practitioner* (St. Paul, Minnesota: Llewellyn Publications, 1989), p.10.

155. John Yarker, *The Arcane Schools* (Belfast, Ireland: William Tait, 1909), p.36.

156. Gaynor, *op. cit.*, p.108.

157. Yarker, *op. cit.*, p.63.

158. *Llewellyn New Times* (January/February 1987; #871), p.32.

159. Joseph Leon Blau, *The Christian Cabala* (Port Washington, New York: Kennikat Press, Inc., 1944), p.118; See also: *Ibid.*

160. Schnoebelen, *Masonry, op. cit.*, p.194; See also: Kunk, *What Is the Secret Doctrine?, op. cit.*, p.17.

161. Arthur Edward Waite, *An Encyclopedia of Freemasonry and of Cognate Instituted Mysteries: Their Rites, Literature and History*, Vol. II (New York: Weathervane Books, 1970), p.61-62.

162. George Oliver, *Signs and Symbols* (New York: Macoy Publishing and Masonic Supply Company, 1906), p.38.

163. Pike, *op. cit.*, p.586; *New Larousse Encyclopedia of Mythology, op. cit.*, p.83.

164. Hutchens, *A Bridge to Light, op. cit.*, p.175; See also: Oliver, *Signs and Symbols, op. cit.*, p.140-142; Pike, *op. cit.*, p.586; Charles H. Vail, *The Ancient Mysteries and Modern Masonry* (New York: Macoy Publishing and Masonic Supply Company, 1909), p.186.

165. Pike, *op. cit.*, p.494.

166. *Ibid.*, p.501; See also: Oliver, *Signs and Symbols, op. cit.*, p.38.

167. Catalog from Isis, p.40; See also: *Short Talk Bulletin*, "Mosaic Pavement and Blazing Star," *op. cit.*, p.8.

168. Pike, *op. cit.*, p.376, 378; See also: *Short Talk Bulletin*, "Mosaic Pavement and Blazing Star," *op. cit.*, p.7-8; Churchward, *op. cit.*, p.206.

169. *Ibid.*, p.430; See also: The Rim Institute (1989 Catalog of Summer Programs), p.16; Gaynor, *op. cit.*, p.13; Thomas Bulfinch, *Bulfinch's Mythology* (New York: Thomas Y. Crowell Company, Inc., 1970), p.907; Fritz, *op. cit.*, p.468.

170. Ions, *op. cit.*, p.83.

171. Catalog from Abyss, p.39; See also: *New Larousse Encyclopedia of Mythology, op. cit.*, p.25; Ions, *op. cit.*, p.83; Charles F. Pfeiffer, Editor, *The Biblical World: A Dictionary of Biblical Archaeology* (New York: Bonanza Books, 1966), p.152.

172. Fritz, *op. cit.*, p.468; See also: *Chrysalis* (Autumn 1987, Vol. 2, Issue 3), p.252.

173. *Circle Network News* (Summer 1987), *op. cit.*, p.15.

174. Pike, *op. cit.*, p.430; *New Larousse Encyclopedia of Mythology, op. cit.*, p.25; Ions, *op. cit.*, p.83; Geoffrey Parrinder, Editor, *World Religions: From Ancient History to the Present* (New York, New York: Facts on File, 1971), p.141; *Circle Network News* (Summer 1987), *op. cit.*, p.14; Percival George Woodcock, *Short Dictionary of Mythology* (Philosophical Library, 1953), p.16; Gaynor, *op. cit.*, p.13; Laurie Cabot with Tom Cowan, *Power of the Witch: The*

Earth, the Moon, and the Magical Path to Enlightenment (New York, New York: Delacorte Press, 1989), p.48; Fritz, *op. cit.*, p.468.

175. *New Larousse Encyclopedia of Mythology, op. cit.*, p.27; Campbell, *The Hero with a Thousand Faces, op. cit.*, p.72; Editors of Time-Life Books, *Magical Arts* (Alexandria, Virginia: Time-Life Books, 1990), p.53; Charles F. Pfeiffer, Editor, *The Biblical World: A Dictionary of Biblical Archaeology* (New York: Bonanza Books, 1966), p.218, 482; Brochure from Wise Woman Center, n.p. listed; Ions, *op. cit.*, p.86-87; Gaynor, *op. cit.*, p.186; Jung, *et. al., op. cit.*, p.156; *The World Book Encyclopedia*, 1961 Edition; Vol. 17, p.206; Cirlot, *op. cit.*, p.155.

176. *The World Book Encyclopedia*, 1961 Edition; Vol. 16, p.250.

177. Ions, *op. cit.*, p.63.

178. Brochure from Wise Woman Center, n.p. listed; Catalog from Abyss, p.39; Geoffrey Parrinder, Editor, *World Religions: From Ancient History to the Present* (New York, New York: Facts on File, 1971), p.141; Ions, *op. cit.*, p.21, 86.

179. Catalog from Sounds True, Inside front cover; *The World Book Encyclopedia*, 1961 Edition; Vol. 14, p.93.

180. Catalog from Abyss, p.39.

181. Frederic Portal (Translated by John W. Simons), *A Comparison of Egyptian Symbols with Those of the Hebrews* (New York: Masonic Publishing and Manufacturing Company, 1866), p.50-51; See also: *Last Trumpet Newsletter* (April 1993, Vol. 12, Issue 4), p.2; John B. Harrison and Richard E. Sullivan, *A Short History of Western Civilization* (New York: Alfred A. Knopf, 1960), p.13-14; Gaynor, *op. cit.*, p.103; Geoffrey Parrinder, Editor, *World Religions: From Ancient History to the Present* (New York, New York: Facts on File, 1971), p.181.

182. *Last Trumpet Newsletter* (April 1993, Vol. 12, Issue 4), p.2.

183. Jim Shaw and Tom McKenney, *The Deadly Deception* (Lafayette, Louisiana: Huntington House, Inc., 1988), p.85; Hutchens, *A Bridge to Light, op. cit.*, p.300-301.

184. Hutchens, *A Bridge to Light, op. cit.*

185. Churchward, *op. cit.*, p.468.

186. John T. Lawrence, *The Perfect Ashlar* (London: A. Lewis, 1912), p.162.

Chapter 5: The Pentagram

1. Albert Pike, *Morals and Dogma of the Ancient and Accepted Scottish Rite of Freemasonry* (Richmond, Virginia: L. H. Jenkins, Inc., 1871), p.15.

2. Albert Churchward, *Signs and Symbols of Primordial Man* (London: George Allen and Company, Ltd., 1913, Second Edition), p.206.

3. *Short Talk Bulletin*, "Blazing Star," Part 1 (March 1965; Vol. 43, No. 3), p.12.

4. *Ibid.*; See also: Mary Ann Slipper, *The Symbolism of the Order of the Eastern Star* (no other information available), p.15.

5. *The F.A.T.A.L. Flaw* (Issaquah, Washington: Free the Masons Ministries, n.d.), p.5.

6. *The World Book Encyclopedia*, 1961 Edition; Vol. 16, p.250; See also: Arthur Lyons, Jr., *The Second Coming: Satanism in America* (Dodd, Mead and Company, 1970), p.23.

7. Churchward, *op. cit.*, p.477; See also: Dave Hunt and T. A. McMahon, *America: The Sorcerer's New Apprentice: The Rise of New Age Shamanism* (Eugene, Oregon: Harvest House Publishers, 1988), p.239; E. A. Wallis Budge, *Amulets and Superstitions* (New York, New York: Dover Publications, Inc., 1978), p.141; Helena Petrovna Blavatsky, *Isis Unveiled*, Vol. I: Science (New York, New York: Trow's Printing and Bookbinding Company, 1877), p.554; Harry E. Wedeck, *Treasury of Witchcraft* (New York, New York: Philosophical Library, 1961), p.89; Anton Szandor LaVey, *The Satanic Bible* (New York: Avon Books, 1969), p.60, 146.

8. John Yarker, *The Arcane Schools* (Belfast, Ireland: William Tait, 1909), p.17.

9. J. S. M. Ward, *Freemasonry and the Ancient Gods* (London: Simpkin, Marshall, Hamilton, Kent and Company, Ltd., 1921), p.64; See also: William J. Schnoebelen, *Twice the Child of Hell* (Issaquah, Washington: Saints Alive in Jesus, n.d.), p.9.

10. *Adelphi Quarterly* (Third Quarter 1992), p.6; See also: *Voyage to the Source* (McMinnville, Oregon: The Aquarian Church of Universal Service, 1986), p.17.

11. Anton Szandor LaVey, *The Satanic Bible* (New York: Avon Books, 1969), p.146.

12. *Ibid.*, p.60, 146.

13. *Ibid.*, p.146.

14. *Ibid.*, p.60; See also: J. Edward Decker, *Freemasonry: Satan's Door to America?* (Issaquah, Washington: Free the Masons Ministries, n.d.), p.3.

15. Harry E. Wedeck, *Treasury of Witchcraft* (New York, New York: Philosophical Library, 1961), p.89; See also: Josh McDowell and Don Stewart, *Understanding the Occult* (San Bernardino, California: Here's Life Publishers, Inc., 1982), p.128; Phil Phillips, *Saturday Morning Mind Control* (Nashville, Tennessee: Oliver-Nelson Books, 1991), p.196.

16. Eklal Kueshana, *The Ultimate Frontier* (Quinlan, Texas: The Stelle Group, 1963), p.89.

17. Helena Petrovna Blavatsky, *Isis Unveiled*, Vol. I: Science (New York, New York: Trow's Printing and Bookbinding Company, 1877), p.554, xxxiii.

18. William Schnoebelen, *Masonry: Beyond the Light* (Chino, California: Chick Publications, 1991), p.106; See also: Arthur Lyons, *Satan Wants You: The Cult of Devil Worship in America* (New York, New York: The Mysterious Press, 1988), p.126.

19. Dave Hunt and T. A. McMahon, *America: The Sorcerer's New Apprentice: The Rise of New Age Shamanism* (Eugene, Oregon: Harvest House Publishers, 1988), p.236; Texe Marrs, *Mystery Mark of the New Age: Satan's Design for World Domination* (Westchester, Illinois: Crossway Books, 1988), p.182; William and Sharon Schnoebelen, *Lucifer Dethroned* (Chino, California: Chick Publications, 1993), p.93; Johanna Michaelsen, *Like Lambs to the Slaughter* (Eugene, Oregon: Harvest House Publishers, 1989), p.257; William J. Schnoebelen, *Twice the Child of Hell* (Issaquah, Washington: Saints Alive in Jesus, n.d.), p.8; Texe Marrs, *Texe Marrs Book of New Age Cults and Religions* (Austin, Texas: Living Truth Publishers, 1990), p.312.

20. Texe Marrs, *Mystery Mark of the New Age: Satan's Design for World Domination* (Westchester, Illinois: Crossway Books, 1988), p.181; Johanna Michaelsen, *Like Lambs to the Slaughter* (Eugene, Oregon: Harvest House Publishers, 1989), p.257; William J. Schnoebelen, *Twice the Child of Hell* (Issaquah, Washington: Saints Alive in Jesus, n.d.), p.8, 9; *Constance Cumbey's New Age Monitor* (June 1986; Vol. 1, No. 2), p.7; Schnoebelen, *Masonry, op. cit.*, p.106; William and Sharon Schnoebelen, *Lucifer Dethroned* (Chino, California: Chick Publications, 1993), p.92; Texe Marrs, *Texe Marrs Book of New Age Cults and Religions* (Austin, Texas: Living Truth Publishers, 1990), p.312.

21. William J. Schnoebelen, *Twice the Child of Hell* (Issaquah, Washington: Saints Alive in Jesus, n.d.), p.9; Johanna Michaelsen, *Like Lambs to the Slaughter* (Eugene, Oregon: Harvest House Publishers, 1989), p.257; Arthur Lyons, Jr., *The Second Coming: Satanism in America* (Dodd, Mead and Company, 1970), p.172, 173; William and Sharon Schnoebelen, *Lucifer Dethroned* (Chino, California: Chick Publications, 1993), p.92; Arthur Lyons, *Satan Wants You: The Cult of Devil Worship in America* (New York, New York: The Mysterious Press, 1988), p.109, 127-128.

22. *Constance Cumbey's New Age Monitor* (June 1986; Vol. 1, No. 2), p.7.

23. *Ibid.;* Marrs, *Mystery Mark of the New Age, op. cit.*, p.181; Hunt and McMahon, *America, op. cit.*, p.233; Texe Marrs, *Texe Marrs Book of New Age Cults and Religions* (Austin, Texas: Living Truth Publishers, 1990), p.312.

24. Hunt and McMahon, quoting Aquino, *America, op. cit.*

25. *Ibid.*, p.238.

26. Marrs, *Mystery Mark of the New Age, op. cit.*, p.181; William and Sharon Schnoebelen, *Lucifer Dethroned* (Chino, California: Chick Publications, 1993), p.108.

27. Schnoebelen, *Twice the Child of Hell, op. cit.*

28. *The F.A.T.A.L. Flaw, op. cit.*, p.5.

29. *New Larousse Encyclopedia of Mythology* (Prometheus Press, 1972 Edition), p.21; Veronica Ions, *Egyptian Mythology* (England: The Hamlyn Publishing Group, Ltd., 1965), p.63; M. Esther Harding, *Woman's Mysteries: Ancient and Modern* (New York: G. P. Putnam's Sons for the C. G. Jung Foundation for Analytical Psychology, 1971 Edition), p.172.

30. Churchward, *op. cit.*, p.478.

31. Veronica Ions, *Egyptian Mythology* (England: The Hamlyn Publishing Group, Ltd., 1965), p.21.

32. M. Esther Harding, *Woman's Mysteries: Ancient and Modern* (New York: G. P. Putnam's Sons for the C. G. Jung Foundation for Analytical Psychology, 1971 Edition), p.48.

33. Arthur Lyons, *Satan Wants You: The Cult of Devil Worship in America* (New York, New York: The Mysterious Press, 1988), p.129.

34. Harding, *op. cit.*, p.168; See also: *Circle Network News* (Summer 1984; Vol. 6, No. 2), p.3.

35. *Ibid.*

36. Schnoebelen, *Twice the Child of Hell, op. cit.;* William and Sharon Schnoebelen, *Lucifer Dethroned* (Chino, California: Chick Publications, 1993), p.95.

37. *Christian News* (April 17, 1989; Vol. 27, No. 16), p.12.

394 HIDDEN SECRETS OF THE EASTERN STAR

38. *What Is the Order of the Eastern Star?* (Newtonville, New York: HRT Ministries, Inc., n.d.), p.2.

39. Marrs, *Mystery Mark of the New Age*, op. cit., p.95; See also: Rudolf Koch, *The Book of Signs* (New York, New York: Dover Publications, Inc., 1955 edition), p.6; John T. Lawrence, *The Perfect Ashlar* (London: A. Lewis, 1912), p.200; *Short Talk Bulletin*, "Blazing Star," op. cit., p.5; Mary Ann Slipper, *The Symbolism of the Order of the Eastern Star* (no other information available), p.15.

40. Rudolf Koch, *The Book of Signs* (New York, New York: Dover Publications, Inc., 1955 edition), p.6.

41. *Short Talk Bulletin*, "Blazing Star," op. cit., p.5, 8; See also: John T. Lawrence, *The Perfect Ashlar* (London: A. Lewis, 1912), p.200.

42. William O. Peterson, Editor, *Masonic Quiz Book: "Ask Me Another, Brother"* (Chicago, Illinois: Charles T. Powner Company, 1950), p.272; Laurie Cabot with Tom Cowan, *Power of the Witch: The Earth, the Moon, and the Magical Path to Enlightenment* (New York, New York: Delacorte Press, 1989), p.94; *Pocket Masonic Dictionary* (Silver Spring, Maryland: The Masonic Service Association of the United States, 1988), p.23; *Short Talk Bulletin*, "Blazing Star," op. cit., p.5, 7, 8; *What? When? Where? Why? Who? in Freemasonry* (Silver Spring, Maryland: Masonic Service Association of the United States, 1956), p.58; W. L. Wilmshurst, *The Masonic Initiation* (Ferndale, Michigan: Trismegistus Press, 1980; Originally published 1924), p.57; E. L. Hawkins, *A Concise Cyclopaedia of Freemasonry* (EC: A. Lewis, 1908), p.172; *Short Talk Bulletin*, "The Significant Numbers" (September 1956; Vol. 34; No. 9), p.6.

43. Colin F. W. Dyer, *Symbolism in Craft Freemasonry* (England: A Lewis [Masonic Publishers], Ltd., 1976), p.36; Henry C. Clausen, *Clausen's Commentaries on Morals and Dogma* (Supreme Council, 33rd Degree, Ancient and Accepted Scottish Rite of Freemasonry, Southern Jurisdiction, USA, 1974), p.2, 125-126; Henry C. Clausen, *Messages for a Mission* (Supreme Council, 1977), p.9; *Short Talk Bulletin*, "Numerology of Masonry" (June 1946; Vol. 24, No. 6; Reprinted November 1984), p.3; *Short Talk Bulletin*, "The Bee Hive" (September 1951; Vol. 29, No. 9; Reprinted April 1990), p.5; *What? When? Where? Why? Who? in Freemasonry* (Silver Spring, Maryland: Masonic Service Association of the United States, 1956), p.33, 54; Henry C. Clausen, *Emergence of the Mystical* (Washington, D.C.: Supreme Council, 1981, Second Edition), p.62; James L. Holly, *The Southern Baptist Convention and Freemasonry* (Beaumont, Texas: Mission and Ministry to Men, Inc., 1992), p.48-49; Christian D. Ginsburg, *The Essenes: Their History and Doctrines: The Kabbalah* (London: Routledge and Kegan Paul, Ltd., 1956 Reprint), p.14; *Short Talk Bulletin*, "The Winding Stairs" (January 1932; Vol. 10, No. 1; Reprinted July 1991), p.7; Arthur Edward Waite, *The Mysteries of Magic: A Digest of the Writings of Eliphas Levi* (Chicago, Illinois: De Laurence, Scott and Company, 1909), p.208-209; J. D. Buck, *Mystic Masonry* (Illinois: Indo-American Book Company, 1913, Sixth Edition), p.248-249; George Oliver, *The Historical Landmarks and Other Evidences of Freemasonry, Explained* (Vol. I & II) (New York: John W. Leonard and Company, 1855), p.186; John J. Robinson, *Born in Blood: The Lost Secrets of Freemasonry* (New York, New York: M. Evans and Company, 1989), p.177, 230; Charles H. Vail, *The Ancient Mysteries and Modern Masonry* (New York: Macoy Publishing and Masonic Supply Company, 1909), p.22, 145, 202, 208; R. Swinburne Clymer, *The Mysticism of Masonry* (Quakertown, Pennsylvania: The Philosophical Publishing Company, 1924), p.47-48; Rex R. Hutchens, *A Bridge to Light* (Washington, D.C.: Supreme Council, 33° Ancient and Accepted Scottish Rite of Freemasonry, Southern Jurisdiction, 1988), p.31, 49, 113,

255, 316, 318; Henry C. Clausen, *Your Amazing Mystic Powers* (Washington, D.C.: Supreme Council of the Inspectors General Knights Commander of the House of the Temple of Solomon of the Thirty-Third Rite of Freemasonry of the Southern Jurisdiction, 1985), p.xxxvii; A. T. C. Pierson, *The Traditions, Origin and Early History of Freemasonry* (New York: Masonic Publishing Company, 1865), p.379; Albert G. Mackey, *The Symbolism of Freemasonry* (New York: Clark and Maynard, 1869), p.133, 183, 219, 350; Paul Foster Case, *The Masonic Letter G* (Los Angeles, California: Builders of the Adytum, Ltd., 1981), p.60-61; Yarker, *op. cit.*, p.109, 141, 147, 221; W. L. Wilmshurst, *The Masonic Initiation* (Ferndale, Michigan: Trismegistus Press, 1980; Originally published 1924), p.57, 99-100; *Pocket Encyclopedia of Masonic Symbols* (Silver Spring, Maryland: The Masonic Service Association of the United States, 1953), p.42-43.

44. J. D. Buck, *Mystic Masonry* (Illinois: Indo-American Book Company, 1913, Sixth Edition), p.78; See also: R. Swinburne Clymer, *The Mysticism of Masonry* (Quakertown, Pennsylvania: The Philosophical Publishing Company, 1924), p.44-45.

45. Editors of Time-Life Books, *Magical Arts* (Alexandria, Virginia: Time-Life Books, 1990), p.26; See also: Arkon Daraul, *Witches and Sorcerers* (New York, New York: The Citadel Press, 1966), p.18; *What? When? Where? Why? Who? in Freemasonry* (Silver Spring, Maryland: Masonic Service Association of the United States, 1956), p.33; Colin Wilson, *The Occult: A History* (New York, Random House, 1971), p.194, 202-203; E. M. Butler, *The Myth of the Magus* (New York: MacMillan Company, 1948), p.50-51, 54, 56.

46. Schnoebelen, *Masonry, op. cit.*, p.163; See also: Arkon Daraul, *Witches and Sorcerers* (New York, New York: The Citadel Press, 1966), p.17, 20; *Short Talk Bulletin*, "Blazing Star," *op. cit.*, p.8; Laurie Cabot with Tom Cowan, *Power of the Witch: The Earth, the Moon, and the Magical Path to Enlightenment* (New York, New York: Delacorte Press, 1989), p.178; E. M. Butler, *The Myth of the Magus* (New York: MacMillan Company, 1948), p.54.

47. Peterson, *op. cit.*, p.259; See also: Laurie Cabot with Tom Cowan, *Power of the Witch: The Earth, the Moon, and the Magical Path to Enlightenment* (New York, New York: Delacorte Press, 1989), p.150; Allen E. Roberts, *The Craft and Its Symbols: Opening the Door to Masonic Symbolism* (Richmond, Virginia: Macoy Publishing and Masonic Supply Company, Inc., 1974), p.16.

48. Schnoebelen, *Masonry, op. cit.*, p.163.

49. Arkon Daraul, *Witches and Sorcerers* (New York, New York: The Citadel Press, 1966), p.25; See also: W. L. Reese, *Dictionary of Philosophy and Religion: Eastern and Western Thought* (Atlantic Highlands, New Jersey: Humanities Press, Inc., 1980), p.20.

50. David L. Carrico, quoting Janet and Stewart Farrar, *The Pentagram, Freemasonry and the Goat* (Evansville, Illinois: Followers of Jesus Christ, 1992), p.1.

51. Sybil Leek, *Numerology: The Magic of Numbers* (New York, New York: The MacMillan Company, 1969), p.21.

52. *Circle Network News* (Summer 1987; Vol. 9, No. 2), p.12; See also: *Llewellyn New Times* (September/October 1988; #885), p.77; Brochure from The Magic Door, p.4; *Short Talk Bulletin*, "Blazing Star," *op. cit.*, p.8; John T. Lawrence, *The Perfect Ashlar* (London: A. Lewis, 1912), p.193.

53. Leek, *op. cit.*, p.124.; See also: Scott Cunningham, *Wicca: A Guide for the Solitary Practitioner* (St. Paul, Minnesota: Llewellyn Publications, 1989), p.33;

Self-Help Update (Issue #26), p.13; E. L. Hawkins, *A Concise Cyclopaedia of Freemasonry* (EC: A. Lewis, 1908), p.172; Carrico, *The Pentagram, Freemasonry and the Goat, op. cit.,* p.1; Phil Phillips, *Turmoil in the Toybox* (Lancaster, Pennsylvania: Starburst Press, 1986), p.77.

54. *Self-Help Update* (1985), Issue 26, p.13.

55. Wedeck, *op. cit.,* p.59; See also: Eric Barger, *From Rock to Rock: The Music of Darkness Exposed!* (Lafayette, Louisiana: Huntington House, Inc., 1990), p.163; Frank Gaynor, Editor, *Dictionary of Mysticism* (New York: Philosophical Library, 1953), p.136.

56. *Complete Occult Digest A to Z,* 1984 catalog from International Imports, p.252; See also: W. J. McCormick, *Christ, the Christian and Freemasonry* (Belfast, Ireland: Great Joy Publications, 1984), p.91; J. E. Cirlot, *A Dictionary of Symbols* (New York, New York: Philosophical Library, Inc., 1972), p.309.

57. *Ibid.,* p.117.

58. *Ibid.*

59. Gary Jennings, *Black Magic, White Magic* (Eau Claire, Wisconsin: The Dial Press, Inc., 1964), p.51.

60. Frank Gaynor, Editor, *Dictionary of Mysticism* (New York: Philosophical Library, 1953), p.136; See also: Stewart Farrar, *What Witches Do: The Modern Coven Revealed* (Custer, Washington: Phoenix Publishing Company, 1983, Revised Edition), p.18.

61. Laurie Cabot with Tom Cowan, *Power of the Witch: The Earth, the Moon, and the Magical Path to Enlightenment* (New York, New York: Delacorte Press, 1989), p.90.

62. Eric Barger, *From Rock to Rock: The Music of Darkness Exposed!* (Lafayette, Louisiana: Huntington House, Inc., 1990), p.143-144.

63. *Ibid.,* p.118.

64. *Llewellyn New Times* (September/October 1988; #885), p.77; *Magical Blend* (February/March/April 1988; Issue #18), p.39.

65. Margot Adler, *Drawing Down the Moon: Witches, Druids, Goddess-Worshippers, and Other Pagans in America Today* (New York, New York: The Viking Press, 1979), p.46.

66. Stewart Farrar, *What Witches Do: The Modern Coven Revealed* (Custer, Washington: Phoenix Publishing Company, 1983, Revised Edition), unnumbered page; Charles H. Vail, *The Ancient Mysteries and Modern Masonry* (New York: Macoy Publishing and Masonic Supply Company, 1909), p.189; S. R. Parchment, *Ancient Operative Masonry* (San Francisco, California: San Francisco Center—Rosicrucian Fellowship, 1930), p.43; *Short Talk Bulletin,* "Symbolism" (March 1925; Vol. 3, No. 3; Reprinted May 1982), p.13; *Christian News* (April 17, 1989; Vol. 27, No. 16), p.12; Barger, *op. cit.,* p.163; Arthur Lyons, Jr., *The Second Coming: Satanism in America* (Dodd, Mead and Company, 1970), p.136; Arthur Edward Waite, *The Mysteries of Magic: A Digest of the Writings of Eliphas Levi* (Chicago, Illinois: De Laurence, Scott and Company, 1909), p.201, 202, 204, 295; Johanna Michaelsen, *Like Lambs to the Slaughter* (Eugene, Oregon: Harvest House Publishers, 1989), p.229-230; *Complete Occult Digest A to Z, op. cit.,* p.99, 106, 252; Editors of Time-Life Books, *Magical Arts, op. cit.,* p.39; Arthur Edward Waite, *The Brotherhood of the Rosy Cross: Being Records of the House of the Holy Spirit in Its Inward and Outward History* (New Hyde Park, New York: University Books, 1961); p.578.

67. Barger, *op. cit.*, p.144.

68. J. Edward Decker, *Freemasonry: Satan's Door to America?* (Issaquah, Washington: Free the Masons Ministries, n.d.), p.3.

69. Marrs, quoting Manly Palmer Hall, *Mystery Mark of the New Age,*, *op. cit.*, p.97; Larry Kunk, *What Is the Secret Doctrine of the Masonic Lodge and How Does It Relate to Their Plan of Salvation?* (1992, Unpublished manuscript), p.16; Carrico, *The Pentagram, Freemasonry and the Goat, op. cit.*, p.11.

70. S. R. Parchment, *Ancient Operative Masonry* (San Francisco, California: San Francisco Center—Rosicrucian Fellowship, 1930), p.39-40.

71. *Llewellyn New Times* (January/February 1987; #871), p.32.

72. Israel Regardie, *The Golden Dawn* (St. Paul, Minnesota: Llewellyn Publications, 1986), p.507.

73. Robert A. Morey, *The Origins and Teachings of Freemasonry* (Southbridge, Massachusetts: Crowne Publications, Inc., 1990), p.39.

74. Regardie, *op. cit.*, Back Cover; See also: Editors of Time-Life Books, *Magical Arts, op. cit.*, p.64; Brochure from Hermetic Society of the Golden Dawn, p.2; Joseph J. Carr, *The Twisted Cross* (Shreveport, Louisiana: Huntington House, Inc., 1985), p.105; Farrar, *op. cit.*, p.28; Morey, *op. cit.*, p.39, 45; Eustace Mullins, *The Curse of Canaan: A Demonology of History* (Staunton, Virginia: Revelation Books, 1987), p.102; Ellic Howe, *Magicians of the Golden Dawn: A Documentary History of a Magical Order 1887-1923* (London: Routledge and Kegan Paul, Ltd., 1972), p.xviii, xxiii, 43

75. *Llewellyn New Times* (January/February 1987; #871), p.32; Brochure from Hermetic Society of the Golden Dawn, p.2.

76. Regardie, *op. cit.*, p.ii.

77. Arthur Edward Waite, *The Brotherhood of the Rosy Cross: Being Records of the House of the Holy Spirit in Its Inward and Outward History* (New Hyde Park, New York: University Books, 1961), p.578.

78. Henry Leonard Stillson and William James Hughan, editors, *History of the Ancient and Honorable Fraternity of Free and Accepted Masons, and Concordant Orders* (Boston, Massachusetts: The Fraternity Publishing Company, 1895), p.49.

79. *Ibid.*, p.101; See also: Arthur Edward Waite, *The Mysteries of Magic: A Digest of the Writings of Eliphas Levi* (Chicago, Illinois: De Laurence, Scott and Company, 1909), p.202; Charles H. Vail, *The Ancient Mysteries and Modern Masonry* (New York: Macoy Publishing and Masonic Supply Company, 1909), p.189. Note: Charles H. Vail, a Mason and the former minister of the Pullman Memorial Church in Albion, New York, agrees with one difference: he states that the inverted pentagram represents Lucifer while the other authors claim that the pentagram with one point up represents Lucifer. "The Blazing Star also represents these two principles. If the point is turned upward it represents God; Good, Order, or the Lamb of Ormuzd and St. John; if the point is turned downward it denotes Lucifer, Evil, Disorder, or the accursed God of Mendes and the Mysteries."

80. Arthur Edward Waite, *A New Encyclopedia of Freemasonry and of Cognate Instituted Mysteries: Their Rites, Literature and History* (New York: Weathervane Books, 1970), Vol. I, p.ix; See also: Arthur Edward Waite, *The Mysteries of Magic: A Digest of the Writings of Eliphas Levi* (Chicago, Illinois: De Laurence,

Scott and Company, 1909), p.202, 206, 212, 442; Joseph Carr, *The Lucifer Connection* (Lafayette, Louisiana: Huntington House, Inc., 1987), p.139; John Sebastian Marlow Ward, *The Sign Language of the Mysteries* (Land's End Press, 1969), p.86; Rex R. Hutchens, *A Bridge to Light* (Washington, D.C.: Supreme Council, 33° Ancient and Accepted Scottish Rite of Freemasonry, Southern Jurisdiction, 1988), p.81; Churchward, *op. cit.*, p.469; *The World Book Encyclopedia*, 1961 Edition; Vol. 18, p.251; Geoffrey Parrinder, Editor, *World Religions: From Ancient History to the Present* (New York, New York: Facts on File, 1971), p.117; Ward, *Freemasonry and the Ancient Gods, op. cit.*, p. before p.111; Starhawk (Miriam Simos), *The Spiral Dance: A Rebirth of the Ancient Religion of the Great Goddess* (New York, New York: Harper-Collins Publishers, 1989 Edition), p.92; John T. Lawrence, *The Perfect Ashlar* (London: A. Lewis, 1912), p.164; Rex R. Hutchens and Donald W. Monson, *The Bible in Albert Pike's Morals and Dogma* (Washington, D.C.: Supreme Council, 33rd Degree, 1992), p.102; Gaynor, *op. cit.*, p.101; Manly Palmer Hall, *America's Assignment with Destiny* (Los Angeles, California: Philosophical Research Society, Inc., 1951), p.19; *Llewellyn New Times* (January/February 1988; #881), p.36; R. Swinburne Clymer, *The Mysteries of Osiris or Ancient Egyptian Initiation* (Quakertown, Pennsylvania: The Philosophical Publishing Company, 1951, Revised Edition), p.124; John J. Robinson, *A Pilgrim's Path: One Man's Road to the Masonic Temple* (New York: New York: M. Evans and Company, Inc., 1993), p.48; Percival George Woodcock, *Short Dictionary of Mythology* (Philosophical Library, 1953), p.87.

81. Pike, *op. cit.*, p.612.

82. *Ibid.*, p.613; See also: Rex R. Hutchens, *A Bridge to Light* (Washington, D.C.: Supreme Council, 33° Ancient and Accepted Scottish Rite of Freemasonry, Southern Jurisdiction, 1988), p.213, 230, 316, 318.

83. *Ibid.*, p.819.

84. *Ibid.*, p.104-105; See also: *Short Talk Bulletin*, "Symbolism" (March 1925; Vol. 3, No. 3; Reprinted May 1982), p.13-14.

85. Jean M'Kee Kenaston, Compiler, *History of the Order of the Eastern Star* (Cedar Rapids, Iowa: The Torch Press, 1917), p.60.

86. *Ibid.*

87. *Ritual of the Order of the Eastern Star* (Washington, D.C.: General Grand Chapter Order of the Eastern Star, 1956), p.9; See also: *Ibid.*, p.53.

88. *Ibid.*, p.9.

89. Willis D. Engle, *A General History of the Order of the Eastern Star* (Indianapolis, Indiana: Willis D. Engle, 1901), p.3.

90. Kenaston, *op. cit.*, p.18.

91. Engle, *op. cit.*, p.135-136; See also: D. Duane Winters, quoting Jim Shaw, *A Search for Light in a Place of Darkness: A Study of Freemasonry* (no other information available), p.64.

92. *Ibid.*, p.511-512.

93. *Ibid.*, p.512.

94. *What? When? Where? Why? Who? in Freemasonry* (Silver Spring, Maryland: Masonic Service Association of the United States, 1956), p.49; See also: Carl H. Claudy, *Masonic Harvest* (Washington, D.C.: The Temple Publishers, 1948), p.171-172.

95. D. Duane Winters, quoting Jim Shaw, *A Search for Light in a Place of Darkness: A Study of Freemasonry* (no other information available), p.64.

96. *Short Talk Bulletin*, "Symbolism" (March 1925; Vol. 3, No. 3; Reprinted May 1982), p.13-14.

97. J. E. Cirlot (Translated by Jack Sage), *A Dictionary of Symbols* (New York: Dorset Press, 1991 Edition), p.143; See also: Arthur Edward Waite, *The Mysteries of Magic: A Digest of the Writings of Eliphas Levi* (Chicago, Illinois: De Laurence, Scott and Company, 1909), p.299.

98. Percival George Woodcock, *Short Dictionary of Mythology* (Philosophical Library, 1953), p.93; See also: Eden Within (1994 Catalog), p.15.

99. Brochure from Nuit Unlimited Imports, p.3.

100. *Ibid.;* See also: Catalog from Occult Emporium, p.26; Cirlot, *op. cit.,* p.80; Brochure from The Wicca describing a course in witchcraft; *Complete Occult Digest A to Z, op. cit.,* p.95, 106; Eric Maple, *The Complete Book of Witchcraft and Demonology* (Cranbury, New Jersey: A. S. Barnes and Company, Inc., 1966 Edition), Caption under picture facing p.145.

Chapter 6: A Look at Baphomet

1. Brochure from Nuit Unlimited Imports, p.3; Lewis Spence, *Myths & Legends of Babylonia & Assyria* (London: George G. Harrap and Company, 1916), p.293.

2. Arthur Edward Waite, *The Mysteries of Magic: A Digest of the Writings of Eliphas Levi* (Chicago, Illinois: De Laurence, Scott and Company, 1909), p.iv; David L. Carrico, *Lucifer—Eliphas Levi—Albert Pike and the Masonic Lodge* (Evansville, Indiana: Followers of Jesus Christ, 1991), p.2, 4; *New Times* (1985; #853), p.21; Robert A. Morey, *The Origins and Teachings of Freemasonry* (Southbridge, Massachusetts: Crowne Publications, Inc., 1990), p.36; J. D. Buck, *Mystic Masonry* (Illinois: Indo-American Book Company, 1913, Sixth Edition), p.xvi; Ellic Howe, *Magicians of the Golden Dawn: A Documentary History of a Magical Order 1887-1923* (London: Routledge and Kegan Paul, Ltd., 1972), p.9; E. M. Butler, *The Myth of the Magus* (New York: MacMillan Company, 1948), p.243; R. Swinburne Clymer, *The Mysteries of Osiris or Ancient Egyptian Initiation* (Quakertown, Pennsylvania: The Philosophical Publishing Company, 1951, Revised Edition), p.324; Maurice Bessy, *A Pictorial History of Magic and the Supernatural* (New York: Hamlyn Publishing Group Limited, 1964), p.260; Editors of Time-Life Books, *Magical Arts* (Alexandria, Virginia: Time-Life Books, 1990), p.60; Norman MacKenzie, Editor, *Secret Societies* (Holt, Rinehart and Winston, 1967), p.144; Rex R. Hutchens and Donald W. Monson, *The Bible in Albert Pike's Morals and Dogma* (Washington, D.C.: Supreme Council, 33rd Degree, 1992), p.243; 70, p.253; Gary Jennings, *Black Magic, White Magic* (Eau Claire, Wisconsin: The Dial Press, Inc., 1964), p.36.

3. Hutchens and Monson, *The Bible in Albert Pike's Morals and Dogma,* (Washington, D.C.: Supreme Council, 33rd Degree, 1992), p.243; See also: Waite, *The Mysteries of Magic, op. cit.,* p.2.

4. Waite, *The Mysteries of Magic, op. cit.,* p.6; R. Swinburne Clymer, *The Mysteries of Osiris or Ancient Egyptian Initiation* (Quakertown, Pennsylvania: The Philosophical Publishing Company, 1951, Revised Edition), p.325; *Ibid.*

5. *Ibid.,* p.6.

6. *Ibid.*, p.7; See also: Hutchens and Monson, *The Bible in Albert Pike's Morals and Dogma, op. cit.*, p.243.

7. Maurice Bessy, *A Pictorial History of Magic and the Supernatural* (New York: Hamlyn Publishing Group Limited, 1964), p.260.

8. Hutchens and Monson, *The Bible in Albert Pike's Morals and Dogma, op. cit.*, p.243-244; See also: Catalog from Occult Emporium, p.26; Arthur Edward Waite, *The Secret Tradition in Freemasonry* (London: Rider and Company, 1937), p.620; Ellic Howe, *Magicians of the Golden Dawn: A Documentary History of a Magical Order 1887-1923* (London: Routledge and Kegan Paul, Ltd., 1972), p.9, 28; *Complete Occult Digest A to Z* (North Hollywood, California: International Imports, 1984), p.106; David L. Carrico, *Lucifer—Eliphas Levi—Albert Pike and the Masonic Lodge* (Evansville, Indiana: Followers of Jesus Christ, 1991), p.2; E. M. Butler, *The Myth of the Magus* (New York: MacMillan Company, 1948), p.243, 244; Arthur Lyons, *Satan Wants You: The Cult of Devil Worship in America* (New York, New York: The Mysterious Press, 1988), p.57; Howard Kerr and Charles L. Crow, Editors, *The Occult in America: New Historical Perspectives* (Urbana, Illinois: University of Illinois Press, 1983), p.128; R. Swinburne Clymer, *The Mysteries of Osiris or Ancient Egyptian Initiation* (Quakertown, Pennsylvania: The Philosophical Publishing Company, 1951, Revised Edition), p.327; Editors of Time-Life Books, *Magical Arts* (Alexandria, Virginia: Time-Life Books, 1990), p.60, 64; Arkon Daraul, *Witches and Sorcerers* (New York, New York: The Citadel Press, 1966), Page following p.239, 255.

9. David L. Carrico, *Lucifer—Eliphas Levi—Albert Pike and the Masonic Lodge* (Evansville, Indiana: Followers of Jesus Christ, 1991), quoting Wade Baskin, p.2; See also: Helena Petrovna Blavatsky, *Isis Unveiled*, Vol. I: Science (New York, New York: Trow's Printing and Bookbinding Company, 1877), p.137; Robert A. Morey, *The Origins and Teachings of Freemasonry* (Southbridge, Massachusetts: Crowne Publications, Inc., 1990), p.36; R. Swinburne Clymer, *The Mysteries of Osiris or Ancient Egyptian Initiation* (Quakertown, Pennsylvania: The Philosophical Publishing Company, 1951, Revised Edition), p.327; E. M. Butler, *The Myth of the Magus* (New York: MacMillan Company, 1948), p.244-245; David L. Carrico, *The Pentagram, Freemasonry and the Goat* (Evansville, Illinois: Followers of Jesus Christ, 1992), p.14.

10. Manly Palmer Hall, *An Encyclopedic Outline of Masonic, Hermetic, Qabbalistic and Rosicrucian Symbolical Philosophy: Being an Interpretation of the Secret Teachings Concealed Within the Rituals, Allegories and Mysteries of All Ages* (San Francisco, California: H. S. Crocker Company, Inc., 1928), p.100; See also: E. M. Butler, *The Myth of the Magus* (New York: MacMillan Company, 1948), p.55, 63; Bessy, *op. cit.*, p.87; Editors of Time-Life Books, *Magical Arts* (Alexandria, Virginia: Time-Life Books, 1990), p.45.

11. Arkon Daraul, *Witches and Sorcerers* (New York, New York: The Citadel Press, 1966), p.25.

12. Carrico, *Lucifer—Eliphas Levi—Albert Pike and the Masonic Lodge, op. cit.*, p.2; See also: *Ibid.*, p.25, 26; W. L. Reese, *Dictionary of Philosophy and Religion: Eastern and Western Thought* (Atlantic Highlands, New Jersey: Humanities Press, Inc., 1980), p.20; Colin Wilson, *The Occult: A History* (New York, Random House, 1971), p.197.

13. Garth Fowden, *The Egyptian Hermes: A Historical Approach to the Late Pagan Mind* (England: Cambridge University Press, 1986), p.28, 196.

14. Carrico, *Lucifer—Eliphas Levi—Albert Pike and the Masonic Lodge, op. cit.*, p.2.

15. *Ibid.*, p.3.

16. *Ibid.*, p.2.

17. Samuel Weiser (1989/1990 Catalog), p.60.

18. Carrico, *Lucifer—Eliphas Levi—Albert Pike and the Masonic Lodge, op. cit.,* p.2; See also: Eustace Mullins, *The Curse of Canaan: A Demonology of History* (Staunton, Virginia: Revelation Books, 1987), p.102; Robert A. Morey, *The Origins and Teachings of Freemasonry* (Southbridge, Massachusetts: Crowne Publications, Inc., 1990), p.39.

19. Rex R. Hutchens and Donald W. Monson, "Signs, Symbols and Silliness," *The Scottish Rite Journal* (May 1993; Vol. 101, No. 5), p.16.

20. Max Wood, *Rock and Roll: An Analysis of the Music* (n.p., n.d.), p.30; *Necronomicon* (New York, New York: Avon Books, 1977), p.xvii; Eric Maple, *The Complete Book of Witchcraft and Demonology* (Cranbury, New Jersey: A. S. Barnes and Company, Inc., 1966 Edition), p.136, 162; David Carrico with Rick Doninger, *The Egyptian-Masonic-Satanic Connection* (Evansville, Indiana: Followers of Jesus Christ, 1991), p.92; Eustace Mullins, *The Curse of Canaan: A Demonology of History* (Staunton, Virginia: Revelation Books, 1987), p.102.

21. *Necronomicon* (New York, New York: Avon Books, 1977), p.vi.

22. *Ibid.*, p.xvii.

23. Ellic Howe, *Magicians of the Golden Dawn: A Documentary History of a Magical Order 1887-1923* (London: Routledge and Kegan Paul, Ltd., 1972), p.xix, 193, 296; See also: *Llewellyn New Times* (January/February 1987; #871), p.32; Editors of Time-Life Books, *Magical Arts* (Alexandria, Virginia: Time-Life Books, 1990), p.64, 65; Bessy, *op. cit.*, p.262; Samuel Weiser (1989/ 1990 Catalog), p.60; Joseph J. Carr, *The Twisted Cross* (Shreveport, Louisiana: Huntington House, Inc., 1985), p.104; Jeff Godwin, *Dancing with Demons: The Music's Real Master* (Chino, California: Chick Publications, 1988), p.92.

24. William O. Peterson, Editor, *Masonic Quiz Book: "Ask Me Another, Brother"* (Chicago, Illinois: Charles T. Powner Company, 1950), p.100.

25. Howe, *op. cit.*, p.192-193; See also: *Christian News* (April 17, 1989; Vol. 27, No. 16), p.14.

26. For example, see: Eustace Mullins, *The Curse of Canaan: A Demonology of History* (Staunton, Virginia: Revelation Books, 1987), p.102; *Christian News* (April 17, 1989; Vol. 27, No. 16), p.14; Harry E. Wedeck, *Treasury of Witchcraft* (New York, New York: Philosophical Library, 1961), p.200; Eric Maple, *The Complete Book of Witchcraft and Demonology* (Cranbury, New Jersey: A. S. Barnes and Company, Inc., 1966 Edition), p.162; Jeff Godwin, *Dancing with Demons: The Music's Real Master* (Chino, California: Chick Publications, 1988), p.92; Carrico, *Lucifer—Eliphas Levi—Albert Pike and the Masonic Lodge, op. cit.*, p.2; David L. Carrico, *The Pentagram, Freemasonry and the Goat* (Evansville, Illinois: Followers of Jesus Christ, 1992), p.4, 14; David Carrico with Rick Doninger, *The Egyptian-Masonic-Satanic Connection* (Evansville, Indiana: Followers of Jesus Christ, 1991), p.39, 118; *Necronomicon, op. cit.*, p.xxvi.

27. Arthur Lyons, *Satan Wants You: The Cult of Devil Worship in America* (New York, New York: The Mysterious Press, 1988), p.81; J. Gordon Melton, *The Encyclopedia of American Religions* (Vol. 2) (Wilmington, North Carolina: McGrath Publishing Company, 1978), p.255; Eric Maple, *The Complete Book of Witchcraft and Demonology* (Cranbury, New Jersey: A. S. Barnes and Company, Inc., 1966 Edition), p.163; Jeff Godwin, *Dancing with Demons: The*

Music's Real Master (Chino, California: Chick Publications, 1988), p.92; David Carrico with Rick Doninger, *The Egyptian-Masonic-Satanic Connection* (Evansville, Indiana: Followers of Jesus Christ, 1991), p.92.

28. *Ibid.*, p.78.

29. Colin Wilson, *The Occult: A History* (New York, Random House, 1971), p.362-363.

30. *Ibid.*, p.365.

31. Lyons, *Satan Wants You, op. cit.*, p.81; See also: *Ibid.*, p.366; David Carrico with Rick Doninger, *The Egyptian-Masonic-Satanic Connection* (Evansville, Indiana: Followers of Jesus Christ, 1991), p.92.

32. Eustace Mullins, *The Curse of Canaan: A Demonology of History* (Staunton, Virginia: Revelation Books, 1987), p.102; See also: J. Gordon Melton, *The Encyclopedia of American Religions* (Vol. 2) (Wilmington, North Carolina: McGrath Publishing Company, 1978), p.255.

33. Arthur Lyons, Jr., *The Second Coming: Satanism in America* (Dodd, Mead and Company, 1970), p.108.

34. *Ibid.*

35. *Ibid.*, p.183; Lyons, *Satan Wants You, op. cit.*, p.114.

36. Wood, *op. cit.*, p.30.

37. *Ibid.*

38. *Ibid.*

39. William Schnoebelen, *Masonry: Beyond the Light* (Chino, California: Chick Publications, 1991), p.168-169; See also: Norman MacKenzie, Editor, *Secret Societies* (Holt, Rinehart and Winston, 1967), p.146.

40. Carrico, *Lucifer—Eliphas Levi—Albert Pike and the Masonic Lodge, op. cit.*, p.2.

41. Wilson, *op. cit.*, p.157.

42. R. Swinburne Clymer, *The Mysteries of Osiris or Ancient Egyptian Initiation* (Quakertown, Pennsylvania: The Philosophical Publishing Company, 1951, Revised Edition), p.362-363; Wilson, *op. cit.*, p.365; Lyons, *Satan Wants You, op. cit.*, p.81; Catalog from Arkana, p.18; Editors of Time-Life Books, *Magical Arts* (Alexandria, Virginia: Time-Life Books, 1990), p.45, 65; Jeff Godwin, *Dancing with Demons: The Music's Real Master* (Chino, California: Chick Publications, 1988), p.92; David Carrico with Rick Doninger, *The Egyptian-Masonic-Satanic Connection* (Evansville, Indiana: Followers of Jesus Christ, 1991), p.92.

43. Wanda Marrs, *New Age Lies to Women* (Austin, Texas: Living Truth Publishers, 1989), p.30.

44. Lyons, *The Second Coming, op. cit.*, p.53.

45. D. Duane Winters, *A Search for Light in a Place of Darkness: A Study of Freemasonry* (no other information available), p.72.

46. Waite, *The Mysteries of Magic, op. cit.*, p.223; See also: *Ibid.*, p.69.

47. Eric Maple, *The Complete Book of Witchcraft and Demonology* (Cranbury, New Jersey: A. S. Barnes and Company, Inc., 1966 Edition), Picture facing p.145; See also: Brochure from Nuit Unlimited Imports, p.3; *Fate* (October 1990; Vol. 43, No. 9 [sic]), p.56; Schnoebelen, *Masonry, op. cit.*, p.169-170.

48. Starhawk (Miriam Simos), *The Spiral Dance: A Rebirth of the Ancient Religion of the Great Goddess* (New York, New York: Harper-Collins Publishers, 1989 Edition), p.108.

49. Waite, *The Mysteries of Magic, op. cit.,* p.135.

50. *Ibid.,* p.222-223.

51. *Ibid.,* p.224.

52. *Ibid.,* p.453.

53. *Ibid.,* p.512-513.

54. Carrico, quoting Eliphas Levi, *Lucifer—Eliphas Levi—Albert Pike and the Masonic Lodge, op. cit.,* p.8.

55. Waite, *The Mysteries of Magic, op. cit.,* p.xi; see also William T. Still, *New World Order: The Ancient Plan of Secret Societies* (Lafayette, Louisiana: Huntington House, Inc., 1990), p.45; Rudolf Steiner (Translated by Max Gysi), *The Way of Initiation* (New York: Macoy Publishing and Masonic Supply Company, 1910), p.33; G. A. Riplinger, *New Age Bible Versions* (Munroe Falls, Ohio: A. V. Publications, 1993), p.25, 412, 413; *The Christian World Report* (February 1991; Vol. 3, No. 2), p.8; Arthur Edward Waite, *The Brotherhood of the Rosy Cross: Being Records of the House of the Holy Spirit in Its Inward and Outward History* (New Hyde Park, New York: University Books, 1961), p.355.

56. J. Gordon Melton, *The Encyclopedia of American Religions* (Vol. 2) (Wilmington, North Carolina: McGrath Publishing Company, 1978), p.253.

57. Carrico, *Lucifer—Eliphas Levi—Albert Pike and the Masonic Lodge, op. cit.,* p.3; Robert A. Morey, *The Origins and Teachings of Freemasonry* (Southbridge, Massachusetts: Crowne Publications, Inc., 1990), p.36; David L. Carrico, *The Pentagram, Freemasonry and the Goat* (Evansville, Illinois: Followers of Jesus Christ, 1992), p.14.

58. *Ibid.,* p.9.

59. Arthur Edward Waite, *The Secret Tradition in Freemasonry* (London: Rider and Company, 1937), p.620.

60. Carrico, *Lucifer—Eliphas Levi—Albert Pike and the Masonic Lodge, op. cit.,* p.18-22; J. D. Buck, *Mystic Masonry* (Illinois: Indo-American Book Company, 1913, Sixth Edition), p.xvi; Arthur Edward Waite, *The Holy Kabbalah* (London: Williams and Norgate Ltd., 1929), p.553; *Ibid.,* p.620; Joseph Fort Newton, *The Builders: A Story and Study of Masonry* (Cedar Rapids, Iowa: The Torch Press, 1914), p.66; Arthur Edward Waite, *An Encyclopedia of Freemasonry and of Cognate Instituted Mysteries: Their Rites, Literature and History,* Vol. II (New York: Weathervane Books, 1970), p.278; Hutchens and Monson, *The Bible in Albert Pike's Morals and Dogma, op. cit.,* p.19, 29, 42, 45, 63, 71, 101, 102, 103, 159, 170, 172, 174, 177, 178, 181, 243, 244, 252; Joseph Fort Newton, *The Men's House* (Washington, D.C.: Masonic Service Association, 1923), p.113; Robert A. Morey, *The Origins and Teachings of Freemasonry* (Southbridge, Massachusetts: Crowne Publications, Inc., 1990), p.37, 38, 49, 75.

61. Jim Shaw and Tom McKenney, *The Deadly Deception* (Lafayette, Louisiana: Huntington House, Inc., 1988), p.62.

62. *Short Talk Bulletin,* "Albert Pike" (July 1923; Vol. 1, No. 7; Reprinted December 1988), p.5; See also: Lucien V. Rule, quoting Lilian Pike Roome, *The Life and Times of Rob Morris* (no other information available), p.161.

63. *Ibid,* p.12; See also: Rule, *The Life and Times of Rob Morris* (no other information available), p.158.

64. *Ibid.,* p.14.

65. "A Bridge to Light," C. Fred Kleinknecht, *The New Age Magazine,* (January 1989; Vol. 97, No. 1), p.1.

66. Henry C. Clausen, *Messages for a Mission* (Supreme Council, 1977), p.20; Peterson, *op. cit.,* p.225; Rex R. Hutchens, *Short Talk Bulletin,* "Albert Pike— The Man Not the Myth" (June 1990; Vol. 68, No. 6), p.3; Robert A. Morey, *The Origins and Teachings of Freemasonry* (Southbridge, Massachusetts: Crowne Publications, Inc., 1990), p.28, 36; *Pike's Poems* (Little Rock, Arkansas: Fred W. Allsopp, 1899), p.26; *What? When? Where? Why? Who? in Freemasonry* (Silver Spring, Maryland: Masonic Service Association of the United States, 1956), p.58; *Ibid.,* p.11; Arthur Edward Waite, *The Holy Kabbalah* (London: Williams and Norgate Ltd., 1929), p.552, 553; Joseph Fort Newton, *The Men's House* (Washington, D.C.: Masonic Service Association, 1923), p.113; Samuel Harrison Baynard, Jr., *History of the Supreme Council, 33rd Degree,* Vol. II (Williamsport, Pennsylvania: Grit Publishing Company, 1938), p.71, 76-77, Vol. II.

67. *The Scottish Rite Journal* (November 1992; Vol. 100, No. 11), p.6.

68. *Ibid.,* p.5; See also: *Pike's Poems* (Little Rock, Arkansas: Fred W. Allsopp, 1899), p.25; Hutchens and Monson, *The Bible in Albert Pike's Morals and Dogma, op. cit.,* p.5.

69. Waite, *The Mysteries of Magic, op. cit.,* p.440.

70. Albert Pike, *Morals and Dogma of the Ancient and Accepted Scottish Rite of Freemasonry* (Richmond, Virginia: L. H. Jenkins, Inc., 1871), p.321.

71. Waite, *The Mysteries of Magic, op. cit.,* p.442.

72. Anton Szandor LaVey, *The Satanic Bible* (New York: Avon Books, 1969), p.39, 57.

73. Manly Palmer Hall, *The Lost Keys of Freemasonry* (Richmond, Virginia: Macoy Publishing and Masonic Supply Company, Inc., 1976; Originally published in 1923), p.48.

74. David Carrico, quoting from *The Scottish Rite Journal,* in *Manly P. Hall: The Honored Masonic Author* (Evansville, Indiana: Followers of Jesus Christ, 1992), p.17.

75. *Adelphi Quarterly* (Third Quarter 1992), p.7.

76. *Ibid.,* p.6-7.

77. Lynn F. Perkins, *Masonry in the New Age* (Lakemont, Georgia: CSA Press, 1971), p.99.

78. *Ibid.*

79. *Ibid.,* p.100.

80. Carrico, *Lucifer—Eliphas Levi—Albert Pike and the Masonic Lodge, op. cit.,* p.30, 16; See also: Gary Kah, *En Route to Global Occupation* (Lafayette, Louisiana: Huntington House Publishers, 1992), p.113.

81. David Carrico, *The Occult Meaning of the Great Seal of the United States* (Evansville, Indiana: Followers of Jesus Christ, 1991), p.57; Des Griffin, *Fourth Reich of the Rich* (Emissary Publications, 1978), p.68-69.

82. Schnoebelen, *Masonry, op. cit.,* p.194.

83. *Ibid.,* quoting Domenico Margiotta, p.193; See also: William T. Still, *New World Order: The Ancient Plan of Secret Societies* (Lafayette, Louisiana: Huntington House, Inc., 1990), p.123; David Carrico, *The Occult Meaning of the Great Seal of the United States, op. cit.,* p.57.

84. Carrico, quoting Domenico Margiotta, *Lucifer—Eliphas Levi—Albert Pike and the Masonic Lodge, op. cit.,* p.30; David Carrico, *The Occult Meaning of the Great Seal of the United States* (Evansville, Indiana: Followers of Jesus Christ, 1991), p.57.

85. Carrico, quoting William Josiah Sutton, *Lucifer—Eliphas Levi—Albert Pike and the Masonic Lodge, op. cit.,* p.16.

86. *Ibid.,* p.31; See also: Schnoebelen, *Masonry, op. cit.,* p.191.

87. William T. Still, *New World Order: The Ancient Plan of Secret Societies* (Lafayette, Louisiana: Huntington House, Inc., 1990), p.124; Gary Kah, *En Route to Global Occupation* (Lafayette, Louisiana: Huntington House Publishers, 1992), p.114.

88. Arthur Edward Waite, *An Encyclopedia of Freemasonry and of Cognate Instituted Mysteries: Their Rites, Literature and History,* Vol. II (New York: Weathervane Books, 1970), p.253; See also: Schnoebelen, *Masonry, op. cit.,* p.191; Sheldon Emry, quoting Eustace Mullins, *America's Promise Newsletter* (January 1988), p.5.

89. *History of the Order of the Eastern Star* (General Grand Chapter in the U. S. A., 1989), p.18; See also: Lucien V. Rule, *The Life and Times of Rob Morris* (no other information available), p.158, 162.

90. Albert G. Mackey, *Encyclopedia of Freemasonry,* Vol. 1 (Chicago, Illinois: The Masonic History Company, 1909), p.302-303; See also: Winters, *op. cit.,* p.61.

91. *Ibid.,* p.303.

92. Arthur Edward Waite, *The Holy Kabbalah* (London: Williams and Norgate Ltd., 1929), p.552-553.

93. *Pike's Poems* (Little Rock, Arkansas: Fred W. Allsopp, 1899), p.13.

94. *Ibid.,* p.35, 36, 37.

95. *Ibid.,* p.40.

96. *Ibid.,* p.53.

97. *Ibid.,* p.55, 56, 58.

98. *Ibid.,* p.64.

99. *Ibid.,* p.75.

100. Carrico, quoting William Guy Carr, *Lucifer—Eliphas Levi—Albert Pike and the Masonic Lodge, op. cit.,* p.15.

101. *Ibid.,* quoting William Guy Carr, p.15.

102. Des Griffin, *Fourth Reich of the Rich* (Emissary Publications, 1978), p.68.

103. *Ibid.;* See also: Robert A. Morey, *The Origins and Teachings of Freemasonry* (Southbridge, Massachusetts: Crowne Publications, Inc., 1990), p.45, 49; Pike, *op. cit.,* p.730-731.

104. Carrico, *Lucifer—Eliphas Levi—Albert Pike and the Masonic Lodge*, op. cit., p.14; Carrico, *The Occult Meaning of the Great Seal of the United States*, op. cit., p.56.

105. *Ibid.*, quoting *Light-bearers of Darkness*, p.14.

106. *Ibid.*, p.14; *Christian News* (June 28, 1993), p.13-15; Dennis Cuddy, *Now Is the Dawning of the New Age New World Order* (Oklahoma City, Oklahoma: Hearthstone Publishing, Ltd., 1991), p.42; *Saints Alive in Jesus Newsletter* (May/June 1993), p.4; Schnoebelen, *Masonry*, op. cit., p.192; Intelligence Examiner Special Edition, "The Masonic Plot Against America" by Texe Marrs, 1993.

107. *Ibid.*, quoting Carl A. Raschke, p.14.

108. *Christian News* (June 28, 1993), p.14.

109. *Ibid.*, quoting Anton Chaitkin, p.15; See also: Dennis Cuddy, *Now Is the Dawning of the New Age New World Order* (Oklahoma City, Oklahoma: Hearthstone Publishing, Ltd., 1991), p.57.

110. Robert A. Morey, *The Origins and Teachings of Freemasonry* (Southbridge, Massachusetts: Crowne Publications, Inc., 1990), p.48.

111. *Ibid.*

112. Hutchens and Monson, *The Bible in Albert Pike's Morals and Dogma*, op. cit., p.2-3.

113. Pike, op. cit., p.719.

114. *Ibid.*, p.719; See also: Hutchens and Monson, *The Bible in Albert Pike's Morals and Dogma*, op. cit., p.7.

115. *Ibid.*, p.524.

116. Winters, op. cit., p.69.

117. Frank Gaynor, Editor, *Dictionary of Mysticism* (New York: Philosophical Library, 1953), p.24, 71.

118. Carrico, *Lucifer—Eliphas Levi—Albert Pike and the Masonic Lodge*, op. cit., p.4.

119. LaVey, op. cit., p.130, 135, 136, 138; See also: Arthur Lyons, *Satan Wants You*, op. cit., p.251.

120. Wanda Marrs, quoting Zeena LaVey, *New Age Lies to Women*, op. cit., p.29.

121. LaVey, op. cit., p.136, 58, 145; See also: Peterson, op. cit., p.72; Eric Barger, *From Rock to Rock: The Music of Darkness Exposed!* (Lafayette, Louisiana: Huntington House, Inc., 1990), p.164; J. E. Cirlot (Translated by Jack Sage), *A Dictionary of Symbols* (New York: Dorset Press, 1991 Edition), p.80; Bessy, op. cit., p.163; Gaynor, op. cit., p.24, 159; Hutchens and Monson, *The Bible in Albert Pike's Morals and Dogma*, op. cit., p.251.

122. Eric Barger, *From Rock to Rock: The Music of Darkness Exposed!* (Lafayette, Louisiana: Huntington House, Inc., 1990), p.64.

123. Still, op. cit., p.112; A. R. Chambers, Editor, *Questions & Answers* (n.p., 1972), p.245; Rex R. Hutchens, *A Bridge to Light* (Washington, D.C.: Supreme Council, 33° Ancient and Accepted Scottish Rite of Freemasonry, Southern Jurisdiction, 1988), p.319; Pike, op. cit., p.815; Peter Partner, *The Knights*

Templar and Their Myth (Rochester, Vermont: Destiny Books, 1990, Revised Edition), p.77.

124. J. S. M. Ward, *Freemasonry and the Ancient Gods* (London: Simpkin, Marshall, Hamilton, Kent and Company, Ltd., 1921), p.277; See also Peter Partner, *The Knights Templar and Their Myth* (Rochester, Vermont: Destiny Books, 1990, Revised Edition), p.77; Still, *op. cit.*, p.112; John J. Robinson, *Born in Blood: The Lost Secrets of Freemasonry* (New York, New York: M. Evans and Company, 1989), p.130, 136; Michael Baigent and Richard Leigh, *The Temple and the Lodge* (New York: Arcade Publishing, Inc., 1989), p.53, 267; Peterson, *op. cit.*, p.193; Gaynor, *op. cit.*, p.183; Lyons, *Satan Wants You, op. cit.*, p.31-32, 50; Norman MacKenzie, Editor, *Secret Societies* (Holt, Rinehart and Winston, 1967), p.127, 129, John J. Robinson, *A Pilgrim's Path: One Man's Road to the Masonic Temple* (New York: New York: M. Evans and Company, Inc., 1993), p.81; David Carrico with Rick Doninger, *The Egyptian-Masonic-Satanic Connection* (Evansville, Indiana: Followers of Jesus Christ, 1991), p.103.

125. G. Legman, Henry Charles Lea, Thomas Wright, George Witt, Sir James Tennent, and Sir William Dugdale, *The Guilt of the Templars* (New York: Basic Books, Inc., 1966), p.39.

126. *New Larousse Encylcopedia of Mythology* (Prometheus Press, 1972 Edition), p.166; J. Gordon Melton, *The Encyclopedia of American Religions* (Vol. 2) (Wilmington, North Carolina: McGrath Publishing Company, 1978), p.252.

127. Schnobelen, *Masonry, op. cit.*, p.166.

128. Gary Kah, quoting Edith Starr Miller, *En Route to Global Occupation* (Lafayette, Louisiana: Huntington House Publishers, 1992), p.102; See also: Peter Partner, *The Knights Templar and Their Myth* (Rochester, Vermont: Destiny Books, 1990, Revised Edition), p.169.

129. *Ibid.*, quoting Edith Starr Miller, p.102; See also: Peter Partner, *The Knights Templar and Their Myth* (Rochester, Vermont: Destiny Books, 1990, Revised Edition), p.169.

130. Schnobelen, *Masonry, op. cit.*, p.87, 166; Legman, *et. al., op. cit.*, p.111; Peter Partner, *The Knights Templar and Their Myth* (Rochester, Vermont: Destiny Books, 1990, Revised Edition), p.77, 140; Ward, *Freemasonry and the Ancient Gods, op. cit.*, p.280; John J. Robinson, *Born in Blood: The Lost Secrets of Freemasonry* (New York, New York: M. Evans and Company, 1989), p.136.

131. A. R. Chambers, Editor, *Questions & Answers* (n.p., 1972), p.245.

132. Still, quoting Albert Pike, *op. cit.*, p.113.

133. Kah, *op. cit.*, p.115, 135; See also: Charles H. Vail, *The Ancient Mysteries and Modern Masonry* (New York: Macoy Publishing and Masonic Supply Company, 1909), p.147; Rex R. Hutchens, *A Bridge to Light* (Washington, D.C.: Supreme Council, 33° Ancient and Accepted Scottish Rite of Freemasonry, Southern Jurisdiction, 1988), p.271, 282, 291, 319; David Carrico with Rick Doninger, *The Egyptian-Masonic-Satanic Connection* (Evansville, Indiana: Followers of Jesus Christ, 1991), p.103, 105.

134. Henry C. Clausen, *Clausen's Commentaries on Morals and Dogma* (Supreme Council, 33rd Degree, Ancient and Accepted Scottish Rite of Freemasonry, Southern Jurisdiction, USA, 1974), p.168.

135. Chambers, *op. cit.*, p.245.

136. Intelligence Examiner Special Edition, "The Masonic Plot Against America" by Texe Marrs, 1993.

137. Ward, *Freemasonry and the Ancient Gods, op. cit.,* p.211, 280.

138. Winters, *op. cit.,* p.64; Jack T. Chick, *The Curse of Baphomet* (Chino, California: Chick Publications, 1991), p.10.. 139. Carrico, quoting Eliphas Levi, *Lucifer—Eliphas Levi—Albert Pike and the Masonic Lodge, op. cit.,* p.8; David L. Carrico, quoting Eliphas Levi, *The Pentagram, Freemasonry and the Goat* (Evansville, Illinois: Followers of Jesus Christ, 1992), p.14.

140. Kah, *op. cit.,* p.104.

141. Schnobelen, *Masonry, op. cit.,* p.87; *Short Talk Bulletin,* "The Masonic Goat" (November 1936, Vol. 14, No. 11), p.3; *The Scottish Rite Journal* (September 1991; Vol. 99, No. 9), p.25.

142. Wilson, *op. cit.,* p.128.

143. Schnobelen, *Masonry, op. cit.,* p.87; See also: Gaynor, *op. cit.,* p.24; John J. Robinson, *Born in Blood: The Lost Secrets of Freemasonry* (New York, New York: M. Evans and Company, 1989), p.136.

144. Pike, *op. cit.,* p.817-818.

145. Howe, *op. cit.,* p.28, 33.

146. David L. Carrico, quoting Kenneth Mackenzie, *The Pentagram, Freemasonry and the Goat* (Evansville, Illinois: Followers of Jesus Christ, 1992), p.15.

147. Waite, *The Mysteries of Magic, op. cit.,* p.68.

148. Carrico, quoting Lynn F. Perkins, *The Pentagram, Freemasonry and the Goat, op. cit.,* p.17.

149. Robert Macoy (Arranged by), *Adoptive Rite Ritual* (Virginia: Macoy Publishing and Masonic Supply Company, 1897), p.293; W. J. Colville, *The Pentagram: Its Symbolism, and the Heroines of the Order of Eastern Star* (New York: Macoy Publishing and Masonic Supply Company, 1914), p.3.

150. John Kennedy Lacock, quoting Rob Morris, *History of the Star Points: Order of the Eastern Star* (Sampson Publications, Inc., 1929), p.7; Mackey, *Encyclopedia of Freemasonry,* Vol. 1, *op. cit.,* p.303.

151. *Ibid.*

152. Pike, *op. cit.,* p.687; See also: Hutchens and Monson, *The Bible in Albert Pike's Morals and Dogma, op. cit.,* p.165; J. D. Buck, *Mystic Masonry* (Illinois: Indo-American Book Company, 1913, Sixth Edition), p.90.

153. LaVey, *op. cit.,* p.30.

154. *Ibid.,* p.39, 57.

155. *Ibid.,* p.131, 57.

156. Harry E. Wedeck, *The Treasury of Witchcraft* (New York: Philosophical Library, 1961), caption under picture between p.170-171..

157. Willis D. Engle, *A General History of the Order of the Eastern Star* (Indianapolis, Indiana: Willis D. Engle, 1901), p.134, 136.

158. Lacock, *op. cit.*

159. Mary Ann Slipper, *The Symbolism of the Order of the Eastern Star* (no other information available), p.18; *Short Talk Bulletin,* "Blazing Star," Part 1 (March

1965; Vol. 43, No. 3), p.5, 7, 12; A. T. C. Pierson, *The Traditions, Origin and Early History of Freemasonry* (New York: Masonic Publishing Company, 1865), p.367-368; Winters, *op. cit.*, p.66, 68; Shirley Plessner, *Symbolism of the Eastern Star* (Cleveland, Ohio: Gilbert Publishing Company, 1956), p.159, 160, 185; George Oliver, *Symbol of Glory Shewing the Object and End of Freemasonry* (New York: John W. Leonard and Company, American Masonic Agency, 1855), p.258, 259, 260; Rex R. Hutchens, *A Bridge to Light* (Washington, D.C.: Supreme Council, 33° Ancient and Accepted Scottish Rite of Freemasonry, Southern Jurisdiction, 1988), p.201; Waite, *The Mysteries of Magic, op. cit.*, p.202.

160. Brochure from the Witches' League for Public Awareness, p.2.

161. Brochure from The Magic Door, p.4.

162. Ed Decker *The Question of Freemasonry Companion* (Issaquah, Washington: Saints Alive in Jesus, 1992), quoting from *Man, Myth and Magic*, p.49.

163. *Short Talk Bulletin*, "Blazing Star," Part 1 (March 1965; Vol. 43, No. 3), p.8.

164. *For Full Moon Workers* (Manhattan Beach, California: Arcana Workshops, n.d.), p.8.

165. LaVey, *op. cit.*, p.51.

166. John Yarker, *The Arcane Schools* (Belfast, Ireland: William Tait, 1909), p.140.

167. *Short Talk Bulletin*, "Blazing Star," *op. cit.*, p.7; See also: Pike, *op. cit.*, p.787; A. T. C. Pierson, *The Traditions, Origin and Early History of Freemasonry* (New York: Masonic Publishing Company, 1865), p.66-67; George Oliver, *Symbol of Glory Shewing the Object and End of Freemasonry* (New York: John W. Leonard and Company, American Masonic Agency, 1855), p.258.

168. Schnoebelen, *Masonry, op. cit.*, p.169; See also: Hutchens and Monson, *The Bible in Albert Pike's Morals and Dogma, op. cit.*, p.251; Waite, *The Mysteries of Magic, op. cit.*, p.299.

169. *Ritual of the Order of the Eastern Star* (Washington, D.C.: General Grand Chapter Order of the Eastern Star, 1956), p.81.

170. Macoy, *op. cit.*, p.293; W. J. Colville, *The Pentagram: Its Symbolism, and the Heroines of the Order of Eastern Star* (New York: Macoy Publishing and Masonic Supply Company, 1914), p.3.

171. George H. Steinmetz, *Freemasonry: Its Hidden Meaning* (New York: Macoy Publishing and Masonic Supply Company, 1948), p.43-44; See also: Charles H. Vail, *The Ancient Mysteries and Modern Masonry* (New York: Macoy Publishing and Masonic Supply Company, 1909), p.182; *Short Talk Bulletin*, "Symbolism" (March 1925; Vol. 3, No. 3; Reprinted May 1982), p.6, 9.

172. J. D. Buck, quoting Albert Pike, *The Lost Word Found in the Great Work* (Chicago, Illinois: Indo-American Book Company, 1913, Third Edition), p.14-15; See also: Pike, *op. cit.*, p.819; *Short Talk Bulletin*, "Behind the Symbol" (July 1954; Vol. 32, No. 7), p.3.

173. J. D. Buck, *Mystic Masonry* (Illinois: Indo-American Book Company, 1913, Sixth Edition), p.xxxvi.

174. Waite, *The Secret Tradition in Freemasonry, op. cit.*, p.633.

175. *Short Talk Bulletin*, "Symbolism" (March 1925; Vol. 3, No. 3; Reprinted May 1982), p.15.

176. Shirley Plessner, *Symbolism of the Eastern Star* (Cleveland, Ohio: Gilbert Publishing Company, 1956), p.195; See also: *What? When? Where? Why? Who? in Freemasonry* (Silver Spring, Maryland: Masonic Service Association of the United States, 1956), p.73; *Short Talk Bulletin*, "Veiled in Allegory and Illustrated by Symbols" (November 1974; Vol. 52, No. 11), p.3.

177. *Ibid.*, p.191.

178. Ward, *Freemasonry and the Ancient Gods, op. cit.*, p.44, 46, See also: p.61.

179. S. R. Parchment, *Ancient Operative Masonry* (San Francisco, California: San Francisco Center—Rosicrucian Fellowship, 1930), p.41.

180. Albert G. Mackey, *The Symbolism of Freemasonry* (New York: Clark and Maynard, 1869), p.185, 339; See also: Albert G. Mackey, *A Manual of the Lodge* (New York: Charles E. Merrill Company, 1870), p.56, 57; Albert G. Mackey, *An Encyclopedia of Freemasonry and Its Kindred Science* (Chicago, Illinois: The Masonic History Company, 1924), p.114; Manly Palmer Hall, *The Lost Keys of Freemasonry* (Richmond, Virginia: Macoy Publishing and Masonic Supply Company, Inc., 1976; Originally published in 1923), p.98; *Mysteries of Mind Space & Time: The Unexplained* (Vol. 1) (Westport, Connecticut: H. S. Stuttman, Inc., 1992), p.40.

181. G. A. Riplinger, *New Age Bible Versions* (Munroe Falls, Ohio: A. V. Publications, 1993), p.401.

182. *Ibid.*, p.400.

183. Parchment, *op. cit.*, p.43.

184. *Ibid.*

185. *Ibid.*, p.116.

186. George Oliver, *Symbol of Glory Shewing the Object and End of Freemasonry* (New York: John W. Leonard and Company, American Masonic Agency, 1855), p.259.

187. Waite, *The Mysteries of Magic, op. cit.*, p.205; Rex R. Hutchens, *A Bridge to Light* (Washington, D.C.: Supreme Council, 33° Ancient and Accepted Scottish Rite of Freemasonry, Southern Jurisdiction, 1988), p.201, 205.

188. *Ibid.*, p.217.

189. *The World Book Encyclopedia*, 1961 Edition; Vol. 18, p.251; *Webster's Seventh New Collegiate Dictionary*, 1967, p.502; Joseph Carr, *The Lucifer Connection* (Lafayette, Louisiana: Huntington House, Inc., 1987), p.139; Manly Palmer Hall, *America's Assignment with Destiny* (Los Angeles, California: Philosophical Research Society, Inc., 1951), p.19.

190. Rex R. Hutchens, *A Bridge to Light* (Washington, D.C.: Supreme Council, 33° Ancient and Accepted Scottish Rite of Freemasonry, Southern Jurisdiction, 1988), p.81.

191. Carrico, quoting John Robison, *The Occult Meaning of the Great Seal of the United States, op. cit.*, p.7-8; See also: Still, *op. cit.*, p.77; Dennis Cuddy, *Now Is the Dawning of the New Age New World Order* (Oklahoma City, Oklahoma: Hearthstone Publishing, Ltd., 1991), p.31; Francois Ribadeau Dumas (Translated by Elisabeth Abbott), *Cagliostro: Scoundrel or Saint?* (New York: The Orion Press, 1967), p.54.

192. Dennis Cuddy, quoting Adam Weishaupt, *Now Is the Dawning of the New Age New World Order* (Oklahoma City, Oklahoma: Hearthstone Publishing, Ltd., 1991), p.31.

193. Still, *op. cit.*, p.77.

194. Quoting Baron von Knigge, *Masonic Institutes* (High Holborn: Richard Spencer, 1847), p.167.

Chapter 7: Symbolism of the Eastern Star

1. Mary Ann Slipper, *The Symbolism of the Eastern Star* (n.p., 1927), p.5, 92; Mary Ann Slipper, *The Symbolism of the Order of the Eastern Star* (no other information available), p.5.

2. *The Authorized Standard Ritual of the Order of the Eastern Star of New York* (New York, Press of Andrew H. Kellogg Company, 1876; Twentieth Edition, 1916), p.14; Shirley Plessner, *Symbolism of the Eastern Star* (Cleveland, Ohio: Gilbert Publishing Company, 1956), p.31, 59, 132, 133; Robert Macoy (Arranged by), *Adoptive Rite Ritual* (Virginia: Macoy Publishing and Masonic Supply Company, 1897), p.30, 49, 114; *Ritual of the Order of the Eastern Star* (Washington, D.C.: General Grand Chapter Order of the Eastern Star, 1956), p.19, 37, 73, 85; F. A. Bell, *Bell's Eastern Star Ritual* (P. R. C. Publications, Inc., 1988 Revised Edition), p.31, 33, 51, 89, 130; Thomas Lowe, *Adoptive Masonry: Eastern Star Ritual* (Chicago, Illinois: Ezra A. Cook, 1913), p.52; William Meyer, *The Order of the Eastern Star* (no other information available), p.4; Lucien V. Rule, *Pioneering in Masonry: The Life and Times of Rob Morris, Masonic Poet Laureate, Together with Story of Clara Barton and the Eastern Star* (Louisville, Kentucky: Brandt and Connors Company, 1922), p.177.

3. Jean M'Kee Kenaston, Compiler, *History of the Order of the Eastern Star* (Cedar Rapids, Iowa: The Torch Press, 1917), p.664; See also: 50, p.210; *Pocket Masonic Dictionary* (Silver Spring, Maryland: The Masonic Service Association of the United States, 1988), p.9; *What? When? Where? Why? Who? in Freemasonry* (Silver Spring, Maryland: Masonic Service Association of the United States, 1956), p.11; Robert Macoy (Arranged by), *Adoptive Rite Ritual* (Virginia: Macoy Publishing and Masonic Supply Company, 1897), p.114-115; W. J. McCormick, *Christ, the Christian and Freemasonry* (Belfast, Ireland: Great Joy Publications, 1984), p.87; F. A. Bell, *Bell's Eastern Star Ritual* (P. R. C. Publications, Inc., 1988 Revised Edition), p.89.

4. Shirley Plessner, *Symbolism of the Eastern Star* (Cleveland, Ohio: Gilbert Publishing Company, 1956), p.31-32, 133.

5. Slipper, *The Symbolism of the Order of the Eastern Star, op. cit.*, p.7; See also: Sarah H. Terry, *The Second Mile* (Corpus Christi, Texas: Christian Triumph Press, 1935), p.5.

6. Edmond Ronayne, quoting Albert Mackey, *The Master's Carpet (Mah-Hah-Bone)* (n.p., 1879), p.132.

7. Plessner, *op. cit.*, p.58.

8. *Ibid.*, p.195; See also: *Short Talk Bulletin*, "Veiled in Allegory and Illustrated by Symbols" (November 1974; Vol. 52, No. 11), p.3.

9. *Ibid.*, p.94; See also: Henry C. Clausen, *Clausen's Commentaries on Morals and Dogma* (Supreme Council, 33rd Degree, Ancient and Accepted Scottish Rite of Freemasonry, Southern Jurisdiction, USA, 1974), p.72.

10. Frank Gaynor, Editor, *Dictionary of Mysticism* (New York: Philosophical Library, 1953), p.128; Lynn F. Perkins, *Masonry in the New Age* (Lakemont, Georgia: CSA Press, 1971), p.145, 341.

11. Sarah H. Terry, *The Second Mile* (Corpus Christi, Texas: Christian Triumph Press, 1935), p.50; See also: J. D. Buck, *Mystic Masonry* (Illinois: Indo-American Book Company, 1913, Sixth Edition), p.257; Charles H. Vail, *The Ancient Mysteries and Modern Masonry* (New York: Macoy Publishing and Masonic Supply Company, 1909), p.182.

12. Slipper, *The Symbolism of the Order of the Eastern Star, op. cit.*, p.6.

13. Plessner, *op. cit.*, p.155.

14. Slipper, *The Symbolism of the Order of the Eastern Star, op. cit.*, p.5.

15. Slipper, *The Symbolism of the Eastern Star, op. cit.*, p.9-10; See also: *History of the Order of the Eastern Star* (General Grand Chapter in the U. S. A., 1989), p.13.

16. *Pocket Encyclopedia of Masonic Symbols* (Silver Spring, Maryland: The Masonic Service Association of the United States, 1953), p.15; See also: *What? When? Where? Why? Who? in Freemasonry* (Silver Spring, Maryland: Masonic Service Association of the United States, 1956), p.11.

17. William O. Peterson, Editor, *Masonic Quiz Book: "Ask Me Another, Brother"* (Chicago, Illinois: Charles T. Powner Company, 1950), p.208; William Hutchinson (Revised by George Oliver), *The Spirit of Masonry,* (New York: Bell Publishing Company, 1982; Originally published in 1775), p.195.

18. Joseph Fort Newton, *The Builders: A Story and Study of Masonry* (Cedar Rapids, Iowa: The Torch Press, 1914), p.9.

19. *Short Talk Bulletin*, "Veiled in Allegory" (September 1949; Vol. 27, No. 9; Reprinted April 1986), p.7.

20. *Short Talk Bulletin*, "The Broken Column" (February 1956; Vol. 34, No. 2; Reprinted January 1985), p.6-7; See also: Ronayne, *op. cit.*, p.387-388; W. J. McCormick, *Christ, the Christian and Freemasonry* (Belfast, Ireland: Great Joy Publications, 1984), p.87; Malcolm Duncan, *Duncan's Ritual of Freemasonry* (New York: David McKay Company, Inc., n.d., 3rd Edition), p.125; Harold Waldwin Percival, *Masonry and Its Symbols in the Light of "Thinking and Destiny"* (New York, New York: The Word Foundation, Inc., 1952), p.35; *What? When? Where? Why? Who? in Freemasonry* (Silver Spring, Maryland: Masonic Service Association of the United States, 1956), p.80.

21. A. T. C. Pierson, *The Traditions, Origin and Early History of Freemasonry* (New York: Masonic Publishing Company, 1865), p.220-221.

22. William Schnoebelen, *Masonry: Beyond the Light* (Chino, California: Chick Publications, 1991), p.158; See also: Percival George Woodcock, *Short Dictionary of Mythology* (Philosophical Library, 1953), p.145; Charles G. Berger, *Our Phallic Heritage* (New York, New York: Greenwich Book Publishers, Inc., 1966), p.40; J. E. Cirlot (Translated by Jack Sage), *A Dictionary of Symbols* (New York: Dorset Press, 1991 Edition), p.278.

23. Pierson, *op. cit.*, p.232.

24. Albert Pike, *Morals and Dogma of the Ancient and Accepted Scottish Rite of Freemasonry* (Richmond, Virginia: L. H. Jenkins, Inc., 1871), p.15, 597; Paul Hamlyn, *Greek Mythology* (London: Paul Hamlyn, Ltd., 1967), p.13; George Oliver, *Signs and Symbols* (New York: Macoy Publishing and Masonic Supply

Company, 1906), p.94; *The World Book Encyclopedia*, 1961 Edition; Vol. 16, p.129; Thomas Bulfinch, *Bulfinch's Mythology* (New York: Thomas Y. Crowell Company, Inc., 1970), p.967; Arthur Coon, *The Theosophical Seal* (no other info available); p.190; J. E. Cirlot (Translated by Jack Sage), *A Dictionary of Symbols* (New York: Dorset Press, 1991 Edition), p.67; *Ibid.*, p.221; Aleister Crowley, *Seven, Seven, Seven* (no other information available), p.73; R. Swinburne Clymer, *The Mysteries of Osiris or Ancient Egyptian Initiation* (Quakertown, Pennsylvania: The Philosophical Publishing Company, 1951, Revised Edition), p.111; J. E. Cirlot (Translated by Jack Sage), *A Dictionary of Symbols* (New York: Dorset Press, 1991 Edition), p.278; M. Esther Harding, *Woman's Mysteries: Ancient and Modern* (New York: G. P. Putnam's Sons for the C. G. Jung Foundation for Analytical Psychology, 1971 Edition), p.94.

25. *The World Book Encyclopedia*, 1961 Edition; Vol. 16, p.129.

26. *Ibid.;* p.129; Thomas Bulfinch, *Bulfinch's Mythology* (New York: Thomas Y. Crowell Company, Inc., 1970), p.920, 967; Percival George Woodcock, *Short Dictionary of Mythology* (Philosophical Library, 1953), p.35; Thomas Bulfinch, *Bulfinch's Mythology: The Age of Fable or Stories of Gods and Heroes* (Garden City, New York: Doubleday and Company, Inc., 1948), p.9; Charles G. Berger, *Our Phallic Heritage* (New York, New York: Greenwich Book Publishers, Inc., 1966), p.40; Gustav Schwab, *Gods and Heroes: Myths and Epics of Ancient Greece* (New York: Pantheon Books, 1946), p.36; Thomas Bulfinch, *Bulfinch's Mythology* (New York: Thomas Y. Crowell Company, Inc., 1970), p.967; Arthur Coon, *The Theosophical Seal* (no other info available), p.190; Edith Hamilton, *Mythology* (Boston, Massachusetts: Little, Brown and Company, 1942), p.21, 51; Helena Petrovna Blavatsky, *Isis Unveiled*, Vol. I: Science (New York, New York: Trow's Printing and Bookbinding Company, 1877), p.263; Clifton L. Fowler, *Santa Claus and Christmas* (Knoxville, Tennessee: Evangelist of Truth, 1982), p.28; Paul Hamlyn, *Greek Mythology* (London: Paul Hamlyn, Ltd., 1967), p.7.

27. J. S. M. Ward, *Freemasonry and the Ancient Gods* (London: Simpkin, Marshall, Hamilton, Kent and Company, Ltd., 1921), p.232; See also: Texe Marrs, *Mystery Mark of the New Age: Satan's Design for World Domination* (Westchester, Illinois: Crossway Books, 1988), p.69.

28. Arthur Edward Waite, *The Mysteries of Magic: A Digest of the Writings of Eliphas Levi* (Chicago, Illinois: De Laurence, Scott and Company, 1909), p.214.

29. Texe Marrs, *Mystery Mark of the New Age: Satan's Design for World Domination* (Westchester, Illinois: Crossway Books, 1988), p.68.

30. Percival George Woodcock, *Short Dictionary of Mythology* (Philosophical Library, 1953), p.135.

31. Marrs, *Mystery Mark of the New Age, op. cit.*, p.65.

32. Helena Petrovna Blavatsky, *Isis Unveiled*, Vol. I: Science (New York, New York: Trow's Printing and Bookbinding Company, 1877), p.263, 578.

33. Waite, *The Mysteries of Magic, op. cit.*, p.217; Woodcock, *op. cit.*, p.135; J. E. Cirlot (Translated by Jack Sage), *A Dictionary of Symbols* (New York: Dorset Press, 1991 Edition), p.281.

34. J. E. Cirlot (Translated by Jack Sage), *A Dictionary of Symbols* (New York: Dorset Press, 1991 Edition), p.281; See also: George Oliver, *Signs and Symbols* (New York: Macoy Publishing and Masonic Supply Company, 1906), p.82; Charles Scott, *The Analogy of Ancient Craft Masonry to Natural and Revealed Religion* (Philadelphia, Pennsylvania: E. H. Butler and Company, 1857), p.311.

35. Veronica Ions, *Egyptian Mythology* (England: The Hamlyn Publishing Group, Ltd., 1965), p.85.

36. *Ibid.*, p.58, 75, 85, 91; *New Larousse Encyclopedia of Mythology* (Prometheus Press, 1972 Edition), p.19; *Ibid.*, p.75, 85, 91; E. A. Wallis Budge, *Amulets and Superstitions* (New York, New York: Dover Publications, Inc., 1978), p.xix.

37. Gaynor, *op. cit.*, p.87.

38. William T. Still, *New World Order: The Ancient Plan of Secret Societies* (Lafayette, Louisiana: Huntington House, Inc., 1990), p.24.

39. R. Swinburne Clymer, *The Mysteries of Osiris or Ancient Egyptian Initiation* (Quakertown, Pennsylvania: The Philosophical Publishing Company, 1951, Revised Edition), p.63.

40. Kenaston, *op. cit.*, p.664; Willis D. Engle, *A General History of the Order of the Eastern Star* (Indianapolis, Indiana: Willis D. Engle, 1901), p.71; Robert Macoy (Arranged by), *Adoptive Rite Ritual* (Virginia: Macoy Publishing and Masonic Supply Company, 1897), p.127; Plessner, *op. cit.*, , p.101; Carl H. Claudy, *Masonic Harvest* (Washington, D.C.: The Temple Publishers, 1948), p.234-235; W. L. Wilmshurst, *The Masonic Initiation* (Ferndale, Michigan: Trismegistus Press, 1980; Originally published 1924), 52-53; Albert G. Mackey, *The Symbolism of Freemasonry* (New York: Clark and Maynard, 1869), p.253, 261; *Short Talk Bulletin*, "Veiled in Allegory" *op. cit.*, p.3; Arthur Edward Waite, *The Secret Tradition in Freemasonry* (London: Rider and Company, 1937), p.646, 650; *Masonic Vocabulary* (Silver Spring, Maryland: Masonic Service Association of the United States, 1955), p.4; *What? When? Where? Why? Who?* in Freemasonry (Silver Spring, Maryland: Masonic Service Association of the United States, 1956), p.2; Schnoebelen, *Masonry, op. cit.*, p.158; *Pocket Encyclopedia of Masonic Symbols, op. cit.*, p.5; *Pocket Masonic Dictionary* (Silver Spring, Maryland: The Masonic Service Association of the United States, 1988), p.6, 14; Manly Palmer Hall, *An Encyclopedic Outline of Masonic, Hermetic, Qabbalistic and Rosicrucian Symbolical Philosophy: Being an Interpretation of the Secret Teachings Concealed Within the Rituals, Allegories and Mysteries of All Ages* (San Francisco, California: H. S. Crocker Company, Inc., 1928), p.36; John J. Robinson, *Born in Blood: The Lost Secrets of Freemasonry* (New York, New York: M. Evans and Company, 1989), p.222, 270, 271.

41. *Pocket Masonic Dictionary* (Silver Spring, Maryland: The Masonic Service Association of the United States, 1988), p.6, 14.

42. *Pocket Encyclopedia of Masonic Symbols, op. cit.*, p.5; See also: *What? When? Where? Why? Who?* in Freemasonry (Silver Spring, Maryland: Masonic Service Association of the United States, 1956), p.2.

43. Kenaston, *op. cit.*, p.664.

44. Albert G. Mackey, *The Symbolism of Freemasonry* (New York: Clark and Maynard, 1869), p.260.

45. *Ibid.*, p.261.

46. *Ibid.*, p.259-260 in correlation with p.261.

47. Waite, *The Mysteries of Magic, op. cit.*, p.217.

48. Schnoebelen, *Masonry, op. cit.*, p.158.

49. *The World Book Encyclopedia*, 1961 Edition; Vol. 16, p.250.

50. Waite, *The Mysteries of Magic, op. cit.*, p.214.

51. Charles G. Berger, *Our Phallic Heritage* (New York, New York: Greenwich Book Publishers, Inc., 1966), p.40, 80; Cirlot, *op. cit.*, p.279; Clifton L. Fowler, *Santa Claus and Christmas* (Knoxville, Tennessee: Evangelist of Truth, 1982), p.28; Al Dager, *Origins of Christmas Traditions* (Costa Mesa, California: Media Spotlight, 1985 Special Report), n.p.; *CIB Bulletin* (December 1989; Vol. 5, No. 12), p.1; Anthony Frewin, *The Book of Days* (St. James Place, London: William Collins Sons and Company, Ltd., 1979), p.384; "Babel Becomes One," *The Omega-Letter* (April 1990; Vol. 5, No. 4), p.7; Ralph Edward Woodrow, *Babylon Mystery Religion: Ancient and Modern* (Riverside, California: Ralph Woodrow Evangelistic Association, Inc., 1990 Edition), p.143; Peter Lalonde, *One World Under Antichrist* (Eugene, Oregon: Harvest House Publishers, 1991), p.59; Woodcock, *op. cit.*, p.134; Dave Hunt, *Whatever Happened to Heaven?* (Eugene, Oregon: Harvest House Publishers, 1988), p.113.

52. Al Dager, *Origins of Christmas Traditions* (Costa Mesa, California: Media Spotlight, 1985 Special Report), n.p.

53. Clifton L. Fowler, *Santa Claus and Christmas* (Knoxville, Tennessee: Evangelist of Truth, 1982), p.28.

54. Anton Szandor LaVey, *The Satanic Bible* (New York: Avon Books, 1969), p.98; Henry C. Clausen, *Clausen's Commentaries on Morals and Dogma* (Supreme Council, 33rd Degree, Ancient and Accepted Scottish Rite of Freemasonry, Southern Jurisdiction, USA, 1974), p.142, Newton, *The Builders: A Story and Study of Masonry, op. cit.*, p.183; George H. Steinmetz, *Freemasonry: Its Hidden Meaning* (New York: Macoy Publishing and Masonic Supply Company, 1948), p.93-94; *What? When? Where? Why? Who? in Freemasonry* (Silver Spring, Maryland: Masonic Service Association of the United States, 1956), p.67-68; Allen E. Roberts, *The Craft and Its Symbols: Opening the Door to Masonic Symbolism* (Richmond, Virginia: Macoy Publishing and Masonic Supply Company, Inc., 1974), p.36; W. L. Wilmshurst, *The Masonic Initiation* (Ferndale, Michigan: Trismegistus Press, 1980; Originally published 1924), p.95, 187-188; *Short Talk Bulletin*, "Sts. Johns' Days" (December 1933; Vol. 11, No. 12; Reprinted July 1986), p.5-6, 8; Texe Marrs, *Millennium: Peace, Promises, and the Day They Take Our Money Away* (Austin, Texas: Living Truth Publishers, 1990), p.50; Albert G. Mackey, *A Manual of the Lodge* (New York: Charles E. Merrill Company, 1870), p.57; Charles H. Vail, *The Ancient Mysteries and Modern Masonry* (New York: Macoy Publishing and Masonic Supply Company, 1909), p.51-52, 135-136, 186; Colin F. W. Dyer, *Symbolism in Craft Freemasonry* (England: A Lewis [Masonic Publishers], Ltd., 1976), p.98, 100-101; Mackey, *The Symbolism of Freemasonry, op. cit.*, p.115; J. D. Buck, *Mystic Masonry* (Illinois: Indo-American Book Company, 1913, Sixth Edition), p.86; Albert Churchward, *Signs and Symbols of Primordial Man* (London: George Allen and Company, Ltd., 1913, Second Edition), p.289.

55. Fowler, *op. cit.*, p.28.

56. Arthur Edward Waite, *A New Encyclopedia of Freemasonry and of Cognate Instituted Mysteries: Their Rites, Literature and History* (New York: Weathervane Books, 1970), Vol. I, p.61-62.

57. Peterson, *op. cit.*, p.32, 133, 271; See also: William Adrian Brown, *Facts, Fables and Fantasies of Freemasonry* (New York, New York: Vantage Press, Inc., 1968), p.169.

58. John T. Lawrence, *The Perfect Ashlar* (London: A. Lewis, 1912), p.295, updated language. The quotation actually reads: "At ye makeing of ye Toure of Babell,

there was Masonrie first much esteemed of, and the King of Babilon yt was called Nimrod was a mason himself and loved well Masons."

59. John Yarker, *The Arcane Schools* (Belfast, Ireland: William Tait, 1909), p.267.

60. William Adrian Brown, *Facts, Fables and Fantasies of Freemasonry* (New York, New York: Vantage Press, Inc., 1968), p.34.

61. For example, see: William Hutchinson, *The Spirit of Masonry*, revised by Rev. George Oliver, originally published in 1775 (New York: Bell Publishing Company, 1982), p.278; Robert Morris and Albert Mackey, *Lights and Shadows of the Mystic Tie* (New York: Masonic Publishing Company, 1878), p.470; Manly Palmer Hall, *The Lost Keys of Freemasonry* (Richmond, Virginia: Macoy Publishing and Masonic Supply Company, Inc., 1976; Originally published in 1923), p.90; Albert G. Mackey, *A Manual of the Lodge* (New York: Charles E. Merrill Company, 1870), p.21; Mackey, *The Symbolism of Freemasonry, op. cit.,* p.158, 356; R. Swinburne Clymer, *The Mysticism of Masonry* (Quakertown, Pennsylvania: The Philosophical Publishing Company, 1924), p.117; Rex R. Hutchens, *A Bridge to Light* (Washington, D.C.: Supreme Council, 33° Ancient and Accepted Scottish Rite of Freemasonry, Southern Jurisdiction, 1988), p.120, 129, 267, 320, 321; Thomas Lowe, *Adoptive Masonry: Eastern Star Ritual* (Chicago, Illinois: Ezra A. Cook, 1913), p.18; Kenaston, *op. cit.,* p.638; *Short Talk Bulletin,* "Kipling and Masonry" (October 1964; Vol. 42, No. 10; Reprinted June 1985), p.6; Albert Churchward, *Signs and Symbols of Primordial Man* (London: George Allen and Company, Ltd., 1913, Second Edition), p.276; Charles H. Vail, *The Ancient Mysteries and Modern Masonry* (New York: Macoy Publishing and Masonic Supply Company, 1909), p.122.

62. H. L. Haywood, *Symbolic Masonry: An Interpretation of the Three Degrees* (Washington, D.C.: Masonic Service Association of the United States, 1923), p.128.

63. George H. Steinmetz, quoting Robert Hewitt Brown, *Freemasonry: Its Hidden Meaning* (New York: Macoy Publishing and Masonic Supply Company, 1948), p.46.

64. Gaynor, *op. cit.,* p.171.

65. Henry C. Clausen, *Clausen's Commentaries on Morals and Dogma* (Supreme Council, 33rd Degree, Ancient and Accepted Scottish Rite of Freemasonry, Southern Jurisdiction, USA, 1974), p.133; See also: Pike, *op. cit.,* p.819.

66. *Ibid.,* p.379.

67. *Ibid.*

68. *Short Talk Bulletin,* "Albert Gallatin Mackey" (February 1936; Vol. 14, No. 2; Reprinted July 1980), p.7.

69. Albert G. Mackey, *A Manual of the Lodge* (New York: Charles E. Merrill Company, 1870), p.56; See also: Mackey, *The Symbolism of Freemasonry, op. cit.,* p.112-113, 192; Cirlot, *op. cit.,* p.60.

70. Harold Waldwin Percival, *Masonry and Its Symbols in the Light of "Thinking and Destiny"* (New York, New York: The Word Foundation, Inc., 1952), p.40; See also: Cirlot, *op. cit.,* p.60.

71. Waite, *The Mysteries of Magic, op. cit.,* p.214.

72. John Kennedy Lacock, *History of the Star Points: Order of the Eastern Star* (Sampson Publications, Inc., 1929), p.97.

73. See: *Ritual of the Order of the Eastern Star* (Washington, D.C.: General Grand Chapter Order of the Eastern Star, 1956), p.21, 120-121; F. A. Bell, *Bell's Eastern Star Ritual* (P. R. C. Publications, Inc., 1988 Revised Edition), p.35, 129-130; Robert Macoy (Arranged by), *Adoptive Rite Ritual* (Virginia: Macoy Publishing and Masonic Supply Company, 1897), p.43-47.

74. Slipper, *The Symbolism of the Eastern Star, op. cit.,* p.33.

75. *The Authorized Standard Ritual of the Order of the Eastern Star of New York, op. cit.,* p.224; Robert Macoy (Arranged by), *Adoptive Rite Ritual* (Virginia: Macoy Publishing and Masonic Supply Company, 1897), p.237.

76. Plessner, *op. cit.,* p.18; Slipper, *The Symbolism of the Eastern Star, op. cit.,* p.26; Robert Macoy (Arranged by), *Adoptive Rite Ritual* (Virginia: Macoy Publishing and Masonic Supply Company, 1897), p.237.

77. Slipper, *The Symbolism of the Order of the Eastern Star, op. cit.,* p.19; Peterson, *op. cit.,* p.272.

78. Slipper, *The Symbolism of the Eastern Star, op. cit.,* p.34.

79. Terry, *op. cit.,* p.70; Steinmetz, *Freemasonry: Its Hidden Meaning, op. cit.,* p.62; Paul Foster Case, *The Masonic Letter G* (Los Angeles, California: Builders of the Adytum, Ltd., 1981), p.50; Thomas Albert Stafford, *Christian Symbolism in the Evangelical Churches* (Nashville, Tennessee: Abingdon Press, 1942), p.35.

80. Plessner, *op. cit.,* p.49; Alice A. Bailey, *A Treatise on White Magic* (or *The Way of the Disciple*) (New York: Lucis Publishing Company, 1951), p.553; *Ibid.,* p.70; Slipper, *The Symbolism of the Eastern Star, op. cit.,* p.29, 30; See also R. Swinburne Clymer, *The Mysticism of Masonry* (Quakertown, Pennsylvania: The Philosophical Publishing Company, 1924), p.157; *Pocket Encyclopedia of Masonic Symbols, op. cit.,* p.36, 56; George Oliver, *Signs and Symbols* (New York: Macoy Publishing and Masonic Supply Company, 1906), p.92-93; Paul Foster Case, *The Masonic Letter G* (Los Angeles, California: Builders of the Adytum, Ltd., 1981), p.50; Thomas Albert Stafford, *Christian Symbolism in the Evangelical Churches* (Nashville, Tennessee: Abingdon Press, 1942), p.35; Charles H. Vail, *The Ancient Mysteries and Modern Masonry* (New York: Macoy Publishing and Masonic Supply Company, 1909), p.190; Rex R. Hutchens, *A Bridge to Light* (Washington, D.C.: Supreme Council, 33° Ancient and Accepted Scottish Rite of Freemasonry, Southern Jurisdiction, 1988), p.15, 247; Mackey, *The Symbolism of Freemasonry, op. cit.,* p.192, 195, 196, 331, 361; Ward, *Freemasonry and the Ancient Gods, op. cit.,* p.10; Steinmetz, *Freemasonry: Its Hidden Meaning, op. cit.,* p.62, 63, 87; *What? When? Where? Why? Who? in Freemasonry* (Silver Spring, Maryland: Masonic Service Association of the United States, 1956), p.74; Pierson, *op. cit.,* p.379; Alain Danielou, *The Gods of India* (New York, New York: Inner Traditions International, Ltd., 1985), p.219, 352; Cirlot, *op. cit.,* p.281, 351; George H. Steinmetz, *The Lost Word: Its Hidden Meaning* (New York: Macoy Publishing and Masonic Supply Company, 1953), p.148, 215; *Report from Concerned Christians* (May/June 1990), p.13; Gary Jennings, *Black Magic, White Magic* (Eau Claire, Wisconsin: The Dial Press, Inc., 1964), p.49; *Short Talk Bulletin,* "The Significant Numbers" (September 1956; Vol. 34; No. 9), p.3; *Short Talk Bulletin,* "Sanctum Sanctorum" (July 1944; Vol. 22, No. 7; Reprinted January 1982), p.5; Wes Cook, Editor, *Did You Know? Vignettes in Masonry from the Royal Arch Mason Magazine* (Missouri Lodge of Research, 1965), p.132; Clausen, *Clausen's Commentaries on Morals and Dogma, op. cit.,* p.72; R. P. Lawrie Krishna, *The Lamb Slain— Supreme Sacrifice,* Part 3 (Medway, Ohio: Manujothi Ashram Publications,

n.d.), p.30; *Complete Occult Digest A to Z* (North Hollywood, California: International Imports, 1984), p.95; Pike, *op. cit.*, p.323, 429, 632, 634, 782, 858, 861.

81. *Ibid.*, p.50; Terry, *op. cit.*, p.70; Heinrich Zimmer with Joseph Campbell as Editor, *Myths and Symbols in Indian Art and Civilization* (New York: Harper and Row, 1962), p.147; Alain Danielou, *The Gods of India* (New York, New York: Inner Traditions International, Ltd., 1985), p.219, 352; Albert Churchward, *Signs and Symbols of Primordial Man* (London: George Allen and Company, Ltd., 1913, Second Edition), p.313; Charles H. Vail, *The Ancient Mysteries and Modern Masonry* (New York: Macoy Publishing and Masonic Supply Company, 1909), p.190; Cirlot, *op. cit.*, p.281, 351; Gary Jennings, *Black Magic, White Magic* (Eau Claire, Wisconsin: The Dial Press, Inc., 1964), p.49.

82. Steinmetz, *Freemasonry: Its Hidden Meaning, op. cit.*, p.63, 67; George H. Steinmetz, *The Lost Word: Its Hidden Meaning* (New York: Macoy Publishing and Masonic Supply Company, 1953), p.148.

83. Anton Szandor LaVey, *The Satanic Bible* (New York: Avon Books, 1969), p.96.

84. Texe Marrs, quoting Michael Aquino, *Ravaged by the New Age* (Austin, Texas: Living Truth Publishers, 1989), p.110.

85. Jon Klino, "The Psychology of Channeling," *New Age Journal*, (November/December 1987), Vol. 3, Issue 6, p.36.

86. Marrs, quoting Penny Torres, *Mystery Mark of the New Age, op. cit.*, p.208.

87. W.L. Wilmshurst, *The Meaning of Masonry* (Bell Publishing Company, 1980 edition), p.147.

88. *Ibid.*, p.46.

89. J. D. Buck, *Mystic Masonry* (Illinois: Indo-American Book Company, 1913, Sixth Edition), p.136-8.

90. Arthur Edward Waite, *A New Encyclopedia of Freemasonry and of Cognate Instituted Mysteries: Their Rites, Literature and History* (New York: Weathervane Books, 1970 edition), p.421.

91. Charles H. Vail, *The Ancient Mysteries and Modern Masonry* (New York: Macoy Publishing and Masonic Supply Company, 1909), p.25, 28.

92. Manly Palmer Hall, *The Lost Keys of Freemasonry* (Richmond, Virginia: Macoy Publishing and Masonic Supply Company, Inc., 1976; Originally published in 1923), p.92; See also: David L. Carrico, quoting Manly Palmer Hall, *Manly P. Hall: The Honored Masonic Author* (Evansville, Indiana: Followers of Jesus Christ, 1992), p.5; Lynn F. Perkins, *Masonry in the New Age* (Lakemont, Georgia: CSA Press, 1971), p.101, 102.

93. George H. Steinmetz, *The Lost Word: Its Hidden Meaning* (New York: Macoy Publishing and Masonic Supply Company, 1953), p.241-242; See also: David L. Carrico, quoting George H. Steinmetz, *George Steinmetz: The Honored Masonic Author* (Evansville, Indiana: Followers of Jesus Christ, 1992), p.8-9.

94. Joseph Fort Newton, *The Religion of Masonry: An Interpretation* (Richmond, Virginia: Macoy Publishing and Masonic Supply Company, Inc., 1969 Edition), p.37.

95. *Ibid.;* W. L. Wilmshurst, *The Masonic Initiation* (Ferndale, Michigan: Trismegistus Press, 1980; Originally published 1924), p.26, 27; Henry C. Clausen, *Emergence of the Mystical* (Washington, D.C.: Supreme Council, 1981, Second Edition),

p.3; Buck, *Mystic Masonry, op. cit.,* p.174, 247; Slipper, *The Symbolism of the Order of the Eastern Star, op. cit.,* p.21; Newton, *The Builders, op. cit.,* p.293; Vail, *op. cit.,* p.28, 33, 49, 68, 88-89, 125-126, 141, 190, 195; Robert A. Morey, *The Origins and Teachings of Freemasonry* (Southbridge, Massachusetts: Crowne Publications, Inc., 1990), p.45; Malcolm Duncan, *Duncan's Ritual of Freemasonry* (New York: David McKay Company, Inc., n.d., 3rd Edition), p.125; Arthur E. Powell, *The Magic of Freemasonry* (Baskerville Press, Ltd., 1924), p.17; Arthur H. Ward, *Masonic Symbolism and the Mystic Way* (London: Theosophical Publishing House, Ltd., 1923, Second Edition), p.130, 160-161; S. R. Parchment, *Ancient Operative Masonry* (San Francisco, California: San Francisco Center—Rosicrucian Fellowship, 1930), p.35, 36, 74; Larry Kunk, quoting from Masonic sources, *What Is the Secret Doctrine of the Masonic Lodge and How Does It Relate to Their Plan of Salvation?* (1992, Unpublished manuscript), p.7, 9, 13, 14; Steinmetz, *Freemasonry: Its Hidden Meaning, op. cit.,* p.67, 87; David Carrico with Rick Doninger, *The Egyptian-Masonic-Satanic Connection* (Evansville, Indiana: Followers of Jesus Christ, 1991), quoting J. D. Buck, p.16; Haywood, *Symbolic Masonry, op. cit.,* p.129, 263; R. Swinburne Clymer, *The Mysticism of Masonry* (Quakertown, Pennsylvania: The Philosophical Publishing Company, 1924), p.14, 16, 47; J. D. Buck, *The Genius of Free-Masonry and the Twentieth Century Crusade* (Chicago, Illinois: Indo-American Book Company, 1907), p.304-305; Steinmetz, *The Lost Word, op. cit.,* p.36; *The Scottish Rite Journal* (May 1992; Vol. 100, No. 5), p.17; David L. Carrico, quoting George H. Steinmetz, *George Steinmetz: The Honored Masonic Author* (Evansville, Indiana: Followers of Jesus Christ, 1992), p.2-3; Arthur Edward Waite, *The Secret Tradition in Freemasonry* (London: Rider and Company, 1937), p.483, 582; Arthur Edward Waite, *Emblematic Freemasonry and the Evolution of Its Deeper Issues* (London: William Rider and Son, Ltd., 1925), p.275

96. Arthur Edward Waite, *The Secret Tradition in Freemasonry* (London: Rider and Company, 1937), p.483, 582; Vail, *op. cit.,* p.33, 68; Arthur Edward Waite, *A New Encyclopedia of Freemasonry and of Cognate Instituted Mysteries, op. cit.,* p.421.; W.L. Wilmshurst, *The Meaning of Masonry* (Bell Publishing Company, 1980 edition), p.147.

97. Charles A. Watts, *Worthy Matrons' Hand Book: Order of the Eastern Star* (Washington, D.C.: General Grand Chapter, Order of the Eastern Star, 1988), p.21.

98. Slipper, *The Symbolism of the Eastern Star, op. cit.,* p.72.

99. *Short Talk Bulletin,* "The Significant Numbers" (September 1956; Vol. 34; No. 9), p.4.

100. Albert Churchward, *Signs and Symbols of Primordial Man* (London: George Allen and Company, Ltd., 1913, Second Edition), p.189, 309, 471.

101. William Meyer, *The Order of the Eastern Star* (no other information available), p.20; See also: R. P. Lawrie Krishna, *The Lamb Slain—Supreme Sacrifice,* Part 3 (Medway, Ohio: Manujothi Ashram Publications, n.d.), p.30-32; Ward, *Freemasonry and the Ancient Gods, op. cit.,* p.10-11.

102. Ward, *Freemasonry and the Ancient Gods, op. cit.,* p.10-11; See also: *Ibid.;* Alain Danielou, *The Gods of India* (New York, New York: Inner Traditions International, Ltd., 1985), p.352.

103. LaVey, *op. cit.,* p.60, 145.

104. Blavatsky, *op. cit.*, p.578; See also: Marrs, *Mystery Mark of the New Age,* *op. cit.*, p.68.

105. Alice A. Bailey, *Discipleship in the New Age* (Vol. II) (New York: Lucis Publishing Company, 1955), p.135-136.

106. Benjamin Creme, *The Reappearance of the Christ and the Masters of Wisdom* (North Hollywood, California: Tara Center, 1980), p.5, 74, 75, 116; See also: Gaynor, *op. cit.*, p.167; *Ibid.*, p.159; *Shamballa: Where the Will of God is Known* (New York, New York: Arcane School, n.d.), p.27; Catalog from All About Pyramids, p.19; *Shamballa: The Centre Where the Will of God Is Known* (New York, New York: World Goodwill, n.d.), n.p.; *Magical Work of the Soul* (New York, New York: The Arcane School, n.d.), p.4, 5; Lynn F. Perkins, *Masonry in the New Age* (Lakemont, Georgia: CSA Press, 1971), p.56; *Transmission.* (April 1983, No. 1), p.2-3; *New Times* (March/April 1986; #862), p.23; John Godwin, *Occult America* (Garden City, New York: Doubleday and Company, Inc., 1972), p.294; Alice A. Bailey, *A Treatise on White Magic* (or *The Way of the Disciple*) (New York: Lucis Publishing Company, 1951), p.378-379; Marrs, *Mystery Mark of the New Age, op. cit.*, p.57-58.

107. Bailey, *Discipleship in the New Age*, Vol. II, *op. cit.*, p.326.

108. *Ibid.*, Vol. I, p.171.

109. Lynn F. Perkins, *Masonry in the New Age* (Lakemont, Georgia: CSA Press, 1971), p.56.

110. *Ibid.*, p.56-57.

111. Terry, *op. cit.*, p.70.

112. C. F. McQuaig, quoting Martin L. Wagner, *The Masonic Report* (Norcross, Georgia: Answer Books and Tapes, 1976), p.52; See also: Heinrich Zimmer with Joseph Campbell as Editor, *Myths and Symbols in Indian Art and Civilization* (New York: Harper and Row, 1962), p.147.

113. *Ibid.*, p.52.

114. O. J. Graham, *The Six-Pointed Star* (New Puritan Library, 1988, Second Edition), p.32, 34; See also Peterson, *op. cit.*, p.277.

115. Slipper, *The Symbolism of the Eastern Star, op. cit.*, p.14; See also Plessner, *op. cit.*, p.125.

116. Terry, *op. cit.*, p.70.

117. Graham, *op. cit.*, p.4, 11; Stewart Farrar, *What Witches Do: The Modern Coven Revealed* (Custer, Washington: Phoenix Publishing Company, 1983, Revised Edition), p.35.

118. *Ibid.*, p.35.

119. E. L. Hawkins, *A Concise Cyclopaedia of Freemasonry* (EC: A. Lewis, 1908), p.124-125.

120. E. A. Wallis Budge, *Amulets and Superstitions* (New York, New York: Dover Publications, Inc., 1978), p.432.

121. Gary Jennings, *Black Magic, White Magic* (Eau Claire, Wisconsin: The Dial Press, Inc., 1964), p.51.; See also Harry E. Wedeck, *Treasury of Witchcraft* (New York, New York: Philosophical Library, 1961), p.135.

122. *Saints Alive in Jesus Newsletter* (March 1992), p.4.

123. Jack T. Chick, *Spellbound* (Chino, California: Chick Publications, 1978), p.7.; See also Eric Barger, *From Rock to Rock: The Music of Darkness Exposed!* (Lafayette, Louisiana: Huntington House, Inc., 1990), p.165; Marrs, *Mystery Mark of the New Age*, op. cit., p.118; David Carrico, *The Occult Meaning of the Great Seal of the United States* (Evansville, Indiana: Followers of Jesus Christ, 1991), p.25; Irene Arrington Park, *Modernized Paganism* (Tampa, Florida: Christ's Deliverance Ministries, 1983), p.8.

124. Slipper, *The Symbolism of the Eastern Star*, op. cit., p.74; Terry, op. cit., p.4.

125. Eric Barger, *From Rock to Rock: The Music of Darkness Exposed!* (Lafayette, Louisiana: Huntington House, Inc., 1990), p.166.

126. Graham, op. cit., p.91; See also Jeff Godwin, *Dancing with Demons: The Music's Real Master* (Chino, California: Chick Publications, 1988), p.279; *Saints Alive in Jesus Newsletter* (March 1992), p.4.

127. *Ibid.*, p.30.

128. Plessner, op. cit., p.50.

129. *Ibid.*, p.197; Slipper, *The Symbolism of the Eastern Star*, op. cit., p.31-32.

130. Slipper, *The Symbolism of the Eastern Star*, op. cit., p.68, 31-32; See also: *Ibid.*, p.159, 185.

131. Plessner, op. cit., p.98.

132. *Ibid.*, p.152.

133. Stewart Farrar, *What Witches Do: The Modern Coven Revealed* (Custer, Washington: Phoenix Publishing Company, 1983, Revised Edition), p.64.

134. *Ibid.*, p.76.

135. Ward, *Freemasonry and the Ancient Gods*, op. cit., p.12, 32.

136. Alain Danielou, *The Gods of India* (New York, New York: Inner Traditions International, Ltd., 1985), p.208.

137. Martin Koblo (Translated by Ian F. Finlay), *World of Color: An Introduction to the Theory and Use of Color in Art* (New York: McGraw-Hill Book Company, 1963), p.19.

138. *Ibid.*

139. Phone conversation with William Schnoebelen on August 23, 1993.

140. Letter on file from David J. Meyer, dated September 5, 1993.

141. Slipper, *The Symbolism of the Eastern Star*, op. cit., p.32.

142. J. Edward Decker, *Freemasonry: Satan's Door to America?* (Issaquah, Washington: Free the Masons Ministries, n.d.), p.3; J. Edward Decker, Jr., *The Question of Freemasonry* (Issaquah, Washington: Free the Masons Ministries, n.d.), p.40; See also Schnoebelen, *Masonry*, op. cit., p.86; George Oliver, *Signs and Symbols* (New York: Macoy Publishing and Masonic Supply Company, 1906), p.22; *Necronomicon* (New York, New York: Avon Books, 1977), p.28.

143. Waite, *The Mysteries of Magic*, op. cit., p.213.

144. *Ibid.*, p.214.

145. Ward, *Freemasonry and the Ancient Gods*, op. cit., p.348; For another Masonic source that refers to a cleansing period that needs to take place, see Perkins, op. cit., p.201, 203-204.

146. Wes Cook, Editor, *Did You Know? Vignettes in Masonry from the Royal Arch Mason Magazine* (Missouri Lodge of Research, 1965), p.132.

147. *Short Talk Bulletin*, "The Significant Numbers," *op. cit.*, p.5; See also *Ibid.*, p.34.

148. Philip G. Zimbardo and Floyd L. Ruch, Editors, *Psychology and Life* (Glenview, Illinois: Scott, Foresman and Company, 1977, Ninth Edition), p.317.

149. Gary Jennings, *op. cit.*, p.50.

150. Sybil Leek, *Reincarnation: The Second Chance* (Briarcliff Manor, New York: Stein and Day, 1974), p.189-190.

151. Heinrich Zimmer with Joseph Campbell as Editor, *Myths and Symbols in Indian Art and Civilization* (New York: Harper and Row, 1962), p.147; See also Danielou, *op. cit.*, p.352; Jeff Godwin, *Dancing with Demons: The Music's Real Master* (Chino, California: Chick Publications, 1988), p.312; Mackey, *The Symbolism of Freemasonry*, *op. cit.*, p.195.

152. *Ibid.*, p.147; See also Danielou, *op. cit.*, p.352; Jeff Godwin, *Dancing with Demons: The Music's Real Master* (Chino, California: Chick Publications, 1988), p.312; Mackey, *The Symbolism of Freemasonry*, *op. cit.*, p.195.

153. Cook, *Did You Know?*, *op. cit.*, p.132; See also Marrs, *Mystery Mark of the New Age*, *op. cit.*, p.118; Graham, *op. cit.*, p.31-32; Thomas Albert Stafford, *Christian Symbolism in the Evangelical Churches* (Nashville, Tennessee: Abingdon Press, 1942), p.50; Pike, *op. cit.*, p.13; Mackey, *The Symbolism of Freemasonry*, *op. cit.*, p.195, 361; Danielou, *op. cit.*, p.219.

154. *Ibid.*, p.209-210.

155. Marrs, *Mystery Mark of the New Age*, *op. cit.*, p.79.

156. *Ibid.*, quoting Barbara Walker.

157. Eustace Mullins, *The Curse of Canaan: A Demonology of History* (Staunton, Virginia: Revelation Books, 1987), p.38-39.

158. Danielou, *op. cit.*, p.219; See also Rex R. Hutchens, *Short Talk Bulletin*, "Albert Pike—The Man Not the Myth" (June 1990; Vol. 68, No. 6), p.190.

159. *The Scottish Rite Journal* (February 1993; Vol. 101, No. 2), p.68; See also *Short Talk Bulletin*, "Some Misconceptions About Freemasonry" (August 1958; Vol. 36, No. 8; Reprinted March 1989), p.8.

160. "Address by George W. Truett, Freemason," *Ibid.*, p.34.

161. *The Evangelical Methodist* (October 1933; Vol. 72, No. 8), p.5.

Chapter 8: More Eastern Star Symbolism

1. Mary Ann Slipper, *The Symbolism of the Eastern Star* (n.p., 1927), p.34-35; See also: Albert G. Mackey, *The Symbolism of Freemasonry* (New York: Clark and Maynard, 1869), p.163; *History of the Order of the Eastern Star* (General Grand Chapter in the U. S. A., 1989), p.21; Starhawk (Miriam Simos), *The Spiral Dance: A Rebirth of the Ancient Religion of the Great Goddess* (New York, New York: Harper-Collins Publishers, 1989 Edition), p.75.

2. *Pocket Encyclopedia of Masonic Symbols* (Silver Spring, Maryland: The Masonic Service Association of the United States, 1953), p.4.

3. Slipper, *The Symbolism of the Eastern Star, op. cit.,* p.35; J. S. M. Ward, *Freemasonry and the Ancient Gods* (London: Simpkin, Marshall, Hamilton, Kent and Company, Ltd., 1921), p.xix; Albert Churchward, *Signs and Symbols of Primordial Man* (London: George Allen and Company, Ltd., 1913, Second Edition), p.482; Henry C. Clausen, *Clausen's Commentaries on Morals and Dogma* (Supreme Council, 33rd Degree, Ancient and Accepted Scottish Rite of Freemasonry, Southern Jurisdiction, USA, 1974), p.61.

4. Albert Churchward, *Signs and Symbols of Primordial Man* (London: George Allen and Company, Ltd., 1913, Second Edition), p.482.

5. J. D. Buck, *Mystic Masonry* (Illinois: Indo-American Book Company, 1913, Sixth Edition), p.156-157; See also: Charles H. Vail, *The Ancient Mysteries and Modern Masonry* (New York: Macoy Publishing and Masonic Supply Company, 1909), p.196.

6. Slipper, *The Symbolism of the Eastern Star, op. cit.,* p.36.

7. Buck, *Mystic Masonry, op. cit.,* p.244; Harold Waldwin Percival, *Masonry and Its Symbols in the Light of "Thinking and Destiny"* (New York, New York: The Word Foundation, Inc., 1952), p.50; C. F. McQuaig, *The Masonic Report* (Norcross, Georgia: Answer Books and Tapes, 1976), quoting J. D. Buck, p.51.

8. Slipper, *The Symbolism of the Eastern Star, op. cit.,* p.35-36.

9. *Ibid.,* p.36.

10. Colin F. W. Dyer, quoting an anonymous author, *Symbolism in Craft Freemasonry* (England: A Lewis [Masonic Publishers], Ltd., 1976), p.36.

11. Albert G. Mackey, *The Symbolism of Freemasonry* (New York: Clark and Maynard, 1869), p.294.

12. *Ibid.,* p.164.

13. *Ibid.,* p.164.

14. Churchward, *op. cit.,* p.289, 303.

15. John Yarker, *The Arcane Schools* (Belfast, Ireland: William Tait, 1909), p.141.

16. Joseph Fort Newton, *The Builders: A Story and Study of Masonry* (Cedar Rapids, Iowa: The Torch Press, 1914), p.28.

17. Churchward, *op. cit.,* p.291; *Short Talk Bulletin,* "The All-Seeing Eye" (December 1932; Vol. 10, No. 12; Reprinted January 1982), p.4.

18. Newton, *The Builders, op. cit.,* p.156; See also: Arthur Edward Waite, *The Mysteries of Magic: A Digest of the Writings of Eliphas Levi* (Chicago, Illinois: De Laurence, Scott and Company, 1909), p.529.

19. George Oliver, *Signs and Symbols* (New York: Macoy Publishing and Masonic Supply Company, 1906), p.8.

20. Arthur Edward Waite, *Emblematic Freemasonry and the Evolution of Its Deeper Issues* (London: William Rider and Son, Ltd., 1925), p.101; Harold Bloom, *Kabbalah and Criticism* (New York, New York: The Seabury Press, Inc., 1975), p.45; *Short Talk Bulletin,* "Albert Pike" (July 1923; Vol. 1, No. 7; Reprinted December 1988), p.3, 19, 21; J. Edward Decker, Jr., *The Question of Freemasonry* (Issaquah, Washington: Free the Masons Ministries, n.d.), p.40; David L. Carrico, *Immorals and Dogma* (Evansville, Indiana: Followers of Jesus Christ, n.d.), p.4; Waite, *The Mysteries of Magic, op. cit.,* p.28, 57, 58, 426, 528; Arthur Edward Waite, *The Holy Kabbalah* (London: Williams and Norgate Ltd., 1929),

p. 33, 437, 518, 519 Moshe Idel, *Kabbalah: New Perspectives* (New Haven, Connecticut: Yale University Press, 1988), p.268, 269, 270, 395; O. J. Graham, *The Six-Pointed Star* (New Puritan Library, 1988, Second Edition), p.22, 80; Joseph Leon Blau, *The Christian Cabala* (Port Washington, New York: Kennikat Press, Inc., 1944), p.79, 85.

21. William Hutchinson, *The Spirit of Masonry*, revised by Rev. George Oliver, originally published in 1775 (New York: Bell Publishing Company, 1982), p.195.

22. *Ibid.*, p.209.

23. Churchward, *op. cit.*, p.189.

24. *Short Talk Bulletin*, "From Whence Came We?" (October 1932; Vol. 10, No. 10; Reprinted December 1983), p.9.

25. Colin Wilson, *The Occult: A History* (New York, Random House, 1971), p.296; See also: *Battle Cry* (March/April 1991), p.4; William Schnoebelen, *Masonry: Beyond the Light* (Chino, California: Chick Publications, 1991), p.204-205; Manly P. Hall, *America's Assignment with Destiny* (Los Angeles, California: Philosophical Research Society, Inc., 1951), p.95; Slipper, *The Symbolism of the Eastern Star, op. cit.*, p.137; Manly Palmer Hall, *The Lost Keys of Freemasonry* (Richmond, Virginia: Macoy Publishing and Masonic Supply Company, Inc., 1976; Originally published in 1923), p.19.

26. David L. Carrico, *The Pentagram, Freemasonry and the Goat* (Evansville, Illinois: Followers of Jesus Christ, 1992), p.549.

27. Manly Palmer Hall, *The Lost Keys of Freemasonry* (Richmond, Virginia: Macoy Publishing and Masonic Supply Company, Inc., 1976; Originally published in 1923), p.19.

28. Thomas Lowe, *Adoptive Masonry: Eastern Star Ritual* (Chicago, Illinois: Ezra A. Cook, 1913), p.20.

29. Malcolm Duncan, *Duncan's Ritual of Freemasonry* (New York: David McKay Company, Inc., n.d., 3rd Edition), p.36.

30. William Schnoebelen, *Masonry: Beyond the Light* (Chino, California: Chick Publications, 1991), p.111, 118; See also: J. S. M. Ward, *Freemasonry and the Ancient Gods* (London: Simpkin, Marshall, Hamilton, Kent and Company, Ltd., 1921), p.241; J. E. Cirlot (Translated by Jack Sage), *A Dictionary of Symbols* (New York: Dorset Press, 1991 Edition), p.61.

31. Jim Shaw and Tom McKenney, *The Deadly Deception* (Lafayette, Louisiana: Huntington House, Inc., 1988), p.143-144; See also: Albert Pike, *Morals and Dogma of the Ancient and Accepted Scottish Rite of Freemasonry* (Richmond, Virginia: L. H. Jenkins, Inc., 1871), p.850-851 for more explanation of these symbols.

32. Schnoebelen, *Masonry, op. cit.*, p.146.

33. Slipper, *The Symbolism of the Eastern Star, op. cit.*, p.9-10.

34. *The Authorized Standard Ritual of the Order of the Eastern Star of New York* (New York, Press of Andrew H. Kellogg Company, 1876; Twentieth Edition, 1916), p.12; Shirley Plessner, *Symbolism of the Eastern Star* (Cleveland, Ohio: Gilbert Publishing Company, 1956), p.59.

35. Shirley Plessner, *Symbolism of the Eastern Star* (Cleveland, Ohio: Gilbert Publishing Company, 1956), p.58.

36. Robert Macoy (Arranged by), *Adoptive Rite Ritual* (Virginia: Macoy Publishing and Masonic Supply Company, 1897), p.208; See also: *Ibid.*, p.200.

37. Sarah H. Terry, *The Second Mile* (Corpus Christi, Texas: Christian Triumph Press, 1935), p.4.

38. *Ibid.*, p.69.

39. Mackey, *The Symbolism of Freemasonry, op. cit.*, p.109, 111, 115, 353; *Short Talk Bulletin*, "Point Within a Circle" (August 1931; Vol. 9, No. 8; Reprinted July 1990), p.4; Mackey, *A Manual of the Lodge, op. cit.*, p.57; *Short Talk Bulletin*, "Blazing Star," Part 1 (March 1965; Vol. 43, No. 3), p.7; F. De P. Castells, *Genuine Secrets in Freemasonry Prior to A.D. 1717* (London: A. Lewis, 1930), p.261; George Oliver, *Symbol of Glory Shewing the Object and End of Freemasonry* (New York: John W. Leonard and Company, American Masonic Agency, 1855), p.152; R. Swinburne Clymer, *The Mysticism of Masonry* (Quakertown, Pennsylvania: The Philosophical Publishing Company, 1924), p.167; George H. Steinmetz, *Freemasonry: Its Hidden Meaning* (New York: Macoy Publishing and Masonic Supply Company, 1948), p.92; See also: J. E. Cirlot (Translated by Jack Sage), *A Dictionary of Symbols* (New York: Dorset Press, 1991 Edition), p.46.

40. Terry, *op. cit.*, p.71.

41. J. S. M. Ward, *Freemasonry and the Ancient Gods* (London: Simpkin, Marshall, Hamilton, Kent and Company, Ltd., 1921), p.30; See also: George Oliver, *Symbol of Glory Shewing the Object and End of Freemasonry* (New York: John W. Leonard and Company, American Masonic Agency, 1855), p.162; Charles Scott, *The Analogy of Ancient Craft Masonry to Natural and Revealed Religion* (Philadelphia, Pennsylvania: E. H. Butler and Company, 1857), p.93.

42. Harold Waldwin Percival, *Masonry and Its Symbols in the Light of "Thinking and Destiny"* (New York, New York: The Word Foundation, Inc., 1952), p.21.

43. *Ibid.*, p.145; See also: *Pocket Masonic Dictionary* (Silver Spring, Maryland: The Masonic Service Association of the United States, 1988), p.23.

44. William O. Peterson, Editor, *Masonic Quiz Book: "Ask Me Another, Brother"* (Chicago, Illinois: Charles T. Powner Company, 1950), p.163; See also: George H. Steinmetz, *Freemasonry: Its Hidden Meaning* (New York: Macoy Publishing and Masonic Supply Company, 1948), p.92.

45. Albert G. Mackey, *A Manual of the Lodge* (New York: Charles E. Merrill Company, 1870), p.56; See also: Edmond Ronayne, quoting Albert Mackey, *The Master's Carpet (Mah-Hah-Bone)* (n.p., 1879), p.324-326.

46. Alain Danielou, *The Gods of India* (New York, New York: Inner Traditions International, Ltd., 1985), p.227.

47. Mackey, *The Symbolism of Freemasonry, op. cit.*, p.112.

48. *Short Talk Bulletin*, "Albert Gallatin Mackey" (February 1936; Vol. 14, No. 2; Reprinted July 1980), p.7.

49. Wes Cook, Editor, *Did You Know? Vignettes in Masonry from the Royal Arch Mason Magazine* (Missouri Lodge of Research, 1965), p.173.

50. William T. Still, *New World Order: The Ancient Plan of Secret Societies* (Lafayette, Louisiana: Huntington House, Inc., 1990), p.73.

51. Oliver, *Signs and Symbols, op. cit.*, p.122; Mackey, *The Symbolism of Freemasonry, op. cit.*, p.109.

52. Churchward, *op. cit.*, p.325; See also: Ward, *Freemasonry and the Ancient Gods, op. cit.*, p.36; F. De P. Castells, *Genuine Secrets in Freemasonry Prior to A.D. 1717* (London: A. Lewis, 1930), p.256.

53. Ward, *Freemasonry and the Ancient Gods, op. cit.*, p.12.

54. *Ibid.*, p.15.

55. Waite, *Emblematic Freemasonry, op. cit.*, p.185.

56. George H. Steinmetz, *Freemasonry: Its Hidden Meaning* (New York: Macoy Publishing and Masonic Supply Company, 1948), p.92; See also: Peterson, *op. cit.*, p.52.

57. A. T. C. Pierson, *The Traditions, Origin and Early History of Freemasonry* (New York: Masonic Publishing Company, 1865), p.84; See also: R. Swinburne Clymer, *The Mysticism of Masonry* (Quakertown, Pennsylvania: The Philosophical Publishing Company, 1924), p.164.

58. Yarker, *op. cit.*, p.61.

59. *Short Talk Bulletin*, "Point Within a Circle" (August 1931; Vol. 9, No. 8; Reprinted July 1990), p.4.

60. Albert Pike, *Morals and Dogma of the Ancient and Accepted Scottish Rite of Freemasonry* (Richmond, Virginia: L. H. Jenkins, Inc., 1871), p.401.

61. Pierson, *op. cit.*, p.87.

62. Oliver, *Signs and Symbols, op. cit.*, p.124-126.

63. Mackey, *A Manual of the Lodge, op. cit.*, p.56-57.

64. J. Edward Decker, Jr., *The Question of Freemasonry* (Issaquah, Washington: Free the Masons Ministries, n.d.), p.39-40.

65. Texe Marrs, *Mystery Mark of the New Age: Satan's Design for World Domination* (Westchester, Illinois: Crossway Books, 1988), p.109.

66. Terry, *op. cit.*, p.71.

67. *History of the Order of the Eastern Star* (General Grand Chapter in the U. S. A., 1989), p.21.

68. Laurie Cabot with Tom Cowan, *Power of the Witch: The Earth, the Moon, and the Magical Path to Enlightenment* (New York, New York: Delacorte Press, 1989), p.95-96.

69. Jean M'Kee Kenaston, Compiler, *History of the Order of the Eastern Star* (Cedar Rapids, Iowa: The Torch Press, 1917), p.502-503.

70. Cabot and Cowan, *op. cit.*, p.207.

71. Frank Gaynor, Editor, *Dictionary of Mysticism* (New York: Philosophical Library, 1953), p.103; See also: Harry E. Wedeck, *Treasury of Witchcraft* (New York, New York: Philosophical Library, 1961), p.60.

72. Maurice Bessy, *A Pictorial History of Magic and the Supernatural* (New York: Hamlyn Publishing Group Limited, 1964), p.200.

73. Harry E. Wedeck, *Treasury of Witchcraft* (New York, New York: Philosophical Library, 1961), p.50.

74. Editors of Time-Life Books, *Magical Arts* (Alexandria, Virginia: Time-Life Books, 1990), p.38.

75. *Ibid.*

76. Starhawk (Miriam Simos), *The Spiral Dance: A Rebirth of the Ancient Religion of the Great Goddess* (New York, New York: Harper-Collins Publishers, 1989 Edition), p.75.

77. *History of the Order of the Eastern Star, op. cit.,* p.21.

78. Pike, *op. cit.,* p.459.

79. J. E. Cirlot (Translated by Jack Sage), *A Dictionary of Symbols* (New York: Dorset Press, 1991 Edition), p.173.

80. Plessner, *op. cit.,* p.126.

81. Willis D. Engle, *A General History of the Order of the Eastern Star* (Indianapolis, Indiana: Willis D. Engle, 1901), p.136; See also: *The Authorized Standard Ritual of the Order of the Eastern Star of New York, op. cit.,* p.64.

82. Slipper, *The Symbolism of the Eastern Star, op. cit.,* p.34-35; See also: Mackey, *The Symbolism of Freemasonry, op. cit.,* p.163; *History of the Order of the Eastern Star, op. cit.,* p.2.

83. Starhawk, *op. cit.,* p.75.

84. Morning Glory and Otter G'Zell, *Who on Earth Is the Goddess?* (Berkeley, California: Covenant of the Goddess, n.d.), p.2.

85. Macoy, *op. cit.,* p.253-256; *The Authorized Standard Ritual of the Order of the Eastern Star of New York, op. cit.,* p.297-304.

86. Steinmetz, *Freemasonry: Its Hidden Meaning, op. cit.,* p.132; *The Scottish Rite Journal* (August 1992; Vol. 100, No. 8), p.43; Mackey, *The Symbolism of Freemasonry, op. cit.,* p.172; *Your Masonic Capital City* (Silver Spring, Maryland: The Masonic Service Association of the United States, n.d.), p.5; *Pocket Encyclopedia of Masonic Symbols, op. cit.,* p.57-58; *Pocket Masonic Dictionary* (Silver Spring, Maryland: The Masonic Service Association of the United States, 1988), p.11, 13, 23, 26, 28; George Oliver, *Symbol of Glory Shewing the Object and End of Freemasonry* (New York: John W. Leonard and Company, American Masonic Agency, 1855), p.280; W. L. Wilmshurst, *The Masonic Initiation* (Ferndale, Michigan: Trismegistus Press, 1980; Originally published 1924), p.106-108; *Short Talk Bulletin,* "The Winding Stairs" (January 1932; Vol. 10, No. 1; Reprinted July 1991), p.3.

87. *Ibid.,* quoting Albert G. Mackey, p.132.

88. *Ibid.,* p.133-134.

89. H. L. Haywood, *Symbolic Masonry: An Interpretation of the Three Degrees* (Washington, D.C.: Masonic Service Association of the United States, 1923), p.98-99.

90. *The Authorized Standard Ritual of the Order of the Eastern Star of New York, op. cit.,* p.304, 305.

91. Haywood, *Symbolic Masonry, op. cit.,* p.153-154; See also: George Oliver, *Symbol of Glory Shewing the Object and End of Freemasonry* (New York: John W. Leonard and Company, American Masonic Agency, 1855), p.203.

92. *Ibid.,* p.240.

93. *Ibid.*

94. Percival, *op. cit.,* p.21.

95. O. J. Graham, *The Six-Pointed Star* (New Puritan Library, 1988, Second Edition), p.28; See also: Pike, *op. cit.,* p.206; Rex R. Hutchens and Donald W.

428 HIDDEN SECRETS OF THE EASTERN STAR

Monson, *The Bible in Albert Pike's Morals and Dogma* (Washington, D.C.: Supreme Council, 33rd Degree, 1992), p.59.

96. J. S. M. Ward, *Freemasonry and the Ancient Gods, op. cit.,* p.232.

97. Decker, *The Question of Freemasonry, op. cit.,* p.39.

Chapter 9: Gavel, Clasped Hands, and Veil

1. *The Authorized Standard Ritual of the Order of the Eastern Star of New York* (New York, Press of Andrew H. Kellogg Company, 1876; Twentieth Edition, 1916), p.12, 14; Shirley Plessner, *Symbolism of the Eastern Star* (Cleveland, Ohio: Gilbert Publishing Company, 1956), p.59, 107.

2. Shirley Plessner, *Symbolism of the Eastern Star* (Cleveland, Ohio: Gilbert Publishing Company, 1956), p.58.

3. *Ibid.,* p.107; See also: *What? When? Where? Why? Who? in Freemasonry* (Silver Spring, Maryland: Masonic Service Association of the United States, 1956), p.36.

4. Anton Szandor LaVey, *The Satanic Bible* (New York: Avon Books, 1969), p.131, 57.

5. Harry E. Wedeck, *The Treasury of Witchcraft* (New York: Philosophical Library, 1961), caption under picture between p.170-171.

6. Sarah H. Terry, *The Second Mile* (Corpus Christi, Texas: Christian Triumph Press, 1935), p.73; See also: George Oliver, *Signs and Symbols* (New York: Macoy Publishing and Masonic Supply Company, 1906), p.14; John Yarker, *The Arcane Schools* (Belfast, Ireland: William Tait, 1909), p.222; Thomas Bulfinch, *Bulfinch's Mythology* (New York: Thomas Y. Crowell Company, Inc., 1970), p.972.

7. Frank Gaynor, Editor, *Dictionary of Mysticism* (New York: Philosophical Library, 1953), p.186.

8. Albert Pike, *Morals and Dogma of the Ancient and Accepted Scottish Rite of Freemasonry* (Richmond, Virginia: L. H. Jenkins, Inc., 1871), p.13, 552; See also: W. L. Wilmshurst, *The Masonic Initiation* (Ferndale, Michigan: Trismegistus Press, 1980; Originally published 1924), p.92; Charles H. Vail, *The Ancient Mysteries and Modern Masonry* (New York: Macoy Publishing and Masonic Supply Company, 1909), p.67; *Pocket Encyclopedia of Masonic Symbols* (Silver Spring, Maryland: The Masonic Service Association of the United States, 1953), p.51; Rex R. Hutchens, *A Bridge to Light* (Washington, D.C.: Supreme Council, 33° Ancient and Accepted Scottish Rite of Freemasonry, Southern Jurisdiction, 1988), p.231; Percival George Woodcock, *Short Dictionary of Mythology* (Philosophical Library, 1953), p.144; *Ibid.*

9. Charles H. Vail, *The Ancient Mysteries and Modern Masonry* (New York: Macoy Publishing and Masonic Supply Company, 1909), p.67-68; See also: George Oliver, *Signs and Symbols* (New York: Macoy Publishing and Masonic Supply Company, 1906), p.95.

10. R. Swinburne Clymer, *The Mysteries of Osiris or Ancient Egyptian Initiation* (Quakertown, Pennsylvania: The Philosophical Publishing Company, 1951, Revised Edition), p.38.

11. *Ibid.*

12. Pike, *op. cit.,* p.368.

13. "Bel," *Encyclopaedia Britannica*, 1964 edition, Vol. 3, p.410.

14. Texe Marrs, *Mystery Mark of the New Age: Satan's Design for World Domination* (Westchester, Illinois: Crossway Books, 1988), p.91.

15. Stephen Knight, *The Brotherhood: The Secret World of the Freemasons* (Briarcliff Manor, New York: Stein and Day, 1984), p.236.

16. *Ibid.*

17. William Schnoebelen, *Masonry: Beyond the Light* (Chino, California: Chick Publications, 1991), p.167.

18. Pike, *op. cit.,* 368.

19. Einar Haugen, "Thor," *The World Book Encyclopedia*, 1961 edition, Vol. 17, p.204.

20. *The World Book Encyclopedia*, 1961 Edition; Vol. 17, p.204; See also: *Pocket Encyclopedia of Masonic Symbols* (Silver Spring, Maryland: The Masonic Service Association of the United States, 1953), p.51; Gaynor, *op. cit.,* p.186; George Oliver, *Signs and Symbols* (New York: Macoy Publishing and Masonic Supply Company, 1906), p.14; Percival George Woodcock, *Short Dictionary of Mythology* (Philosophical Library, 1953), p.144; Thomas Bulfinch, *Bulfinch's Mythology* (New York: Thomas Y. Crowell Company, Inc., 1970), p.972.

21. Max Wood, *Rock and Roll: An Analysis of the Music* (n.p., n.d.), p.30.

22. *Ibid.,* p.31.

23. J. S. M. Ward, *Freemasonry and the Ancient Gods* (London: Simpkin, Marshall, Hamilton, Kent and Company, Ltd., 1921), p.238.

24. *Ibid.,* p.241.

25. A. T. C. Pierson, *The Traditions, Origin and Early History of Freemasonry* (New York: Masonic Publishing Company, 1865), p.42.

26. Ward, *Freemasonry and the Ancient Gods, op. cit.,* p.236.

27. J. D. Buck, *Mystic Masonry* (Illinois: Indo-American Book Company, 1913, Sixth Edition), p.244-245.

28. Plessner, *op. cit.,* p.191; See also: Sarah H. Terry, Compiler, *History of the Order of the Eastern Star* (n.p., 1914), p.37.

29. Jean M'Kee Kenaston, Compiler, *History of the Order of the Eastern Star* (Cedar Rapids, Iowa: The Torch Press, 1917), p.63; Sarah H. Terry, Compiler, *History of the Order of the Eastern Star* (n.p., 1914), p.38.

30. *Ibid.,* p.588. The *Manual of the Eastern Star Degree* was included as part of this book.; See also: Sarah H. Terry, Compiler, *History of the Order of the Eastern Star* (n.p., 1914), p.38.

31. *Ibid.,* p.489. The *Mosaic Book* was included as part of this book.

32. John Yarker, *The Arcane Schools* (Belfast, Ireland: William Tait, 1909), p.146; Vail, *op. cit.,* p.190.

33. *Pocket Masonic Dictionary* (Silver Spring, Maryland: The Masonic Service Association of the United States, 1988), p.17, 18, 24; *What? When? Where? Why? Who? in Freemasonry* (Silver Spring, Maryland: Masonic Service Association of the United States, 1956), p.39; Albert G. Mackey, *A Manual of the Lodge* (New York: Charles E. Merrill Company, 1870), p.40; R. Swinburne Clymer, *The Mysticism of Masonry* (Quakertown, Pennsylvania: The Philosophical

Publishing Company, 1924), p.146; Daniel Sickles, Editor, *The Freemason's Monitor* (New York: Macoy Publishing and Masonic Supply Company, 1901), p.38; George Oliver, *The Historical Landmarks and Other Evidences of Freemasonry, Explained* (Vol. I & II) (New York: John W. Leonard and Company, 1855), p.132; Malcolm Duncan, *Duncan's Ritual of Freemasonry* (New York: David McKay Company, Inc., n.d., Third Edition), p.50; W. J. McCormick, *Christ, the Christian and Freemasonry* (Belfast, Ireland: Great Joy Publications, 1984), p.89, etc.

34. Albert G. Mackey, *A Manual of the Lodge* (New York: Charles E. Merrill Company, 1870), p.40-41; See also: Daniel Sickles, Editor, *The Freemason's Monitor* (New York: Macoy Publishing and Masonic Supply Company, 1901), p.38; Edmond Ronayne, *The Master's Carpet (Mah-Hah-Bone)* (n.p., 1879), p.276, quoting A. T. C. Pierson, and p.276-277, quoting Albert Mackey.

35. R. Swinburne Clymer, quoting Daniel Sickles, *The Mysticism of Masonry* (Quakertown, Pennsylvania: The Philosophical Publishing Company, 1924), p.146; See also: Edmond Ronayne, *The Master's Carpet (Mah-Hah-Bone)* (n.p., 1879), p.275.

36. Malcolm Duncan, *Duncan's Ritual of Freemasonry* (New York: David McKay Company, Inc., n.d., Third Edition), p.50.

37. *The Authorized Standard Ritual of the Order of the Eastern Star of New York*, op. cit., p.12, Plessner, op. cit., p.59; Lucien V. Rule, *Pioneering in Masonry: The Life and Times of Rob Morris, Masonic Poet Laureate, Together with Story of Clara Barton and the Eastern Star* (Louisville, Kentucky: Brandt and Connors Company, 1922), p.177; F. A. Bell, *Bell's Eastern Star Ritual* (P. R. C. Publications, Inc., 1988 Revised Edition), p.31; Terry, op. cit., p.11.

38. *Ibid.*, p.55; William J. Whalen, *Handbook of Secret Organizations* (Milwaukee, Wisconsin: The Bruce Publishing Company, 1966), p.27; Robert Macoy (Arranged by), *Adoptive Rite Ritual* (Virginia: Macoy Publishing and Masonic Supply Company, 1897), p.88; Alvin J. Schmidt and Nicholas Babchuk, editors, *The Greenwood Encyclopedia of American Institutions: Fraternal Organizations* (Westport, Connecticut: Greenwood Press, 1980), p.98; Willis D. Engle, *A General History of the Order of the Eastern Star* (Indianapolis, Indiana: Willis D. Engle, 1901), p.132.

39. *Ibid.*, p.12, 56, 62; F. A. Bell, *Bell's Eastern Star Ritual* (P. R. C. Publications, Inc., 1988 Revised Edition), p.61, 68; Mary Ann Slipper, *The Symbolism of the Eastern Star* (n.p., 1927), p.53.

40. Willis D. Engle, *A General History of the Order of the Eastern Star* (Indianapolis, Indiana: Willis D. Engle, 1901), p.132; See also: *Ibid.*, p.62; Robert Macoy (Arranged by), *Adoptive Rite Ritual* (Virginia: Macoy Publishing and Masonic Supply Company, 1897), p.94.

41. *Ibid.*, p.64; Robert Macoy (Arranged by), *Adoptive Rite Ritual* (Virginia: Macoy Publishing and Masonic Supply Company, 1897), p.94.

42. J. E. Cirlot (Translated by Jack Sage), *A Dictionary of Symbols* (New York: Dorset Press, 1991 Edition), p.359.

43. *Pocket Masonic Dictionary*, op. cit., p.34, 17.

44. H. L. Haywood, *Symbolic Masonry: An Interpretation of the Three Degrees* (Washington, D.C.: Masonic Service Association of the United States, 1923), p.71-72; See also: Duncan, op. cit., p.28, 31, 48, 88, 163; Harold Waldwin Percival, *Masonry and Its Symbols in the Light of "Thinking and Destiny"* (New

York, New York: The Word Foundation, Inc., 1952), p.8; Larry Kunk, *Sons of Light? or Sons of Darkness?* (Fishers, Indiana: Ephesians 5:11, n.d.), p.2.

45. Joseph Fort Newton, *The Religion of Masonry: An Interpretation* (Washington, D.C.: The Masonic Service Association of the United States, 1927), p.54.

46. *The Authorized Standard Ritual of the Order of the Eastern Star of New York, op. cit.,* p.62.

47. Harold Waldwin Percival, *Masonry and Its Symbols in the Light of "Thinking and Destiny"* (New York, New York: The Word Foundation, Inc., 1952), p.8.

48. Haywood, *Symbolic Masonry, op. cit.,* p.71-72.

49. *Ibid.*

50. Larry Kunk, *Sons of Light? or Sons of Darkness?* (Fishers, Indiana: Ephesians 5:11, n.d.), p.2, quoting from *The Ahiman Rezon.*

51. *Ibid.,* quoting from *The Ahiman Rezon.*

52. *Ibid.,* quoting from *The Ahiman Rezon.*

53. Haywood, *Symbolic Masonry, op. cit.,* p.71; See also: *The Authorized Standard Ritual of the Order of the Eastern Star of New York, op. cit.,* p.64; Robert Macoy (Arranged by), *Adoptive Rite Ritual* (Virginia: Macoy Publishing and Masonic Supply Company, 1897), p.94.

54. Albert Churchward, *Signs and Symbols of Primordial Man* (London: George Allen and Company, Ltd., 1913, Second Edition), p.331.

55. Catalog from Abyss, p.39; See also: *The World Book Encyclopedia,* 1961 Edition; Vol. 17, p.206; Veronica Ions, *Egyptian Mythology* (England: The Hamlyn Publishing Group, Ltd., 1965), p.85; *Necronomicon* (New York, New York: Avon Books, 1977), p.xix.

56. Cirlot, *op. cit.,* p.155.

57. Dave Hunt and T. A. McMahon, *The Seduction of Christianity: Spiritual Discernment in the Last Days* (Eugene, Oregon: Harvest House Publishers, 1985), p.140; Robert Sessler, *To Be God of One World: The French Revolution Globalized* (Merlin, Oregon: Let There Be Light Publications, 1992), p.132; Johanna Michaelsen, *Like Lambs to the Slaughter* (Eugene, Oregon: Harvest House Publishers, 1989), p.121; *Mysteries of Mind Space & Time: The Unexplained* (Vol. 1) (Westport, Connecticut: H. S. Stuttman, Inc., 1992), p.41.

58. LaVey, *op. cit.,* p.146.

59. Helena Petrovna Blavatsky, *Isis Unveiled,* Vol. I: Science (New York, New York: Trow's Printing and Bookbinding Company, 1877), p.554, xxxiii.

Chapter 10: Eastern Star Goddesses

1. Albert G. Mackey, quoting Rob Morris, *Encyclopedia of Freemasonry,* Vol. 1 (Chicago, Illinois: The Masonic History Company, 1909), p.303; See also: Robert Macoy (Arranged by), *Adoptive Rite Ritual* (Virginia: Macoy Publishing and Masonic Supply Company, 1897), p.17.

2. *Ibid.,* quoting Rob Morris; See also: Jean M'Kee Kenaston, Compiler, quoting Rob Morris, *History of the Order of the Eastern Star* (Cedar Rapids, Iowa: The Torch Press, 1917), p.17-18, 21.

3. Henry Wilson Coil, *Coil's Masonic Encyclopedia* (New York, New York: Macoy Publishing and Masonic Supply Company, Inc., 1961), p.11; See also: Willis D. Engle, *A General History of the Order of the Eastern Star* (Indianapolis, Indiana: Willis D. Engle, 1901), p.25; *History of the Order of the Eastern Star* (General Grand Chapter in the U. S. A., 1989), p.11.

4. Jean M'Kee Kenaston, Compiler, *History of the Order of the Eastern Star* (Cedar Rapids, Iowa: The Torch Press, 1917), p.503; See also: Willis D. Engle, *A General History of the Order of the Eastern Star* (Indianapolis, Indiana: Willis D. Engle, 1901), p.27, 31, 70-71; Harold Van Buren Voorhis, *The Eastern Star: The Evolution from a Rite to an Order* (Richmond, Virginia: Macoy Publishing and Masonic Supply Company, Inc., 1938), p.50; *History of the Order of the Eastern Star* (General Grand Chapter in the U. S. A., 1989), p.12.

5. *History of the Order of the Eastern Star* (General Grand Chapter in the U. S. A., 1989), p.14, 21; See also: Sarah H. Terry, Compiler, *History of the Order of the Eastern Star* (n.p., 1914), p.14; *Ibid.;* p.108; Mary Ann Slipper, *The Symbolism of the Order of the Eastern Star* (no other information available), p.15; Sarah H. Terry, *The Second Mile* (Corpus Christi, Texas: Christian Triumph Press, 1935), p.21.

6. *Ibid.,* p.21, 12, 23, 30; See also: Sarah H. Terry, *The Second Mile* (Corpus Christi, Texas: Christian Triumph Press, 1935), p.21; Sarah H. Terry, Compiler, *History of the Order of the Eastern Star* (n.p., 1914), p.14.

7. R. Swinburne Clymer, *The Mysteries of Osiris or Ancient Egyptian Initiation* (Quakertown, Pennsylvania: The Philosophical Publishing Company, 1951, Revised Edition), p.120.

8. *History of the Order of the Eastern Star, op. cit.,* p.30.

9. J. E. Cirlot, *A Dictionary of Symbols* (New York, New York: Philosophical Library, Inc., 1972), p.249; See also: *Complete Occult Digest A to Z* (North Hollywood, California: International Imports, 1984), p.115; *What? When? Where? Why? Who? in Freemasonry* (Silver Spring, Maryland: Masonic Service Association of the United States, 1956), p.37.

10. Willis D. Engle, *A General History of the Order of the Eastern Star* (Indianapolis, Indiana: Willis D. Engle, 1901), p.52-53; See also: *History of the Order of the Eastern Star, op. cit.,* p.14.

11. *Ibid.,* p.25.

12. Engle, *op. cit.,* p.70; *Ibid.,* p.12.

13. Encyclopedia article entitled "Luna" by Pearl Cleveland Wilson, p.325; See also: *Academic American Encyclopedia,* 1982, Vol. 12, p.459; *Encyclopedia Americana,* 1979, Vol. 17, p.851; John T. Lawrence, *The Perfect Ashlar* (London: A. Lewis, 1912), p.197; Jacques Duchesne-Guillemin (Edited by Ruth Nanda Anshen) *Symbols and Values in Zoroastrianism: Their Survival and Renewal* (New York, New York: Harper and Row, 1966), p.96, 99, 100; Thomas Bulfinch, *Bulfinch's Mythology* (New York: Thomas Y. Crowell Company, Inc., 1970), p.355; Eric Barger, *From Rock to Rock: The Music of Darkness Exposed!* (Lafayette, Louisiana: Huntington House, Inc., 1990), p.163; M. Esther Harding, *Woman's Mysteries: Ancient and Modern* (New York: G. P. Putnam's Sons for the C. G. Jung Foundation for Analytical Psychology, 1971 Edition), p.53.

14. Edith Hamilton, *Mythology* (Boston, Massachusetts: Little, Brown and Company, 1942), p.32; See also: Laurie Cabot with Tom Cowan, *Power of the Witch: The Earth, the Moon, and the Magical Path to Enlightenment* (New York, New

York: Delacorte Press, 1989), p.32; Percival George Woodcock, *Short Dictionary of Mythology* (Philosophical Library, 1953), p.20; Cirlot, *op. cit.*, p.81, 143; Harry E. Wedeck, *Treasury of Witchcraft* (New York, New York: Philosophical Library, 1961), p.39, 72.

15. Laurie Cabot with Tom Cowan, *Power of the Witch: The Earth, the Moon, and the Magical Path to Enlightenment* (New York, New York: Delacorte Press, 1989), p.32; See also: Harry E. Wedeck, *Treasury of Witchcraft* (New York, New York: Philosophical Library, 1961), p.39, 72; Eden Within (1994 Catalog), p.12.

16. Albert E. Bedworth and David A. Bedworth, *Health for Human Effectiveness* (Englewood Cliffs, New Jersey: Prentice-Hall, Inc., 1982), p.6; *Chrysalis* (Autumn 1987, Vol. 2, Issue 3), p.253; Cirlot, *op. cit.*, p.207; Paul Hamlyn, *Greek Mythology* (London: Paul Hamlyn, Ltd., 1967), p.5, 52; Frank Gaynor, Editor, *Dictionary of Mysticism* (New York: Philosophical Library, 1953), p.77; Carl Jung, M.-L. Von Franz, Joseph L. Henderson, Jolande Jacobi, and Aniela Jaffe, *Man and His Symbols* (Garden City, New York: Doubleday and Company, Inc. 1964), p.156; Joseph Campbell, *The Hero with a Thousand Faces* (Princeton, New Jersey: Princeton University Press, 1968, Second Edition), p.72; *New Larousse Encyclopedia of Mythology* (Prometheus Press, 1972 Edition), p.123; Geoffrey Parrinder, Editor, *World Religions: From Ancient History to the Present* (New York, New York: Facts on File, 1971), p.148; William O. Peterson, Editor, *Masonic Quiz Book: "Ask Me Another, Brother"* (Chicago, Illinois: Charles T. Powner Company, 1950), p.256; Thomas Bulfinch, *Bulfinch's Mythology* (New York: Thomas Y. Crowell Company, Inc., 1970), p.934.

17. Percival George Woodcock, *Short Dictionary of Mythology* (Philosophical Library, 1953), p.20, 65, 88, 98; See also: Thomas Bulfinch, *Bulfinch's Mythology* (New York: Thomas Y. Crowell Company, Inc., 1970), p.134; Jeff Godwin, *Dancing with Demons: The Music's Real Master* (Chino, California: Chick Publications, 1988), p.161; Clymer, *The Mysteries of Osiris, op. cit.*, p.63.

18. Thomas Bulfinch, *Bulfinch's Mythology* (New York: Thomas Y. Crowell Company, Inc., 1970), p.934; G. A. Riplinger, *New Age Bible Versions* (Munroe Falls, Ohio: A. V. Publications, 1993), p.125; Frank Gaynor, Editor, *Dictionary of Mysticism* (New York: Philosophical Library, 1953), p.76; Editors of Time-Life Books, *Magical Arts* (Alexandria, Virginia: Time-Life Books, 1990), p.22.

19. Eric Barger, *From Rock to Rock: The Music of Darkness Exposed!* (Lafayette, Louisiana: Huntington House, Inc., 1990), p.163.

20. G. A. Riplinger, *New Age Bible Versions* (Munroe Falls, Ohio: A. V. Publications, 1993), p.125.

21. Woodcock, *op. cit.*, p.46; See also: Frank Gaynor, Editor, *Dictionary of Mysticism* (New York: Philosophical Library, 1953), p.48.

22. Texe Marrs, *Ravaged by the New Age: Satan's Plan to Destroy Our Kids* (Austin, Texas: Living Truth Publishers, 1989), p.58.

23. Bulfinch, *Bulfinch's Mythology, op. cit.*, p.939.

24. Charles M. Skinner, *Myths and Legends of Flowers, Trees, Fruits, and Plants* (Philadelphia, Pennsylvania: J. B. Lippincott Company, 1911), p.280; See also: *Ibid.*, p.939.

25. Robert Macoy (Arranged by), *Adoptive Rite Ritual* (Virginia: Macoy Publishing and Masonic Supply Company, 1897), p.127; Shirley Plessner, *Symbolism of the Eastern Star* (Cleveland, Ohio: Gilbert Publishing Company, 1956), p.101,

197; Lucien V. Rule, *Pioneering in Masonry: The Life and Times of Rob Morris, Masonic Poet Laureate, Together with Story of Clara Barton and the Eastern Star* (Louisville, Kentucky: Brandt and Connors Company, 1922), p.177; F. A. Bell, *Bell's Eastern Star Ritual* (P. R. C. Publications, Inc., 1988 Revised Edition), p.106; *History of the Order of the Eastern Star* (General Grand Chapter in the U. S. A., 1989), p.12; Engle, *op. cit.*, p.70.

26. Aleister Crowley, *Seven, Seven, Seven* (no other information available), p.68.

27. Engle, *op. cit.*, p.71; *History of the Order of the Eastern Star, op. cit.*, p.12; Kenaston, *op. cit.*, p.534.

28. Encyclopedia article entitled "Hebe" by Pearl Cleveland Wilson; See also: *Encyclopedia Britannica*, 1982, Vol. 4, p.982; *Academic American Encyclopedia*, 1982, Vol. 10, p.100; *Encyclopedia Americana*, 1979, Vol. 14, p.33; *Collier's Encyclopedia*, 1991 Edition, Vol. 12, p.4; Maria Leach, Editor, *Funk and Wagnalls Standard Dictionary of Folklore Mythology and Legend*, Vol. II (New York: Funk and Wagnalls, 1950), p.564; Woodcock, *op. cit.*, p.60, p.65; Paul Hamlyn, *Greek Mythology* (London: Paul Hamlyn, Ltd., 1967), p.25, 82; *New Larousse Encyclopedia of Mythology* (Prometheus Press, 1972 Edition), p.137; Bulfinch, *Bulfinch's Mythology, op. cit.*, p.39, 135, p.934; Thomas Bulfinch, *Bulfinch's Mythology: The Age of Fable or Stories of Gods and Heroes* (Garden City, New York: Doubleday and Company, Inc., 1948), p.163-164; Hamilton, *Mythology, op. cit.*, p.39.

29. *History of the Order of the Eastern Star, op. cit.*, p.12; Engle, *op. cit.*, p.71; Kenaston, *op. cit.*, p.531.

30. Hamilton, *Mythology, op. cit.*, p.483; p.659, p.64; *Pike's Poems* (Little Rock, Arkansas: Fred W. Allsopp, 1899), p.72; Charles G. Berger, *Our Phallic Heritage* (New York, New York: Greenwich Book Publishers, Inc., 1966), p.78; Woodcock, *op. cit.*, p.35, 58; *Report from Concerned Christians* (September/October 1990; Vol. 24), p.15; *New Larousse Encyclopedia of Mythology* (Prometheus Press, 1972 Edition), p.210. 211, 217; John Lust, *The Herb Book* (New York, New York: Bantam Books, Inc., 1974), p.614; Thomas Bulfinch, *Bulfinch's Mythology: The Age of Fable or Stories of Gods and Heroes* (Garden City, New York: Doubleday and Company, Inc., 1948), p.10, 12; Thomas Bulfinch, *The Age of Fable or the Beauties of Mythology* (New York: The Heritage Press, 1942), p.12; Bulfinch, *Bulfinch's Mythology, op. cit.*, p.928.

31. *Pike's Poems* (Little Rock, Arkansas: Fred W. Allsopp, 1899), p.72.

32. Encyclopedia article entitled "Flora," p.64; See also: Woodcock, *op. cit.*, p.58; Charles G. Berger, *Our Phallic Heritage* (New York, New York: Greenwich Book Publishers, Inc., 1966), p.78; *New Larousse Encyclopedia of Mythology* (Prometheus Press, 1972 Edition), p.210; Anthony Frewin, *The Book of Days* (St. James Place, London: William Collins Sons and Company, Ltd., 1979), p.137, 139.

33. Charles G. Berger, *Our Phallic Heritage* (New York, New York: Greenwich Book Publishers, Inc., 1966), p.78-79.

34. Lucien V. Rule, *Pioneering in Masonry: The Life and Times of Rob Morris, Masonic Poet Laureate, Together with Story of Clara Barton and the Eastern Star* (Louisville, Kentucky: Brandt and Connors Company, 1922), p.177.

35. *The Authorized Standard Ritual of the Order of the Eastern Star of New York* (New York, Press of Andrew H. Kellogg Company, 1876; Twentieth Edition, 1916), p.14; William Meyer, *The Order of the Eastern Star* (no other information available), p.17; *Ibid.*; Shirley Plessner, *Symbolism of the Eastern Star* (Cleveland,

Ohio: Gilbert Publishing Company, 1956), p.63, p.59; F. A. Bell, *Bell's Eastern Star Ritual* (P. R. C. Publications, Inc., 1988 Revised Edition), p.31; Sarah H. Terry, *The Second Mile* (Corpus Christi, Texas: Christian Triumph Press, 1935), p.21.

36. Cirlot, *op. cit.,* p.93.

37. Shirley Plessner, *Symbolism of the Eastern Star* (Cleveland, Ohio: Gilbert Publishing Company, 1956), p.58.

38. Kenaston, *op. cit.,* p.518; Engle, *op. cit.,* p.71; *History of the Order of the Eastern Star, op. cit.,* p.12.

39. Encyclopedia article entitled "Thetis";*The World Book Encyclopedia,* 1961 Edition; Vol. 1, p.22; Encyclopedia article entitled "Thetis" by George E. Duckworth; Woodcock, *op. cit.,* p.3, 144; *New Larousse Encyclopedia of Mythology* (Prometheus Press, 1972 Edition), p.136; 146; Paul Hamlyn, *Greek Mythology* (London: Paul Hamlyn, Ltd., 1967), p.24-25, 59; Thomas Bulfinch, *Bulfinch's Mythology: The Age of Fable or Stories of Gods and Heroes* (Garden City, New York: Doubleday and Company, Inc., 1948), p.189; Thomas Bulfinch, *The Age of Fable or the Beauties of Mythology* (New York: The Heritage Press, 1942), p.177-178; Bulfinch, *Bulfinch's Mythology, op. cit.,* p.972.

40. Woodcock, *op. cit.,* p.3, 144; See also: Thomas Bulfinch, *Bulfinch's Mythology: The Age of Fable or Stories of Gods and Heroes* (Garden City, New York: Doubleday and Company, Inc., 1948), p.189.

41. Padraic Colum, "Styx," *The World Book Encyclopedia,* 1961 Edition; Vol. 16, p.748.

42. *What? When? Where? Why? Who? in Freemasonry* (Silver Spring, Maryland: Masonic Service Association of the United States, 1956), p.5; See also: *Pocket Encyclopedia of Masonic Symbols* (Silver Spring, Maryland: The Masonic Service Association of the United States, 1953), p.8-9.

43. Frederic Portal (Translated by John W. Simons), *A Comparison of Egyptian Symbols with Those of the Hebrews* (New York: Masonic Publishing and Manufacturing Company, 1866), p.68.

44. *Ibid.,* p.69.

45. Crowley, *op. cit.,* p.68.

46. John Algeo, "The Wizard of Oz: The Perilous Journey," *The Quest* (Summer 1993; Vol. 6, No. 2), p.50.

47. *Ibid.,* p.49; Dennis Cuddy, *Now Is the Dawning of the New Age New World Order* (Oklahoma City, Oklahoma: Hearthstone Publishing, Ltd., 1991), p.61; See also: Dennis L. Cuddy, "The Deceptive New Age 'Service' and 'Light,'" *The Christian World Report* (February 1991; Vol. 3, No. 2), p.8.

48. Dennis Cuddy, quoting Michael Patrick Hearn, *Now Is the Dawning of the New Age New World Order* (Oklahoma City, Oklahoma: Hearthstone Publishing, Ltd., 1991), p.62.

49. *Ibid.,* p.63.

50. Manly Palmer Hall, *An Encyclopedic Outline of Masonic, Hermetic, Qabbalistic and Rosicrucian Symbolical Philosophy: Being an Interpretation of the Secret Teachings Concealed Within the Rituals, Allegories and Mysteries of All Ages* (San Francisco, California: H. S. Crocker Company, Inc., 1928), p.53.

51. Plessner, *op. cit.,* p.110.

52. Algeo, op. cit., p.54.

53. Engle, op. cit., p.71; F. A. Bell, Bell's Eastern Star Ritual (P. R. C. Publications, Inc., 1988 Revised Edition), p.106; Macoy, Adoptive Rite Ritual, op. cit., p.127; History of the Order of the Eastern Star, op. cit., p.12; History of the Order of the Eastern Star (General Grand Chapter in the U. S. A., 1989), p.12.

54. Cirlot op. cit., p.256.

55. Ibid., p.82, 256; See also: Hall, An Encyclopedic Outline, op. cit., p.95.

56. Berger, op. cit., p.54.

57. Skinner, op. cit., p.217.

58. Albert James Dager, Facts and Fallacies of the Resurrection (Costa Mesa, California: Media Spotlight), p.1; Alice A. Bailey, From Bethlehem to Calvary: The Initiations of Jesus (New York: Lucis Publishing Company, 1965), p.61.

59. Plessner, op. cit., p.53, 130.

60. What? When? Where? Why? Who? in Freemasonry, op. cit., p.49; Skinner, op. cit., Carl H. Claudy, Masonic Harvest (Washington, D.C.: The Temple Publishers, 1948), p.171-172; Clymer, The Mysteries of Osiris, op. cit., p.50-51.

61. Geoffrey Parrinder, Editor, World Religions: From Ancient History to the Present (New York, New York: Facts on File, 1971), p.116-117.

62. Macoy, Adoptive Rite Ritual, op. cit., Syllabus.

63. George Oliver, Signs and Symbols (New York: Macoy Publishing and Masonic Supply Company, 1906); p.47; H. L. Haywood, Symbolic Masonry: An Interpretation of the Three Degrees (Washington, D.C.: Masonic Service Association of the United States, 1923), p.279-280.

64. Phone conversation with William Schnoebelen on August 23, 1993.

65. Starhawk (Miriam Simos), The Spiral Dance: A Rebirth of the Ancient Religion of the Great Goddess (New York, New York: Harper-Collins Publishers, 1989 Edition), p.254.

66. Personal letter from David J. Meyer dated September 5, 1993.

67. Harry E. Wedeck, Treasury of Witchcraft (New York, New York: Philosophical Library, 1961), p.39, 71; Mary Ann Slipper, The Symbolism of the Eastern Star (n.p., 1927), p.76.

68. Albert Pike, Morals and Dogma of the Ancient and Accepted Scottish Rite of Freemasonry (Richmond, Virginia: L. H. Jenkins, Inc., 1871), p.548.

69. Mysteries of Mind Space & Time: The Unexplained (Vol. 1) (Westport, Connecticut: H. S. Stuttman, Inc., 1992), p.83.

70. Robert Macoy, Burial Service for the Order of the Eastern Star (Richmond, Virginia: Macoy Publishing and Masonic Supply Company, Inc., 1905), p.16.

71. F. A. Bell, Bell's Eastern Star Ritual (P. R. C. Publications, Inc., 1988 Revised Edition), p.155.

72. David Haddon and Vail Hamilton, TM Wants You! A Christian Response to Transcendental Meditation (Grand Rapids, Michigan: Baker Book House, 1976), p.44, 46, 48.

73. Kenaston, *op. cit.*, p.92; See also: Harold Van Buren Voorhis, *The Eastern Star: The Evolution from a Rite to an Order* (Richmond, Virginia: Macoy Publishing and Masonic Supply Company, Inc., 1938), p.114.

74. *Ibid.*

75. *Ibid.*, p.90-91.

76. J. Edward Decker, Jr. *The Question of Freemasonry* (Issaquah, Washington: Free the Masons Ministries, n.d.), p.12.

77. Pike, *op. cit.*, p.15-16.

78. *Ibid.*, p.477.

79. *History of the Order of the Eastern Star, op. cit.*, p.14, 21; See also: Sarah H. Terry, *The Second Mile* (Corpus Christi, Texas: Christian Triumph Press, 1935), p.21; Sarah H. Terry, Compiler, *History of the Order of the Eastern Star* (n.p., 1914), p.14.

Chapter 11: What Is the Cabalistic Motto?

1. *New Times* (1985; #855), p.29.

2. *Llewellyn New Times* (January/February 1987; #871), p.7.

3. Catalog from Isis, p.35.

4. *New Times* (1984; #884), p.28.

5. See also: *What Is the Order of the Eastern Star?* (Newtonville, New York: HRT Ministries, Inc., n.d.), p.2; Eustace Mullins, *The Curse of Canaan: A Demonology of History* (Staunton, Virginia: Revelation Books, 1987), p.47; J. Gordon Melton, *The Encyclopedia of American Religions* (Vol. 2) (Wilmington, North Carolina: McGrath Publishing Company, 1978), p.185; Stewart Farrar, *What Witches Do: The Modern Coven Revealed* (Custer, Washington: Phoenix Publishing Company, 1983, Revised Edition), p.121, 181; E. A. Wallis Budge, *Amulets and Superstitions* (New York, New York: Dover Publications, Inc., 1978), p.xxxviii; Nat Freedland, *The Occult Explosion* (New York: G. P. Putnam's and Sons, 1972), p.71; J. Edward Decker, Jr., *The Question of Freemasonry* (Lafayette, Louisiana: Huntington House Publishers, 1992), p.5; *The F.A.T.A.L. Flaw* (Issaquah, Washington: Free the Masons Ministries, n.d.), p.6; *New Times* (March/April 1986; #862), p.12; John Godwin, *Occult America* (Garden City, New York: Doubleday and Company, Inc., 1972), p.292; *Self-Help Update* (Issue #27), p.16; *Llewellyn New Times* (May/June 1987; #873), p.6; *Llewellyn New Times* (January/February 1987; #871), p.7; Brochure from Coleman Publishing; Stewart Farrar, *What Witches Do: The Modern Coven Revealed* (Custer, Washington: Phoenix Publishing Company, 1983, Revised Edition), p.181; Joseph Wallman, *The Kabalah: From Its Inception to Its Evanescence* (Brooklyn, New York: Theological Research Publishing Company, 1958), p.1, 205; Moshe Idel, *Kabbalah: New Perspectives* (New Haven, Connecticut: Yale University Press, 1988), p.394; Harold Bloom, *Kabbalah and Criticism* (New York, New York: The Seabury Press, Inc., 1975), p.15, 32; Arthur Edward Waite, *The Holy Kabbalah* (London: Williams and Norgate Ltd., 1929), p.xiii, 4, 186, 557; Mary Ann Slipper, *The Symbolism of the Eastern Star* (n.p., 1927), p.136; David L. Carrico, *Immorals and Dogma* (Evansville, Indiana: Followers of Jesus Christ, n.d.), p.4; Joseph Leon Blau, *The Christian Cabala* (Port Washington, New York: Kennikat Press, Inc., 1944), p.6, 85; Rex R. Hutchens, *A Bridge to Light* (Washington, D.C.: Supreme Council, 33° Ancient and Accepted Scottish

Rite of Freemasonry, Southern Jurisdiction, 1988), p.249; Arthur Edward Waite, *The Mysteries of Magic: A Digest of the Writings of Eliphas Levi* (Chicago, Illinois: De Laurence, Scott and Company, 1909), p.97; H. L. Haywood, *The Great Teachings of Masonry* (New York: George H. Doran Company, 1923), p.95; Rex R. Hutchens and Donald W. Monson, *The Bible in Albert Pike's Morals and Dogma* (Washington, D.C.: Supreme Council, 33rd Degree, 1992), p.242; Editors of Time-Life Books, *Magical Arts* (Alexandria, Virginia: Time-Life Books, 1990), p.26; Paul Foster Case, *The Masonic Letter G* (Los Angeles, California: Builders of the Adytum, Ltd., 1981), p.14; William O. Peterson, Editor, *Masonic Quiz Book: "Ask Me Another, Brother"* (Chicago, Illinois: Charles T. Powner Company, 1950), p.143, 266; Lynn F. Perkins, *Masonry in the New Age* (Lakemont, Georgia: CSA Press, 1971), p.75; p.310; Catalog from Research Centre of Kabbalah, p.2; Shirley Plessner, *Symbolism of the Eastern Star* (Cleveland, Ohio: Gilbert Publishing Company, 1956), p.33, 34; Colin Wilson, *The Occult: A History* (New York: Random House, 1971), p.104; *New Times* (1984; #884), p.28, article entitled "Jung and the Qabalah".

6. Colin Wilson, *The Occult: A History* (New York, Random House, 1971), p.511; Editors of Time-Life Books, *Magical Arts* (Alexandria, Virginia: Time-Life Books, 1990), p.26, 61; John Maxson Stillman, *The Story of Alchemy and Early Chemistry* (New York, New York: Dover Publications, Inc., 1960), p.367; Wilson, *op. cit.*, p.513.

7. Editors of Time-Life Books, *Magical Arts* (Alexandria, Virginia: Time-Life Books, 1990), p.54.

8. Frank Gaynor, Editor, *Dictionary of Mysticism* (New York: Philosophical Library, 1953), p.92.

9. Mary Ann Slipper, *The Symbolism of the Eastern Star* (n.p., 1927), p.136.

10. Joseph Leon Blau, *The Christian Cabala* (Port Washington, New York: Kennikat Press, Inc., 1944), p.21-22.

11. William O. Peterson, Editor, *Masonic Quiz Book: "Ask Me Another, Brother"* (Chicago, Illinois: Charles T. Powner Company, 1950), p.215.

12. W. L. Reese, *Dictionary of Philosophy and Religion: Eastern and Western Thought* (Atlantic Highlands, New Jersey: Humanities Press, Inc., 1980), p.575.

13. H. M. Kallen, "Theosophist," *The World Book Encyclopedia*, 1961 Edition; Vol. 17, p.192.

14. Wilson, *op. cit.*, p.332.

15. Blau, *op. cit.*, p.52.

16. *Ibid.*, p.83.

17. Wilson, *op. cit.*, p.331.

18. David L. Carrico, *Lucifer—Eliphas Levi—Albert Pike and the Masonic Lodge* (Evansville, Indiana: Followers of Jesus Christ, 1991), p.14; See also: David L. Carrico, *Manly P. Hall: The Honored Masonic Author* (Evansville, Indiana: Followers of Jesus Christ, 1992), p.12; Gary Kah, *En Route to Global Occupation* (Lafayette, Louisiana: Huntington House Publishers, 1992), p.89; John Yarker, *The Arcane Schools* (Belfast, Ireland: William Tait, 1909), p.492; Gaynor, *op. cit.*, p.185; David Carrico, *The Occult Meaning of the Great Seal of the United States* (Evansville, Indiana: Followers of Jesus Christ, 1991), p.51, 55; E. M. Butler, *The Myth of the Magus* (New York: MacMillan Company, 1948), p.247; R. Swinburne Clymer, *The Mysteries of Osiris or Ancient Egyptian Initiation*

(Quakertown, Pennsylvania: The Philosophical Publishing Company, 1951, Revised Edition), p.331, 349; Norman MacKenzie, Editor, *Secret Societies* (Holt, Rinehart and Winston, 1967), p.144; Howard Kerr and Charles L. Crow, Editors, *The Occult in America: New Historical Perspectives* (Urbana, Illinois: University of Illinois Press, 1983), p.2, 7, 116; G. A. Riplinger, *New Age Bible Versions* (Munroe Falls, Ohio: A. V. Publications, 1993), p.412; "Where Did the New Age Come From?," *The Front Page* (September 1993; Vol. 7, No. 9), p.10; John Algeo, "One Life: A Theosophical View of the Global Challenge," *The Quest* (Autumn 1993; Vol. 6, No. 3), p.43; Richard Leviton, "The Imagination of Pentecost: Rudolf Steiner and Contemporary Spirituality," *The Quest* (Autumn 1993; Vol. 6, No. 3), p.73; *The World Book Encyclopedia*, 1961 Edition; Vol. 17, p.192; Pamphlet entitled "Theosophy Simply Stated", p.5; Wilson, *op. cit.*, p.332-333; *New Age Journal* (March/April 1987; Vol. 3; Issue 2), p.26; *The Christian World Report* (February 1991; Vol. 3, No. 2), p.8.

19. Gaynor, *op. cit.*, p.185; See also: E. M. Butler, *The Myth of the Magus* (New York: MacMillan Company, 1948), p.247, 259.

20. Arthur Edward Waite, *The Mysteries of Magic: A Digest of the Writings of Eliphas Levi* (Chicago, Illinois: De Laurence, Scott and Company, 1909), p.xi; William T. Still, *New World Order: The Ancient Plan of Secret Societies* (Lafayette, Louisiana: Huntington House, Inc., 1990), p.45; Rudolf Steiner (Translated by Max Gysi), *The Way of Initiation* (New York: Macoy Publishing and Masonic Supply Company, 1910), p.33; Constance Cumbey, *The Hidden Dangers of the Rainbow: The New Age Movement and Our Coming Age of Barbarism* (Shreveport, Louisiana: Huntington House, Inc., Revised Edition, 1983), p.46; G. A. Riplinger, *New Age Bible Versions* (Munroe Falls, Ohio: A. V. Publications, 1993), p.25, 412, 413; Manly P. Hall, *America's Assignment with Destiny* (Los Angeles, California: Philosophical Research Society, Inc., 1951), p.27.

21. Carrico, *Lucifer—Eliphas Levi—Albert Pike and the Masonic Lodge, op. cit.*, p.14; David Carrico, *The Occult Meaning of the Great Seal of the United States* (Evansville, Indiana: Followers of Jesus Christ, 1991), p.56; Gary Kah, *En Route to Global Occupation* (Lafayette, Louisiana: Huntington House Publishers, 1992), p.88, 89, 90.

22. G. A. Riplinger, *New Age Bible Versions* (Munroe Falls, Ohio: A. V. Publications, 1993), p.412.

23. Gary Kah, *En Route to Global Occupation* (Lafayette, Louisiana: Huntington House Publishers, 1992), p.89; John Yarker, *The Arcane Schools* (Belfast, Ireland: William Tait, 1909), p.486; William Schnoebelen, *Masonry: Beyond the Light* (Chino, California: Chick Publications, 1991), p.204; *Battle Cry* (March/April 1991), p.4.

24. David Carrico, *The Occult Meaning of the Great Seal of the United States* (Evansville, Indiana: Followers of Jesus Christ, 1991), p.51; *Ibid.;* William Schnoebelen, *Masonry: Beyond the Light* (Chino, California: Chick Publications, 1991), p.204.

25. *Ibid.*, p.83.

26. William Schnoebelen, *Masonry: Beyond the Light* (Chino, California: Chick Publications, 1991), p.205; *Battle Cry* (March/April 1991), p.4; Constance Cumbey, *The Hidden Dangers of the Rainbow: The New Age Movement and Our Coming Age of Barbarism* (Shreveport, Louisiana: Huntington House, Inc., Revised Edition, 1983), p.49.

27. David L. Carrico with Rick Doninger, *The Egyptian-Masonic-Satanic Connection* (Evansville, Indiana: Followers of Jesus Christ, 1991), p.12, 13; Texe Marrs, *Texe Marrs Book of New Age Cults and Religions* (Austin, Texas: Living Truth Publishers, 1990), 199, 238.

28. Waite, *The Mysteries of Magic, op. cit.,* p.213.

29. Riplinger, quoting Blavatsky, *op. cit.,* p.121.

30. Albert Pike, *Morals and Dogma of the Ancient and Accepted Scottish Rite of Freemasonry* (Richmond, Virginia: L. H. Jenkins, Inc., 1871), p.734.

31. Rex R. Hutchens, *A Bridge to Light* (Washington, D.C.: Supreme Council, 33□ Ancient and Accepted Scottish Rite of Freemasonry, Southern Jurisdiction, 1988), p.253.

32. Waite, *The Mysteries of Magic, op. cit.,* p.68, 453.

33. Albert Churchward, *Signs and Symbols of Primordial Man* (London: George Allen and Company, Ltd., 1913, Second Edition), p.199.

34. William T. Still, *New World Order: The Ancient Plan of Secret Societies* (Lafayette, Louisiana: Huntington House, Inc., 1990), p.122; Arthur Edward Waite, *The Holy Kabbalah* (London: Williams and Norgate Ltd., 1929), p.550.

35. Reese, *Dictionary of Philosophy and Religion, op. cit.,* p.575; See also: Waite, *The Mysteries of Magic, op. cit.,* p.58, 80; Prepared under the supervision of H. Spencer Lewis with revision by Ralph M. Lewis, *Rosicrucian Manual* (San Jose, California: Grand Lodge of AMORC, 1987, 27th Edition), p.204; Gaynor, *op. cit.,* p.184, 185, 186.

36. Eustace Mullins, *The Curse of Canaan: A Demonology of History* (Staunton, Virginia: Revelation Books, 1987), p.48.

37. Still, *op. cit.,* p.78; Carrico and Doninger, *The Egyptian-Masonic-Satanic Connection, op. cit.,* p.97-98.

38. Editors of Time-Life Books, *Magical Arts, op. cit.,* , p.42-43.

39. *Ibid.,* p.43-44.

40. Francois Ribadeau Dumas (Translated by Elisabeth Abbott), *Cagliostro: Scoundrel or Saint?* (New York: The Orion Press, 1967), p.96; See also: Arkon Daraul, *Witches and Sorcerers* (New York, New York: The Citadel Press, 1966), p.238.

41. *Ibid.*

42. Waite, *The Mysteries of Magic, op. cit.,* p.x.

43. S. R. Parchment, *Ancient Operative Masonry* (San Francisco, California: San Francisco Center—Rosicrucian Fellowship, 1930), p.76.

44. Blau, *op. cit.,* p.118.

45. Arthur Edward Waite, *The Holy Kabbalah* (London: Williams and Norgate Ltd., 1929), p.33, footnote.

46. *Ibid.,* p.186.

47. *Ibid.,* p.437.

48. *Ibid.,* p.518.

49. F. De P. Castells, *Genuine Secrets in Freemasonry Prior to A.D. 1717* (London: A. Lewis, 1930), p.8.

50. Pike, *op. cit.,* p.741.

51. *Ibid.*, p.626.

52. *Llewellyn New Times* (January/February 1987; #871), p.32.

53. Paul Foster Case, *The Masonic Letter G* (Los Angeles, California: Builders of the Adytum, Ltd., 1981), p.v.

54. *Ibid.*, p.vi.

55. Hutchens, quoting Albert Mackey, *A Bridge to Light, op. cit.,* p.250.

56. Blau, *op. cit.,* p.9; Moshe Idel, *Kabbalah: New Perspectives* (New Haven, Connecticut: Yale University Press, 1988), p.349; Adolphe Franck *The Kabbalah: The Religious Philosophy of the Hebrews* (University Books, Inc., 1967), p.97; Joseph Wallman, *The Kabalah: From Its Inception to Its Evanescence* (Brooklyn, New York: Theological Research Publishing Company, 1958), p.58, 128; Harold Bloom, *Kabbalah and Criticism* (New York, New York: The Seabury Press, Inc., 1975), p.24.

57. Case, *op. cit.,* p.15.

58. George Oliver, *Signs and Symbols* (New York: Macoy Publishing and Masonic Supply Company, 1906), p.101-102; James L. Holly, *The Southern Baptist Convention and Freemasonry* (Beaumont, Texas: Mission and Ministry to Men, Inc., 1992), p.23; Carrico, *Lucifer—Eliphas Levi—Albert Pike and the Masonic Lodge, op. cit.,* p.21.

59. Brochure from Nuit Unlimited Imports, p.3.

60. Waite, *The Holy Kabbalah, op. cit.,* p.170-171, 206-208, 210; See also: Pike, *op. cit.,* p.771-772; Wilson, *op. cit.,* p.206; Moshe Idel, *Kabbalah: New Perspectives* (New Haven, Connecticut: Yale University Press, 1988), p.128; Harold Bloom, *Kabbalah and Criticism* (New York, New York: The Seabury Press, Inc., 1975), p.31; Case, *op. cit.,* p.72.

61. Reese, *op. cit.,* p.75; "The Kabbalah," *Fertile Soil* (Fall 1993, No. 1), p.37.

62. *Ibid.*, p.643; See also: "The Kabbalah," *Fertile Soil* (Fall 1993, No. 1), p.38; Gaynor, *op. cit.,* p.207.

63. Waite, *The Holy Kabbalah, op. cit.,* p.599.

64. Moshe Idel, *Kabbalah: New Perspectives* (New Haven, Connecticut: Yale University Press, 1988), p.128.

65. *Ritual of the Order of the Eastern Star* (Washington, D.C.: General Grand Chapter Order of the Eastern Star, 1956), p.18; Robert Macoy (Arranged by), *Adoptive Rite Ritual* (Virginia: Macoy Publishing and Masonic Supply Company, 1897), p.28, 34; F. A. Bell, *Bell's Eastern Star Ritual* (P. R. C. Publications, Inc., 1988 Revised Edition), p.32, 34, 118.

66. Robert Macoy (Arranged by), *Adoptive Rite Ritual* (Virginia: Macoy Publishing and Masonic Supply Company, 1897), p.208; See also: Shirley Plessner, *Symbolism of the Eastern Star* (Cleveland, Ohio: Gilbert Publishing Company, 1956), p.200.

67. Schnoebelen, *Masonry, op. cit.,* p.111, 118; See also: J. S. M. Ward, *Freemasonry and the Ancient Gods* (London: Simpkin, Marshall, Hamilton, Kent and Company, Ltd., 1921), p.241; J. E. Cirlot (Translated by Jack Sage), *A Dictionary of Symbols* (New York: Dorset Press, 1991 Edition), p.61.

68. Hutchens, *A Bridge to Light, op. cit.,* p.254.

69. Christian D. Ginsburg, *The Essenes: Their History and Doctrines; The Kabbalah* (London: Routledge and Kegan Paul, Ltd., 1956 Reprint), p.84; See also: Arthur Edward Waite, *Emblematic Freemasonry and the Evolution of Its Deeper Issues* (London: William Rider and Son, Ltd., 1925), p.99-101.

70. Albert G. Mackey, quoting Rob Morris, *Encyclopedia of Freemasonry*, Vol. 1 (Chicago, Illinois: The Masonic History Company, 1909), p.303.

71. Alvin J. Schmidt and Nicholas Babchuk, editors, *The Greenwood Encyclopedia of American Institutions: Fraternal Organizations* (Westport, Connecticut: Greenwood Press, 1980), p.98-99; See also: F. A. Bell, *Bell's Eastern Star Ritual* (P. R. C. Publications, Inc., 1988 Revised Edition), p.99; *Order of the Eastern Star: Recognition Test* (Chicago, Illinois: Ezra A. Cook Publications, Inc., n.d.), p.3.

72. *Order of the Eastern Star: Recognition Test* (Chicago, Illinois: Ezra A. Cook Publications, Inc., n.d.), p.2-3; F. A. Bell, *Bell's Eastern Star Ritual* (P. R. C. Publications, Inc., 1988 Revised Edition), p.98-100.

73. F. A. Bell, *Bell's Eastern Star Ritual* (P. R. C. Publications, Inc., 1988 Revised Edition), p.107.

74. Jean M'Kee Kenaston, Compiler, *History of the Order of the Eastern Star* (Cedar Rapids, Iowa: The Torch Press, 1917), p.565.

75. *Ibid.*, p.572.

76. H. D. M. Spence and Joseph S. Exell, Editors, *The Pulpit Commentary* (Vol. 9), p.128, 129, 133, 137, 143.

77. Bell, *op. cit.*, p.107; See also: Kenaston, *op. cit.*, p.588.

78. Kenaston, *op. cit.*, p.506-507.

79. Willis D. Engle, *A General History of the Order of the Eastern Star* (Indianapolis, Indiana: Willis D. Engle, 1901), p.134.

80. Wilson, *op. cit.*, p.311.

81. Arthur Lyons, *Satan Wants You: The Cult of Devil Worship in America* (New York, New York: The Mysterious Press, 1988), p.38; See also: Carrico, *The Occult Meaning of the Great Seal of the United States, op. cit.*, p.37; Waite, *The Mysteries of Magic, op. cit.*, p.298.

82. *What Is* (1987; Vol. 1, No. 2), p.13.

83. Mustaga El-Amin, *Freemasonry: Ancient Egypt and the Islamic Destiny* (Jersey City, New Jersey: New Mind Productions, 1988), p.23.

84. Stewart Farrar, *What Witches Do: The Modern Coven Revealed* (Custer, Washington: Phoenix Publishing Company, 1983, Revised Edition), p.106.

85. *Ibid.*

86. Blau, *op. cit.*, p.52.

87. Charles A. Watts, *Worthy Matrons' Hand Book: Order of the Eastern Star* (Washington, D.C.: General Grand Chapter, Order of the Eastern Star, 1988), p.21, reprint from the July 1913 issue of the *National-Mizpah Eastern Star Magazine*.

88. R. Swinburne Clymer, *The Mysticism of Masonry* (Quakertown, Pennsylvania: The Philosophical Publishing Company, 1924), p.14.

89. *Ibid.*, p.55.

90. *Ibid.,* quoting A. T. C. Pierson, p.116-117.

91. J. D. Buck, *Mystic Masonry* (Illinois: Indo-American Book Company, 1913, Sixth Edition), p.130.

92. Larry Kunk, quoting Lynn F. Perkins, *Sons of Light? or Sons of Darkness?* (Fishers, Indiana: Ephesians 5:11, n.d.), p.3.

93. Henry C. Clausen, *Clausen's Commentaries on Morals and Dogma* (Supreme Council, 33rd Degree, Ancient and Accepted Scottish Rite of Freemasonry, Southern Jurisdiction, USA, 1974), p.96.

94. Forrest D. Haggard, *The Clergy and the Craft* (Ovid Bell Press, Inc., 1970); p.59.

Chapter 12: Is Death a Victor?

1. Robert Macoy (Arranged by), *Adoptive Rite Ritual* (Virginia: Macoy Publishing and Masonic Supply Company, 1897), p.279; *Ritual of the Order of the Eastern Star* (Washington, D.C.: General Grand Chapter Order of the Eastern Star, 1956), p.153; F. A. Bell, *Bell's Eastern Star Ritual* (P. R. C. Publications, Inc., 1988 Revised Edition), p.197; Robert Macoy, *Burial Service for the Order of the Eastern Star* (Richmond, Virginia: Macoy Publishing and Masonic Supply Company, Inc., 1905), p.5.

2. *Ibid.,* p.279-280.

3. Colin F. W. Dyer, quoting J. S. M. Ward, *Symbolism in Craft Freemasonry* (England: A Lewis [Masonic Publishers], Ltd., 1976), p.119.

4. Macoy, *Adoptive Rite Ritual, op. cit.,* p.281; Robert Macoy, *Burial Service for the Order of the Eastern Star* (Richmond, Virginia: Macoy Publishing and Masonic Supply Company, Inc., 1905), p.10.

5. *Pocket Encyclopedia of Masonic Symbols* (Silver Spring, Maryland: The Masonic Service Association of the United States, 1953), p.4.

6. *Pocket Masonic Dictionary* (Silver Spring, Maryland: The Masonic Service Association of the United States, 1988), p.22.

7. Albert Churchward, *Signs and Symbols of Primordial Man* (London: George Allen and Company, Ltd., 1913, Second Edition), p.289.

8. *Ibid.,* p.348.

9. *Ibid.,* p.27, 196, 199, 347.

10. *Ibid.,* quoting from an Egyptian ritual, p.347.

11. Ed Decker *The Question of Freemasonry Companion* (Issaquah, Washington: Saints Alive in Jesus, 1992), p.32; J. Edward Decker, Jr., *The Question of Freemasonry* (Issaquah, Washington: Free the Masons Ministries, n.d.), p.10-11.

12. Macoy, *Adoptive Rite Ritual, op. cit.,* p.263-264, 282; Robert Macoy, *Burial Service for the Order of the Eastern Star* (Richmond, Virginia: Macoy Publishing and Masonic Supply Company, Inc., 1905), p.11; *The Authorized Standard Ritual of the Order of the Eastern Star of New York* (New York, Press of Andrew H. Kellogg Company, 1876; Twentieth Edition, 1916), p.132. This book has the Matron giving this speech rather than the Patron.

13. G. W. Brown, *The Ladies' Friend* (Ann Arbor, Michigan: Press of Dr. A. W. Chase, 1866), p.76-77.

14. Mary Ann Slipper, *The Symbolism of the Eastern Star* (n.p., 1927), quoting from *Bacon Essays*, p.125.

15. *The Authorized Standard Ritual of the Order of the Eastern Star of New York* (New York, Press of Andrew H. Kellogg Company, 1876; Twentieth Edition, 1916), p.160, 161; F. A. Bell, *Bell's Eastern Star Ritual* (P. R. C. Publications, Inc., 1988 Revised Edition), p.210; See also: William Meyer, *The Order of the Eastern Star* (no other information available), p.5.

[16. Albert Pike, *Morals and Dogma of the Ancient and Accepted Scottish Rite of Freemasonry* (Richmond, Virginia: L. H. Jenkins, Inc., 1871), p.283.

17. David L. Carrico, *Lucifer—Eliphas Levi—Albert Pike and the Masonic Lodge* (Evansville, Indiana: Followers of Jesus Christ, 1991), p.2.

18. *The Authorized Standard Ritual of the Order of the Eastern Star of New York*, *op. cit.*, p.136; Macoy, *Adoptive Rite Ritual*, *op. cit.*, p.272; Robert Macoy, *Burial Service for the Order of the Eastern Star* (Richmond, Virginia: Macoy Publishing and Masonic Supply Company, Inc., 1905), p.18.

19. Arthur Edward Waite, *The Mysteries of Magic: A Digest of the Writings of Eliphas Levi* (Chicago, Illinois: De Laurence, Scott and Company, 1909), p.399; See also: Henry C. Clausen, *Emergence of the Mystical* (Washington, D.C.: Supreme Council, 1981, Second Edition), p.25.

20. For example, see: George H. Steinmetz, *The Lost Word: Its Hidden Meaning* (New York: Macoy Publishing and Masonic Supply Company, 1953), p.203; Joseph Fort Newton, *The Men's House* (Washington, D.C.: Masonic Service Association, 1923), p.83; Rex R. Hutchens, *A Bridge to Light* (Washington, D.C.: Supreme Council, 33° Ancient and Accepted Scottish Rite of Freemasonry, Southern Jurisdiction, 1988), p.248; Texe Marrs, quoting Ruth Montgomery, *Dark Secrets of the New Age: Satan's Plan for a One World Religion* (Westchester, Illinois: Crossway Books, 1987), p.142; Agnes Sanford, *The Healing Light: The Art and Method of Spiritual Healing* (St. Paul, Minnesota: MacAlester Park Publishing Company, 1947), p.142; *Christianity Today* (May 16, 1986; Vol. 30, No. 8), p.17, article entitled "Americans Get Religion in the New Age" by Robert J. L. Burrows, quoting a New Ager; Alice A. Bailey, *A Treatise on White Magic* (or *The Way of the Disciple*) (New York: Lucis Publishing Company, 1951), p.300, 301, 308; *Alpha...and Beyond* (West Allis, Wisconsin: Lor 'd Industries Ltd., n.d.), p.44; *Shepherdsfield* (March 1989), p.10; Dave Hunt and Ed Decker, quoting W. Grant Bangerter, *The God Makers: A Shocking Expose of What the Mormon Church Really Believes* (Eugene, Oregon: Harvest House Publishers, 1984), p.67; Letter from Cosmic Awareness Communications; Florence Graves, "Searching for the Truth: Ruth Montgomery Investigates Life, Death and the Hereafter," *New Age Journal* (January/February 1987; Vol. 3; Issue 1), p.24, 26; *New Age Journal* (July/August 1987; Vol. 3; Issue 4), p.47; *News and Views* (1987), p.1, quoting Richard Bach; *The Peetham: A Center for Well-Being* (Stroudsburg, Pennsylvania: The Peetham, n.d.), p.6; "Yahoshua-Joseph's Birthday," *Kingdom Voice* (August 1990), p.20-21; R. Paulaseer Lawrie, *Unwritten Thunders Revealed by Lord God Almighty* (Medway, Ohio: Manujothi Ashram Publications, n.d.), p.5; "Autumn Rain" (Card handed out at my great uncle's funeral); Joseph Murphy, *The Amazing Laws of Cosmic Mind Power* (West Nyack, New York: Parker Publishing Company, Inc., 1965), p.22; Corinne Heline, *Color and Music in the New Age* (Marina Del Rey, California: DeVorss and Company, 1964), p.51; John Randolph Price, *The Superbeings* (New York:

Ballantine Books, 1981), p.13; Matthew Fox, "Hospice: Denying the Denial of Death," *Creation* (July/August 1986; Vol. 2, No. 3), p.26; A. Wassink, quoting Mary Baker Eddy, *The Bible and Christian Science* (Grand Rapids, Michigan: Faith, Prayer and Tract League, n.d.), p.11-12; Charles H. Vail, *The Ancient Mysteries and Modern Masonry* (New York: Macoy Publishing and Masonic Supply Company, 1909), p.131.

21. Joseph Fort Newton, *The Men's House* (Washington, D.C.: Masonic Service Association, 1923), p.253-254.

22. Macoy, *Adoptive Rite Ritual, op. cit.*, p.282; Robert Macoy, *Burial Service for the Order of the Eastern Star* (Richmond, Virginia: Macoy Publishing and Masonic Supply Company, Inc., 1905), p.11.

23. *Ritual of the Order of the Eastern Star* (Washington, D.C.: General Grand Chapter Order of the Eastern Star, 1956), p.153-154.

24. F. A. Bell, *Bell's Eastern Star Ritual* (P. R. C. Publications, Inc., 1988 Revised Edition), p.198.

25. *Ibid.*, p.201.

26. *Short Talk Bulletin*, "Acacia Leaves and Easter Lilies" (April 1929; Vol. 7, No. 4; Reprinted March 1985), p.7.

27. George Oliver, *Symbol of Glory Shewing the Object and End of Freemasonry* (New York: John W. Leonard and Company, American Masonic Agency, 1855), p.280.

28. *Ibid.*, p.284-285.

29. Arthur E. Powell, *The Magic of Freemasonry* (Baskerville Press, Ltd., 1924), p.10-11.

30. Malcolm Duncan, *Duncan's Ritual of Freemasonry* (New York: David McKay Company, Inc., n.d., 3rd Edition), p.7.

31. J. S. M. Ward, *Freemasonry and the Ancient Gods* (London: Simpkin, Marshall, Hamilton, Kent and Company, Ltd., 1921), p.ix.

32. Churchward, *op. cit.*, p.195; See also: Albert G. Mackey, *A Manual of the Lodge* (New York: Charles E. Merrill Company, 1870), p.43-44.

33. *Short Talk Bulletin*, "The All-Seeing Eye" (December 1932; Vol. 10, No. 12; Reprinted January 1982), p.11.

34. For instance, see: *Pocket Encyclopedia of Masonic Symbols, op. cit.*, p.54; William Schnoebelen, *Masonry: Beyond the Light* (Chino, California: Chick Publications, 1991), p.25; Charles Scott, *The Analogy of Ancient Craft Masonry to Natural and Revealed Religion* (Philadelphia, Pennsylvania: E. H. Butler and Company, 1857), p.110; John Yarker, *The Arcane Schools* (Belfast, Ireland: William Tait, 1909), p.187; *Pocket Masonic Dictionary, op. cit.*, p.12; Arthur Edward Waite, *The Secret Tradition in Freemasonry* (London: Rider and Company, 1937), p.37; Carl H. Claudy, *Masonic Harvest* (Washington, D.C.: The Temple Publishers, 1948), p.247.

35. Carl H. Claudy, *Masonic Harvest* (Washington, D.C.: The Temple Publishers, 1948), p.253.

36. Bell, *op. cit.*, p.56.

37. *Ibid.*, p.212.

38. Robert Macoy, *Burial Service for the Order of the Eastern Star* (Richmond, Virginia: Macoy Publishing and Masonic Supply Company, Inc., 1905), p.31.

Chapter 13: Secrecy and the Eastern Star

1. *The Authorized Standard Ritual of the Order of the Eastern Star of New York* (New York, Press of Andrew H. Kellogg Company, 1876; Twentieth Edition, 1916), p.22.

2. Robert Macoy (Arranged by), *Adoptive Rite Ritual* (Virginia: Macoy Publishing and Masonic Supply Company, 1897), p.86.

3. *Ibid.*, p.88, 131, 132; *The Authorized Standard Ritual of the Order of the Eastern Star of New York, op. cit.*, p.56; F. A. Bell, *Bell's Eastern Star Ritual* (P. R. C. Publications, Inc., 1988 Revised Edition), p.63, 65, 66.

4. *The Authorized Standard Ritual of the Order of the Eastern Star of New York, op. cit.*, p.60-61; See also: William Meyer, *The Order of the Eastern Star* (no other information available), p.3; F. A. Bell, *Bell's Eastern Star Ritual* (P. R. C. Publications, Inc., 1988 Revised Edition), p.64, 65, 66, 98, 151, 169; Alvin J. Schmidt and Nicholas Babchuk, editors, *The Greenwood Encyclopedia of American Institutions: Fraternal Organizations* (Westport, Connecticut: Greenwood Press, 1980), p.97, 98; Thomas Lowe, *Adoptive Masonry: Eastern Star Ritual* (Chicago, Illinois: Ezra A. Cook, 1913), p.24; *Ibid.*, Syllabus.

5. *Ibid.*, p.15, 14; William J. Whalen, *Handbook of Secret Organizations* (Milwaukee, Wisconsin: The Bruce Publishing Company, 1966), p.28; F. A. Bell, *Bell's Eastern Star Ritual* (P. R. C. Publications, Inc., 1988 Revised Edition), p.38; Charles A. Watts, *Worthy Matrons' Hand Book: Order of the Eastern Star* (Washington, D.C.: General Grand Chapter, Order of the Eastern Star, 1988), p.21.

6. Malcolm Duncan, *Duncan's Ritual of Freemasonry* (New York: David McKay Company, Inc., n.d., 3rd Edition), p.33.

7. *Ibid.*, p.34.

8. *Ibid.*, p.94; Jim Shaw and Tom McKenney, *The Deadly Deception* (Lafayette, Louisiana: Huntington House, Inc., 1988), p.137; Stephen Knight, *The Brotherhood* (Briarcliff Manor, New York: Stein and Day, 1984), p.234.

9. *Ibid.*, p.230.

10. Jim Shaw and Tom McKenney, *The Deadly Deception* (Lafayette, Louisiana: Huntington House, Inc., 1988), p.137.

11. *Ibid.*, quoting Edmond Ronayne, p.137.

12. F. A. Bell, *Bell's Eastern Star Ritual* (P. R. C. Publications, Inc., 1988 Revised Edition), p.20.

13. *Ibid.*, p.94; Albert G. Mackey, *The Symbolism of Freemasonry* (New York: Clark and Maynard, 1869), p.29; William J. Whalen, *Handbook of Secret Organizations* (Milwaukee, Wisconsin: The Bruce Publishing Company, 1966), p.27, 29; Thomas Lowe, *Adoptive Masonry: Eastern Star Ritual* (Chicago, Illinois: Ezra A. Cook, 1913), p.20-21; *Ritual of the Order of the Eastern Star* (Washington, D.C.: General Grand Chapter Order of the Eastern Star, 1956), p.56, 77.

14. Lucien V. Rule, *The Life and Times of Rob Morris* (no other information available), p.11.

15. William D. Hawkland, *Law and Banking* (American Institute of Banking, 1971), p.183.

16. *Ibid.,* p.70.

17. Macoy, *Adoptive Rite Ritual, op. cit.,* p.93, 133.

18. W. J. McCormick, quoting J. S. M. Ward, *Christ, the Christian and Freemasonry* (Belfast, Ireland: Great Joy Publications, 1984), p.36.

19. Macoy, *Adoptive Rite Ritual, op. cit.,* p.57.

20. Lewis Spence, *Myths & Legends of Babylonia & Assyria* (London: George G. Harrap and Company, 1916), p.14; Shirley Plessner, *Symbolism of the Eastern Star* (Cleveland, Ohio: Gilbert Publishing Company, 1956), p.59.

21. Macoy, *Adoptive Rite Ritual, op. cit.,* p.57-58; See also: Bell, *op. cit.,* p.25, 43, 127, 145.

22. Edmond Ronayne, *The Master's Carpet (Mah-Hah-Bone)* (n.p., 1879), p.273; William O. Peterson, Editor, *Masonic Quiz Book: "Ask Me Another, Brother"* (Chicago, Illinois: Charles T. Powner Company, 1950), p.263; David Stevenson, *The Origins of Freemasonry: Scotland's Century, 1590-1710* (Cambridge: Press Syndicate of the University of Cambridge, 1988), p.97; Rex R. Hutchens, *A Bridge to Light* (Washington, D.C.: Supreme Council, 33° Ancient and Accepted Scottish Rite of Freemasonry, Southern Jurisdiction, 1988), p.18, 177; Veronica Ions, *Egyptian Mythology* (England: The Hamlyn Publishing Group, Ltd., 1965), p.78; George Oliver, *The Historical Landmarks and Other Evidences of Freemasonry, Explained* (Vol. I & II) (New York: John W. Leonard and Company, 1855), p.113, 136; John Lust, *The Herb Book* (New York, New York: Bantam Books, Inc., 1974), p.615; Percival George Woodcock, *Short Dictionary of Mythology* (Philosophical Library, 1953), p.65; Thomas Bulfinch, *Bulfinch's Mythology: The Age of Fable or Stories of Gods and Heroes* (Garden City, New York: Doubleday and Company, Inc., 1948), p.316; Thomas Bulfinch, *Bulfinch's Mythology* (New York: Thomas Y. Crowell Company, Inc., 1970), p.937; E. A. Wallis Budge, *Amulets and Superstitions* (New York, New York: Dover Publications, Inc., 1978), p.206.

23. *New Larousse Encyclopedia of Mythology* (Prometheus Press, 1972 Edition), p.23; See also: Albert Churchward, *Signs and Symbols of Primordial Man* (London: George Allen and Company, Ltd., 1913, Second Edition), p.418; Rex R. Hutchens, *A Bridge to Light* (Washington, D.C.: Supreme Council, 33° Ancient and Accepted Scottish Rite of Freemasonry, Southern Jurisdiction, 1988), p.18; Veronica Ions, *Egyptian Mythology* (England: The Hamlyn Publishing Group, Ltd., 1965), p.78; E. A. Wallis Budge, *Amulets and Superstitions* (New York, New York: Dover Publications, Inc., 1978), p.206.

24. George Oliver, *The Historical Landmarks and Other Evidences of Freemasonry, Explained* (Vol. I & II) (New York: John W. Leonard and Company, 1855), p.113; See also: *Ibid.,* p.23; William O. Peterson, Editor, *Masonic Quiz Book: "Ask Me Another, Brother"* (Chicago, Illinois: Charles T. Powner Company, 1950), p.263.

25. Ronayne, *op. cit.,* p.273.

26. McCormick, *op. cit.,* p.39.

27. C. Penney Hunt, quoting J. S. M. Ward, *Masons and Christ: The Menace of Freemasonry* (Finleyville, Pennsylvania: The Voice of the Nazarene Press, 1967), p.9.; *Ibid.,* p.39.

28. Harold Van Buren Voorhis, *The Eastern Star: The Evolution from a Rite to an Order* (Richmond, Virginia: Macoy Publishing and Masonic Supply Company, Inc., 1938), p.xv.

29. Jean M'Kee Kenaston, Compiler, *History of the Order of the Eastern Star* (Cedar Rapids, Iowa: The Torch Press, 1917), p.484.

30. *Ibid.*, p.491.

31. *The Authorized Standard Ritual of the Order of the Eastern Star of New York*, *op. cit.*, p.15; Macoy, *Adoptive Rite Ritual*, *op. cit.*, p.13-14.

32. William Meyer, *The Order of the Eastern Star* (no other information available), p.11.

33. *Ibid.*, p.11-12.

34. Letter on file dated January 2, 1992.

35. Letter on file dated November 17, 1991.

36. Manly Palmer Hall, *An Encyclopedic Outline of Masonic, Hermetic, Qabbalistic and Rosicrucian Symbolical Philosophy: Being an Interpretation of the Secret Teachings Concealed Within the Rituals, Allegories and Mysteries All Ages* (San Francisco, California: H. S. Crocker Company, Inc., 1928), p.101.

37. David Carrico, quoting from *The Scottish Rite Journal*, in *Manly P. Hall: The Honored Masonic Author* (Evansville, Indiana: Followers of Jesus Christ, 1992), p.17.

38. See: Recent catalogs from Macoy Publishing and Masonic Supply Company.

39. Manly Palmer Hall, *The Lost Keys of Freemasonry* (Richmond, Virginia: Macoy Publishing and Masonic Supply Company, Inc., 1976; Originally published in 1923), Title Page.

40. G. W. Brown, *The Ladies' Friend* (Ann Arbor, Michigan: Press of Dr. A. W. Chase, 1866), p.116.

41. Macoy, *Adoptive Rite Ritual*, *op. cit.*, Syllabus.

42. *Ibid.*

43. *Ibid.*

44. *Ibid.*

45. *Ibid.*

46. Bell, *op. cit.*, p.18, 53, 64, 94; Albert G. Mackey, *The Symbolism of Freemasonry* (New York: Clark and Maynard, 1869), p.29; William J. Whalen, *Handbook of Secret Organizations* (Milwaukee, Wisconsin: The Bruce Publishing Company, 1966), p.25, 27, 29; Thomas Lowe, *Adoptive Masonry: Eastern Star Ritual* (Chicago, Illinois: Ezra A. Cook, 1913), p.19-21; *Ritual of the Order of the Eastern Star* (Washington, D.C.: General Grand Chapter Order of the Eastern Star, 1956), p.56, 77; Rule, *The Life and Times of Rob Morris*, *op. cit.*, p.11; *Ibid.*, p.67; Kenaston, *op. cit.*, p.75, 95, 582-584; Brown, *op. cit.*, p.7-8.

Chapter 14: The Four Elements

1. J. E. Cirlot (Translated by Jack Sage), *A Dictionary of Symbols* (New York: Dorset Press, 1991 Edition), p.6, 35, 80, 95; Mustaga El-Amin, *Freemasonry: Ancient Egypt and the Islamic Destiny* (Jersey City, New Jersey: New Mind Productions, 1988), p.32, 34; Margot Adler, *Drawing Down the Moon: Witches,*

Druids, Goddess-Worshippers, and Other Pagans in America Today (New York, New York: The Viking Press, 1979), p.107; Helena Petrovna Blavatsky, *Isis Unveiled*, Vol. I: Science (New York, New York: Trow's Printing and Bookbinding Company, 1877), p.312; Scott Cunningham, *Wicca: A Guide for the Solitary Practitioner* (St. Paul, Minnesota: Llewellyn Publications, 1989), p.44; Stewart Farrar, *What Witches Do: The Modern Coven Revealed* (Custer, Washington: Phoenix Publishing Company, 1983, Revised Edition), p.103, 122; Frank Gaynor, Editor, *Dictionary of Mysticism* (New York: Philosophical Library, 1953), p.55, 169; Phil Phillips, *Saturday Morning Mind Control* (Nashville, Tennessee: Oliver-Nelson Books, 1991), p.189; Albert G. Mackey, *The Symbolism of Freemasonry* (New York: Clark and Maynard, 1869), p.107; Rex R. Hutchens, *A Bridge to Light* (Washington, D.C.: Supreme Council, 33□ Ancient and Accepted Scottish Rite of Freemasonry, Southern Jurisdiction, 1988), p.149; Brochure from Nuit Unlimited Imports, p.3; Arthur Edward Waite, *The Mysteries of Magic: A Digest of the Writings of Eliphas Levi* (Chicago, Illinois: De Laurence, Scott and Company, 1909), p.201; *What Is* (1987; Vol. 1, No. 2), p.2; Israel Regardie, *The Golden Dawn* (St. Paul, Minnesota: Llewellyn Publications, 1986), p.11-12, 456, 507; *Master of Life: Tools & Teachings to Create Your Own Reality* (1986; Issue #32), p.45; *What Is* (Summer 1986; Vol. 1, No. 1), p.2; *Llewellyn New Times* (March/April 1988; #882), p.76; *Self-Help Update* (Issue #28), p.60; *Self-Help Update* (Issue #30), p.8; Stuart Holroyd, *Psychic Voyages* (Garden City, New York: Doubleday and Company, Inc., 1977), p.64; Charles H. Vail, *The Ancient Mysteries and Modern Masonry* (New York: Macoy Publishing and Masonic Supply Company, 1909), p.179; Frederic Portal (Translated by John W. Simons), *A Comparison of Egyptian Symbols with Those of the Hebrews* (New York: Masonic Publishing and Manufacturing Company, 1866), p.68; Henry C. Clausen, *Clausen's Commentaries on Morals and Dogma* (Supreme Council, 33rd Degree, Ancient and Accepted Scottish Rite of Freemasonry, Southern Jurisdiction, USA, 1974), p.132; S. R. Parchment, *Ancient Operative Masonry* (San Francisco, California: San Francisco Center—Rosicrucian Fellowship, 1930), p.79, 125; Laurie Cabot with Tom Cowan, *Power of the Witch: The Earth, the Moon, and the Magical Path to Enlightenment* (New York, New York: Delacorte Press, 1989), p.114, 128; Albert Pike, *Morals and Dogma of the Ancient and Accepted Scottish Rite of Freemasonry* (Richmond, Virginia: L. H. Jenkins, Inc., 1871), p.459, 634, 784, 791; *The Masonry of Adoption* (no other information available), p.62, Second section, p.34, Third Section, p.87, Third Section; *Personal Energy Patterns: How They Affect Your Personality, Health, and Relationships* (Albany, California: Taoist Healing Centre, n.d.), p.3.

2. *Ibid.*, p.95; Albert Pike, *Morals and Dogma of the Ancient and Accepted Scottish Rite of Freemasonry* (Richmond, Virginia: L. H. Jenkins, Inc., 1871), p.469, 634; *Circle Network Bulletin* (Spring 1989), p.3; *Fate* (October 1990; Vol. 43, No. 9 [sic]), p.58; *Circle Network News* (Summer 1987; Vol. 9, No. 2), p.12; Stuart Holroyd, *Psychic Voyages* (Garden City, New York: Doubleday and Company, Inc., 1977), p.66.

3. *Circle Network News* (Summer 1987; Vol. 9, No. 2), p.12; See also: *Llewellyn New Times* (September/October 1988; #885), p.77; *Prediction* (March 1986; Vol. 52, No. 3), p.69; *Circle Network Bulletin* (Spring 1989), p.3.

4. Frank Gaynor, Editor, *Dictionary of Mysticism* (New York: Philosophical Library, 1953), p.202; *Personal Energy Patterns: How They Affect Your Personality, Health, and Relationships* (Albany, California: Taoist Healing Centre, n.d.), p.3.

5. S. R. Parchment, *Ancient Operative Masonry* (San Francisco, California: San Francisco Center—Rosicrucian Fellowship, 1930), p.125.

6. Albert Pike, *Morals and Dogma of the Ancient and Accepted Scottish Rite of Freemasonry* (Richmond, Virginia: L. H. Jenkins, Inc., 1871), p.773, 775, 778, 791, 850.

7. John Yarker, *The Arcane Schools* (Belfast, Ireland: William Tait, 1909), p.207-208.

8. Gaynor, *op. cit.*, p.184; Mustaga El-Amin, *Freemasonry: Ancient Egypt and the Islamic Destiny* (Jersey City, New Jersey: New Mind Productions, 1988), p.34; Arthur Lyons, *Satan Wants You: The Cult of Devil Worship in America* (New York, New York: The Mysterious Press, 1988), p.57; *The Masonry of Adoption* (no other information available), p.34, Third section, p.87, Third section.

9. *Ibid.*; See also: Arthur Lyons, *Satan Wants You: The Cult of Devil Worship in America* (New York, New York: The Mysterious Press, 1988), p.57.

10. Laurie Cabot with Tom Cowan, *Power of the Witch: The Earth, the Moon, and the Magical Path to Enlightenment* (New York, New York: Delacorte Press, 1989), p.226.

11. *Ibid.*; See also: Gaynor, *op. cit.*; 207; *What? When? Where? Why? Who? in Freemasonry* (Silver Spring, Maryland: Masonic Service Association of the United States, 1956), p.74; *Pocket Masonic Dictionary* (Silver Spring, Maryland: The Masonic Service Association of the United States, 1988), p.27; R. Swinburne Clymer, *The Mysticism of Masonry* (Quakertown, Pennsylvania: The Philosophical Publishing Company, 1924), p.48; J. S. M. Ward, *Freemasonry and the Ancient Gods* (London: Simpkin, Marshall, Hamilton, Kent and Company, Ltd., 1921), p.xix; Charles H. Vail, *The Ancient Mysteries and Modern Masonry* (New York: Macoy Publishing and Masonic Supply Company, 1909), p.63, 197, 199; Albert G. Mackey, *The Symbolism of Freemasonry* (New York: Clark and Maynard, 1869), p.181, 187; J. D. Buck, *Mystic Masonry* (Illinois: Indo-American Book Company, 1913, Sixth Edition), p.248; *Short Talk Bulletin*, "The Letter 'G'" (June 1933; Vol. 11, No. 6; Reprinted April 1986), p.8; Arthur Edward Waite, *The Mysteries of Magic: A Digest of the Writings of Eliphas Levi* (Chicago, Illinois: De Laurence, Scott and Company, 1909), p.102, 207.

12. Manly Palmer Hall, *The Secret Destiny of America* (New York, New York: Philosophical Library, Inc., 1958), p.179; See also: Albert G. Mackey, *The Symbolism of Freemasonry* (New York: Clark and Maynard, 1869), p.181.

13. Anton Szandor LaVey, *The Satanic Bible* (New York: Avon Books, 1969), p.130; See also: John Godwin, *Occult America* (Garden City, New York: Doubleday and Company, Inc., 1972), p.247-248.

14. Rex R. Hutchens, *A Bridge to Light* (Washington, D.C.: Supreme Council, 33° Ancient and Accepted Scottish Rite of Freemasonry, Southern Jurisdiction, 1988), p.15.

15. *Ibid.*, p.113.

16. George Oliver, *The Historical Landmarks and Other Evidences of Freemasonry, Explained* (Vol. I & II) (New York: John W. Leonard and Company, 1855), p.378; *Masonic Vocabulary* (Silver Spring, Maryland: Masonic Service Association of the United States, 1955), p.54; *What? When? Where? Why? Who? in Freemasonry* (Silver Spring, Maryland: Masonic Service Association of the United States, 1956), p.74; *Pocket Masonic Dictionary* (Silver Spring,

Maryland: The Masonic Service Association of the United States, 1988), p.27; R. Swinburne Clymer, *The Mysticism of Masonry* (Quakertown, Pennsylvania: The Philosophical Publishing Company, 1924), p.47-48; J. S. M. Ward, *Freemasonry and the Ancient Gods* (London: Simpkin, Marshall, Hamilton, Kent and Company, Ltd., 1921), p.xvii; Charles H. Vail, *The Ancient Mysteries and Modern Masonry* (New York: Macoy Publishing and Masonic Supply Company, 1909), p.63, 197, 199; Albert G. Mackey, *The Symbolism of Freemasonry* (New York: Clark and Maynard, 1869), p.176, 181, 184, 185, 187, 188, 189, 192, 195, 283, 297, 299, 322, 339, 361, 364; J. D. Buck, *Mystic Masonry* (Illinois: Indo-American Book Company, 1913, Sixth Edition), p.248; *Short Talk Bulletin*, "The Letter 'G'" (June 1933; Vol. 11, No. 6; Reprinted April 1986), p.8; Arthur Edward Waite, *The Mysteries of Magic: A Digest of the Writings of Eliphas Levi* (Chicago, Illinois: De Laurence, Scott and Company, 1909), p.102, 104, 170, 191, 204, 208, 295, 297; William O. Peterson, Editor, *Masonic Quiz Book: "Ask Me Another, Brother"* (Chicago, Illinois: Charles T. Powner Company, 1950), p.255, 266; William Adrian Brown, *Facts, Fables and Fantasies of Freemasonry* (New York, New York: Vantage Press, Inc., 1968), p.165; Pike, *op. cit.*, p.104, 323, 620, 633, 698, 700, 732, 757, 795.

17. Albert G. Mackey, *The Symbolism of Freemasonry* (New York: Clark and Maynard, 1869), p.188.

18. Charles H. Vail, *The Ancient Mysteries and Modern Masonry* (New York: Macoy Publishing and Masonic Supply Company, 1909), p.198; See also: Pike, *op. cit.*, p.323, 698, 700, 757.

19. Mackey, *The Symbolism of Freemasonry, op. cit.*, p.339.

20. Pike, *op. cit.*, p.732.

21. *Ibid.*, p.851.

22. Margot Adler, *Drawing Down the Moon: Witches, Druids, Goddess-Worshippers, and Other Pagans in America Today* (New York, New York: The Viking Press, 1979), p.107.

23. Brochure from Nuit Unlimited Imports, p.3; Arthur Edward Waite, *The Mysteries of Magic: A Digest of the Writings of Eliphas Levi* (Chicago, Illinois: De Laurence, Scott and Company, 1909), p.299; Cirlot *op. cit.*, p.80.

24. *Ibid.*; Arkon Daraul, *Witches and Sorcerers* (New York, New York: The Citadel Press, 1966), page following p.239.

25. *Ibid.*

26. *Ibid.*

27. *Ibid.*

28. *Ibid.*

29. Cirlot *op. cit.*; See also: Arthur Edward Waite, *The Mysteries of Magic: A Digest of the Writings of Eliphas Levi* (Chicago, Illinois: De Laurence, Scott and Company, 1909), p.299.

30. Sarah H. Terry, *The Second Mile* (Corpus Christi, Texas: Christian Triumph Press, 1935), p.65.

31. Brochure from The Wicca describing a course in witchcraft.

32. Cirlot, *op. cit.*, p.35.

33. LaVey, *op. cit.*, p.126.

452 HIDDEN SECRETS OF THE EASTERN STAR

34. Brochure from Nuit Unlimited Imports.

35. M. Randall Mueller, "A Critique of Anton Szandor LaVey's The Satanic Bible," *Christian News* (April 17, 1989; Vol. 27, No. 16), p.9; *Ibid.*

36. Helena Petrovna Blavatsky, *Isis Unveiled*, Vol. I: Science (New York, New York: Trow's Printing and Bookbinding Company, 1877), p.312.

37. Arthur Edward Waite, *The Mysteries of Magic: A Digest of the Writings of Eliphas Levi* (Chicago, Illinois: De Laurence, Scott and Company, 1909), p.201-202; See also: Samuel, "Helpers," *Connecting Link* (November/December 1989; Vol. 1, No. 5), p.4.

38. Pike, *op. cit.*, p.787.

39. Waite, *The Mysteries of Magic, op. cit.*, p.205.

40. Stuart Holroyd, *Psychic Voyages* (Garden City, New York: Doubleday and Company, Inc., 1977), p.64.

41. Terry, *The Second Mile, op. cit.*, p.69; See also: *Pocket Encyclopedia of Masonic Symbols* (Silver Spring, Maryland: The Masonic Service Association of the United States, 1953), p.26.

42. *Ibid.*, p.70.

43. Waite, *The Mysteries of Magic, op. cit.*, p.202.

44. Stewart Farrar, *What Witches Do: The Modern Coven Revealed* (Custer, Washington: Phoenix Publishing Company, 1983, Revised Edition), p.57.

45. W. L. Wilmshurst, *The Masonic Initiation* (Ferndale, Michigan: Trismegistus Press, 1980; Originally published 1924), p.57.

46. Mary Ann Slipper, *The Symbolism of the Order of the Eastern Star* (no other information available), p.129.

47. For example, see: Scott Cunningham, *Cunningham's Encyclopedia of Crystal, Gem & Metal Magic* (St. Paul, Minnesota: Llewellyn Publications, 1988, p.198; Farrar, *op. cit.*, p.35, 183, 416; Sybil Leek, *Numerology: The Magic of Numbers* (New York, New York: The MacMillan Company, 1969), p.119; *What? When? Where? Why? Who? in Freemasonry* (Silver Spring, Maryland: Masonic Service Association of the United States, 1956), p.31; Wilmshurst, *The Masonic Initiation, op. cit.*, p.57; Vail, *op. cit.*, p.189; Hutchens, *A Bridge to Light, op. cit.*, p.254; Editors of Time-Life Books, *Magical Arts* (Alexandria, Virginia: Time-Life Books, 1990), p.39; Starhawk (Miriam Simos), *The Spiral Dance: A Rebirth of the Ancient Religion of the Great Goddess* (New York, New York: Harper-Collins Publishers, 1989 Edition), p.79; Arthur Edward Waite, *The Secret Tradition in Freemasonry* (London: Rider and Company, 1937), p.648; *Mystic Moon* (February 1988, No. 2), Inside Front Cover; Terry, *The Second Mile, op. cit.*, p.47, 69.

48. Sybil Leek, *Numerology: The Magic of Numbers* (New York, New York: The MacMillan Company, 1969), p.119.

49. Slipper, *The Symbolism of the Order of the Eastern Star, op. cit.*, p.19; See also: Shirley Plessner, *Symbolism of the Eastern Star* (Cleveland, Ohio: Gilbert Publishing Company, 1956), p.162.

50. William Schnoebelen, *Masonry: Beyond the Light* (Chino, California: Chick Publications, 1991), p.204; *Battle Cry* (March/April 1991), p.4.

51. Alice A. Bailey, *A Treatise on White Magic* (or *The Way of the Disciple*) (New York: Lucis Publishing Company, 1951), p.42.

52. Texe Marrs, *Big Sister Is Watching You: Hillary Clinton and the White House Feminists Who Now Control America—and Tell the President What to Do* (Austin, Texas: Living Truth Publishers, 1993), p.68; Summit University Press (30th Anniversary Sale), p.6.

53. *Mysteries of Mind Space & Time: The Unexplained* (Vol. 1) (Westport, Connecticut: H. S. Stuttman, Inc., 1992), p.43; Cirlot, *op. cit.*, p.36, 285, 288.

54. Cirlot, *op. cit.*, p.288.

55. Marrs, quoting Matthew Fox, *Big Sister Is Watching You*, *op. cit.*, p.68.

56. Cirlot, *op. cit.*, Arthur Lyons, *Satan Wants You: The Cult of Devil Worship in America* (New York, New York: The Mysterious Press, 1988), p.78.

57. *Mysteries of Mind Space & Time*, *op. cit.*, p.43.

58. Bailey, *A Treatise on White Magic*, *op. cit.*, p.593.

59. *Truth Journal* (January/February 1991), p.4.

60. *Ibid.;* Waite, quoting Eliphas Levi, *The Mysteries of Magic*, *op. cit.*, p.76-77; See also: Hutchens, *A Bridge to Light*, *op. cit.*

61. David L. Carrico, *The Heart of Freemasonry Exposed! Who Is Hiram Abiff?* (Evansville, Indiana: Followers of Jesus Christ, 1991), p.4; See also: David Carrico with Rick Doninger, *The Egyptian-Masonic-Satanic Connection* (Evansville, Indiana: Followers of Jesus Christ, 1991), p.28.

62. *Ibid.*, quoting Charles W. Leadbeater, p.5.

63. R. Swinburne Clymer, *The Mysticism of Masonry* (Quakertown, Pennsylvania: The Philosophical Publishing Company, 1924), p.65.

64. Arthur H. Ward, *Masonic Symbolism and the Mystic Way* (London: Theosophical Publishing House, Ltd., 1923, Second Edition), p.36-37.

65. Bailey, *A Treatise on White Magic*, *op. cit.*, p.398.

66. *Ibid.*

67. *Ibid.*, p.399.

68. *Ibid.*, p.399-401.

69. *Ibid.*, p.414.

70. Slipper, *The Symbolism of the Order of the Eastern Star*, *op. cit.*, p.129.

71. Terry, *The Second Mile*, *op. cit.*, p.70.

72. Jean M'Kee Kenaston, Compiler, *History of the Order of the Eastern Star* (Cedar Rapids, Iowa: The Torch Press, 1917), p.588.

73. Vail, *op. cit.*, p.123-124, 128-129.

74. *Ibid.*, p.124-124; See also: Alice A. Bailey, quoting Annie Besant, *From Bethlehem to Calvary: The Initiations of Jesus* (New York: Lucis Publishing Company, 1965), p.237-238.

75. Gaynor, *op. cit.*, p.77; See also: George Oliver, *Signs and Symbols* (New York: Macoy Publishing and Masonic Supply Company, 1906), p.91, 140; A. T. C. Pierson, *The Traditions, Origin and Early History of Freemasonry* (New York: Masonic Publishing Company, 1865), p.228, 286; Wilmshurst, *The Masonic Initiation*, *op. cit.*, p.104, 187; R. Swinburne Clymer, *The Mysteries of Osiris or Ancient Egyptian Initiation* (Quakertown, Pennsylvania: The Philosophical Publishing Company, 1951, Revised Edition), p.70, 191; Albert Churchward,

Signs and Symbols of Primordial Man (London: George Allen and Company, Ltd., 1913, Second Edition), p.40; J. S. M. Ward, *Freemasonry and the Ancient Gods* (London: Simpkin, Marshall, Hamilton, Kent and Company, Ltd., 1921), p.252; *Ibid.*, p.41-43, 69, 76, 124, 135, 186; *The Full Moon Story* (Manhattan Beach, California: Rams' Dell Press, July 1967; Revised September 1974), p.17; Mackey, *The Symbolism of Freemasonry, op. cit.*, p.42, 107-108, 322; Paul Foster Case, *The Masonic Letter G* (Los Angeles, California: Builders of the Adytum, Ltd., 1981), p.67-68; Parchment, *Ancient Operative Masonry, op. cit.*, p.11, 24, 79, 140; Albert G. Mackey, *A Manual of the Lodge* (New York: Charles E. Merrill Company, 1870), p.27-28; Henry C. Clausen, *Clausen's Commentaries on Morals and Dogma* (Supreme Council, 33rd Degree, Ancient and Accepted Scottish Rite of Freemasonry, Southern Jurisdiction, USA, 1974), p.128; Francois Ribadeau Dumas (Translated by Elisabeth Abbott), *Cagliostro: Scoundrel or Saint?* (New York: The Orion Press, 1967), p.56, 129.

76. Mackey, *The Symbolism of Freemasonry, op. cit.*, p.37, 339; Edmond Ronayne, *The Master's Carpet (Mah-Hah-Bone)* (n.p., 1879), p.230.

77. Catalog from House of Avalon, p.34; Israel Regardie, *The Golden Dawn* (St. Paul, Minnesota: Llewellyn Publications, 1986), p.507; Colin Wilson, *The Occult: A History* (New York: Random House, 1971), p.232; Catalog from Papa Jim, p.107; Hutchens, *A Bridge to Light, op. cit.*, p.254; Waite, *The Mysteries of Magic, op. cit.*, p.203, 207, 487.

78. Gaynor, *op. cit.*, p.112; See also: Editors of Time-Life Books, *Magical Arts* (Alexandria, Virginia: Time-Life Books, 1990), p.26.

79. CASH (brochure from Continental Association of Satan's Hope).

80. *Ibid.*

81. *Ibid.*

82. Cabot and Cowan, *op. cit.*, p.95.

83. Waite, *The Mysteries of Magic, op. cit.*, p.487.

84. Colin Wilson, *The Occult: A History* (New York, Random House, 1971), p.231.

85. Vail, *op. cit.*, p.189.

86. D. Duane Winters, quoting Spence, *A Search for Light in a Place of Darkness: A Study of Freemasonry* (no other information available), p.67.

87. Shirley Plessner, *Symbolism of the Eastern Star* (Cleveland, Ohio: Gilbert Publishing Company, 1956), p.102.

88. *New Larousse Encyclopedia of Mythology* (Prometheus Press, 1972 Edition), p.40.

89. Sir Wallis Budge, *Egyptian Magic* (Secaucus, New Jersey: University Books, Inc., n.d.), p.89.

90. Pike, *op. cit.*, p.15.

91. Plessner, *op. cit.*, p.188; See also: p.3, 54, 134, 166; Terry, *The Second Mile, op. cit.*, p.58.

92. Blavatsky, *op. cit.*, p.146-147.

93. LaVey, *op. cit.*, p.98.

94. Henry C. Clausen, *Clausen's Commentaries on Morals and Dogma* (Supreme Council, 33rd Degree, Ancient and Accepted Scottish Rite of Freemasonry, Southern Jurisdiction, USA, 1974), p.142, Joseph Fort Newton, *The Builders:*

A Story and Study of Masonry (Cedar Rapids, Iowa: The Torch Press, 1914), p.183; George H. Steinmetz, *Freemasonry: Its Hidden Meaning* (New York: Macoy Publishing and Masonic Supply Company, 1948), p.93-94; *What? When? Where? Why? Who? in Freemasonry* (Silver Spring, Maryland: Masonic Service Association of the United States, 1956), p.67-68; Allen E. Roberts, *The Craft and Its Symbols: Opening the Door to Masonic Symbolism* (Richmond, Virginia: Macoy Publishing and Masonic Supply Company, Inc., 1974), p.36; Wilmshurst, *The Masonic Initiation*, op. cit., p.95, 187-188; *Short Talk Bulletin*, "Sts. Johns' Days" (December 1933; Vol. 11, No. 12; Reprinted July 1986), p.5-6, 8; Blavatsky, op. cit., *Pocket Encyclopedia of Masonic Symbols* (Silver Spring, Maryland: The Masonic Service Association of the United States, 1953), p.50; Albert G. Mackey, *A Manual of the Lodge* (New York: Charles E. Merrill Company, 1870), p.57; Vail, op. cit., p.51-52, 135-136, 186; Colin F. W. Dyer, *Symbolism in Craft Freemasonry* (England: A Lewis [Masonic Publishers], Ltd., 1976), p.98, 100-101; Mackey, *The Symbolism of Freemasonry, op. cit.*, p.115; J. D. Buck, *Mystic Masonry* (Illinois: Indo-American Book Company, 1913, Sixth Edition), p.86; Albert Churchward, *Signs and Symbols of Primordial Man* (London: George Allen and Company, Ltd., 1913, Second Edition), p.289.

95. *Short Talk Bulletin*, "Sts. Johns' Days" (December 1933; Vol. 11, No. 12; Reprinted July 1986), p.5-6.

96. Mary Ann Slipper, *The Symbolism of the Order of the Eastern Star, op. cit.*, p.135.

97. *The Externalization of the Hierarchy: Emergence of the Kingdom of God on Earth* (New York, New York: School for Esoteric Studies, n.d.), p.30.

98. Prepared under the supervision of H. Spencer Lewis with revision by Ralph M. Lewis, *Rosicrucian Manual* (San Jose, California: Grand Lodge of AMORC, 1987, 27th Edition), p.192.

99. Leek, *op. cit.*, p.115.

100. Cabot and Cowan, *op. cit.*, p.203.

101. Farrar, *op. cit.*, p.122; Don Elkins and Carla Rueckert, *The Crucifixion of Esmerelda Sweetwater* (Louisville, Kentucky: L/L Research, 1986), p.34.

102. *The F.A.T.A.L. Flaw* (Issaquah, Washington: Free the Masons Ministries, n.d.) p.3; See also: *Ibid.*

103. Farrar, *op. cit.*, p.64, 122.

104. Plessner, *op. cit.*, p.102.

105. Oliver, *The Historical Landmarks, op. cit.*, p.112.

106. Frederic Portal (Translated by John W. Simons), *A Comparison of Egyptian Symbols with Those of the Hebrews* (New York: Masonic Publishing and Manufacturing Company, 1866), p.68.

107. Plessner, *op. cit.*, p.152.

108. Brochure from The Magic Door, p.2.

109. Cabot and Cowan, *op. cit.*, p.128; See also: Scott Cunningham, *Wicca: A Guide for the Solitary Practitioner* (St. Paul, Minnesota: Llewellyn Publications, 1989), p.16.

110. Scott Cunningham, *Wicca: A Guide for the Solitary Practitioner* (St. Paul, Minnesota: Llewellyn Publications, 1989), p.50.

111. Mary Ann Slipper, *The Symbolism of the Eastern Star* (n.p., 1927), p.62-63.

112. Manly Palmer Hall, *An Encyclopedic Outline of Masonic, Hermetic, Qabbalistic and Rosicrucian Symbolical Philosophy: Being an Interpretation of the Secret Teachings Concealed Within the Rituals, Allegories and Mysteries of All Ages* (San Francisco, California: H. S. Crocker Company, Inc., 1928), p.95.

113. *Ibid.*

114. Kenaston, *op. cit.,* p.664; Willis D. Engle, *A General History of the Order of the Eastern Star* (Indianapolis, Indiana: Willis D. Engle, 1901), p.71; Robert Macoy (Arranged by), *Adoptive Rite Ritual* (Virginia: Macoy Publishing and Masonic Supply Company, 1897), p.127; Plessner, *op. cit.,* p.101; Carl H. Claudy, *Masonic Harvest* (Washington, D.C.: The Temple Publishers, 1948), p.234-235; Wilmshurst, *The Masonic Initiation, op. cit.,* 52-53; Mackey, *The Symbolism of Freemasonry, op. cit.,* p.253, 261; *Short Talk Bulletin,* "Veiled in Allegory" (September 1949; Vol. 27, No. 9; Reprinted April 1986), p.3; Arthur Edward Waite, *The Secret Tradition in Freemasonry* (London: Rider and Company, 1937), p.646, 650; *Masonic Vocabulary* (Silver Spring, Maryland: Masonic Service Association of the United States, 1955), p.4; *What? When? Where? Why? Who? in Freemasonry* (Silver Spring, Maryland: Masonic Service Association of the United States, 1956), p.2; Schnoebelen, *Masonry, op. cit.,* p.158; Blavatsky, *op. cit., Pocket Encyclopedia of Masonic Symbols* (Silver Spring, Maryland: The Masonic Service Association of the United States, 1953), p.5; *Pocket Masonic Dictionary* (Silver Spring, Maryland: The Masonic Service Association of the United States, 1988), p.6, 14; *Ibid.,* p.36.

115. Willis D. Engle, *A General History of the Order of the Eastern Star* (Indianapolis, Indiana: Willis D. Engle, 1901), p.71; Terry, *The Second Mile, op. cit.,* p.21; Robert Macoy (Arranged by), *Adoptive Rite Ritual* (Virginia: Macoy Publishing and Masonic Supply Company, 1897), p.127; Plessner, *op. cit.,* p.101, 119-120, 122, 165.

116. Hall, *An Encyclopedic Outline, op. cit.*

117. *Ibid.*

118. Robert Macoy (Arranged by), *Adoptive Rite Ritual* (Virginia: Macoy Publishing and Masonic Supply Company, 1897), p.127; Engle, *op. cit.,* p.71; Plessner, *op. cit.,* p.101.

119. Charles M. Skinner, *Myths and Legends of Flowers, Trees, Fruits, and Plants* (Philadelphia, Pennsylvania: J. B. Lippincott Company, 1911), p.151.

120. *Ibid.*

121. *The World Book Encyclopedia,* 1961 Edition; Vol. 18, p.251.

122. Skinner, *op. cit.,* p.244; See also: Oliver, *The Historical Landmarks, op. cit.,* p.136; David Stevenson, *The Origins of Freemasonry: Scotland's Century, 1590-1710* (Cambridge: Press Syndicate of the University of Cambridge, 1988), p.97; John Lust, *The Herb Book* (New York, New York: Bantam Books, Inc., 1974), p.615.

123. *Ibid.,* p.244.

124. Macoy, *Adoptive Rite Ritual, op. cit.,* p.127.

125. Dennis L. Cuddy, "The Deceptive New Age 'Service' and 'Light,'" *The Christian World Report* (February 1991; Vol. 3, No. 2), p.8.

126. Plessner, *op. cit.,* p.123.

127. *Ibid.*

128. Cabot and Cowan, *op. cit.*, p.133.

129. *Ibid.*

130. Alex Horne, *King Solomon's Temple in the Masonic Tradition* (London: The Aquarian Press, 1971), Back Cover.

131. *Ibid.*

132. Waite, *The Mysteries of Magic, op. cit.*, p.217.

133. Horne, *op. cit.*

134. Parchment, *Ancient Operative Masonry, op. cit.*, p.63.

135. Robert Morris and Albert Mackey, *Lights and Shadows of the Mystic Tie* (New York: Masonic Publishing Company, 1878), p.392.

136. Vail, *op. cit.*, p.213-214.

137. Macoy, *Adoptive Rite Ritual, op. cit.*, p.263; G. W. Brown, *The Ladies' Friend* (Ann Arbor, Michigan: Press of Dr. A. W. Chase, 1866), p.104.

138. Starhawk (Miriam Simos), *The Spiral Dance: A Rebirth of the Ancient Religion of the Great Goddess* (New York, New York: Harper-Collins Publishers, 1989 Edition), p.74.

139. Vail, *op. cit.*, p.213.

Chapter 15: A Look at the Rainbow Girls

1. W. Mark Sexson, *Ritual—Supreme Assembly International Order of the Rainbow for Girls* (McAlester, Oklahoma: Office of Supreme Assembly, 1948), Title page; *Allied Masonic Groups and Rites* (Silver Spring, Maryland: Masonic Service Association of the United States, 1956; Revised 1988), p.22; William J. Whalen, *Handbook of Secret Organizations* (Milwaukee, Wisconsin: The Bruce Publishing Company, 1966), p.132; *Pennsylvania Youth Foundation* (Elizabethtown, Pennsylvania: Pennsylvania Youth Foundation, n.d.), p.3; *The Scottish Rite Journal* (November 1992; Vol. 100, No. 11), p.13; Harold Van Buren Voorhis, *The Eastern Star: The Evolution from a Rite to an Order* (Richmond, Virginia: Macoy Publishing and Masonic Supply Company, Inc., 1938), p.114.

2. *Ibid,* p.93.

3. *Ibid.*

4. *Ibid.*

5. *Ibid.*, p.94-95; See also: *Allied Masonic Groups and Rites* (Silver Spring, Maryland: Masonic Service Association of the United States, 1956; Revised 1988), p.22; Stephen Brent Morris, *Masonic Philanthropies: A Tradition of Caring* (Lexington, Massachusetts and Washington, D.C.: The Supreme Councils, 33rd Degree, Northern Masonic Jurisdiction and Southern Jurisdiction, 1991), p.11.

6. *Ibid.*, p.25, 26, 27, 28, 59.

7. *Ibid.*, p.29, 39, 41, 59, 60, 62, 77, 89.

8. *Ibid.*, p.39.

9. *Ibid.*, p.77.

10. Laura Burton, tape of her address on the Rainbow Girls given at the June 1993 Knoxville Leadership Conference.

11. *Ibid.*

12. *Allied Masonic Groups and Rites* (Silver Spring, Maryland: Masonic Service Association of the United States, 1956; Revised 1988), p.22. This book states that the age is between twelve and eighteen (p.22). Another book, *The Eastern Star: The Evolution from a Rite to an Order*, claims that the age is between thirteen and twenty. [Harold Van Buren Voorhis, *The Eastern Star: The Evolution from a Rite to an Order* (Richmond, Virginia: Macoy Publishing and Masonic Supply Company, Inc., 1938), p.114]; See also: William J. Whalen, *Handbook of Secret Organizations* (Milwaukee, Wisconsin: The Bruce Publishing Company, 1966), p.131. *The Pennsylvania Youth Foundation* pamphlet says the age for acceptance is between eleven and twenty (p.3). Laura Burton, a former Rainbow Girl, gives the membership age as between twelve and twenty. She was a member from the time she turned twelve until she reached twenty.

13. Harold Van Buren Voorhis, *The Eastern Star: The Evolution from a Rite to an Order* (Richmond, Virginia: Macoy Publishing and Masonic Supply Company, Inc., 1938), p.114.

14. *Allied Masonic Groups and Rites, op. cit.,* p.22; William J. Whalen, *Handbook of Secret Organizations* (Milwaukee, Wisconsin: The Bruce Publishing Company, 1966), p.131.

15. William Schnoebelen, *Masonry: Beyond the Light* (Chino, California: Chick Publications, 1991), p.110.

16. *Allied Masonic Groups and Rites, op. cit.,* p.22.

17. *Ibid.,* Foreword; Voorhis, *op. cit.,* p.113; See also: *What? When? Where? Why? Who? in Freemasonry* (Silver Spring, Maryland: Masonic Service Association of the United States, 1956), p.83.

18. *Ibid.*

19. Stephen Brent Morris, *Masonic Philanthropies: A Tradition of Caring* (Lexington, Massachusetts and Washington, D.C.: The Supreme Councils, 33rd Degree, Northern Masonic Jurisdiction and Southern Jurisdiction, 1991), p.11.

20. *What? When? Where? Why? Who? in Freemasonry* (Silver Spring, Maryland: Masonic Service Association of the United States, 1956), p.83.

21. *Allied Masonic Groups and Rites, op. cit.,* p.22.

22. William J. Whalen, *Handbook of Secret Organizations* (Milwaukee, Wisconsin: The Bruce Publishing Company, 1966), p.132; See also: Voorhis, *op. cit.,* p.114.

23. Sexson, *op. cit.,* p.30; *Ibid.,* p.132.

24. *Ibid.,* p.31; Whalen, *op. cit.,* p.132.

25. *Ibid.,* p.28-29.

26. For instance, see: Schnoebelen, *Masonry, op. cit.,* p.133, 134; *Pocket Encyclopedia of Masonic Symbols* (Silver Spring, Maryland: The Masonic Service Association of the United States, 1953), p.13; Shirley Plessner, *Symbolism of the Eastern Star* (Cleveland, Ohio: Gilbert Publishing Company, 1956), p.2; Joseph Fort Newton, *The Religion of Masonry: An Interpretation* (Washington, D.C.: The Masonic Service Association of the United States, 1927), p.93; Tape from World Goodwill entitled: "Democracy: Its Esoteric Dimension", p.7, p.2-3; H. L. Haywood, *Symbolic Masonry: An Interpretation of the Three Degrees* (Washington, D.C.: Masonic Service Association of the United States, 1923), p.118-119; Mary Ann Slipper, *The Symbolism of the Eastern Star* (n.p., 1927),

p.91; *Short Talk Bulletin*, "Symbolism" (March 1925; Vol. 3, No. 3; Reprinted May 1982), p.11; Joseph Fort Newton, *The Religion of Masonry: An Interpretation* (Richmond, Virginia: Macoy Publishing and Masonic Supply Company, Inc., 1969 Edition), p.93; Joseph Fort Newton, *The Men's House* (Washington, D.C.: Masonic Service Association, 1923), p.83-84; C. F. McQuaig, *The Masonic Report* (Norcross, Georgia: Answer Books and Tapes, 1976), p.48.

27. *Short Talk Bulletin*, "The Nature of Symbols" (July 1957; Vol. 35, No. 7; Reprinted May 1982), p.4.

28. Joseph Fort Newton, *The Religion of Masonry: An Interpretation* (Washington, D.C.: The Masonic Service Association of the United States, 1927), p.93; See also: W. J. McCormick, quoting Joseph Fort Newton, *Christ, the Christian and Freemasonry* (Belfast, Ireland: Great Joy Publications, 1984), p.59.

29. Schnoebelen, quoting Oliver Day Street, *Masonry, op. cit.*, p.134-135.

30. W. J. McCormick, quoting the *Masonic Record* in *Christ, the Christian and Freemasonry* (Belfast, Ireland: Great Joy Publications, 1984), p.59.

31. *Ibid.*, quoting G. Wingate Chase, p.59.

32. Newton, *The Religion of Masonry, op. cit.*, p.82-83; H. L. Haywood, *Symbolic Masonry: An Interpretation of the Three Degrees* (Washington, D.C.: Masonic Service Association of the United States, 1923), p.118.

33. *Ibid.*, p.30, 32, 33, 63, 64.

34. Alice A. Bailey, *A Treatise on White Magic* (or *The Way of the Disciple*) (New York: Lucis Publishing Company, 1951), p.345.

35. *Ibid.*

36. Barbara Powell, "Touching Mother Earth: Seeing the Past and Future in a Handful of Sand," *New Times* (March/April 1986; #862), p.28.

37. *Transmission* (April 1983, No. 1), p.3.

38. Benjamin Creme, *The Reappearance of the Christ and the Masters of Wisdom* (North Hollywood, California: Tara Center, 1980), p.5.

39. "How to Meditate: Physical Considerations," *Circle Network News* (Spring 1988; Vol. 10, No. 1), p.9.

40. Dennis Carpenter, "A Special Place in Nature, *Circle Network News* (Spring 1988; Vol. 10, No. 1), p.12.

41. *Voices from Spirit* (May 1989; Vol. 3, No. 1), Back Cover.

42. Van Ault, "Lazaris," *Magical Blend* (February/March/April 1988; Issue #18), p.77.

43. Brochure from Royal Teton Ranch.

44. Corinne Heline, *Color and Music in the New Age* (Marina Del Rey, California: DeVorss and Company, 1964), p.44.

45. *Ibid.*

46. *Ibid.*

47. Timothy Green Beckley, "The Spirits Speak,"*Inner Light: The Voice of the New Age* (1988, No. 13), p.22.

48. For instance, see the following: Newton, *The Religion of Masonry, op. cit.*, p.82; Shirley MacLaine, *Dancing in the Light* (New York, New York: Bantam

Books, Inc., 1985), p.36-37; Carla L. Rueckert, *A Channeling Handbook* (Amherst, Wisconsin: Palmer Publications, Inc., 1987), p.21; *Master of Life* (1987, Issue #37), p.17; *Master of Life: Tools & Teachings to Create Your Own Reality* (1986; Issue #32), p.42, 43, 44, 47; *Master of Life: Tools & Teachings to Create Your Own Reality* (1986; Issue #33), p.21; *Master of Life: Tools & Teachings to Create Your Own Reality* (1987; Issue #35), p.8, 11, 13; Don Elkins, Carla Rueckert, and James Allen McCarty *The Ra Material* (Norfolk, Virginia: The Donning Company, 1984), p.30-31; Bernard Gunther, *Energy Ecstasy and Your Seven Vital Chakras* (Van Nuys, California: Newcastle Publishing Company, Inc., 1978), p.6, 91; *Siva's Cosmic Dance* (San Francisco, California: Himalayan Academy, n.d.), p.17; Dave Hunt and T. A. McMahon, *America: The Sorcerer's New Apprentice: The Rise of New Age Shamanism* (Eugene, Oregon: Harvest House Publishers, 1988), p.64-65; p.108, quoting from the Creativity in Business course offered by Stanford Graduate School of Business; Scott Malcolmson, "Sex and Death in Key West," *Mother Jones* (February/March 1988; Vol. 13, No. 2), p.45, 31; Agnes Sanford, *The Healing Light: The Art and Method of Spiritual Healing* (St. Paul, Minnesota: MacAlester Park Publishing Company, 1947), p.146; *Prophecy Newsletter* (Vol. 1, No. 6), p.12-13, quoting Benjamin Creme; Kirstine Tomasik, "Your Body, Your Self," *Jr. High Ministry* (September/October 1986; Vol. 1, No.5), p.69-70; Esalen (January-June 1985 Catalog), p.17; Kenneth Ring interview with *Psychic Guide* (March/April/May 1985), p.17; Psychic BookShop, p.8; *Complete Occult Digest A to Z* (North Hollywood, California: International Imports, 1984), p.207; *Self-Help Update* (Issue #26), p.21, 45, 49, 50, 51, 52; David Spangler, *Emergence: The Rebirth of the Sacred* (New York, New York: Dell Publishing, 1984), p.62; Johanna Michaelsen, *The Beautiful Side of Evil* (Eugene, Oregon: Harvest House Publishers, 1982), p.103; *Self-Help Update* (Issue #30), p.11; *Self-Help Update* (Issue #31), p.32; Summit University Press (30th Anniversary Sale), p.6, 21; *Llewellyn New Times* (July/August 1986; #864), p.51; Baraka Bashad, "Trance of the Meeting of Magickal Energies East and West," *Circle Network News* (Spring 1988; Vol. 10, No. 1), p.10; Michael Harismides, "Basic Tree Meditation," p.11, and Selena Fox, "Pennsylvania Dutch Hex Signs," *Circle Network News* (Summer 1987; Vol. 9, No. 2), p.11; Gerald Tros, *New Age Notes* (IBM disk); Maureen Murdock, *Spinning Inward: Using Guided Imagery with Children for Learning, Creativity & Relaxation* (Boston, Massachusetts: Shambhala Publications, Inc., 1987, Revised and Expanded Edition), p.22; "Changing Our Reality," Rita Lynne interview with *Aquarian Voices* (August 1989), p.10; Martin and Deidre Bobgan, quoting Bill Wilson, *12 Steps to Destruction: Codependency/Recovery Heresies* (Santa Barbara, California: EastGate Publishers, 1991), p.98; *Pass It On: The Story of Bill Wilson and How the A.A. Message Reached the World* (New York, New York: Alcoholics Anonymous World Services, Inc., 1984), p.120-121; Lily Dale Summer Workshop (Catalog), p.8; Texe Marrs, quoting Elizabeth Clare Prophet, *America Shattered* (Austin, Texas: Living Truth Publishers, 1991), p.70; "Teaching Children to Contact Evil Spirits?," compiled from a report issued by the National Association of Christian Educators in *"God's Watchman"* and the Hope of Israel (Vol. 18, No. 1), p.14-15.

49. J. Gordon Melton, *The Encyclopedia of American Religions* (Vol. 2) (Wilmington, North Carolina: McGrath Publishing Company, 1978), p.262.

50. *Circle Network News* (Summer 1987; Vol. 9, No. 2), p.20.

51. Melton, *The Encyclopedia of American Religions*, op. cit., p.262.

52. Letter on file from David J. Meyer, dated September 5, 1993.

53. Bailey, *A Treatise on White Magic*, op. cit., p.593.

54. Summit University Press (30th Anniversary Sale), p.6.

55. Arthur H. Ward, *Masonic Symbolism and the Mystic Way,* (London: Theosophical Publishing House, Ltd., 1923, Second Edition), p.149-150.

56. Whalen, *op. cit.,* p.133; Sexson, *op. cit.,* p.61.

57. *Ibid.,* p.32.

58. *Ibid.*

59. *Ibid.,* p.57; See also: Whalen, *op. cit.,* p.133.

60. Sexson, *op. cit.,* p.5, 12, 57-59; See also: *Ibid.,* p.133.

61. George Oliver, *Signs and Symbols* (New York: Macoy Publishing and Masonic Supply Company, 1906), p.124; R. Swinburne Clymer, *The Mysteries of Osiris or Ancient Egyptian Initiation* (Quakertown, Pennsylvania: The Philosophical Publishing Company, 1951, Revised Edition), p.185.

62. Texe Marrs, *Mystery Mark of the New Age: Satan's Design for World Domination* (Westchester, Illinois: Crossway Books, 1988), p.97.

63. Edith Hamilton, *Mythology* (Boston, Massachusetts: Little, Brown and Company, 1942), p.459; *New Larousse Encyclopedia of Mythology* (Prometheus Press, 1972 Edition), p.249, 268; Helena Petrovna Blavatsky, *Isis Unveiled,* Vol. I: Science (New York, New York: Trow's Printing and Bookbinding Company, 1877), p.161; Edmond Ronayne, *The Master's Carpet (Mah-Hah-Bone)* (n.p., 1879), p.323.

64. R. Swinburne Clymer, *The Mysteries of Osiris or Ancient Egyptian Initiation* (Quakertown, Pennsylvania: The Philosophical Publishing Company, 1951, Revised Edition), p.185.

65. *Ibid.*

66. Rex R. Hutchens, *A Bridge to Light* (Washington, D.C.: Supreme Council, 33□ Ancient and Accepted Scottish Rite of Freemasonry, Southern Jurisdiction, 1988), p.ii.

67. *The Scottish Rite Journal* (November 1993; Vol. 101, No. 11), p.57; See also:, *The Scottish Rite Journal* (November 1992; Vol. 100, No. 11), p.46.

68. Hutchens, *A Bridge to Light, op. cit.,* p.ii.

69. Canon Richard Tydeman, "Let Us Pontificate," *The New Age Magazine,* (January 1989; Vol. 97, No. 1), p.12-13.

70. J. E. Cirlot, *A Dictionary of Symbols* (New York, New York: Philosophical Library, Inc., 1972), p.33.

71. Eustace Mullins, *The Curse of Canaan: A Demonology of History* (Staunton, Virginia: Revelation Books, 1987), p.55.

72. *Ibid.,* p.45; See also: *The New Age Movement—Age of Aquarius—Age of Antichrist,* Interview with Constance Cumbey (Oklahoma City, Oklahoma: Southwest Radio Church, 1982), p.5; Phil Phillips, *Turmoil in the Toybox* (Lancaster, Pennsylvania: Starburst Press, 1986), p.83; Johanna Michaelsen, *Like Lambs to the Slaughter* (Eugene, Oregon: Harvest House Publishers, 1989), p.218; Phil Phillips, *Saturday Morning Mind Control* (Nashville, Tennessee: Oliver-Nelson Books, 1991), p.111.

73. For instance, see: Alice A. Bailey, *Discipleship in the New Age* (Vol. II) (New York: Lucis Publishing Company, 1955), p.268, 408; *Shamballa: Where the Will of God is Known* (New York, New York: Arcane School, n.d.), p.19; *The*

Beacon (July/August 1985; Vol. 51, No. 4), p.119-120; *Spiritual Mothering Journal* (Winter 1986; Vol. 6, No. 4), p.22; Alice A. Bailey, *Education in the New Age* (New York: Lucis Publishing Company, 1954), p.96-97; Alice A. Bailey, *Discipleship in the New Age* (Vol. I) (New York: Lucis Publishing Company, 1972); Alice A. Bailey, *The Soul: Quality of Life* (New York: Lucis Publishing Company, 1974), p.243; Pamphlet from Energy Systems Parameters, p.2-3; Brochure from Harmony Horizons, Inc.; *Thoughtline* (August 1990), p.3; Lynn F. Perkins, *Masonry in the New Age* (Lakemont, Georgia: CSA Press, 1971), p.241, 307; Brochure from Sancta Sophia Seminary, p.5; Gary Doore, Editor and Compiler, *Shaman's Path: Healing, Personal Growth and Empowerment* (Boston, Massachusetts: Shambhala, 1988), p.66-71; *New Teachings for an Awakening Humanity* (Santa Clara, California: S. E. E. Publishing Company, n.d.), p.1; Wendell C. Beane and William G. Doty, *Myths, Rites, Symbols: A Mircea Eliade Reader* (Vol. II) (New York, New York: Harper Colophon Books, 1975), p.409-411; Colin Wilson, *The Occult: A History* (New York, Random House, 1971), p.207. Books written from a Christian perspective that warn about the occult teachings of the rainbow are: Marrs, *Mystery Mark of the New Age, op. cit.,* p.97-98; Texe Marrs, *Ravaged by the New Age: Satan's Plan to Destroy Our Kids* (Austin, Texas: Living Truth Publishers, 1989), p.63; *The New Age Movement—Age of Aquarius—Age of Antichrist,* Interview with Constance Cumbey (Oklahoma City, Oklahoma: Southwest Radio Church, 1982), p.5.

74. Dennis L. Cuddy, "The Deceptive New Age 'Service' and 'Light,'" *The Christian World Report* (February 1991; Vol. 3, No. 2), p.8.

75. Lynn F. Perkins, *Masonry in the New Age* (Lakemont, Georgia: CSA Press, 1971), p.307.

76. Marrs, *Mystery Mark of the New Age, op. cit.,* p.97.

77. *Ibid.*

78. Sexson, *op. cit.,* p.57.

79. *Ibid.,* p.12.

80. *Ibid.,* p.57.

81. *Ibid.,* p.58-59, 88.

82. *Ibid.,* p.88.

83. *Ibid.,* p.88-89.

84. Harold Waldwin Percival, *Masonry and Its Symbols in the Light of "Thinking and Destiny"* (New York, New York: The Word Foundation, Inc., 1952), p.11.

85. W. L. Wilmshurst, *The Meaning of Masonry* (Bell Publishing Company, reprint of fifth edition published in 1927), p.31.

86. Arthur Edward Waite, *A New Encyclopedia of Freemasonry and of Cognate Instituted Mysteries: Their Rites, Literature and History* (New York: Weathervane Books, 1970), Vol. II, p.38.

87. Wilmshurst, *The Meaning of Masonry, op. cit.,* p.136; Ed Decker, *A Biblical Look at the Lodge* (Issaquah, Washington: Free the Masons Ministries, n.d.), p.3; Ed Decker *The Question of Freemasonry Companion* (Issaquah, Washington: Saints Alive in Jesus, 1992), p.52; Percival, *op. cit.,* p.11; William Adrian Brown, *Facts, Fables and Fantasies of Freemasonry* (New York, New York: Vantage Press, Inc., 1968), p.138; A. T. C. Pierson, *The Traditions, Origin and Early History of Freemasonry* (New York: Masonic Publishing Company, 1865),

p.45; *Short Talk Bulletin*, "Veiled in Allegory" (September 1949; Vol. 27, No. 9; Reprinted April 1986), p.3; *Masonic Institutes* (Various Authors) (High Holborn: Richard Spencer, 1847), p.203; *What Is* (1987; Vol. 1, No. 2), p.69; George Oliver, *Symbol of Glory Shewing the Object and End of Freemasonry* (New York: John W. Leonard and Company, American Masonic Agency, 1855), p.195; Charles H. Vail, *The Ancient Mysteries and Modern Masonry* (New York: Macoy Publishing and Masonic Supply Company, 1909), p.194; Albert G. Mackey, *The Symbolism of Freemasonry* (New York: Clark and Maynard, 1869), p.131; John J. Robinson, *Born in Blood: The Lost Secrets of Freemasonry* (New York, New York: M. Evans and Company, 1989), p.239; George H. Steinmetz, *The Lost Word: Its Hidden Meaning* (New York: Macoy Publishing and Masonic Supply Company, 1953), p.200; *Short Talk Bulletin*, "The Apron" (June 1932; Vol. 10, No. 6; Reprinted March 1986), p.8, 9.

88. Albert Pike, *Morals and Dogma of the Ancient and Accepted Scottish Rite of Freemasonry* (Richmond, Virginia: L. H. Jenkins, Inc., 1871), p.407.

89. *Ibid.*

90. William Hutchinson (Revised by George Oliver), *The Spirit of Masonry,* (New York: Bell Publishing Company, 1982; Originally published in 1775), p.82.

91. *Ibid.*, p.82-83.

92. Pike, *op. cit.*

93. Charles H. Vail, *The Ancient Mysteries and Modern Masonry* (New York: Macoy Publishing and Masonic Supply Company, 1909), p.193-194.

94. John T. Lawrence, *The Perfect Ashlar* (London: A. Lewis, 1912), p.60; See also: William Adrian Brown, *Facts, Fables and Fantasies of Freemasonry* (New York, New York: Vantage Press, Inc., 1968), p.138; H. L. Haywood, *Symbolic Masonry: An Interpretation of the Three Degrees* (Washington, D.C.: Masonic Service Association of the United States, 1923), p.141; A. T. C. Pierson, *The Traditions, Origin and Early History of Freemasonry* (New York: Masonic Publishing Company, 1865), p.45; J. S. M. Ward, *Freemasonry and the Ancient Gods* (London: Simpkin, Marshall, Hamilton, Kent and Company, Ltd., 1921), p.62-63; Albert G. Mackey, *The Symbolism of Freemasonry* (New York: Clark and Maynard, 1869), p.131; *Pocket Encyclopedia of Masonic Symbols* (Silver Spring, Maryland: The Masonic Service Association of the United States, 1953), p.9; Albert G. Mackey, *A Manual of the Lodge* (New York: Charles E. Merrill Company, 1870), p.32; *Short Talk Bulletin*, "The Apron" (June 1932; Vol. 10, No. 6; Reprinted March 1986), p.7; Edmond Ronayne, *The Master's Carpet (Mah-Hah-Bone)* (n.p., 1879), p.294-295.

95. William Adrian Brown, *Facts, Fables and Fantasies of Freemasonry* (New York, New York: Vantage Press, Inc., 1968), p.138.

96. *Ibid.*

97. W. L. Wilmshurst, *The Masonic Initiation* (Ferndale, Michigan: Trismegistus Press, 1980; Originally published 1924), p.92.

98. Paul Foster Case, *The Masonic Letter G* (Los Angeles, California: Builders of the Adytum, Ltd., 1981), p.v.

99. *Ibid.*, p.67-68.

100. Schnoebelen, *Masonry, op. cit.*, p.214.

101. *Ibid.*, p.137.

102. Arthur E. Powell, *The Magic of Freemasonry* (Baskerville Press, Ltd., 1924), p.57.

103. Ed Decker, *A Biblical Look at the Lodge* (Issaquah, Washington: Free the Masons Ministries, n.d.), p.3; Ed Decker *The Question of Freemasonry Companion* (Issaquah, Washington: Saints Alive in Jesus, 1992), p.52; See also: Larry Kunk *Sons of Light? or Sons of Darkness?* (Fishers, Indiana: Ephesians 5:11, n.d.), p.5; Schnoebelen, *Masonry, op. cit.*, p.137.

104. *Ibid.*; Larry Kunk, *Sons of Light? or Sons of Darkness?* (Fishers, Indiana: Ephesians 5:11, n.d.), p.5.

105. Thomas Lowe, *Adoptive Masonry: Eastern Star Ritual* (Chicago, Illinois: Ezra A. Cook, 1913), p.18; Jean M'Kee Kenaston, Compiler, *History of the Order of the Eastern Star* (Cedar Rapids, Iowa: The Torch Press, 1917), p.639; F. A. Bell, *Bell's Eastern Star Ritual* (P. R. C. Publications, Inc., 1988 Revised Edition), p.108.

106. *Ibid.*, p.24.

107. F. A. Bell, *Bell's Eastern Star Ritual* (P. R. C. Publications, Inc., 1988 Revised Edition), p.56; Jean M'Kee Kenaston, Compiler, *History of the Order of the Eastern Star* (Cedar Rapids, Iowa: The Torch Press, 1917), p.638.

108. Pike, *op. cit.*, p.321; See also: Arthur Edward Waite, *The Mysteries of Magic: A Digest of the Writings of Eliphas Levi* (Chicago, Illinois: De Laurence, Scott and Company, 1909), p.442.

109. Gary Kah, *En Route to Global Occupation* (Lafayette, Louisiana: Huntington House Publishers, 1992), p.89; John Yarker, *The Arcane Schools* (Belfast, Ireland: William Tait, 1909), p.486; Schnoebelen, *Masonry, op. cit.*, p.204; *Battle Cry* (March/April 1991), p.4.

110. Israel Regardie, quoting Helena Petrovna Blavatsky, *The Golden Dawn* (St. Paul, Minnesota: Llewellyn Publications, 1986), p.34.

111. Manly P. Hall, *America's Assignment with Destiny* (Los Angeles, California: Philosophical Research Society, Inc., 1951), p.19.

112. Perkins, *op. cit.*, p.144.

113. *Order of DeMolay* (Newtonville, New York: HRT Ministries, Inc., n.d.; Prepared by Commission of Fraternal Organizations), p.7.

114. Zeb E. Blanton, Jr., "Masonic Youth Have We Forgotten," *The Scottish Rite Journal* (August 1991; Vol. 99, No. 8), p.20; See also: Arthur R. Herrmann, *Designs upon the Trestleboard* (New York, New York: Press of Henry Emmerson, 1957), p.134.

115. Alberto Mansur, "DeMolay in Brazil, *The Scottish Rite Journal* (February 1992; Vol. 100, No. 2), p.44.

116. Schnoebelen, *Masonry, op. cit.*, p.110; See also: Michael Baigent and Richard Leigh, *The Temple and the Lodge* (New York: Arcade Publishing, Inc., 1989), p.266.

117. *Ibid.*, p.110-111.

118. *Ibid.*, p.113.

BIBLIOGRAPHY

(The following is a partial listing of the reference materials that were used in preparing this book.)

Academic American Encyclopedia, 1982.

Adams, John Quincy. *Letters and Opinions of the Masonic Institution* (Cincinnati, Ohio: Lorenzo Stratton, 1851).

Adams, Ruth. *One Little Candle* (Richmond, Virginia: Macoy Publishing and Masonic Company, Inc., 1966).

Adelphi Quarterly (Third Quarter 1992).

Adler, Margot. *Drawing Down the Moon: Witches, Druids, Goddess-Worshippers, and Other Pagans in America Today* (New York, New York: The Viking Press, 1979).

Aldridge, K. W. *Short Talk Bulletin,* "Ancient *Symbolic* Penalties" (August 1988; Vol. 66, No. 8).

Algeo, John, "The Wizard of Oz: The Perilous Journey." *The Quest* (Summer 1993; Vol. 6, No. 2).

Allied Masonic Groups and Rites (Silver Spring, Maryland: Masonic Service Association of the United States, 1956; Revised 1988).

Alpha...and Beyond (West Allis, Wisconsin: Lor 'd Industries Ltd., n.d.).

Ancient Arabic Order of the Nobles of the Mystic Shrine, The (Chicago, Illinois: Ezra A. Cook Publications, Inc., n.d.).

Ancient Arabic Order Nobles of the Mystic Shrine: The Shriners (Newtonville, New York: HRT Ministries, Inc., n.d.).

Aquarian Collection (Wellingborough: Thorsons Publishing Group, n.d.).

Aquarian Voices (August 1989).

Armstrong, Herbert W. *The Plain Truth About Easter* (no other information available).

Aurea Flamma, The (July 1986; Vol. 1, No. 10).

Authorized Standard Ritual of the Order of the Eastern Star of New York, The (New York: Press of Andrew H. Kellogg Company, 1876; Twentieth Edition, 1916).

Baigent, Michael and Leigh, Richard. *The Temple and the Lodge* (New York: Arcade Publishing, Inc., 1989).

Bailey, Alice A. *A Treatise on White Magic* (or *The Way of the Disciple*) (New York: Lucis Publishing Company, 1951).

Bailey, Alice A. *Discipleship in the New Age* (Vol. I) (New York: Lucis Publishing Company, 1972).

Bailey, Alice A. *Discipleship in the New Age* (Vol. II) (New York: Lucis Publishing Company, 1955).

Bailey, Alice A. *Education in the New Age* (New York: Lucis Publishing Company, 1954).

Bailey, Alice A. *From Bethlehem to Calvary: The Initiations of Jesus* (New York: Lucis Publishing Company, 1965).

Bailey, Alice A. *Reappearance of the Christ* (New York: Lucis Publishing Company, 1948).

Bailey, Alice A. *The Soul: Quality of Life* (New York: Lucis Publishing Company, 1974).

Bailey, Foster. *The Spirit of Masonry* (England: Lucis Press Limited, 1957).

Barger, Eric. *From Rock to Rock: The Music of Darkness Exposed!* (Lafayette, Louisiana: Huntington House, Inc., 1990).

Battle Cry (March/April 1991).

Battle Cry (May/June 1991).

Baynard, Samuel Harrison, Jr. *History of the Supreme Council, 33rd Degree,* Vol. I (Williamsport, Pennsylvania: Grit Publishing Company, 1938).

Baynard, Samuel Harrison, Jr. *History of the Supreme Council, 33rd Degree,* Vol. II (Williamsport, Pennsylvania: Grit Publishing Company, 1938).

Beacon, The (July/August 1985; Vol. 51, No. 4).

Beane, Wendell C. and Doty, William G. *Myths, Rites, Symbols: A Mircea Eliade Reader* (Vol. I) (New York, New York: Harper Colophon Books 1975).

Beane, Wendell C. and Doty, William G. *Myths, Rites, Symbols: A Mircea Eliade Reader* (Vol. II) (New York, New York: Harper Colophon Book 1975).

Bedworth, Albert E. and Bedworth, David A. *Health for Human Effectiveness* (Englewood Cliffs, New Jersey: Prentice-Hall, Inc., 1982).

Bell, F. A. *Bell's Eastern Star Ritual* (P. R. C. Publications, Inc., 1988 Revised Edition).

Berger, Charles G. *Our Phallic Heritage* (New York, New York: Greenwich Book Publishers, Inc., 1966).

Berry, Harold J. *Rosicrucians: What They Believe* (Lincoln, Nebraska: Back to the Bible, 1987).

Bessy, Maurice. *A Pictorial History of Magic and the Supernatural* (New York: Hamlyn Publishing Group Limited, 1964).

Blau, Joseph Leon. *The Christian Cabala* (Port Washington, New York: Kennikat Press, Inc., 1944).

Blavatsky, Helena Petrovna. *Isis Unveiled,* Vol. I: Science (New York, New York: Trow's Printing and Bookbinding Company, 1877).

Blofeld, John. *The Tantric Mysticism of Tibet* (Boston, Massachusetts: Shambhala Publications, Inc., 1970).

Bloom, Harold. *Kabbalah and Criticism* (New York, New York: The Seabury Press, Inc., 1975).

Bobgan, Martin and Deidre. *12 Steps to Destruction: Codependency/Recovery Heresies* (Santa Barbara, California: EastGate Publishers, 1991).

Boyd, James P. *Bible Dictionary* (Ottenheimer Publishers, Inc., 1958).

Bracelin, J. L. *Gerald Gardner: Witch* (London: The Octagon Press, 1960).

Brief History of the Order of the Eastern Star (General Grand Chapter in the U. S. A., 1989).

Brooke-Little, J. P. *An Heraldic Alphabet* (New York: Arco Publishing Company, Inc., 1973).

Brown, G. W. *The Ladies' Friend* (Ann Arbor, Michigan: Press of Dr. A. W. Chase, 1866).

Brown, William Adrian. *Facts, Fables and Fantasies of Freemasonry* (New York, New York: Vantage Press, Inc., 1968).

Brown, William Moseley. *Short Talk Bulletin,* "A Stairway and a Ladder" (November 1962; Vol. 40, No. 11).

Buck, J. D. *Mystic Masonry* (Illinois: Indo-American Book Company, 1913, Sixth Edition).

Buck, J. D. *The Genius of Free-Masonry and the Twentieth Century Crusade* (Chicago, Illinois: Indo-American Book Company, 1907).

Buck, J. D. *The Lost Word Found in the Great Work* (Chicago, Illinois: Indo-American Book Company, 1913, Third Edition).

Budge, E. A. Wallis. *Amulets and Superstitions* (New York, New York: Dover Publications, Inc., 1978).

Budge, Sir Wallis. *Egyptian Magic* (Secaucus, New Jersey: University Books, Inc., n.d.).

Bulfinch, Thomas. *Bulfinch's Mythology: The Age of Fable or Stories of Gods and Heroes* (Garden City, New York: Doubleday and Company, Inc., 1948).

Bulfinch, Thomas. *Bulfinch's Mythology* (New York: Thomas Y. Crowell Company, Inc., 1970).

Bulfinch, Thomas. *The Age of Fable or the Beauties of Mythology* (New York: The Heritage Press, 1942).

Burton, Juliette T. *The Five Jewels of the Orient* (New York City: New York: Macoy Publishing and Masonic Supply Company, 1928).

Butler, E. M. *The Myth of the Magus* (New York: MacMillan Company, 1948).

Cabot, Laurie with Cowan, Tom. *Power of the Witch: The Earth, the Moon, and the Magical Path to Enlightenment* (New York, New York: Delacorte Press, 1989).

Campbell, Joseph with Moyers, Bill; Flowers, Betty Sue, Editor, *The Power of Myth* (New York, New York: Doubleday, 1988).

Campbell, Joseph, Editor. *Philosophies of India* (Princeton, New Jersey: Princeton University Press, 1951).

Campbell, Joseph. *The Hero with a Thousand Faces* (Princeton, New Jersey: Princeton University Press, 1968, Second Edition).

Campbell, Joseph. *The Masks of God: Creative Mythology* (New York, New York: The Viking Press, 1968).

Cannon, Alexander. *The Power of Karma: In Relation to Destiny* (E. P. Dutton and Company, Inc., 1937).

Carr, Joseph *The Lucifer Connection* (Lafayette, Louisiana: Huntington House, Inc., 1987).

Carr, Joseph J. *The Twisted Cross* (Shreveport, Louisiana: Huntington House, Inc., 1985).

Carrico, David L. *George Steinmetz: The Honored Masonic Author* (Evansville, Indiana: Followers of Jesus Christ, 1992).

Carrico, David L. *Immorals and Dogma* (Evansville, Indiana: Followers of Jesus Christ, n.d.).

Carrico, David L. *Lucifer—Eliphas Levi—Albert Pike and the Masonic Lodge* (Evansville, Indiana: Followers of Jesus Christ, 1991).

Carrico, David L. *Manly P. Hall: The Honored Masonic Author* (Evansville, Indiana: Followers of Jesus Christ, 1992).

Carrico, David L. *The Heart of Freemasonry Exposed! Who Is Hiram Abiff?* (Evansville, Indiana: Followers of Jesus Christ, 1991).

Carrico, David L. *The Jews—A Perspective Study Guide* (Evansville, Indiana: Followers of Jesus Christ, 1991).

Carrico, David L. *The Occult Meaning of the Great Seal of the United States* (Evansville, Indiana: Followers of Jesus Christ, 1991).

Carrico, David L. *The Pentagram, Freemasonry and the Goat* (Evansville, Illinois: Followers of Jesus Christ, 1992).

Carrico, David L. *Why a Christian Can't Be a Freemason, If He Knows the Truth About the Lodge!* (Evansville, Indiana: Followers of Jesus Christ, 1991).

Carrico, David L. with Doninger, Rick. *The Egyptian-Masonic-Satanic Connection* (Evansville, Indiana: Followers of Jesus Christ, 1991).

Case, Paul Foster. *The Masonic Letter G* (Los Angeles, California: Builders of the Adytum, Ltd., 1981).

Castells, F. De P. *Genuine Secrets in Freemasonry Prior to A.D. 1717* (London: A. Lewis, 1930).

Cerminara, Gina. *Many Lives, Many Loves* (New York: William Morrow and Company, Inc., 1963.

Cerza, Alphonse. *Short Talk Bulletin*, "The Origins of Freemasonry" (September 1985; Vol. 63, No. 9).

Chambers, A. R., Editor. *Questions & Answers* (n.p., 1972).

Chambers, Joseph R. *Spirit of Babylon: A New World Order* (Charlotte, North Carolina: Paw Creek Ministries, n.d.).

Chick, Jack T. *The Curse of Baphomet* (Chino, California: Chick Publications, 1991).

Chick, Jack T. *The Death Cookie* (Chino, California: Chick Publications, 1988).

Christian News (April 17, 1989; Vol. 27, No. 16).

Christian News (July 27, 1992; Vol. 30, No. 30).

Christian News (June 28, 1993).

Christian News (November 11, 1991; Vol. 29, No. 41).

Christian World Report, The (December 1990; Vol. 2, No. 9).

Christian World Report, The (February 1991; Vol. 3, No. 2).

Christian World Report, The (September 1989; Vol. 1, No. 7).

Christianity Today (May 16, 1986; Vol. 30, No. 8).

Chrysalis (Autumn 1987, Vol. 2, Issue 3).

Church and State (March 1993; Vol. 46, No. 3).

Churchward, Albert. *Signs and Symbols of Primordial Man* (London George Allen and Company, Ltd., 1913, Second Edition).

CIB Bulletin (December 1989; Vol. 5, No. 12).

CIB Bulletin (June 1988; Vol. 4, No. 6).

CIB Bulletin (May 1990; Vol. 6, No. 5).

Circle Network Bulletin (Spring 1989).

Circle Network News (Spring 1985; Vol. 7, No. 1).

Circle Network News (Spring 1986; Vol. 8, No. 1).

Circle Network News (Spring 1988; Vol. 10, No. 1).

Circle Network News (Summer 1984; Vol. 6, No. 2).

Circle Network News (Summer 1987, Vol. 9, No. 2).

Circle Network News (Winter 1984; Vol. 6, No. 4).

Circle Network News (Winter 80-81).

Cirlot, J. E. (Translated by Jack Sage). *A Dictionary of Symbols* (New York: Dorset Press, 1991 Edition).

Cirlot, J. E. *A Dictionary of Symbols* (New York, New York: Philosophical Library, Inc., 1972).

Clarke, Adam. *Clarke's Commentary, Volume II—Joshua to Esther,* (Abindgon-Cokesbury Press, Nashville, Tennessee, n.d.).

Clarke, Arthur C. *2010: Odyssey Two* (Ballantine Books, 1982).

Claudy, Carl H. *Masonic Harvest* (Washington, D.C.: The Temple Publishers, 1948).

Claudy, Carl H. *The Lion's Paw* (Washington, D.C.: The Temple Publishers, 1944).

Clausen, Henry C. *Beyond the Ordinary—Toward a Better, Wiser, and Happier World* (Washington, D.C., Supreme Council, 33rd Degree, 1983).

Clausen, Henry C. *Clausen's Commentaries on Morals and Dogma* (Supreme Council, 33rd Degree, Ancient and Accepted Scottish Rite of Freemasonry, Southern Jurisdiction, USA, 1974).

Clausen, Henry C. *Emergence of the Mystical* (Washington, D.C.: Supreme Council, 1981, Second Edition).

Clausen, Henry C. *Messages for a Mission* (Supreme Council, 1977).

Clausen, Henry C. *To a Non-Mason: You Must Seek Masonic Membership!* (Washington, D.C.: Supreme Council, Mother Council of the World, Southern Jurisdiction, 1977).

Clausen, Henry C. *Why Public Schools?* (Supreme Council, 1979).

Clausen, Henry C. *Your Amazing Mystic Powers* (Washington, D.C.: Supreme Council of the Inspectors General Knights Commander of the House of the Temple of Solomon of the Thirty-Third Rite of Freemasonry of the Southern Jurisdiction, 1985).

Clymer, R. Swinburne. *The Mysteries of Osiris or Ancient Egyptian Initiation* (Quakertown, Pennsylvania: The Philosophical Publishing Company, 1951, Revised Edition).

Clymer, R. Swinburne. *The Mysticism of Masonry* (Quakertown, Pennsylvania: The Philosophical Publishing Company, 1924).

Coil, Henry Wilson. *Coil's Masonic Encyclopedia* (New York, New York: Macoy Publishing and Masonic Supply Company, Inc., 1961).

Collier's Encyclopedia, 1991 Edition, Vol. 12.

Colville, W. J. *The Pentagram: Its Symbolism, and the Heroines of the Order of Eastern Star* (New York: Macoy Publishing and Masonic Supply Company, 1914).

Complete Occult Digest A to Z (North Hollywood, California: International Imports, 1984).

Connecting Link (January/February 1990, Issue 6).

Connecting Link (November/December 1989; Vol. 1, No. 5).

Constance Cumbey's New Age Monitor (June 1986; Vol. 1, No. 2).

Cook, Wes, Editor. *Did You Know? Vignettes in Masonry from the Royal Arch Mason Magazine* (Missouri Lodge of Research, 1965).

Cook, Wes, Editor. *Masonic Curiosa from the Desk of H. L. Haywood* (Fulton, Missouri: The Ovid Bell Press, Inc., 1968).

Coon, Arthur. *The Theosophical Seal* (no other info available).

Creation (July/August 1986; Vol. 2, No. 3).

Creme, Benjamin. *The Reappearance of the Christ and the Masters of Wisdom* (North Hollywood, California: Tara Center, 1980).

Crowley, Aleister. *Seven, Seven, Seven* (no other information available).

Cuddy, Dennis. *Now Is the Dawning of the New Age New World Order* (Oklahoma City, Oklahoma: Hearthstone Publishing, Ltd., 1991).

Cumbey, Constance. *The Hidden Dangers of the Rainbow: The New Age Movement and Our Coming Age of Barbarism* (Shreveport, Louisiana: Huntington House, Inc., Revised Edition, 1983).

Cunningham, Scott. *Cunningham's Encyclopedia of Crystal, Gem & Metal Magic* (St. Paul, Minnesota: Llewellyn Publications, 1988).

Cunningham, Scott. *Magical Herbalism: The Secret Craft of the Wise* (St. Paul, Minnesota: Llewellyn Publications, 1982).

Cunningham, Scott. *Wicca: A Guide for the Solitary Practitioner* (St. Paul, Minnesota: Llewellyn Publications, 1989).

Dager, Albert James. *A Masonic History of America* (Redmond, Washington: Media Spotlight, 1990 Special Report).

Dager, Albert James. *Facts and Fallacies of the Resurrection* (Costa Mesa, California: Media Spotlight,n.d.).

Dager, Albert James. *Origins of Christmas Traditions* (Costa Mesa, California: Media Spotlight, 1985 Special Report).

Daily Press (December 10, 1991).

Dake, Finis Jennings. *Dake's Annotated Reference Bible* (Lawrenceville, Georgia: Dake Bible Sales, Inc., 1979).

Danielou, Alain. *The Gods of India* (New York, New York: Inner Traditions International, Ltd., 1985).

Daraul, Arkon. *Witches and Sorcerers* (New York, New York: The Citadel Press, 1966).

De Riencourt, Amaury. *The Eye of Shiva: Eastern Mysticism and Science* (New York, New York: William Morrow and Company, Inc., 1980).

Decker, Ed. *A Biblical Look at the Lodge* (Issaquah, Washington: Free the Masons Ministries, n.d.).

Decker, Ed. *The Question of Freemasonry Companion* (Issaquah, Washington: Saints Alive in Jesus, 1992).

Decker, J. Edward, Jr. *The Question of Freemasonry* (Issaquah, Washington: Free the Masons Ministries, n.d.).

Decker, J. Edward, Jr., *The Question of Freemasonry* (Lafayette, Louisiana: Huntington House Publishers, 1992).

Decker, J. Edward. *Freemasonry: Satan's Door to America?* (Issaquah, Washington: Free the Masons Ministries, n.d.).

Desautels, Paul E. *The Gem Kingdom* (New York: Random House, Inc., n.d.).

Doane, Doris Chase and Keyes, King. *Tarot-Card Spread Reader* (West Nyack, New York: Parker Publishing Company, Inc., 1967).

Doore, Gary, Editor and Compiler. *Shaman's Path: Healing, Personal Growth and Empowerment* (Boston, Massachusetts: Shambhala, 1988).

Duchesne-Guillemin, Jacques (Edited by Anshen, Ruth Nanda). *Symbols and Values in Zoroastrianism: Their Survival and Renewal* (New York, New York: Harper and Row, 1966).

Dumas, Francois Ribadeau (Translated by Elisabeth Abbott). *Cagliostro: Scoundrel or Saint?* (New York: The Orion Press, 1967).

Duncan, Malcolm. *Duncan's Ritual of Freemasonry* (New York: David McKay Company, Inc., n.d., Third Edition).

Dyer, Colin F. W. *Symbolism in Craft Freemasonry* (England: A. Lewis [Masonic Publishers], Ltd., 1976).

Eastern Star Journal, The (Summer Edition, 1993).

El-Amin, Mustaga. *Freemasonry: Ancient Egypt and the Islamic Destiny* (Jersey City, New Jersey: New Mind Productions, 1988).

Elkins, Don and Rueckert, Carla. *The Crucifixion of Esmerelda Sweetwater* (Louisville, Kentucky: L/L Research, 1986).

Elkins, Don; Rueckert, Carla; and McCarty, James Allen. *The Ra Material* (Norfolk, Virginia: The Donning Company, 1984).

Emry, Sheldon. *America's Promise Newsletter* (January 1988).

Encyclopedia Americana, 1979.

Encyclopedia Britannica, 1982.

Engle, Willis D. *A General History of the Order of the Eastern Star* (Indianapolis, Indiana: Willis D. Engle, 1901).

Epperson, A. Ralph. *The Unseen Hand: An Introduction to the Conspiratorial View of History* (Tucson, Arizona: Publius Press, 1985).

Evangel, The (December 1990; Vol. 37, No. 9).

Evangelical Methodist, The (October 1933; Vol. 72, No. 8).

Evangelist, The (June 1986).

Externalization of the Hierarchy: Emergence of the Kingdom of God on Earth, The (New York, New York: School for Esoteric Studies, n.d.).

F.A.T.A.L. Flaw, The (Issaquah, Washington: Free the Masons Ministries, n.d.).

Farrar, Stewart. *What Witches Do: The Modern Coven Revealed* (Custer, Washington: Phoenix Publishing Company, 1983, Revised Edition).

Fate (October 1990; Vol. 43, No. 9 [sic]).

Feininger, Andreas. *The Color Photo Book* (Englewood Cliffs, New Jersey: Prentice-Hall, Inc., 1969).

Ferguson, Marilyn. *The Aquarian Conspiracy: Personal and Social Transformation in the 1980s* (Los Angeles, California: J. P. Tarcher, Inc. 1980).

Fertile Soil (Fall 1993, No. 1).

FES (July 1984; Issue #12).

Festivals (June/July 1987; Vol. 6, No. 3).

Finney, Charles G. *The Character, Claims and Practical Workings of Freemasonry* (Chicago, Illinois: National Christian Association, 1938).

Flashpoint (April/May 1991).

Flashpoint (August 1991).

Flashpoint (December 1992).

Flashpoint (July 1992).

Flashpoint (November 1992).

"Follow the Star: Together We Build a Better Life" (Washington, D.C.: General Grand Chapter Order of the Eastern Star, 1989).

For Full Moon Workers (Manhattan Beach, California: Arcana Workshops, n.d.).

Fowden, Garth. *The Egyptian Hermes: A Historical Approach to the Late Pagan Mind* (England: Cambridge University Press, 1986).

Fowler, Clifton L. *Santa Claus and Christmas* (Knoxville, Tennessee: Evangelist of Truth, 1982).

Fox, Matthew. *The Coming of the Cosmic Christ* (New York, New York: Harper and Row, Inc., 1988).

Fox, Robin Lane. *Pagans and Christians* (New York: Alfred A. Knopf, Inc., 1986).

Franck, Adolphe. *The Kabbalah: The Religious Philosophy of the Hebrews* (University Books, Inc., 1967).

Frazer, James. *The New Golden Bough (Abridged)* (New York, New York: Criterion Books, Inc., 1959).

Free the Masons Ministries (January 1991).

Free the Masons Ministries (May 1991).

Freedland, Nat. *The Occult Explosion* (New York: G. P. Putnam's and Sons, 1972).

Freemasonry and Religion (Washington, D.C.: Supreme Council, 33rd Degree, Ancient and Accepted Scottish Rite of Freemasonry, Mother Jurisdiction of the World, Southern Jurisdiction, U. S. A., 1977).

Freemasonry: A Way of Life (The Right Worshipful Grand Lodge of the Most Ancient and Honorable Fraternity of Free and Accepted Masons of Pennsylvania, 1982).

Frewin, Anthony. *The Book of Days* (St. James Place, London: William Collins Sons and Company, Ltd., 1979).

Fritz, James S., "Alchemy." *The World Book Encyclopedia,* 1961 Edition; Vol. 1.

Front Page, The (September 1993; Vol. 7, #9).

Full Moon Story, The (Manhattan Beach, California: Rams' Dell Press, July 1967; Revised September 1974).

Fundamentalist Journal (October 1989; Vol. 8, No. 9).

Gaiagape (Spring 1988).

Gaynor, Frank, Editor. *Dictionary of Mysticism* (New York: Philosophical Library, 1953).

Ginsburg, Christian D. *The Essenes: Their History and Doctrines: The Kabbalah* (London: Routledge and Kegan Paul, Ltd., 1956 Reprint).

Glory, Morning and G'Zell, Otter. *Who on Earth is the Goddess?* (Berkeley, California: Covenant of the Goddess, n.d.).

"God's Watchman" and the Hope of Israel (Vol. 18, No. 1).

Godwin, Jeff. *Dancing with Demons: The Music's Real Master* (Chino, California: Chick Publications, 1988).

Godwin, Jeff. *The Devil's Disciples: The Truth About Rock* (Chino, California: Chick Publications, 1985).

Godwin, John. *Occult America* (Garden City, New York: Doubleday and Company, Inc., 1972).

Goldenberg, Naomi R. *Changing of the Gods: Feminism and the End of Traditional Religions* (Boston, Massachusetts: Beacon Press, 1979).

Graham, O. J. *The Six-Pointed Star* (New Puritan Library, 1988, Second Edition).

Grieve, M. *A Modern Herbal,* Vol. 1 (New York, New York: Hafner Publishing Company, Inc., 1967).

Grieve, M. *A Modern Herbal,* Vol. 2 (London, England: Jonathan Cape, 1931).

Griffin, Des. *Fourth Reich of the Rich* (Emissary Publications, 1978).

Gunther, Bernard. *Energy Ecstasy and Your Seven Vital Chakras* (Van Nuys, California: Newcastle Publishing Company, Inc., 1978).

Haddon, David and Hamilton, Vail. *TM Wants You! A Christian Response to Transcendental Meditation* (Grand Rapids, Michigan: Baker Book House, 1976).

Haffner, Christopher. *Workman Unashamed: The Testimony of a Christian Freemason* (England: Lewis Masonic, 1989).

Haggard, Forrest D. *The Clergy and the Craft* (Ovid Bell Press, Inc., 1970).

Hall, Manly Palmer. *America's Assignment with Destiny* (Los Angeles, California: Philosophical Research Society, Inc., 1951).

Hall, Manly Palmer. *An Encyclopedic Outline of Masonic, Hermetic, Qabbalistic and Rosicrucian Symbolical Philosophy: Being an Interpretation of the Secret Teachings Concealed Within the Rituals, Allegories and Mysteries All Ages* (San Francisco, California: H. S. Crocker Company, Inc., 1928).

Hall, Manly Palmer. *The Lost Keys of Freemasonry* (Richmond, Virginia: Macoy Publishing and Masonic Supply Company, Inc., 1976; Originally published in 1923).

Hall, Manly Palmer. *The Secret Destiny of America* (New York, New York: Philosophical Library, Inc., 1958).

Hamilton, Edith. *Mythology* (Boston, Massachusetts: Little, Brown and Company, 1942).

Hamlyn, Paul. *Greek Mythology* (London: Paul Hamlyn, Ltd., 1967).

Harding, M. Esther. *Woman's Mysteries: Ancient and Modern* (New York: G. P. Putnam's Sons for the C. G. Jung Foundation for Analytical Psychology, 1971 Edition).

Harrison, John B. and Sullivan, Richard E. *A Short History of Western Civilization* (New York: Alfred A. Knopf, 1960).

Hawkins, E. L. *A Concise Cyclopaedia of Freemasonry* (EC: A. Lewis, 1908).

Hawkland, William D., *Law and Banking* (American Institute of Banking, 1971).

Hayden, Sidney. *Washington and His Masonic Compeers* (New York: Masonic Publishing and Manufacturing Company, 1868).

Haywood, H. L. *Symbolic Masonry: An Interpretation of the Three Degrees* (Washington, D.C.: Masonic Service Association of the United States, 1923).

Haywood, H. L. *The Great Teachings of Masonry* (New York: George H. Doran Company, 1923).

Health (February 1986).

Heline, Corinne. *Color and Music in the New Age* (Marina Del Rey California: DeVorss and Company, 1964).

Herrmann, Arthur R. *Designs upon the Trestleboard* (New York, New York: Press of Henry Emmerson, 1957).

Hieronimus, Robert. *America's Secret Destiny: Spiritual Vision and the Founding of a Nation* (Rochester, Vermont: Destiny Books, 1989).

Hinduism Today (February 1992; Vol. 14, No. 2).

Historical Basis of Modern Theosophy, The (Wheaton, Illinois: The Theosophical Society in America, n.d.).

History of the Order of the Eastern Star (General Grand Chapter in the U. S. A., 1989).

Holly, James L. *The Southern Baptist Convention and Freemasonry* (Beaumont, Texas: Mission and Ministry to Men, Inc., 1992).

Holroyd, Stuart. *Psychic Voyages* (Garden City, New York: Doubleday and Company, Inc., 1977).

Home Mission Board, Southern Baptist Convention. *A Report on Freemasonry* (March 17, 1993).

Home Mission Board, Southern Baptist Convention. *A Study of Freemasonry* (Atlanta, Georgia, 1993).

Horne, Alex. *King Solomon's Temple in the Masonic Tradition* (London: The Aquarian Press, 1971).

Howe, Ellic. *Magicians of the Golden Dawn: A Documentary History of Magical Order 1887-1923* (London: Routledge and Kegan Paul, Ltd., 1972).

HRT Ministries Inc. Newsletter (January/February/March 1991; Vol. 4, No. 1).

HRT Ministries Inc. Newsletter (July/August/September 1990; Vol. 3, No. 3).

HRT Ministries Inc. Newsletter (July/August/September 1991; Vol. 4, No. 3).

Hunt, Dave. *Beyond Seduction: A Return to Biblical Christianity* (Eugene, Oregon: Harvest House Publishers, 1987).

Hunt, Dave. *Global Peace and the Rise of Antichrist* (Eugene, Oregon: Harvest House Publishers, 1990).

Hunt, Dave. *Whatever Happened to Heaven?* (Eugene, Oregon: Harvest House Publishers, 1988).

Hunt, Dave and Decker, Ed. *The God Makers: A Shocking Expose of What the Mormon Church Really Believes* (Eugene, Oregon: Harvest House Publishers, 1984).

Hunt, Dave and McMahon, T. A. *America: The Sorcerer's New Apprentice: The Rise of New Age Shamanism* (Eugene, Oregon: Harvest House Publishers, 1988).

Hunt, Dave and McMahon, T. A. *The Seduction of Christianity: Spiritual Discernment in the Last Days* (Eugene, Oregon: Harvest House Publishers, 1985).

Hutchens, Rex R. *A Bridge to Light* (Washington, D.C.: Supreme Council, 33□ Ancient and Accepted Scottish Rite of Freemasonry, Southern Jurisdiction, 1988).

Hutchens, Rex R. "Albert Pike—The Man Not the Myth," *Short Talk Bulletin* (June 1990; Vol. 68, No. 6).

Hutchens, Rex R. and Monson, Donald W. *The Bible in Albert Pike's Morals and Dogma* (Washington, D.C.: Supreme Council, 33rd Degree, 1992).

Hutchinson, William (Revised by George Oliver). *The Spirit of Masonry*, (New York: Bell Publishing Company, 1982; Originally published 1775).

Idel, Moshe. *Kabbalah: New Perspectives* (New Haven, Connecticut Yale University Press, 1988).

Inner Light: The Voice of the New Age (1988, No. 13).

Institute for Spiritual Development (November/December).

Ions, Veronica. *Egyptian Mythology* (England: The Hamlyn Publishing Group, Ltd., 1965).

Is the Antichrist in the World Today?, Interview with Constance Cumbey (Oklahoma City, Oklahoma: Southwest Radio Church, 1982).

Jennings, Gary. *Black Magic, White Magic* (Eau Claire, Wisconsin The Dial Press, Inc., 1964).

Johnson, Mike. *Rock Music Revealed* (n.p., n.d.).

Jr. High Ministry (September/October 1986; Vol. 1, No.5).

Jung, Carl; Von Franz, M.-L.; Henderson, Joseph L.; Jacobi, Jolande; and Jaffe, Aniela. *Man and His Symbols* (Garden City, New York: Doubleday and Company, Inc. 1964).

Kah, Gary. *En Route to Global Occupation* (Lafayette, Louisiana: Huntington House Publishers, 1992).

Kenaston, Jean M'Kee, Compiler. *History of the Order of the Eastern Star* (Cedar Rapids, Iowa: The Torch Press, 1917).

Kerr, Howard and Crow, Charles L., Editors. *The Occult in America: New Historical Perspectives* (Urbana, Illinois: University of Illinois Press, 1983).

Kingdom Voice (August 1990).

Kingdom Voice (May 1989).

Kingston, Jeremy. *Healing Without Medicine* (Garden City, New York: Doubleday and Company, Inc., 1976).

Knight, Stephen. *The Brotherhood* (Briarcliff Manor, New York: Stein and Day, 1984).

Koblo, Martin (Translated by Ian F. Finlay). *World of Color: An Introduction to the Theory and Use of Color in Art* (New York: McGraw-Hill Book Company, 1963).

Koch, Rudolf (Translated by Dyvyan Holland). *The Book of Signs* (New York, New York: Dover Publications, 1955).

Krishna, R. P. Lawrie. *The Lamb Slain—Supreme Sacrifice*, Part (Medway, Ohio: Manujothi Ashram Publications, n.d.).

Kueshana, Eklal. *The Ultimate Frontier* (Quinlan, Texas: The Stelle Group, 1963).

Kunk, Larry. *Sons of Light? or Sons of Darkness?* (Fishers, Indiana: Ephesians 5:11, n.d.).

Kunk, Larry. *What Is the Secret Doctrine of the Masonic Lodge and How Does It Relate to Their Plan of Salvation?* (Unpublished manuscript, 1992).

Lacock, John Kennedy. *History of the Star Points: Order of the Eastern Star* (Sampson Publications, Inc., 1929).

Lady Queenborough (Edith Starr Miller). *Occult Theocrasy* (Christian Book Club of America, First published in 1933).

Lalonde, Peter. *One World Under Antichrist* by Peter Lalonde (Eugene, Oregon: Harvest House Publishers, 1991).

Last Trumpet Newsletter (April 1993, Vol. 12, Issue 4).

LaVey, Anton Szandor. *The Satanic Bible* (New York: Avon Books, 1969).

Lawrence, John T. *By-Ways of Freemasonry* (London: A. Lewis, 1911).

Lawrence, John T. *Sidelights on Freemasonry* (London, A. Lewis, 1909).

Lawrence, John T. *The Perfect Ashlar* (London: A. Lewis, 1912).

Lawrie, R. Paulaseer. *Unwritten Thunders Revealed by Lord God Almighty* (Medway, Ohio: Manujothi Ashram Publications, n.d.).

Leach, Maria, Editor. *Funk and Wagnalls Standard Dictionary of Folklore Mythology and Legend*, Vol. I (New York: Funk and Wagnalls, 1949).

Leach, Maria, Editor. *Funk and Wagnalls Standard Dictionary of Folklore Mythology and Legend*, Vol. II (New York: Funk and Wagnalls, 1950).

Leek, Sybil. *Numerology: The Magic of Numbers* (New York, New York: The MacMillan Company, 1969).

Leek, Sybil. *Reincarnation: The Second Chance* (Briarcliff Manor New York: Stein and Day, 1974).

Legman, G.; Lea, Henry Charles; Wright, Thomas; Witt, George; Tennent, Sir James; and Dugdale, Sir William. *The Guilt of the Templars* (New York: Basic Books, Inc., 1966).

Listen My Children (October 1989).

Living Unicorn, The (Carver, Minnesota: The Living Unicorn, Inc. 1980).

Llewellyn New Times (January/February 1987; #871).

Llewellyn New Times (January/February 1988; #881).

Llewellyn New Times (July/August 1986; #864).

Llewellyn New Times (July/August 1990; #904).

Llewellyn New Times (March/April 1988; #882).

Llewellyn New Times (May/June 1986; #863).

Llewellyn New Times (May/June 1987; #873).

Llewellyn New Times (May/June 1988; #883).

Llewellyn New Times (November/December 1986; #866).

Llewellyn New Times (November/December 1988; #886).

Llewellyn New Times (November/December 1989; #896).

Llewellyn New Times (September/October 1988; #885).

Lochhaas, Philip. *American Rite Masonry or York Rite Masonry* (Newtonville, New York: HRT Ministries, Inc., n.d.).

Lowe, Thomas. *Adoptive Masonry: Eastern Star Ritual* (Chicago, Illinois: Ezra A. Cook, 1913).

Lunar Lights (July/August 1989; Issue 1, No. 4).

Lust, John. *The Herb Book* (New York, New York: Bantam Books, Inc., 1974).

Lyons, Arthur, Jr., *The Second Coming: Satanism in America* (Dodd, Mead and Company, 1970).

Lyons, Arthur. *Satan Wants You: The Cult of Devil Worship in America* (New York, New York: The Mysterious Press, 1988).

Mackenzie, Kenneth R. H., Editor. *The Royal Masonic Cyclopaedia* (England: The Aquarian Press, 1987; First published in 1877).

MacKenzie, Norman, Editor. *Secret Societies* (Holt, Rinehart and Winston, 1967).

Mackey, Albert G. *A Manual of the Lodge* (New York: Charles E. Merrill Company, 1870).

Mackey, Albert G. *An Encyclopedia of Freemasonry and Its Kindred Science* (Chicago, Illinois: The Masonic History Company, 1924).

Mackey, Albert G. *Encyclopedia of Freemasonry*, Vol. 1 (Chicago, Illinois: The Masonic History Company, 1909).

Mackey, Albert G. *The Symbolism of Freemasonry* (New York: Clark and Maynard, 1869).

MacLaine, Shirley. *Dancing in the Light* (New York, New York: Bantam Books, Inc., 1985).

MacLaine, Shirley. *Going Within: A Guide for Inner Transformation* (New York, New York: Bantam Books, 1989).

Macoy, Robert. *A Dictionary of Freemasonry: A Compendium of Masonic History, Symbolism, Rituals, Literature, and Myth* (New York: Bell Publishing Company, n.d.).

Macoy, Robert (Arranged by). *Adoptive Rite Ritual* (Virginia: Macoy Publishing and Masonic Supply Company, 1897).

Macoy, Robert. *Burial Service for the Order of the Eastern Star* (Richmond, Virginia: Macoy Publishing and Masonic Supply Company, Inc., 1905.

Magical Blend (February/March/April 1988; Issue #18).

Magical Work of the Soul (New York, New York: The Arcane School, n.d.).

Maple, Eric. *The Complete Book of Witchcraft and Demonology* (Cranbury, New Jersey: A. S. Barnes and Company, Inc., 1966 Edition).

Marrs, Texe. *America Shattered* (Austin, Texas: Living Truth Publishers, 1991).

Marrs, Texe. *Big Sister Is Watching You: Hillary Clinton and the White House Feminists Who Now Control America—and Tell the President What to Do* (Austin, Texas: Living Truth Publishers, 1993).

Marrs, Texe. *Dark Majesty: The Secret Brotherhood and the Magic of Thousand Points of Light* (Austin, Texas: Living Truth Publishers, 1992).

Marrs, Texe. *Dark Secrets of the New Age: Satan's Plan for a One World Religion* (Westchester, Illinois: Crossway Books, 1987).

Marrs, Texe. "Masonic Plot Against America, The" (Intelligence Examiner Special Edition, 1993).

Marrs, Texe. *Millennium: Peace, Promises, and the Day They Take Our Money Away* (Austin, Texas: Living Truth Publishers, 1990).

Marrs, Texe. *Mystery Mark of the New Age: Satan's Design for World Domination* (Westchester, Illinois: Crossway Books, 1988).

Marrs, Texe. *Ravaged by the New Age: Satan's Plan to Destroy Our Kids* (Austin, Texas: Living Truth Publishers, 1989).

Marrs, Texe. *Texe Marrs Book of New Age Cults and Religions* (Austin, Texas: Living Truth Publishers, 1990).

Marrs, Wanda. *New Age Lies to Women* (Austin, Texas: Living Truth Publishers, 1989).

Masonic Institutes (Various Authors). (High Holborn: Richard Spencer, 1847).

Masonic Vocabulary (Silver Spring, Maryland: Masonic Service Association of the United States, 1955).

Masonry Beyond the Third Degree (Washington, D.C.: Supreme Council, 33rd Degree, n.d.).

Masonry of Adoption, The (no other information available).

Master of Life: Tools & Teachings to Create Your Own Reality (1986; Issue #32).

Master of Life: Tools & Teachings to Create Your Own Reality (1986; Issue #33).

Master of Life: Tools & Teachings to Create Your Own Reality (1987; Issue #35).

Master of Life (1987, Issue #37).

McCormick, W. J. *Christ, the Christian and Freemasonry* (Belfast, Ireland: Great Joy Publications, 1984).

McDowell, Josh and Stewart, Don. *Understanding the Occult* (San Bernardino, California: Here's Life Publishers, Inc., 1982).

McLeod, Walter, Editor. *Beyond the Pillars* (Grand Lodge A.F.& A.M. of Canada, 1973).

McQuaig, C. F., *The Masonic Report* (Norcross, Georgia: Answer Books and Tapes, 1976).

Melton, J. Gordon. *The Encyclopedia of American Religions* (Vol. 2) (Wilmington, North Carolina: McGrath Publishing Company, 1978).

Metaphysical Literature (Newberry, Florida: The Arcane Wisdom, n.d.).

Meyer, William. *The Order of the Eastern Star* (no other information available).

Michaelsen, Johanna. *Like Lambs to the Slaughter* (Eugene, Oregon: Harvest House Publishers, 1989).

Michaelsen, Johanna. *The Beautiful Side of Evil* (Eugene, Oregon: Harvest House Publishers, 1982).

Miller, Betty. *Exposing Satan's Devices* (Dewey, Arizona: Christ Unlimited Ministries, Inc., 1980).

Montgomery, Ruth. *The World Before* (New York, New York: Coward, McCann and Geoghegan, Inc., 1976).

Moran, Hugh A. and Kelley, David H. *The Alphabet and the Ancient Calendar Signs* (Palo Alto, California: Daily Press, 1969, Second Edition).

More Startling Facts Behind the 33° (Newtonville, New York: HRT Ministries, Inc., n.d.).

Morey, Robert A. *Horoscopes and the Christian* (Minneapolis, Minnesota: Bethany House Publishers, 1981).

Morey, Robert A. *The Origins and Teachings of Freemasonry* (Southbridge, Massachusetts: Crowne Publications, Inc., 1990).

Morris, Rob. *Lights and Shadows of Freemasonry,* Universal Masonic Library, Vol. 14 (John W. Leonard and Company, American Masonic Agency, 1855, Sixth Edition).

Morris, Robert and Mackey, Albert. *Lights and Shadows of the Mystic Tie* (New York: Masonic Publishing Company, 1878).

Morris, Stephen Brent. *Masonic Philanthropies: A Tradition of Caring* (Lexington, Massachusetts and Washington, D.C.: The Supreme Councils, 33rd Degree, Northern Masonic Jurisdiction and Southern Jurisdiction, 1991).

Mother Jones (February/March 1988; Vol. 13, No. 2).

MSA *"Freemasonry's Servant": How It Works* (Silver Spring, Maryland: The Masonic Service Association of the United States, n.d.).

Mullins, Eustace. *The Curse of Canaan: A Demonology of History* (Staunton, Virginia: Revelation Books, 1987).

Murdock, Maureen. *Spinning Inward: Using Guided Imagery with Children for Learning, Creativity & Relaxation* (Boston, Massachusetts: Shambhala Publications, Inc., 1987, Revised and Expanded Edition).

Murphy, Joseph. *The Amazing Laws of Cosmic Mind Power* (West Nyack, New York: Parker Publishing Company, Inc., 1965).

Mysteries of Mind Space & Time: The Unexplained (Vol. 1) (Westport, Connecticut: H. S. Stuttman, Inc., 1992).

Mystic Moon (February 1988, No. 2).

Necronomicon (New York, New York: Avon Books, 1977).

New Age Journal (January/February 1987; Vol. 3; Issue 1).

New Age Journal (July/August 1987; Vol. 3; Issue 4).

New Age Journal (June 1985).

New Age Journal (March 1985).

New Age Journal (March/April 1987; Vol. 3; Issue 2).

New Age Magazine, The (January 1989; Vol. 97, No. 1).

New Age Movement—Age of Aquarius—Age of Antichrist, The Interview with Constance Cumbey (Oklahoma City, Oklahoma: Southwest Radio Church, 1982).

New Larousse Encyclopedia of Mythology (Prometheus Press, 1972 Edition).

New Teachings for an Awakening Humanity (Santa Clara, California: S. E. E. Publishing Company, n.d.).

New Times (1984; #884).

New Times (1985; #852).

New Times (1985; #853).

New Times (1985; #855).

New Times (March/April 1986; #862).

New Times (September/October 1985; #854).

News and Views (1987).

Newsletter from a Christian Ministry (October 1992; Vol. 1, No. 8).

Newswatch Magazine (May/June 1991; Vol. 11, No. 5).

Newton, Joseph Fort. *Modern Masonry* (Washington, D.C.: Masonic Service Association of the United States, 1924).

Newton, Joseph Fort. *The Builders: A Story and Study of Masonry* (Cedar Rapids, Iowa: The Torch Press, 1914).

Newton, Joseph Fort. *The Men's House* (Washington, D.C.: Masonic Service Association, 1923).

Newton, Joseph Fort. *The Religion of Masonry: An Interpretation* (Washington, D.C.: The Masonic Service Association of the United States, 1927).

Newton, Joseph Fort. *The Religion of Masonry: An Interpretation* (Richmond, Virginia: Macoy Publishing and Masonic Supply Company, Inc., 1969 Edition).

Northern Light, The (February 1992, Vol. 24, No. 1).

Old Egypt Imports, Ltd. (Vol. 5; #3).

Old Testament According to the Authorised Version Historical Books—Joshua to Esther, The (Various Authors). (London: Society for Promoting Christian Knowledge, 1887).

Oliver, George. *Signs and Symbols* (New York: Macoy Publishing and Masonic Supply Company, 1906).

Oliver, George. *Symbol of Glory Shewing the Object and End of Freemasonry* (New York: John W. Leonard and Company, American Masonic Agency, 1855).

Oliver, George. *The Historical Landmarks and Other Evidences of Freemasonry, Explained* (Vol. I & II) (New York: John W. Leonard and Company, 1855).

Oliver, George. *The Star in the East* (London: Richard Spencer, 1842).

Omega-Letter, The (April 1990; Vol. 5, No. 4).

Order of DeMolay (Newtonville, New York: HRT Ministries, Inc., n.d.; Prepared by Commission of Fraternal Organizations).

Order of the Eastern Star: Recognition Test (Chicago, Illinois: Ezra A. Cook Publications, Inc., n.d.).

Order of the Eastern Star, The (Newtonville, New York: HRT Ministries, Inc., n.d.).

Oxley, Mick. *Masonry, the Occult, and Eastern Mysticism* (Crescent City, Florida: n.p., n.d.).

Pallenberg, Corrado. *Inside the Vatican* (New York City, New York: Hawthorn Books, Inc., 1960).

Parchment, S. R. *Ancient Operative Masonry* (San Francisco, California: San Francisco Center—Rosicrucian Fellowship, 1930).

Park, Irene Arrington. *Modernized Paganism* (Tampa, Florida: Christ's Deliverance Ministries, 1983).

Parrinder, Geoffrey, Editor. *World Religions: From Ancient History to the Present* (New York, New York: Facts on File, 1971).

Partner, Peter. *The Knights Templar and Their Myth* (Rochester, Vermont: Destiny Books, 1990, Revised Edition).

Pass It On: The Story of Bill Wilson and How the A.A. Message Reach the World (New York, New York: Alcoholics Anonymous World Services, Inc. 1984).

Patrick, Richard. *All Color Book of Greek Mythology* (London, England: Octopus Books Limited, 1972).

Peetham: A Center for Well-Being, The (Stroudsburg, Pennsylvania: The Peetham, n.d.).

Pennsylvania Freemason, The (February 1988; Vol. 35, No. 1).

Pennsylvania Freemason, The (May 1990; Vol. 37, No. 2).

Pennsylvania Freemason, The (November 1989; Vol. 36, No. 4).

Pennsylvania Freemason, The (August 1990; Vol. 37, No. 3).

Pennsylvania Youth Foundation (Elizabethtown, Pennsylvania: Pennsylvania Youth Foundation, n.d.).

Perceptions (Summer 1993, Vol. 1, Issue 2).

Percival, Harold Waldwin. *Masonry and Its Symbols in the Light of "Thinking and Destiny"* (New York, New York: The Word Foundation, Inc., 1952).

Perkins, Lynn F. *Masonry in the New Age* (Lakemont, Georgia: CSA Press, 1971).

Personal Energy Patterns: How They Affect Your Personality, Health, and Relationships (Albany, California: Taoist Healing Centre, n.d.).

Peterson, William O., Editor. *Masonic Quiz Book: "Ask Me Another, Brother"* (Chicago, Illinois: Charles T. Powner Company, 1950).

Petrie, Sidney with Stone, Robert B. *What Modern Hypnotism Can Do For You* (New York City, New York: Hawthorn Books, Inc., 1968).

Pfeiffer, Charles F., Editor. *The Biblical World: A Dictionary of Biblical Archaeology* (New York: Bonanza Books, 1966).

Phillips, Phil. *Saturday Morning Mind Control* (Nashville, Tennessee: Oliver-Nelson Books, 1991).

Phillips, Phil. *Turmoil in the Toybox* (Lancaster, Pennsylvania: Starburst Press, 1986).

Phillips, Robert. *A Little Light on the Heroines of the Order of the Eastern Star* (Goldwater, Michigan, n.p., 1910).

Pierson, A. T. C. *The Traditions, Origin and Early History of Freemasonry* (New York: Masonic Publishing Company, 1865).

Pike, Albert. *Morals and Dogma of the Ancient and Accepted Scottish Rite of Freemasonry* (Richmond, Virginia: L. H. Jenkins, Inc., 1871).

Pike's Poems (Little Rock, Arkansas: Fred W. Allsopp, 1899).

Plessner, Shirley. *Symbolism of the Eastern Star* (Cleveland, Ohio: Gilbert Publishing Company, 1956).

Pocket Encyclopedia of Masonic Symbols (Silver Spring, Maryland: The Masonic Service Association of the United States, 1953).

Pocket Masonic Dictionary (Silver Spring, Maryland: The Masonic Service Association of the United States, 1988).

Pollard, Steward M. L., Compiler. *The Lighter Side of Masonry* (n.p., 1983).

Portal, Frederic (Translated by John W. Simons). *A Comparison of Egyptian Symbols with Those of the Hebrews* (New York: Masonic Publishing and Manufacturing Company, 1866).

Powell, Arthur E. *The Magic of Freemasonry* (Baskerville Press, Ltd., 1924).

Prediction (March 1986; Vol. 52, No. 3).

Price, John Randolph. *The Superbeings* (New York: Ballantine Books, 1981).

Prophecy Newsletter (Vol. 1, No. 6).

Psychic Guide Bookshop (Fall/Winter 1986-1987).

Psychic Guide Bookshop (Spring 1986).

Psychic Guide (March/April/May 1985).

Quest, The (Autumn 1993; Vol. 6, No. 3).

Rainbows (May 1987; Vol. 7, No. 2).

Rainbows (May 1988; Vol. 8, No. 2).

Rays from the Rose Cross (April/May 1988).

Ransom, Ira T. *Is Mormonism Based on the Bible?* (La Mesa, California: Utah Christian Tract Society, n.d.).

Reese, Edward, Editor. *The Chronological Bible* (Nashville, Tennessee: Regal Publishers, Inc., 1977).

Reese, W. L. *Dictionary of Philosophy and Religion: Eastern and Western Thought* (Atlantic Highlands, New Jersey: Humanities Press, Inc., 1980).

Regardie, Israel. *The Golden Dawn* (St. Paul, Minnesota: Llewellyn Publications, 1986).

Report from Concerned Christians (May/June 1990).

Report from Concerned Christians (September/October 1990; Vol. 24).

Rest, Friedrich. *Our Christian Symbols* (Philadelphia, Pennsylvania: The Christian Education Press, 1954).

Revesz, Terese Ruth. *Witches* (New York, New York: Contemporary Perspectives, Inc., 1977).

Richardson, Jabez. *Richardson's Monitor of Free-Masonry* (n.p., 1860).

Riplinger, G. A. *New Age Bible Versions* (Munroe Falls, Ohio: A. V. Publications, 1993).

Ritual National Imperial Court of the Daughters of Isis North and South America (Chicago, Illinois: Ezra A. Cook Publications, Inc., n.d.).

Ritual of the Order of the Eastern Star (Washington, D.C.: General Grand Chapter Order of the Eastern Star, 1956).

Roberts, Allen E. *The Craft and Its Symbols: Opening the Door to Masonic Symbolism* (Richmond, Virginia: Macoy Publishing and Masonic Supply Company, Inc., 1974).

Robinson, John J. *A Pilgrim's Path: One Man's Road to the Masonic Temple* (New York: New York: M. Evans and Company, Inc., 1993).

Robinson, John J. *Born in Blood: The Lost Secrets of Freemasonry* (New York, New York: M. Evans and Company, 1989).

Rompage, Marguerite. *Arcana Workshop: An Ancient Yoga Leads to a New Winter Solstice Festival* (December 1985).

Ronayne, Edmond. *The Master's Carpet (Mah-Hah-Bone)* (n.p., 1879).

Rosicrucian Manual (Prepared under the supervision of H. Spence Lewis with revision by Ralph M. Lewis) (San Jose, California: Grand Lodge of AMORC, 1987, 27th Edition).

Rudolf Steiner: A Sketch of His Life and Work (Hudson, New York Anthroposophic Press, n.d.).

Rueckert, Carla L. *A Channeling Handbook* (Amherst, Wisconsin: Palmer Publications, Inc., 1987).

Rule, Lucien V. *Pioneering in Masonry: The Life and Times of Rob Morris, Masonic Poet Laureate, Together with Story of Clara Barton and the Eastern Star* (Louisville, Kentucky: Brandt and Connors Company, 1922).

Rule, Lucien V. *The Life and Times of Rob Morris* (no other information available).

Runes, Dagobert D. *Treasury of Philosophy* (New York, New York: Philosophical Library, 1955).

Sacred Name Broadcaster, The (November 1987).

Saints Alive in Jesus Newsletter (March 1991).

Saints Alive in Jesus Newsletter (March 1992).

Saints Alive in Jesus Newsletter (May/June 1993).

Saints Alive in Jesus Newsletter (November/December 1992).

Sanderson, Ivan T. *Investigating the Unexplained: A Compendium of Disquieting Mysteries of the Natural World* (Englewood Cliffs, New Jersey; Prentice-Hall, Inc., 1972).

Sanford, Agnes. *The Healing Light: The Art and Method of Spiritual Healing* (St. Paul, Minnesota: MacAlester Park Publishing Company, 1947).

Schmidt, Alvin J. and Babchuk, Nicholas, editors. *The Greenwood Encyclopedia of American Institutions: Fraternal Organizations* (Westport, Connecticut: Greenwood Press, 1980).

Schnoebelen, William and Sharon. *Lucifer Dethroned* (Chino, California: Chick Publications, 1993).

Schnoebelen, William J. *Twice the Child of Hell* (Issaquah, Washington: Saints Alive in Jesus, n.d.).

Schnoebelen, William. *Masonry: Beyond the Light* (Chino, California: Chick Publications, 1991).

Schwab, Gustav. *Gods and Heroes: Myths and Epics of Ancient Greece* (New York: Pantheon Books, 1946).

Scott, Charles. *The Analogy of Ancient Craft Masonry to Natural and Revealed Religion* (Philadelphia, Pennsylvania: E. H. Butler and Company, 1857).

Scottish Rite Freemasonry (Newtonville, New York: HRT Ministries, Inc.).

Scottish Rite Journal, The (August 1991; Vol. 99, No. 8).

Scottish Rite Journal, The (August 1992; Vol. 100, No. 8).

Scottish Rite Journal, The (August 1993; Vol. 101, No. 8).

Scottish Rite Journal, The (December 1991; Vol. 99, No. 12).

Scottish Rite Journal, The (December 1992; Vol. 100, No. 12).

Scottish Rite Journal, The (February 1992; Vol. 100, No. 2).

Scottish Rite Journal, The (February 1993; Vol. 101, No. 2).

Scottish Rite Journal, The (January 1992; Vol. 100, No. 1).

Scottish Rite Journal, The (January 1993; Vol. 101, No. 1).

Scottish Rite Journal, The (July 1992; Vol. 100, No. 7).

Scottish Rite Journal, The (June 1992; Vol. 100, No. 6).

Scottish Rite Journal, The (March 1992; Vol. 100, No. 3).

Scottish Rite Journal, The (March 1993; Vol. 101, No. 3).

Scottish Rite Journal, The (May 1992; Vol. 100, No. 5).

Scottish Rite Journal, The (May 1993; Vol. 101, No. 5).

Scottish Rite Journal, The (November 1992; Vol. 100, No. 11).

Scottish Rite Journal, The (November 1993; Vol. 101, No. 11).

Scottish Rite Journal, The (October 1991; Vol. 99, No. 10).

Scottish Rite Journal, The (October 1992; Vol. 100, No. 10).

Scottish Rite Journal, The (September 1991; Vol. 99, No. 9).

Scottish Rite Journal, The (September 1992; Vol. 100, No. 9).

Scottish Rite Journal, The (September 1993; Vol. 101, No. 9).

Self-Help Update (Issue #26).

Self-Help Update (Issue #27).

Self-Help Update (Issue #28).

Self-Help Update (Issue #30).

Self-Help Update (Issue #31).

Sessler, Robert. *To Be God of One World: The French Revolution Globalized* (Merlin, Oregon: Let There Be Light Publications, 1992).

Sexson, W. Mark *Ritual—Supreme Assembly International Order of the Rainbow for Girls* (McAlester, Oklahoma: Office of Supreme Assembly, 1948).

Shamballa: The Centre Where the Will of God Is Known (New York, New York: World Goodwill, n.d.).

Shamballa: Where the Will of God is Known (New York, New York: Arcane School, n.d.).

Shaw, Jim and McKenney, Tom. *The Deadly Deception* (Lafayette, Louisiana: Huntington House, Inc., 1988).

Shepherdsfield (March 1989).

Short Talk Bulletin, "3—5—7" (June 1925; Vol. 3, No. 6; Reprinted December 1990).

Short Talk Bulletin, "Acacia Leaves and Easter Lilies" (April 1929; Vol. 7, No. 4; Reprinted March 1985).

Short Talk Bulletin, "Albert Gallatin Mackey" (February 1936; Vol. 14, No. 2; Reprinted July 1980).

Short Talk Bulletin, "Albert Pike" (July 1923; Vol. 1, No. 7; Reprinted December 1988).

Short Talk Bulletin, "Behind the Symbol" (July 1954; Vol. 32, No. 7).

Short Talk Bulletin, "Blazing Star," Part 1 (March 1965; Vol. 43 No. 3).

Short Talk Bulletin, "Brother Francis Bellamy" (March 1982; Vol. 60; No. 3).

Short Talk Bulletin, "Cord, Rope and Cable-Tow" (September 1950; Vol. 28; No. 9).

Short Talk Bulletin, "Elias Ashmole" (October 1947; Vol. 25, No. 10; Reprinted December 1980).

Short Talk Bulletin, "Fiction—A Tool of Masonic Education" (December 1986; Vol. 64, No. 12).

Short Talk Bulletin, "Formula for L.M.W.W.B.A.O." (September 1943; Vol. 21, No. 9).

Short Talk Bulletin, "Frank S. Land: DeMolay 'Dad' No. 1" (March 1969; Vol. 47, No. 3; Reprinted September 1987).

Short Talk Bulletin, "From Whence Came We?" (October 1932; Vol. 10, No. 10; Reprinted December 1983).

Short Talk Bulletin, "Globes" (July 1967; Vol. 45, No. 7).

Short Talk Bulletin, "Good Masonic Books" (II) (June 1985; Vol. 63; No. 6).

Short Talk Bulletin, "Good Masonic Books" (November 1945; Vol. 23, No. 11; Reprinted June 1985).

Short Talk Bulletin, "Green Trees—High Hills" (August 1955; Vol. 33; No. 8).

Short Talk Bulletin, "Hoodwink" (August 1957; Vol. 35, No. 8; Reprinted September 1981).

Short Talk Bulletin, "Illustrated by Symbols" (March 1941; Vol. 19; No. 3; Reprinted January 1989).

Short Talk Bulletin, "In the Beginning, God" (January 1967; Vol. 45, No. 1; Reprinted January 1982).

Short Talk Bulletin, "Kipling and Masonry" (October 1964; Vol. 42, No. 10; Reprinted June 1985).

Short Talk Bulletin, "Masonic Clothing" (June 1950; Vol. 28, No. 6; Reprinted June 1978).

Short Talk Bulletin, "Moon Lodges" (January 1958; Vol. 36, No. Reprinted June 1978).

Short Talk Bulletin, "Mosaic Pavement and Blazing Star" (April 1951; Vol. 29, No. 4; Reprinted April 1990).

Short Talk Bulletin, "Mummies" (January 1926; Vol. 4, No. 1; Reprinted November 1990).

Short Talk Bulletin, "Numerology of Masonry" (June 1946; Vol. 2, No. 6; Reprinted November 1984).

Short Talk Bulletin, "Our Relations with the Knights of Columbus" (March 1974, Vol. 52, No. 3; Reprinted December 1982).

Short Talk Bulletin, "Planning for Spiritual Growth," Part 1 (October 1974; Vol. 52, No. 10).

Short Talk Bulletin, "Point Within a Circle" (August 1931; Vol. 9, No. 8; Reprinted July 1990).

Short Talk Bulletin, "Ritual in Freemasonry" (August 1990; Vol. 68, No. 8).

Short Talk Bulletin, "Rob Morris" (May 1957; Vol. 35, No. 5; Reprinted July 1981).

Short Talk Bulletin, "Sanctum Sanctorum" (July 1944; Vol. 22, No. 7; Reprinted January 1982).

Short Talk Bulletin, "Secrecy in Symbolism" (July 1981; Vol. 50 No. 7).

Short Talk Bulletin, "Shekinah" (June 1942; Vol. 22, No. 6).

Short Talk Bulletin, "Signs" (August 1937; Vol. 15, No. 8; Reprinted March 1989).

Short Talk Bulletin, "So Mote It Be" (June 1927; Vol. 5, No. 6; Reprinted September 1981).

Short Talk Bulletin, "Some Misconceptions About Freemasonry" (August 1958; Vol. 36, No. 8; Reprinted March 1989).

Short Talk Bulletin, "Sts. Johns' Days" (December 1933; Vol. 11, No. 12; Reprinted July 1986).

Short Talk Bulletin, "Sun, Moon and Stars" (March 1930; Vol. 8, No. 3).

Short Talk Bulletin, "Symbolism" (March 1925; Vol. 3, No. 3; Reprinted May 1982).

Short Talk Bulletin, "The All-Seeing Eye" (December 1932; Vol. 10, No. 12; Reprinted January 1982).

Short Talk Bulletin, "The Altar Is Born" (January 1955; Vol. 33 No. 1).

Short Talk Bulletin, "The Apron" (June 1932; Vol. 10, No. 6; Reprinted March 1986).

Short Talk Bulletin, "The Bee Hive" (September 1951; Vol. 29, No. 9; Reprinted April 1990).

Short Talk Bulletin, "The Broken Column" (February 1956; Vol. 3 No. 2; Reprinted January 1985).

Short Talk Bulletin, "The Handicapped Brother" (September 1989; Vol. 67; No. 9).

Short Talk Bulletin, "The Holy Saints John" (December 1975; Vol. 53, No. 12).

Short Talk Bulletin, "The Legend of the Lost Word" (May 1928; Vol. 6; No. 5; Reprinted March 1986).

Short Talk Bulletin, "The Letter 'G'" (June 1933; Vol. 11, No. Reprinted April 1986).

Short Talk Bulletin, "The Lost Word" (November 1955; Vol. 33, No. 11).

Short Talk Bulletin, "The Masonic Firmament" (January 1945; Vol. 23, No. 1; Reprinted March 1985).

Short Talk Bulletin, "The Masonic Goat" (November 1936, Vol. 14, No. 11).

Short Talk Bulletin, "The Masonic Rod" (September 1957; Vol. 35, No. 9; Reprinted March 1986).

Short Talk Bulletin, "The Mystic Tie" (October 1940; Vol. 28, No. 10; Reprinted March 1982).

Short Talk Bulletin, "The Nature of Symbols" (July 1957; Vol. 3, No. 7; Reprinted May 1982).

Short Talk Bulletin, "The Ritual Is Important" (July 1965; Vol. 43; No. 7; Reprinted April 1983).

Short Talk Bulletin, "The Significant Numbers" (September 1956; Vol. 34; No. 9).

Short Talk Bulletin, "The Winding Stairs" (January 1932; Vol. 1, No. 1; Reprinted July 1991).

Short Talk Bulletin, "Those Terrible Exposes!" (July 1952; Vol. 30; No. 7; Reprinted September 1986).

Short Talk Bulletin, "Two Pillars" (September 1935; Vol. 13, No. 9; Reprinted September 1978).

Short Talk Bulletin, "Veiled in Allegory and Illustrated by Symbols" (November 1974; Vol. 52, No. 11).

Short Talk Bulletin, "Veiled in Allegory" (September 1949; Vol. 27, No. 9; Reprinted April 1986).

Short Talk Bulletin, "What Should a Mason Know About Masonry?" (March 1959; Vol. 37, No. 3; Reprinted March 1984).

Short Talk Bulletin, "What to Tell Your Wife" (July 1939; Vol. 17, No. 7; Reprinted March 1985).

Short Talk Bulletin, "Women Freemasons" (November 1933; Vol. 11, No. 11; Reprinted November 1990).

Shosteck, Robert. *Flowers and Plants: An International Lexicon with Biographical Notes* (New York: Quadrangle, 1974).

Should a Christian Be a Shriner? (Newtonville, New York: HRT Ministries, Inc.).

Shriner's Red Fez: Know the Truth Behind This Symbol of Charity, The (Newtonville, New York: HRT Ministries, Inc., n.d.).

Sickles, Daniel, Editor. *The Freemason's Monitor* (New York: Macoy Publishing and Masonic Supply Company, 1901).

Simon, Edith. *The Piebald Standard: A Biography of the Knights Templar* (Boston, Massachusetts: Little, Brown and Company, 1959).

Siva's Cosmic Dance (San Francisco, California: Himalayan Academy, n.d.).

Skinner, Charles M. *Myths and Legends of Flowers, Trees, Fruits, and Plants* (Philadelphia, Pennsylvania: J. B. Lippincott Company, 1911).

Slipper, Mary Ann. *The Symbolism of the Order of the Eastern Star* (no other information available).

Slipper, Mary Ann. *The Symbolism of the Eastern Star* (n.p., 1927).

South Haven (Michigan) Daily Tribune (April 24, 1987).

Spangler, David. *Emergence: The Rebirth of the Sacred* (New York, New York: Dell Publishing, 1984).

Spangler, David. "Finding Heaven on Earth, *New Age Journal* (January/February 1988; Vol. 4, Issue 1).

Spangler, David. *Links with Space* (Marina Del Rey, California: DeVorss and Company, 1971).

Spangler, David. *Reflections on the Christ* (Scotland: Findhorn Publications, 1977).

Spangler, David. *Revelation: The Birth of a New Age* (Middleton, Wisconsin: The Lorian Press, 1976).

Spence, H. D. M. and Exell, Joseph S., Editors. *The Pulpit Commentary* (Vol. 9).

Spence, Lewis. *Myths & Legends of Babylonia & Assyria* (London: George G. Harrap and Company, 1916).

Sphaera Imaginatio (1986, Issue #16).

Spirit Speaks: Me and My Shadow (1986; Issue #10).

Spiritual Mothering Journal (Winter 1986; Vol. 6, No. 4).

Stafford, Thomas Albert. *Christian Symbolism in the Evangelical Churches* (Nashville, Tennessee: Abingdon Press, 1942).

Star-Spangled Banner, The (Washington, D.C.: Supreme Council, 33rd Degree, Ancient and Accepted Scottish Rite of Freemasonry, Southern Jurisdiction, n.d.).

Starhawk (Miriam Simos). *The Spiral Dance: A Rebirth of the Ancient Religion of the Great Goddess* (New York, New York: Harper-Collins Publishers, 1989 Edition).

Startling Facts Behind the 33☐, The (Newtonville, New York: HRT Ministries, Inc., n.d.).

Stearn, Jess. *Soul Mates: Perfect Partners Past, Present, and Beyond* (New York, New York: Bantam Books, 1984).

Steinbrenner, G. W. *The Origin and Early History of Masonry* (no other information available).

Steiner, Rudolf (Translated by Max Gysi). *The Way of Initiation* (New York: Macoy Publishing and Masonic Supply Company, 1910).

Steinmetz, George H. *Freemasonry: Its Hidden Meaning* (New York: Macoy Publishing and Masonic Supply Company, 1948).

Steinmetz, George H. *The Lost Word: Its Hidden Meaning* (New York: Macoy Publishing and Masonic Supply Company, 1953).

Stevenson, David. *The Origins of Freemasonry: Scotland's Century, 1590-1710* (Cambridge: Press Syndicate of the University of Cambridge, 1988).

Still, William T. *New World Order: The Ancient Plan of Secret Societies* (Lafayette, Louisiana: Huntington House, Inc., 1990).

Stillman, John Maxson. *The Story of Alchemy and Early Chemistry* (New York, New York: Dover Publications, Inc., 1960).

Stillson, Henry Leonard and Hughan, William James, Editors. *History of the Ancient and Honorable Fraternity of Free and Accepted Masons, and Concordant Orders* (no other information available).

Tarkowski, Ed and Mary. *The Origins, Practices and Traditions of Halloween* (Erie, Pennsylvania: Guardians of the Heart, n.d.).

Taylor, Harmon. *Christian Freemason?* (Newtonville, New York: HRT Ministries, Inc., n.d.).

Taylor, Harmon. *Freemasonry: A Grand Chaplain Speaks Out* (Issaquah, Washington: Free the Masons Ministries, n.d.).

Tennessean, The (no other information available).

Tennessean, The (October 25, 1992).

Terry, Sarah H., Compiler. *History of the Order of the Eastern Star* (n.p., 1914).

Terry, Sarah H. *The Second Mile* (Corpus Christi, Texas: Christian Triumph Press, 1935).

Thompson, Frank Charles, Editor. *The New Chain-Reference Bible,* (Indianapolis, Indiana: B. B. Kirkbride Bible Company, Inc., 1957).

Thoughtline (August 1990).

Time-Life Books, Editors. *Magical Arts* (Alexandria, Virginia: Time-Life Books, 1990).

Transmission (April 1983, No. 1).

Tros, Gerald. *New Age Notes* (IBM disk).

Truth Journal (January/February 1991).

Truth Journal (October 1988).

Utne Reader (January/February 1988).

Utne Reader (March/April 1992, No. 50).

Vail, Charles H. *The Ancient Mysteries and Modern Masonry* (New York: Macoy Publishing and Masonic Supply Company, 1909).

Voices from Spirit (May 1989; Vol. 3, No. 1).

Voice of Revolution (July 4, 1990; #88).

Voorhis, Harold Van Buren. *The Eastern Star: The Evolution from a Rite to an Order* (Richmond, Virginia: Macoy Publishing and Masonic Supply Company, Inc., 1938).

Voyage to the Source (McMinnville, Oregon: The Aquarian Church of Universal Service, 1986).

Waite, Arthur Edward. *An Encyclopedia of Freemasonry and of Cognate Instituted Mysteries: Their Rites, Literature and History,* Vol. I (New York: Weathervane Books, 1970).

Waite, Arthur Edward. *An Encyclopedia of Freemasonry and of Cognate Instituted Mysteries: Their Rites, Literature and History,* Vol. II (New York: Weathervane Books, 1970).

Waite, Arthur Edward. *Emblematic Freemasonry and the Evolution of Its Deeper Issues* (London: William Rider and Son, Ltd., 1925).

Waite, Arthur Edward. *The Brotherhood of the Rosy Cross: Being Records of the House of the Holy Spirit in Its Inward and Outward History* (New Hyde Park, New York: University Books, 1961).

Waite, Arthur Edward. *The Holy Kabbalah* (London: Williams and Norgate Ltd., 1929).

Waite, Arthur Edward. *The Mysteries of Magic: A Digest of the Writings of Eliphas Levi* (Chicago, Illinois: De Laurence, Scott and Company, 1909).

Waite, Arthur Edward. *The Secret Tradition in Freemasonry* (London: Rider and Company, 1937).

Wallman, Joseph. *The Kabalah: From Its Inception to Its Evanescence* (Brooklyn, New York: Theological Research Publishing Company 1958).

Ward, Arthur H. *Masonic Symbolism and the Mystic Way* (London: Theosophical Publishing House, Ltd., 1923, Second Edition).

Ward, J. S. M. *Freemasonry and the Ancient Gods* (London: Simpkins, Marshall, Hamilton, Kent and Company, Ltd., 1921).

Ward, John Sebastian Marlow. *The Sign Language of the Mysteries* (Land's End Press, 1969).

Wassink, A. *The Bible and Christian Science* (Grand Rapids, Michigan: Faith, Prayer and Tract League, n.d.).

Watts, Charles A. *Worthy Matrons' Hand Book: Order of the Eastern Star* (Washington, D.C.: General Grand Chapter, Order of the Eastern Star 1988).

Webb, Thomas Smith. *The Freemason's Monitor* (Cincinnati, Ohio: The Pettibone Brothers Manufacturing Company, 1797).

Wedeck, Harry E. *Treasury of Witchcraft* (New York, New York: Philosophical Library, 1961).

Whalen, William J. *Handbook of Secret Organizations* (Milwaukee, Wisconsin: The Bruce Publishing Company, 1966).

What Every Freemason Should Know (Newtonville, New York: HRT Ministries, Inc., n.d.).

What is the Order of the Eastern Star? (Newtonville, New York: HRT Ministries, Inc., n.d.).

What Is (1987; Vol. 1, No. 2).

What Is (Summer 1986; Vol. 1, No. 1).

What? When? Where? Why? Who? in Freemasonry (Silver Spring, Maryland: Masonic Service Association of the United States, 1956).

Whole Life Times (November/December 1984).

illcock, Shaun. *The Pagan Festivals of Christmas and Easter* (South Africa: Bible Based Ministries, 1992).

ilmshurst, W. L. *The Masonic Initiation* (Ferndale, Michigan: Trismegistus Press, 1980; Originally published 1924).

ilmshurst, W. L. *The Meaning of Masonry* (Bell Publishing Company, Reprint of fifth edition published in 1927).

ilson, Colin. *The Occult: A History* (New York, Random House, 1971).

inters, D. Duane. *A Search for Light in a Place of Darkness: A Study of Freemasonry* (no other information available).

ood, Max. *Rock and Roll: An Analysis of the Music* (n.p., n.d.).

oodcock, Percival George. *Short Dictionary of Mythology* (Philosophical Library, 1953).

oodrow, Ralph Edward. *Babylon Mystery Religion: Ancient and Modern* (Riverside, California: Ralph Woodrow Evangelistic Association, Inc., 1990 Edition).

orld Book Encyclopedia, The (1961 Edition).

orth, Fred L. *The Trivia Encyclopedia* (Los Angeles, California: Brooke House, 1974).

rker, John. *The Arcane Schools* (Belfast, Ireland: William Tait, 1909).

ur *Masonic Capital City* (Silver Spring, Maryland: The Masonic Service Association of the United States, n.d.).

mbardo, Philip G. and Ruch, Floyd L., Editors. *Psychology and Life* (Glenview, Illinois: Scott, Foresman and Company, 1977, Ninth Edition).

mmer, Heinrich with Campbell, Joseph as Editor, *Myths and Symbols in Indian Art and Civilization* (New York: Harper and Row, 1962).

OTHER LITERATURE
BY CATHY BURNS

BOOKS:

Alcoholics Anonymous Unmasked (126 pages) .. $5.95
Hidden Secrets of Masonry (64 pages) .... $ 4.95
Hidden Secrets of the Eastern Star $15.95

BOOKLETS: .... **$0.50 each**

Astrology and Your Future
Eternal Life
Hypnosis: Cure or Curse?
Questions and Answers About the New Age Movement
To Catholics with Love
What Is Your I.Q.?

ARTICLES: .... **$0.50 each**
(except where noted)

Chart Your Course with Orion International
Different Kinds of Friendship
Divination
Divorce and Remarriage
Dowsing Is in the Bible!
Hidden Dangers of Reflexology

I Have Sinned

Jason Winters and His Herbal Tea

March for Jesus?

Miscegenation

New Age Love

Some Occult Terms Explained

The Rapture—When Will It Occur?

Unity or D-i-v-i-s-i-o-n?

Witchcraft in the Church

Ye Shall Not Surely Die (on Reincarnation)

A Scriptural View of Hell and Soul Sleep **$1.00**
    (2 part series)

Mormonism (3 part series) **$1.50**

    1. Mormonism and Its History

    2. Some Doctrines of Mormonism

    3. Mormonism and Godhood

Tongues and Related Issues (14 part series) **$5.00**

    1. Do All Speak in Tongues?

    2. Baptism in the Holy Ghost

    3. Sinful Lives and Tongues

    4. Signs and Wonders

    5. Prosperity and Riches

    6. The Power of Words

    7. Can We Create Our Own Reality?

    8. What Is Visualization?

    9. A Look at Inner Healing

    10. Are You a God?

11. Misfits Removed!

12. Renegades Excluded!

13. Thy Kingdom Come!

14. Will the Church Be Raptured?

World Government (6 part series) **$3.00**

1. A One World Order Is Coming

2. World Citizenship

3. A New Economic Order

4. His Number Is 666

5. What Will the Antichrist Be Like?

6. Differences Between Christ and Antichrist

TRACTS:

ABC's of Salvation

My God Cannot Do Everything

What Is Sin?

Please include postage for all literature.

SHARING

212-S East Seventh Street

Mt. Carmel, PA 17851-2211

The Shocking Truth Revealed!

- Does Masonry promote astrology and reincarnation?
- Are Masonry and Christianity compatible?
- What do the Masonic symbols represent?
- Who is the REAL god of Masonry?

Discover hidden meanings, sexual overtones, the god they conceal, and much more. Fully documented with 276 footnotes.

For your gift of $3.95 (plus $1.05 postage and handling)

SHARING
212-S East 7th Street
Mt. Carmel, Pennsylvania 17851-2211